INSIGHTFUL ILLUSTRATIONS: MAKING SENSE OF LIFE'S UPS AND DOWNS

STORIES, PARABLES, AND ANALOGIES THAT HELP PIECE TOGETHER LIFE'S PUZZLE

BY

DAVID C. CAUSEY

January

January 1

WHAT IS GOD LOOKING FOR?

Animal celebrities have been some of the most popular stars and box office draws in Hollywood history. But what few fans realize is that most of them are throwaways, i.e. they had been homeless and did time in "the pound." For instance, *Benji* of the "Benji" series of movies, was rescued from an animal shelter. So was *Morris* the cat – a 15-pound orange tabby named "Lucky." He was rescued from an Illinois animal shelter *just twenty minutes* before he was to be "put to sleep." Similar stories could be told of *Buddy* of the motion picture "Air Bud," *Tramp* of television's "My Three Sons," *Max* of "How the Grinch Stole Christmas," and *Sammy* of the "Dr. Doolittle" movies. *Fang* (a.k.a. Bully), of "Harry Potter" fame, was a junkyard dog in his previous career. All these animals were virtually abandoned. We could add many more to the list. In fact, the American Humane Society estimates that *eighty percent* of all animals used by Hollywood motion pictures were previously homeless – *80%!* Add to this the fact that nearly none of dog stars are of pedigreed breeding. This includes the dog *Pal* and his descendants – who have played the part of *Lassie* in movies and TV.

In the final analysis, previous history, pedigree, and purity of breeding meant nothing to Hollywood executives. They chose the discarded and disreputable and used them to do marvelous things.

Does any of this sound familiar? It should. The Scripture reminds us that God is in the habit of rescuing the throwaways of humanity, the unwanted, the disreputable, and the abandoned. God is in the habit of taking zeroes and making them heroes. Don't ever think that you disqualify for God's mercy and saving grace because of what you are or what you've done. You're the stuff God's looking for.

Look at what St. Paul wrote: *"Brothers, think of what you were when you were called. Not many of you were wise by human standards; not many were influential; not many were of noble birth. But God chose the foolish things of the world to shame the wise; God chose the weak things of the world to shame the strong. He chose the lowly things of this world and the despised things—and the things that are not—to nullify the things that are, so that no one may boast before him."* (1 Corinthians 1:26-29)

PRAYER: Dear Father in heaven, I thank You for Your unconditional love and acceptance of me with all my problems and faults. Please forgive me, cleanse me, heal me, save me, and use me to be a blessing to others and to be a credit to You. Amen.

January 2

GOD KNOWS YOUR TRUE POTENTIAL AND WORTH

The palm tree *Lodoicea seychellarum* has the distinction of producing the largest seeds of any living plant. Just one of these seeds (referred to as the Seychelles Nut, the Sea Coconut or the Double Coconut) weighs a staggering *thirty to forty pounds!* Yet for all its size, the Seychelles Palm Tree grows to a very slender sixty to ninety feet tall.

In contrast, consider the tree, *Sequoia sempervirens*, the California Coastal Redwood. Just one of these seeds weighs a mere $1/7700^{th}$ of an ounce – this means it takes more than 123,000 to measure one pound. Yet from this tiny seed grows a virtual skyscraper – twenty feet wide at its base and over 350 feet tall – the tallest, the recently discovered Hyperion, is just over 379 feet tall. The Coastal Redwood's "thicker sister," *Sequoiadendron giganteum,* or Giant Sequoia, is the largest living thing, and although at 267 feet tall it does not reach the height of the redwood, is far more massive – up to 40 feet in diameter at its base. Yet the mammoth tree spouts from a tiny seed that weighs only $1/3000^{th}$ of an ounce.

So what's the lesson – just as you cannot determine the size of a tree based on the size of its seed, so no one knows the potential that God packs into a human being. Also, it is clear that our early successes or failures in life can be very misleading. Like the Sequoia seed, our lives may not seem very promising at times. But locked away in our hearts is the potential to become a champion – if only we will place our lives and our futures in God's hands. For, as George Washington Carver, once said, "Anyone can count the seeds in an apple, but only God can count the apples in a seed."

In Jeremiah 29:11 God states: "For I know the plans I have for you, declares the LORD, plans to prosper you and not to harm you, plans to give you hope and a future." And in 2 Corinthians 2:9 God again says, "No eye has seen, no ear has heard, no mind has conceived what God has prepared for those who love him!"

PRAYER: Almighty and All-Wise God, please take the raw material of my life and fashion it into something of beauty and purpose that brings glory to You. Amen.

January 3

CLUTTERED LIVES

Do you recall that example that generals were using in their speeches on how we could "do more with less?" The general would place a bucket on a table. Then he would take a container of fist-sized rocks and fill up the bucket, and ask the question, "Is the bucket filled?" Naturally, all of us would answer, "Yes, the bucket is filled." "No it's not," the general would reply, and would then take a container of marbles and pour them into the bucket of rocks. The smooth, smaller marbles would easily find their way in between the jagged, angular rocks. "There," said the general, "now is the bucket filled?" With far less enthusiasm we would answer again, "Yes." "No it ain't," the general would answer. Then he would take a container of sand and pour it into the bucket of rocks and marbles. A third time, the general would ask, "Now is the bucket full?" A few of us would again answer, "Yes, the bucket is full." "You're wrong," said the general, as he took a fourth container – this one of water – and poured its contents into the bucket of rocks, marbles and sand.

What was the general's point? That no matter how busy you are, you can always squeeze more into your schedule and no matter how heavy your workload, you can always do more. That example became the primary illustration of how we all can do more with less during the military draw-down of the 1990s.

I've thought about that demonstration over the years and I believe I've heard a far better application. It is this: *Our lives will tend to get cluttered with lots of things, so be sure to put in the "big things" (like "the rocks"), the most important things first. Otherwise the little things (like the tiny grains of sand), the unimportant things, will crowd them out.*

That's right. Before you clutter your life with little, purposeless activities to kill your boredom or to give you a sense of importance or purpose, make room for the "big things:" your spouse, your children and your God. The Scripture commands us that above all things God should have the preeminence in our lives (Colossians 1:19).

PRAYER: Dear Father in heaven, open my eyes to the treasure I have in you and in my family. Keep my life from purposeless clutter and help me to give my undivided attention to those who matter most. Amen.

January 4

BENEVOLENT FURY

One of the most terrifying of spectacles is lightning. A single bolt of lightning may give off 3,750 million kilowatts of electrical energy and can instantly heat the surrounding air to more than 27,000 degrees Fahrenheit – creating massive compression waves that reach us as "thunder." Lightning can instantly split trees, generate massive forest fires (75,000 each year in the U.S.), and fuse the ground it strikes into glass.

But another strange side of this fearsome phenomenon is that lightening is absolutely essential to plant life. That's right. For one thing, the "devastating" forest fires created by lightning serve to burn away dense underbrush that prevents new growth, adds critical nutrients to the soil and actually facilitates the opening of pine cones so that their seeds can disperse. Even the disastrous fires at Yellowstone Park in 1988 created an ecological boom for the Nation's oldest National Park.

But it is also true no plant life could exist on earth at all if not for lightning. Here's why. All plants need nitrogen to survive. The problem is that, although our atmosphere is 78% nitrogen, it is not in a soluble form nor can it otherwise be absorbed by plants. However, the intense heat generated by lightning causes the nitrogen in the air to combine with oxygen, thus creating nitrogen oxides that are soluble and fall to the earth in rain to nourish all plant life on earth. In fact, each year lightning is responsible for bringing 10 million tons of nitrogen into the earth.

Interesting how something so dangerous and devastating as lightning can also be so necessary to life on earth. But as the lightning bolts of nature are essential to the survival of all plant life, so are the painful jolts of life essential to our spiritual and emotional development. Those things that we expect to devastate or destroy us, will (if our faith and attitude remain positive) in fact promote our spiritual and emotional growth and development.

The shocks and jolts of this life shake us from our complacency, make us far more accepting of others, and lead us to draw strength from others and from God. The Scripture says, "We rejoice in our tribulation, knowing that tribulation brings about perseverance" (Romans 5:3), and "Count it all joy my brothers when you experience various trials, knowing that the testing of your faith produces perseverance" (James 1:3). So take heart. There is a divine benevolence in the fury of the storm.[i]

PRAYER: Dear Father in heaven, please fortify me against the storms of life. Help me to be strong and to absorb wisdom, power and grace from the shocks and jolts of this life. Amen.

January 5

LIVING LIFE "IN A PANIC"

In 1862 John Randolph Bryan was the Confederacy's premiere, and at one time *only*, balloonist. After a number of harrowing experiences, like being shot down by Union gunfire, he tried to resign. His commander, General Joe Johnston, wouldn't let him. But after a last frightful event, Captain Bryan gave up ballooning for good.

His last flight began well enough. Then everything went wrong. His balloon came untethered and drifted over enemy lines. Frantically, Captain Bryan tried to destroy all his notes, orders, and other incriminating evidence. But the balloon continued to drift and Bryan soon found himself heading for deep water. In a panic, Captain Bryan whipped off his clothing and prepared to swim for his life. But the balloon just kept drifting - until it landed right in the heart of a Confederate camp. What relief!

But his relief was short-lived. Having never before seen Captain Bryan or a balloon on the side of the Confederacy, the soldiers suspected he was a spy for the Union. And Captain Bryan had nothing with which to prove his identity or his allegiance. He was stripped down to his long johns and had discarded his orders, maps, notes, uniform and rank. In desperation the poor captain fell to his knees and gave an impassioned plea for his life. The soldiers relented and Captain Bryan escaped with his life – though he was greatly humiliated by the experience.

The picture of Captain Bryan overreacting to each changing situation – over enemy lines, over water, then back over Confederate lines – resembles the way people tend to live their lives. We spend our days in hurried anxiety. We see a small cloud on the horizon and prepare for a hurricane. But God has an answer to our troubled souls: "Come to me, all of you who are weary and carry heavy burdens, and I will give you rest. Take my yoke upon you. Let me teach you, because I am humble and gentle at heart, and you will find rest for your souls. For my yoke is easy to bear, and the burden I give you is light." (Matthew 11:28-30, *New Living Translation*) We were never meant to walk alone, carry our burdens in our own strength, or survive life's jungle by our own wits. We were created for fellowship with our Heavenly Father and to walk hand in hand with our Savior.

PRAYER: Dear Lord Jesus, to You I come for rest in my soul and relief from my burdens. Please speak peace to the storm that rages within me. Please empower me and make me equal to the challenges I face. And through it all, draw me nearer to You. Amen.

January 6

BLOWS THAT BLESS

Chuck Shepherd, who runs the Tampa-based "News of the Weird" syndicated column, reported on a spree of blessings in disguise earlier this year.

In February 2006, Donald Blatsch was wounded twice during the robbery of his grocery store in Bakersfield, California – in the abdomen and left arm. While being operated on for the gunshot wound, doctors discovered a malignant tumor in his abdomen which they successfully removed. Since Donald was completely unaware of the tumor that hadn't caused him any pain or discomfort, doctors believed that the gunshot wounds may have very likely saved his life. Donald went so far as to describe the misfortune as a saving "act of God."

In the same month, an elderly woman, Ms. Arnie Fairclaw of Alamonte Springs, Florida, had to be rushed to the emergency room after a fall left her with a broken hip. A "bad break," you say? Not quite. Later that evening, as nurses were caring for Arnie, a drunk driver lost control of his pick-up truck and plowed into Arnie's house at a high rate of speed. His truck actually went "airborne" before crashing into Arnie's bedroom and landing smack on her bed. She would have been killed instantly.

The next month, Ronald Mann of South Hampton, England, suffered a fatal heart attack while driving. He slumped forward as his car crashed into a tree. The impact of the car against the tree and the compression of steering column against his chest triggered a "defibrillation" of his heart, *saving his life!* The doctors who treated Ronald's injuries suspect that, in this case, the cushioning of an airbag would have left him a dead man.

These events are reminders that the painful events of life can have an amazing redemptive value – especially when touched by God who can turn every curse into a blessing and remove the sting from life's tragedies (Deuteronomy 23:5). The patriarch Joseph, who suffered betrayal from his brothers, slavery, slander, and unjust imprisonment, went on to say, "What others intended for evil, God intended for good." (Genesis 50:20) Don't be too quick to judge the blows that hit you with the speed of a bullet or the force of a car crash. Through the blow, God may be blessing you.

PRAYER: Dear Father in heaven, when life's adversity hammers me into discouragement and disbelief, please come to my aid. Breathe new life into my soul and turn my curses into blessings, my hurts into halos, and my scars into stars. Amen.

January 7

WHEN WE FEEL LIMITED

Dr. Richard Phillips Feynman (pronounced *fin-mun*), winner of the Nobel Prize (1965) for his work in quantum electrodynamics, was a graduate of both MIT (B.S.) and Princeton University (Ph.D), and professor of theoretical physics at both Cornel University and the California Institute of Technology. He contributed extensively to the development of the atomic bomb during the Manhattan Project.

He introduced some of the most innovative and "mind-blowing" theories, theories that pass way over the heads of most people (e.g. theories of super fluidity, weak nuclear force, and the modern theory of quantum electrodynamics). He wrote more than a dozen books, including the bestseller, *Surely You're Joking Mr. Feynman.* If any human being embodied the image of an intellectual egghead, it was Professor Richard Feynman.

Yet Feynman remained a surprisingly humble and approachable man throughout his life. You see, Dr. Feynman made a shocking little discovery one day. At the peak of his career, after winning the Nobel Prize, Dr. Feynman took a trip to his old high school and checked on his academic records. Two things stunned him immediately. First, Feynman realized that he was no stellar student – his grades were only average. The second discovery "knocked his socks off." He looked at his IQ and saw that it was not 160-180, as he had supposed for so long, but *only 124 – just a little above average!*

This raised serious questions in his mind, questions that we should all consider for ourselves: "If I had known how intellectually-limited I was, would I have ever achieved such scientific greatness in life? Would I have even tried? And if I had known how 'limited' I was, would my limitations only be imaginary, for the reality is I've succeeded in the very world for which I'm not supposed to be equipped?"

Dr. Feynman's discovery causes us all to wonder, before the days of IQ tests, how many statesmen, inventors, world-leaders and other shapers of history, were nothing more than average people who dreamed big and paid the price to make those dreams come true. And what about each of us? What imaginary limitations have we, or others, placed upon us? What can we do in life if we will only dream and dare to try?

Remember the story of the polar bear that the Denver Zoo received as a gift years ago? Though ill-prepared to house such a large animal, the zoo gladly accepted this fine exhibit and placed him in an-undersized cage with the intent to build a much larger one. So small was the cage that the polar bear could only take three steps, turn around and take three steps and turn around again. Several years passed before the new and larger cage was finished. With much fanfare and publicity the new cage, complete with plenty of room to wander and a large pool, was opened. Before cheering crowds the bear was released into his new home. He entered, took three steps and turned around, took three more steps and turned around again. What that bear believed about his living area, we believe about ourselves – our limitations are only in our heads. God help us all to understand and fulfill our true potential for goodness and greatness for which He has created us.

Upon rising to the zenith of his power, David, the former shepherd boy and present King of Israel, received this message from God: "I took you from the pasture and from *following* the flock to *leading* the nation of Israel." (2 Samuel 7:8) Only God could look at the little boy David, being led by his own sheep, and see the greatest of Israel's kings leading the most powerful kingdom of his day.

Remember: "Anyone can count the seeds in an apple, but only God can count the apples in a seed."

PRAYER: Dear Father in heaven, I recognize You as my creator and as the one who knows me better than I know myself. Dear Lord, whatever plans you have for me and whatever potential for good and greatness you have packed into me – please fulfill them all. Guide me with your love and counsel and please help me to listen and to follow. Amen.

January 8

DISTURBED ABOUT YOUR FAILURES?

Few men have had as many strikes against them as John did. He was born in Scotland to an unwed mother. He worked briefly as an actor at the age of eleven in the West Indies. At thirteen, he shipped out aboard a slave ship. The slave trade and piracy went on to blemish his career at sea. He was wanted by the authorities for two separate murder charges and he was later tried, but acquitted, for rape. His later years were spent in bitter anonymity and failing health. He died penniless in France and was buried in an unmarked grave.

But we do not remember John Paul Jones for his checkered past. Instead, he is immortalized in U.S. history as the Father of the United States Navy, as the formidable commander of the "Bonhomme Richard" that defeated the far superior "Serapis" off the coast of Flamborough Head. We remember him for his reply to the captain of the Serapis when asked if he wished to surrender, as Jones' own ship was sinking: *"Sir, I have not yet begun to fight!"*

The "Richard" sank the next day, but John Paul Jones had already captured the "Serapis" and taken 500 British prisoners. John Paul Jones went on to help organize the infant United States Navy, advise Congress on the training of its officers, and to command its squadrons. After the Revolution, John Paul Jones won his most stunning successes as an admiral in Catherine the Great's navy during its war against the Turks – destroying 15 warships, killing 3000 and capturing 1600 of the enemy. For these things we remember John Paul Jones.

And what about the "bad things" in his life? Are we naïve? No, we are not naïve. We acknowledge the man's dark side, but we simply refuse to define his life by his failures.

A pastor once held up a large sheet of plain white poster board before his congregation. Then he drew a black dot in the center of it and asked, "What do you see?" Invariably, they all replied, "We see a black dot." "Does no one see a sheet of white poster board?" he asked. Then the pastor admonished, "Don't define this sheet by the dark blotch made upon it, nor define a person's life by any stain it has." The Scripture reminds us that "All have sinned and fallen short of the glory of God," (Romans 3:23) yet "God so loved the word that he gave his one and only Son, that whoever believes in him should not perish but have everlasting life." (John 3:16)

PRAYER: Dear Father in heaven, grant that I may not define my life or anyone else's by its failures and blemishes. Open my eyes to the good in me and in others. Open my eyes to the love you have for me. Amen.

January 9

WHEN YOU FAIL AGAIN AND AGAIN

How many failures should a person allow himself in pursuit of success with a project? How many times should someone fail before she calls it quits? How many times can success elude them before we consider them a failure? Consider the story of Cyrus W. Field and his efforts to lay the first Trans-Atlantic Cable.

Cyrus Field cooked up the idea to lay a telegraph cable across the Atlantic Ocean from Great Britain to the United States as early as 1854. By March 1857, he had convinced both governments to invest millions into the project and by July of that year work was ready to begin. Both countries agreed to lend large frigates (the U.S.'s *Niagara* and the UK's *Agamemnon*) for the task of laying the 2,300-mile long, 2,500-ton cable. But disaster struck on this first attempt. 335 miles away from the coast of Ireland, the *Niagara*'s section of the cable broke and $500,000-worth of cable (a staggering sum for that time) plummeted into the ocean.

A year later both ships tried again, using better equipment and a different method. This time they met midway in the Atlantic, spliced their cables and headed in opposite directions, the *Agamemnon* toward the UK and the *Niagara* toward the U.S. After repeated breaks and the loss of hundreds of miles of cable, the two ships returned in defeat to Great Britain and to a furious public outcry.

In despair numerous members of the project resigned. Yet at a gloomy meeting of the remaining partners, Fields and his associates reluctantly agreed to try one more time to lay the 2,300-mile-long cable. Initially, it seemed like they had finally succeeded. By August of 1858, the long stretch from Ireland to Newfoundland was complete and Cyrus Field tapped out the world's first trans-Atlantic telegraph message. But this success was short-lived. At the worst possible time – while a banquet in Cyrus Field's honor was being held – the cable suddenly ceased to function. Both governments, as well as the public, were outraged and demanded a thorough investigation. By this time the project resulted in wasted millions of dollars and had nothing to show for it.

Seven years and a civil war passed before the project was revived. This time a greatly improved cable (twice as thick and twice as heavy as previous cables) and the huge steamer, the *Great Eastern*, were employed. Cyrus Field made this latest attempt in July 1865. Though greatly optimistic, Cyrus Field saw this effort end in disaster as well.

What did Cyrus do? Call it quits? Resign himself to failure? No, he took all the lessons he learned from each and every failure and used the knowledge to improve on his methods and his equipment. And one year later, on July 27, 1866, Cyrus Field tapped out this message across the Atlantic: *"All well. Thank God, the cable is laid and in perfect working order!"*

Now, answer the question. Does history regard Cyrus W. Field as a flop, as a failure? Not at all. History only records his success. But if he had quit while he was behind, how would history have judged him? You see, persistence and the refusal to accept defeat make the difference between dismal failure and stunning achievement. God promises us in his word, "I will never leave you nor forsake you; therefore we can say with confidence, 'The Lord is my Helper, I will not be afraid. What can man do to me?'" (Hebrews 13:5-6)

PRAYER: Dear God, help me this day, and always, to learn from my failures, to persistently pursue my tasks, and to never quit until my work is done. Amen.

A LESSON FROM AN OLD PAINTING

One of the most popular works from Japan's celebrated artist of the Edo period, Katsushika Hokusai, is *Beneath the Great Wave off Kanagawa*. This woodblock print portrays a thunderous wave towering over the viewer, the barges transporting fish, and (in the distance) Mount Fuji. This woodblock print is just one of a series of the artist's *36 Views of Mount Fuji*, in which Japan's highest mountain is the centerpiece.

However, *The Great Wave* is different. In this picture you are eye-level with the fishermen. You see things as they see them. And

from a fisherman's point of view, the waves are scary. From the fisherman's view Mount Fuji is tiny and almost out of sight, and appears overshadowed by the towering waves. In fact, from the fisherman's view, Mount Fuji appears vulnerable and threatened by the frenzied waves.

Of course the artist and the audience know better. The audience knows, regardless of how things *look*, the waves are no threat to Mount Fuji. In fact, the mountain is quite large - 12,388 feet (3,776 meters) above sea level– 100 times higher than any wave that has ever been. From the Mountain's point of view the waves are the tiniest ripples. From the fisherman's perspective the waves are angry and noisy and Fuji seems distant and silent. But the artist knows that Fuji can also thunder – it last erupted about 300 years ago. And when it thunders again, it will be the waters that quake at the sound of its voice.

In Psalm 46 the hostile nations of the world are pictured as furious waves whose thundering seems to make even the mountains quake. But the psalmist assures us, "God is our refuge and strength, a very present help in times of trouble … the nations will make an uproar, but when God raises His voice, they will melt away." (Psalm 46:1, 6)

Turbulent times may be ahead and you may feel like you're in one of those fishing boats in the midst of the frenzied waves. But God's kingdom and his purpose will prevail upon the earth. And God is an unfailing refuge from the storms of this life for all who put their trust in Him.

PRAYER: Almighty and merciful Father, glorify Your name in all the earth and may Your reign of righteousness, peace and love prevail upon this planet. Please, dear Lord, begin your reign first in my own heart. Amen.

January 11

ARE YOU IN "OVER YOUR HEAD"?

Every parent has had this experience. You're holding your child while wading in the water and then, as you enter deeper water and it touches your child's toes, your child suddenly clings tight to you. When my daughter Laura was just 2 or 3 years old, I held her and waded into the pool at a motel. We began at the shallow end of the pool (3 feet deep) and walked toward the deep end (5 feet deep). She was calm and confident until the water touched her toes – then she clamped onto me like a little leech. As we walked further and further into the deep end of the pool, she clung tighter and tighter to me. I tried to re-assure her, "Everything's OK. I've got you. I won't let you go." But it was to no avail. The water was touching her toes, then her waist, then her shoulders and that was too far. So I did an about face and brought her out of the water.

I've reflected on those times and wondered. "Did it ever occur to Laura that she was in "over her head" at every point in that pool?" My daughter was less than three feet tall, too small for even the shallowest point. Yet she only sensed her need to hang onto daddy when the water touched her. In reality, she was as dependent upon me at the 3-foot mark, as at the 5-foot mark. At the same time, at no point was the water over my head.

This applies to all of us as God's children. When we trust in our Heavenly Father, we are safe in his almighty arms. But we have this mistaken notion that we need Him more in times of trial and less in times of joy and prosperity. The reality is – we need Him every hour.

Like the little child, we frail creatures are always, always "in over our heads."

Early in our faith walk, we naively assume that God will never allow the "water to touch us" – i.e. God will never let trouble break into our lives. But he does. He takes us deeper and the water touches our toes. Sensing the "crisis," we cry out to Him, "Oh God, save me; deliver me from death!" But He takes us deeper, and the water envelops us more until it reaches our waist. Never before, have we sensed our need for our heavenly Father. Never have we clung so close to the Savior. Then he takes us even deeper until the water reaches our shoulders. "Do not forsake me, Oh Lord. Save me, I pray." Then the Lord brings us back to where it's "safer." And we, thinking we're "in the clear," let go of God, assuming our need for him is not as great. Yet if God were to drop us at that point – we would perish, just as surely as if we were in the deepest waters. Because we are always in "over our heads" and there is no time when God does not hold our life and breath in his hands. But there will never be a time when God is in over His head, nor will he ever drop us. No loving parent would ever do so. Are we to expect less from God?

Consider the words of Scripture that say, "In all their suffering he also suffered, and he personally rescued them. In his love and mercy he redeemed them. He lifted them up and carried them through all the years." (Isaiah 63:9, New Living Translation) Trust in God and He will carry you, and there will truly never be a crisis in your life. Ignore and reject Him, and all of life will be a crisis, whether you know it or not.

PRAYER: Dear Father in heaven, help me to understand your love for me and your power to save and protect me. Help me to rest peacefully in Your almighty and all-loving arms. Amen.

January 12

FEARFULLY AND WONDERFULLY MADE

Would you love to get away? Do you yearn to travel to exotic places and lands? How about the crescent of Gianuzzi, the isles of Langerhans, the crypts of Lieberkuhn, the canal of Gugier, the circle of Willis, the area of Cohnheim, the pyramids of Malpighi, the antrum of Highmore, the spaces of Fontana, the cistern of Pecquet, Scarpa's triangle, Gower's tract, and the angle of Ludwig?

Any of those sound interesting? If they do, you're in luck. Not only can you go to them, you carry them with you – all the time. They are parts and areas of the human body, mostly named after the anatomists who discovered or first described them. The point is, within your own body is a veritable gold mine of treasures, an entire world of fascination.

Even at birth you already possessed more than 26 billion cells. And now? If you're just an average adult, your body is made up of between 75 to 100 trillion (100,000,000,000,000) cells. Consider the other resources you possess:

- 1.3 to 1.6 gallons of blood.
- 206 bones.
- Over 650 muscles, from the tiny muscles that move your ears to your largest muscle, the *gluteus maximus* (that big muscle you sit on).
- 10,000 taste buds in your tongue, palate, and cheeks.
- So many arteries, capillaries, and veins that if you laid them end to end, they'd stretch for about 100,000 miles – enough to wrap around the world four times!
- 1 million tubes in your kidneys, which add up to a hefty 40 miles!
- About 13.5 neurons (nerve cells) in your spinal cord.
- 19 million cells in every square inch of your skin.
- About 40 million olfactory receptor cells to help you smell.
- 6,000 million, million, million hemoglobin molecules in your blood stream.
- A digestive system that works 12-15 hours digesting each meal.
- A liver that performs at least 561 known functions to keep you alive, including removing bacteria from the bloodstream, regulating blood clotting, producing bile to digest foods, and storing vitamins and minerals.
- A heart that pumps 8,000 gallons of blood every day and that beats 2.5 billion times in your lifetime.
- A cardio-vascular system that replaces 3 million red blood cells that are lost *every second!*
- DNA molecules that, if unraveled, one would stretch out to almost 80 inches and if all were unraveled they would stretch out so long that they could reach to the sun and back again *600 times!*

- A genetic code which, at conception, contains enough information in your genetic blueprint to fill *200 New York City telephone books of 1000 pages each!*
- A brain that, although it only consists of 2 percent of your body weight, uses 20 to 30 percent of your calorie intake and 20 percent of your blood, but has an incredible 1,000 trillion connections that conduct electrical impulses for everything from creative thoughts to involuntary body functions.

Yes, you and I are engineering marvels, richly endowed and marvelously designed by a loving Creator. In the Scripture the psalmist declared: "I will praise you for I am fearfully and wonderfully made." (Psalm 139:14)[ii]

PRAYER: Dear Father in heaven, in my pursuit after happiness, excitement and wonder, help me not to overlook those people and things that you have already brought into my life. Help me to never lose my sense of wonder at all this is about me and even in me. Thank you, that I am fearfully and wonderfully made. Amen.

January 13

IT'S OK TO HAVE LIMITATIONS

A recent Associated Press article (Arthur Max, September 15, 2006) stated that the Dutch are the tallest people on earth – averaging over six feet tall for men and five-foot seven inches for women. It states further that Scandinavian men had previously had this distinction, but the Dutch have passed them up. What are the reasons for this increase in stature? The source is improved nutrition beginning with a mother's prenatal care of her child, particularly from a diet rich in protein. The article further stated that the Dutch may reach a height of six-feet three inches as a national average within this century.

But they can only grow so tall. The Scandinavians, the article stated, will not get any taller. They've gone as far as they can on the strength of better nutrition. And the Dutch will only get *so* tall themselves by virtue of eating the right things. Why is this so? It's all about genetics. People can only grow as tall they are genetically programmed to grow. For all the article's hoopla about the large size of Europeans, it frankly acknowledged something that we humans have trouble admitting – we all have limitations.

In the military we all desire to have those words in our fitness reports, "He is a leader of *unlimited* potential." And the most hurtful thing to say about someone is that he or she is "a person of limitations." But the truth is that everyone is limited.

Does that disturb you? But having limitations is part of being human. And coming to grips with who and what we are, with what our God-given strengths are and with what our weaknesses are, is one of the greatest lessons we can ever learn.

Do limitations apply to the spiritual realm as well? Yes and no. "You can go as far as your faith and imagination can take you," we have heard it said. There is no denying the truth of this statement. But the other side of the truth is this - both faith and imagination are limited as well. "God has given to everyone a *measure* of faith" (Romans 12:3). So declares the Scripture. But what is "a measure?" It is exactly that, a measured or limited amount. Therefore, we are told not to think more highly of ourselves than we ought to, but to assess ourselves soberly (Romans 12:3).

This is not a condemnation of conceit, but consolation that we do not have to "do it all" and "be it all." We don't have to be a super-hero. And we certainly don't have to be God. We are free to be ourselves – with our specific mix of strengths and weaknesses.

But how do we deal with our limitations in the face of life's impossible tasks? We accomplish our tasks with the help of those around us. The Scripture tells us that each of us is an individual part of a greater whole, like the parts that make up a body (Romans 12:4-8). Together, with each of us doing our part with the faith and grace that God has measured out to us, we can do the impossible.

PRAYER: Dear Father in heaven, thank you for my limitations. Now, lead me on the path of self-discovery, that I may understand the gifts and abilities You have given me and the way You want me to use them – that I may accomplish your good and perfect will and be a blessing to others. Amen.

January 14

HOW DOES IT SUCCEED?

The mighty giant Sequoia tree is truly a wonder. Though beginning as one of the smallest seeds found among plants (a mere 1/5000 of an ounce) this tiny seed contains a blueprint for growing into a virtual skyscraper, thirty stories tall. Consider a premiere example of the Sequoia, the General Sherman tree. The General Sherman is 36.5 feet across at its base, stands 274 feet tall and constitutes the largest living thing on earth.

Besides its magnificence in growth and size, there is another aspect of this giant's wonder – the amazing coordination and cooperation among its trillions of cells for the common survival of the tree. Nutrients and resources gathered through its roots and its leaves via photosynthesis are channeled upward and outward to support this tree's phenomenal growth. In glorious unison, this magnificent giant nurtures and feeds its city of cells, bends its massive frame toward the sun, and fights off the constant invasions of bacteria and disease.

One example of this amazing cooperation and coordination is the way this towering tree, as well as most plants, fights infections. When the tree detects an invading disease or bacterium, signals travel throughout the tree. Cells all around the infected area abruptly die and form a barrier of dead tissue through which the disease cannot penetrate. And it does all this *without a brain*, without any central command dictating orders to subordinate systems and cells.

If only people, like the cells of the tree, could work and live together for the common good. If only we could submit our own personal goals and needs to the needs of the many. The Scripture says: "Make my joy complete by being like-minded, having the same love, being one in spirit and purpose. Do nothing out of selfish ambition or vain conceit, but in humility consider others more important than yourselves. Each one of you should look out not only to your own interests, but also to the interests of others. (Philippians 2:2-4)

PRAYER: Dear Father in heaven, please bless our home, our work place, and our country with unity of purpose and vision. Grant that we may all be willing to set aside our personal interests in order to seek for the common good and peace. Amen.

January 15

DO YOURSELF A FAVOR

An African fable tells the story of an ant carrying a large grain of corn who fell into a pond. The corn sank deep below the surface, but the ant managed to stay afloat, though he struggled to keep his head above water. A pigeon chanced to be nearby for a drink. He felt sorry for the little fellow, so he plucked a leave and tossed it in the direction of the ant. A grateful ant climbed aboard the floating leaf that eventually brought him safely to the shore.

But no sooner had the ant reached the shore that he saw a boy, with bow and arrow in hand, crouching down and aiming for the pigeon. The grateful ant charged after the would-be hunter, climbed on top of his foot and bit him on the toe. "Yeeeoow!" the boy cried out, alerting the pigeon to the danger, who flew away to safety.

In so short a time, each had saved the other. The pigeon, feeling compassion for the little ant, saved the very one who would so soon be his savior. If the pigeon had let the little ant drown, he would have doomed himself.

In a real-life story, the late Stevie Ray Vaughn, rose to become one of the most influential blues guitarists of the 20th Century. But how did he get his start? Stevie's inspiration was the famed blues guitarist of a previous generation – Buddy Guy. Along with fellow blues musicians, Muddy Waters and Howlin' Wolf, Buddy Guy is considered one of the great precursors to the Rock n' Roll era. But by the 1980s Buddy Guy had fallen on hard times and felt he had "lost it." His musical gift and inspiration had died. Then he heard Stevie Ray Vaughn play. He was spellbound by the younger artist. Vaughn's performance energized the Elder Statesman of Rhythm and Blues and he launched on a highly successful comeback. The man he inspired had become his inspiration.

The scripture tells us "Blessed are the merciful, for they shall obtain mercy" (Matthew 5:7), "give and it shall be given unto you" (Luke 6:38), and "by your standard of measure, it will be measured to you." (Matthew 7:2) God has built a law of reciprocation into his universe. The good or the bad that we do to others will come back to either bless or curse us.

PRAYER: Dear Father in heaven, though I am tempted to be selfish and vengeful, make me an instrument of your healing and peace. Grant that I may help and not hurt. I leave the rewards for every good deed in your hands and humbly thank you for your love and forgiveness – which I need every hour. Amen.

January 16

PREDATORS ARE OVERRATED

Great white sharks are the world's largest and most feared predatory fish. They can reach lengths of 20 feet and can weigh-in at over 4,000 pounds. They are widely recognized as nature's ultimate killing machines and consummate predators. But last Christmas Eve a 36-year-old surfer of slight build put a serious dent in the great white's image.

The surfer was Brian Anderson. He was having a great time on Christmas Eve, 2005, riding waves off the Oregon coast, near the town of Seaside. Suddenly, something clamped hard on his leg – "like a bear trap," Anderson explained. A twelve-foot great white shark had just taken a chunk out of his leg and was coming back for the kill.

As the massive beast grabbed him again, Brian had the presence of mind to remember something he learned during the Discovery Channel's "Shark Week": the most sensitive part of a shark's body is his nose. So, as hard as he could, Brian repeatedly punched the shark in the nose with his right hand while clutching his surfboard with his left.

It worked! The "killer beast" swam away and did not pursue again, even though Brian left a trail of blood as he paddled to the shore. Fellow surfers assisted Brian Anderson and brought him to the hospital where he was treated for multiple lacerations before being released to his wife and 10-year-old son.

Our culture is far too enamored with predators. We give the title "predator" to our war machines and to scary science fiction creatures. But the fact is, predators are over-rated. With only a few exceptions (e.g. the wolverine and shrew), predators are nothing but well-armed bullies who are looking for the easiest kill. Predators are **not** looking for a fight – Brian Anderson proved that. Predators pick on the young, the weak, and the sickly. Nor are predators very good survivors. Just check out the fossil record sometime and you'll find that the most terrifying creatures who have ever walked the earth or swam its seas (e.g. Tyrannosaurus Rex, the Ichthyosaur, the saber-toothed tiger, the bone-crushing dog, etc.) are *all extinct!*. In contrast, far smaller and gentler creatures – which also appear in the fossil record (e.g. turtles, opossums, mole rats) – still thrive to this day. The reality is that the "fittest" and strongest of creatures are the gentle ones.

And what is true among God's creatures is also true among his children. As the Scriptures proclaimed so long ago: "the gentle shall inherit the earth." (Psalm 37:11; Matthew 5:5). Therefore, we are told not to "fret" (i.e. "get ourselves agitated and upset") when violent and wicked people rise up to do evil (Psalm 37:1, 7-9). For God will see to it that the gentle and the merciful, not the predators among humanity, will survive and flourish.

PRAYER: Dear Father in heaven, help my troubled heart, for I see so much violence and evil around me. In accordance to your promise, O Lord, please bless and protect the gentle and merciful among humanity, and cause them to prevail upon the earth. Amen.

January 17

CHANGING VALUES

In the late 1800s aluminum was considered a precious metal, fit only for fashioning the helmets and scepters for royalty. Like other precious metals, it did not rust. Unlike them, it was lightweight and strong, and it was these qualities that made it a greatly desired, but rare and expensive commodity. Yet aluminum was not rare at all. In fact, it is the most abundant metals on earth. Trouble is, there existed no feasible way of extracting aluminum ore from the ground. Then, in 1886, two inventors, Charles Hall and Paul Heroult, discovered an inexpensive process of obtaining aluminum ore from the earth's crust using electricity. Their process reduced the price of aluminum to less than 1% of its earlier cost and made it the third most used metal in industry – behind iron and steel. The sad part of the story is that aluminum has fallen from its status as a precious metal. Once it stood alongside gold, silver and platinum. Now it's just a cheap building material. There are some countries that use aluminum in their coinage – but only for the smallest coins of the lowest denominations.

Many material things, things that we once treasured, have decreased in value immensely. Information and technology advances are partly responsible for this. Consider the following. The first marketed microwave oven, Raytheon's "Radarange," was 6 feet tall, weighed 750 pounds, and cost *$4000* in 1947. Today a small microwave can be purchased for less than $50. In 1976 a VCR would put you out $1600. Today you can pick up a new one for $50. And did you know that today a $10 computer chip can do what it took a $100,000 computer to do twenty years ago? Or, that the equivalent of an RCA Color TV in 1956 – then priced at $895 – today costs only about $199?

The list goes on. But these examples are reason enough not to put too much faith in material things or to make them our heart's desire. Family, friends and faith in our loving and saving God are the greatest assets any of us can have. These relationships are worthy of the investment of our time, resources, and devotion. In all our earthly pursuits we should never neglect the things that truly define our lives and will never diminish in value.[iii]

Our Lord warned that "a man's life does not consist in the abundance of his possessions" (Luke 12:15) and that life's true treasures are those things that endure for eternity (John 6:27; Matthew 6:21).

PRAYER: Dear Father, open my eyes to the true treasures I have in my spouse, my children and in You. Help me also, O God, to live with eternity's values in mind. Amen.

January 18

THESE STUPID JOBS

There is a scene in the 1984 blockbuster movie, *The Karate Kid* which contains an important faith lesson. The movie depicts the struggles of a teenage boy, Daniel LaRusso (Ralph Macchio), who is uprooted from his friends and familiar surroundings in Newark, NJ and transplanted on the West Coast in southern California. After finding it impossible to find acceptance from fellow students and enduring several beatings from a gang of martial arts bullies, Daniel is befriended by a local handyman, Mr. Miyagi (Pat Morita).

In the course of time Daniel discovers that Japan-born Mr. Miyagi is well-versed in Karate. At Daniel's request, Mr. Miyagi agrees to teach the boy Karate. However, instead of Karate lessons, Mr. Miyagi seems only interested in getting Daniel to wax his fleet of cars, paint his fence, and sand his deck.

What annoys Daniel most is the *particular way* Mr. Miyagi demands that he apply and wipe off the wax. *"Wax on, wax off,"* is the recurring command, as Miyagi moves Daniel's hands in a specific pattern. He does the same with Daniel's hands as he sands, varnishes, and paints. As the senseless tasks becomes more and more tedious, Daniel grumbles: *"What has this got to do with Karate? I came here to learn how to defend myself. 'Wax on – wax off!' This is stupid. What a waste of time!"* The viewer is just as mystified as Daniel. Finally, Daniel's frustration bubbles over. He erupts in an angry outburst at Mr. Miyagi.

Just then Mr. Miyagi tells him to defend himself. He throws a series of Karate punches at Daniel. But Daniel, whose hands are now conditioned to the hand motions from waxing, painting, and sanding easily blocks every punch. "First lesson complete. Come back tomorrow" Mr. Miyagi congratulates him.

Daniel stands in stunned silence. What he thought was a stupid task and a waste of his time, suddenly takes on a profound meaning. He was being taught Karate all along – and didn't even know it!

If you turn to the Scriptures you see the same pattern. Men and women of God who long to use their talents for something *really important,* but who are forced to waste their time with senseless jobs. Joseph spends wasted years as a prison administrator. Moses and David both spend wasted years as shepherds. Peter spends wasted years as a fisherman. Paul spends wasted years in obscurity as student. Yet, every one of them was learning priceless lessons for the future through those "stupid jobs."

Where has God has placed you? It's hard at the present to understand the significance of your work. But trust in God and be faithful in your work, and He will one day reveal the hidden fruitfulness of this phase of your life. A familiar passage tells us: "Trust in the LORD with all your heart and do not lean on your own understanding. In all your ways acknowledge Him, and He shall direct your paths." (Proverbs 3:5-6)

PRAYER: Dear Father in heaven, I trust that You see my future and have the wisdom to order the events of my life to best prepare me for it. In times of obscurity and tedious and senseless tasks, help me to trust that You will work out everything for my good and for your glory. Amen.

January 19

ARE WE CURING OR KILLING?

It was the saddest affair. James Garfield had come so far in life. Born in a log cabin amidst abject poverty and orphaned when he was only two years old, Garfield rose to become a Christian minister, a college president, a crime-fighting attorney, United States Congressman and Senator, as well as a successful Civil War general. He reached the pinnacle of his career when he was elected President in 1881. But James Garfield had only been in office for four months when he was gunned down by Charles Julius Guiteau on July 2, 1881. Guiteau was a mentally ill attorney who was embittered because the President had not appointed him as a diplomat to France.

But the president didn't die from Guiteau's senseless act. In fact, President Garfield remained alive and conscious for eighty days after the shooting. Tragically, his death was the result of his doctors' well-intentioned efforts.

His primary physician, Dr. Willard Bliss, created complications for the wounded head of state when he stuck a metal probe into the wound to find the bullet. By doing so he cut a path that misled every subsequent examining doctor. He introduced infection into Garfield's wound by poking it with his unwashed finger. Another doctor, desperate to find the bullet, forced his hand wrist-deep into the wound. He didn't find the bullet, but he did manage to puncture Garfield's liver. A total of sixteen well-meaning doctors scrutinized the President's wound, each trying their hand at finding that mysterious bullet with bacteria-laden fingers and probes. They never found the bullet. They only added to Garfield's suffering, greatly enlarged the size of his wound and infected his body with bacteria. On September 14, 1881, James Garfield died from heart failure, following a bout with pneumonia and blood poisoning. An autopsy revealed that the bullet was not located in any life-threatening area and was surrounded by a protective cyst. Medical examiners concluded that the President would surely have lived if his doctors had just left him alone.

The well-intentioned, but deadly, efforts President Garfield's doctors are not unlike some of the things we do to our fellow human beings who are emotionally and spiritually wounded. All around us are deeply wounded, flawed and hurting people. They desperately need our love and understanding. But too often we add to their sorrows by probing into their lives and into their wounds, looking for some hidden flaw or some secret sin.[iv]

We somehow forget the words of our Lord, when he asked: *"Why do you look at the speck that is in your brother's eye, but do not notice the log that is in your own eye? Or how can you say to your brother, 'Let me take the speck out of your eye,' and behold, the log is in your own eye? You hypocrite, first take the log out of your own eye and then you will see clearly to take the speck out of your brother's eye."* (Matthew 7:4-6) Someone has wisely said, "When looking for faults use a mirror, not a telescope."

PRAYER: Lord, make me an instrument of your peace;
Where there is hatred, let me sow love;
    Where there is injury, pardon;
    Where there is doubt, faith;
    Where there is despair, hope;
    Where there is darkness, light;
    Where there is sadness, joy.
Divine Master, grant that I may not so much seek
    To be consoled as to console;
    To be understood as to understand;
    To be loved as to love.
For it is in giving that we receive;
It is in pardoning that we are pardoned;
And it is in dying that we are born to eternal life. Amen.

January 20

WHEN WE CLOSE OUR MINDS

Opinionated! It is the state of mind when someone is obstinately attached to only one view and refuses to consider alternate views. There is no discussion, no debate, and, sadly, no learning.

Some people are opinionated and proud of it. But a closed and narrow mind can sometimes have tragic results. Take, for instance, Lieutenant Hiroo Onada during WWII in the Philippines. Lieutenant Onada was a fine soldier and leader of men. But above all he prized his own devotion to duty and the meticulous care with which he followed instructions. "Hold out to the last man! Do not surrender! Do not take your own life!" These were the parting words of his commanding general, Akira Muto. And hold out he did. Onada held out after the last of his soldiers had died or deserted. He held out when spies tried to impersonate Japanese officers, telling him the war was over. He held out when a spy pretended to be his brother, urging him to lay down his arms and come home. He held out against forged letters from his relatives who pleaded with him to return to Japan. Lieutenant Onada knew better than to trust these lies. Yet even Lieutenant Onada had limitations. And loneliness got the best of him.

Then he did the unthinkable. Lieutenant Onada, now the only survivor of his platoon, surrendered to his former superior officer, Yoshimi Taniguchi – *almost twenty-nine years after the WWII had ended!* That's right. On March 9, 1974, the day he laid down his arms, Lieutenant Hiroo Onada received the shock of his life. All those spies were *not* spies at all. The man impersonating his brother, *was* his brother. That "forged" letter *was* from his family after all. And the war truly *was* over. Lieutenant Onada had been consummately wrong.

Like the stubborn, hard-headed soldier, many a person holds out against the Lord. The Lord announces His victory over Satan, over sin, over the world. Yet precious years go by as we "hunker down" and disbelieve our Creator's word that He loves us and only wishes to bless us. Yet God sends out his invitation again and again: "Come now, and let us reason together, says the Lord. Though your sins be as scarlet they shall be white as snow. Though they be red like crimson, they shall be as wool." (Isaiah 1:18)

PRAYER: Dear Father in heaven, open my blind eyes and deaf ears to your love. Help me to realize you are not the enemy, but the greatest friend. Amen.

GOD CAN MAKE US EQUAL TO THE TASK

Climb the highest point in all fifty States in just 100 days! No big deal, you say? But just think of some of those "highest points" and their remote locations: Mount McKinley in Alaska – 20,320 feet above sea level and thousands of miles from most Americans; Mauna Kea in far off Hawaii – 13,796 feet high; the foreboding Mount Whitney in the impassable Sierra Nevada of California – 14,494 feet; Mount Elbert in the heart of Colorado's Rocky Mountains – 14,443 feet; and the towering Mount Rainier of Washington – 14,441 feet. Included among America's giants are, in descending order: Wyoming's Gannet Peak – 13,804 feet; Utah's Kings Peak – 13,528; New Mexico's Wheeler Peak – 13,161 feet high; Boundary Peak in Nevada – 13,143 feet; Granite Peak in Montana – 12,799 feet; Idaho's Borah Peak – 12,662 feet; Arizona's Humphreys Peak – 12,633 feet; and Oregon's Mount Hood – 11,239 high. The eastern United States also boasts of some challenging peaks: North Carolina's Mount Mitchell – 6,684 feet, Tennessee's Clingmans Dome – 6,664 feet and the unassuming but very dangerous Mount Washington in New Hampshire – 6,288 feet.

The challenge to climb all 50 "high points" in all 50 states in just 100 days came from an organization to all mountaineers who wanted to set a new record. A young man named Todd Huston heard the challenge and decided to go for it. Seeking the advice of expert climbers, he trained hard. The expedition was scheduled to begin in April 1994.

Preparations were on track up until the last two months. Todd lost all support from the companies that pledged to sponsor him. It seemed like all his hard work had been a waste and his dream was dead. But he refused to accept defeat. In the days that followed, Todd went to work organizing funding for a new expedition. He told himself and his supporters, "God willing, I'll find a way to make this expedition happen." His hard work and determination paid off. With the logistics of each climb in place, Todd called the project "Summit America." On June 1, 1994, Todd's first climb began on Mt. McKinley in Alaska. One by one the highest point in each state was conquered.

All went well until the 47th climb. Two days before Todd's arrival, two climbers were killed on Mt. Hood, Oregon. Everyone advised Todd the climb was too dangerous. But he was working against time in a race with many competitors. Though filled with apprehension, Todd made the climb safely with an old high school friend and expert mountaineer, Fred Zalokar.

Then, on August 7, 1994, just 66 days after he started, Todd climbed the last peak in Hawaii. His expedition shattered the old climbing record *by 35 days!* Todd had triumphed over many obstacles, fulfilling his dream project—"Summit America."

There is one thing you should know about Todd, one detail that made him a very unlikely mountain climber. Todd had only one leg – he had lost his left leg thirteen years earlier. But because of his faith in God and heart of determination, Todd - the one-legged, unlikely "climber of mountains," became a champion mountaineer.^v

To look at Todd one would think – "No way is this guy going to beat out the best mountaineers in America." Yet God is in the business of taking zeroes and making them heroes. He can put a dream in our heart and empower us to make it come true. The Scripture reminds us, "God chooses the foolish things of the world to shame the wise, and God chooses the weak things of the world to put to shame the things that are mighty … that no one should boast in God's presence." (1 Corinthians 1:27-29)

PRAYER: Dear Lord, please set my feet on the path that leads to your perfect will and, as you first breathed into man the breath of life, so breath into me the inspiration, motivation and strength to pursue and reach the dreams you've placed in my heart. Amen.

January 22

A SMALL SPARK CAN START A HUGE FIRE

Ever become embroiled in an extended fight with your spouse or close friend and then be unable to recall how the fight started or even what you're fighting about? Upon reflection, we may even find that the initial cause of the fight is ridiculously small and insignificant. Would you believe that even wars have erupted from very minor events?

Ever hear of the *War of the Oaken Bucket*? This war occurred in 1325 between the Italian states of Modena and Bologna. And, yes, it was fought over a wooden bucket that had been stolen by some Modena soldiers who invaded Bologna. This tragic war lasted for twelve years and resulted in the deaths of hundreds of civilians and soldiers. And the bucket was never returned.

Then there was the War of the Stray Dog. This conflict exploded in 1925 when a Greek soldier's dog strayed across the Bulgarian border. When the soldier crossed over to retrieve his dog the Bulgarian border guard shot and killed him. An enraged Greek government declared war on and invaded Bulgaria. Only after the League of Nations intervened was the war brought to a halt.

Much more recently, in 1969, the neighboring countries of El Salvador and Honduras duked it out, resulting in the deaths of 2,000 civilians and soldiers. And what were they fighting about? The survival of their economies or governments? No, their bloody war began over a soccer game.

The Book of Proverbs tells us, "The beginning of strife is like breaching a dam; therefore stop contention before a quarrel starts (Proverbs 17:14)." It's difficult to take back words. A raised gun, a fist, and a voice are all alike-they are easier to lift than to put down. Avoid an outbreak of hostility by practicing the words of Proverbs 15:1: "A gentle answer turns away wrath, but harsh words only stir up anger."

PRAYER: Dear Lord, help me to treat others the way I would like to be treated. When anger rises within me, help me not lose control or do anything I will later regret. Amen.

January 23

WHEN PAIN IS GAIN

Can the painful events of our lives be blessings in disguise? Consider these true stories.

Lt.Cmdr. Robert W. Goehring had walked the decks of his Coast Guard cutter, the *USS Duane*, hundreds of times. But this time would change his life forever. He had just stepped out on deck when a huge wave crashed against the boat and swept him overboard. Immediately, the officer of the deck ordered the ship to turn around and initiate a search for the lost captain. But no sooner had the vessel turned, when another huge wave crashed against the cutter, carefully depositing the lost skipper safely upon the deck of the ship.

Roy Dikkers was a Merchant Marine during WWII. When his ship was torpedoed in the North Atlantic, the explosion blasted the door to his quarters shut. A second torpedo blasted the door open, through which he escaped – only to find himself surrounded by a wall of approaching and inescapable flames. "This is it," he thought, and prayed, "God forgive me!" Just then a third torpedo blasted him clear of the deck and away from the deadly flames. He swam to safety and was later rescued by a Norwegian vessel.[vi]

Sometimes the blows of life can bless us. Sometimes the very things that we fear will destroy us, will save us. The famed English poet, William Cowper, had this idea in mind when he wrote:

God moves in a mysterious way, His wonders to perform; he plants His footsteps in the sea and rides upon the storm.
You fearful saints, fresh courage take; the clouds you so much dread, are big with mercy and shall break with blessings on your head.
Judge not the Lord by feeble sense, but trust Him for His grace; behind a frowning providence faith sees a smiling face.
Blind unbelief is sure to err and scan His work in vain; God is His own interpreter, and He shall make it plain.

The Scripture tells us: "Your God turned the curse into a blessing" (Deuteronomy 23:5). This is what God does for those who place their lives in his hands – he takes the blows, the hard knocks, and the painful events of our lives and uses them to do us ultimate good.

PRAYER: Almighty Father, I put my life, my plans, and my future into your hands. I ask that you will, please, take all my tragedies, hard knocks, and painful blows and turn them all into blessings that will bring about ultimate good in my life. Amen.

January 24

DON'T BE FOOLED

In a documentary on the making of the 1963 Alfred Hitchcock classic, *The Birds*, actress Veronica Cartwright recalls one of the movie's most frightening scenes - when a mass of ravens attacks a group of small school children.

The scene begins with actress Tipi Hedrin sitting outside a country schoolhouse in Bodega Bay, California, waiting for the children to be released. A raven lands on the monkey bars behind her, then another, then a few more. For the next minute the camera focuses on Tipi Hedrin's face and lets the audience speculate as to how many birds have gathered in the lapse of time. Suddenly, a flying raven catches the attention of Hedrin. Her eyes follow its flight overhead to the monkey bars behind her. She turns and gasps as she sees the entire playground literally covered with hundreds of ravens. In retrospect Ms. Cartwright admits it was a very scary scene. However, she confesses that most of the ravens sitting on the monkey bars and perched along the crest of the schoolhouse were nothing but cardboard cutouts painted black.

During the shooting of the scene the actress was concerned that the audience would easily detect the fakery of the cardboard silhouettes. But Hitchcock assured her the mere "cardboard birds" would present a very effective image to fool the audience. Hitchcock was right. In the few seconds you see the hundreds of sinister ravens perched everywhere, they look frighteningly real.

Just as Hitchcock plays tricks on the eyes of his audience, so Satan plays tricks on our minds. He consistently creates the illusion of problems – problems that do not exist or are so small they are hardly worth our attention. He constantly portrays our fellow human beings as evil and threatening. It is a constant battle to shield our minds from the steady bombardment of his poisonous lies. But the Scripture admonishes us: "Resist the devil and he will flee" (James 4:7) and "You shall know the truth and the truth shall make you free" (John 8:32).

PRAYER: Dear Father in heaven, help me to fill my mind with that which is true, honorable, right, pure, lovely, and noble. Deliver me from thoughts and feelings of racism, sexism and bigotry. Amen.

January 25

ARE YOU LAGGING BEHIND?

Thomas Alva Edison, Isaac Newton, and Albert Einstein – what do these men have in common? All geniuses? Yes. All made stunning achievements in the world of science. Yes. Also note that they all were poor students and were considered unfit for academics as children.

What about Christian Heinrich Heinecken, Kim Ung-Yong, or Pierre Bouguer? Never hear of them? Christian Heinecken only lived to be four years old, but by the time he was two and a half he had read the Old and New Testaments of the Bible, and by the age of 3, he could read and speak in German, French and Latin. By the age of 4 Kim Ung-Yong composed and published a book of poetry and spoke Korean, English, German and Japanese. At the age of 10, Pierre Bouguer was teaching math to his instructors and became a professor at the age of 15.

So what's the point? That all of us develop at different rates and reach our most productive years at different ages. Actually, Isaac Newton made his greatest scientific contributions (e.g. the method of calculus, the spectral composition of light along with the fundamentals of optics, and the law of universal gravitation and the basic laws of mechanics) by the age of twenty-three, while during the last third of his life he made none at all.

In contrast, many individuals have proven far more productive in the later part of their lives. Fanny Crosby is considered to be America's greatest hymn writer. Her songs number more than 8,000 (some number them at nearly 9,000). Yet she didn't write her first hymn until her mid-forties. At the age of 50 Plato was still a student and produced his greatest works after he reached 60. Cornelius Vanderbilt's ocean liner empire exploded from 100 miles to more than 10,000 and added more than $100 million to his fortunes between his 70th and 83rd birthdays. Noah Webster wrote his monumental *Dictionary of the American English Language* at the age of 70.

The great scientist, Francis Bacon, produced his greatest literary works on the scientific method after the age of 60. The great French scientist, Jean Baptiste Lamark, completed his greatest work, *The Natural History of Invertebrates* at 78. The great Italian composer, Giuseppe Verdi, was 74 when he produced his masterpiece "Othello," 80 when he wrote "Falstaff," and 85 when he composed "Stabat Mater," "Te Deum," and one of the most beloved works of all time, "Ave Maria."

General Douglas MacArthur was commander of all allied forces during the Korean War and pulled off the most brilliant military operation of his 50-year-career (the Inchon Invasion) when he was *70 years old!*

So if you don't seem to be "in-step" with your peers, if you feel like you're lagging behind, if you feel like you've been left in a cloud of dust by all your brilliant contemporaries, Don't worry. Your best and most productive years are probably yet to come.

The Scripture says, "The righteous person will flourish like a palm tree, he will grow like a cedar in Lebanon. …They will still be fruitful in old age; they shall be full of life and very young at heart, to testify that the Lord is upright, steadfast and there is no unrighteousness in him." (Psalm 92:12-15)

PRAYER: Dear God of peace and hope, fill my heart with hope for the future. Bless my life with fruitful and productive years, that I may bless others and honor your name to my dying day. Amen.

January 26

DEATH IS NOT THE END

One undeniable reality of human existence is that a person's death does not signal the end of his or her influence and impact. This is common in the secular world. Quite often, a person's greatest work takes place after death.

John Kennedy Toole wrote the novel *Confederacy of Dunces* but never lived to see it printed. Tragically, the rejection of eight consecutive publishers led him to believe he would never see success and he took his own life in 1969. Fortunately his mother believed in him more than he believed in himself and pursued the novel's publication and it became a national bestseller and won the Pulitzer Prize for fiction in 1981.

Unknown singer-songwriter Otis Redding had just finished performing at the Monterey Pop Festival in 1967, with such stars as Janis Joplin and Jimi Hendrix – it was the pinnacle of his career. He rented a houseboat for a week on San Francisco Bay to ponder his future. While "wasting time" Otis got the inspiration to write his "Sittin' on the Dock o' the Bay." But he died three days later in a plane crash, not living to see his song rocket to the top of the charts and become one of the most enduring songs of the Sixties.

Jonathan Larson wrote what seemed to be an unpromising musical, entitled *Rent*. Sadly, he died just hours after the final dress rehearsal of a brain aneurysm. He never lived to see his play open to rave reviews at an off Broadway theater, then move on to Broadway and win the Pulitzer Prize for drama in 1996.

At the time of her death in 1886, Emily Dickinson had only published seven poems – hardly an auspicious ending to an obscure, secluded life. While going through her personal effects, her sister, Lavinia, discovered more than 800 of her previously unknown poems, many of which she published in 1890, *The Poems of Emily Dickinson*. Today Emily Dickinson is known to have authored 1,789 poems and is recognized as one of the most towering figures of American literature.

Similarly, Herman Mellville (1819-1891), died in obscurity, long before he was recognized for his literary genius. His most famous novel, *Moby Dick* (published 1851) was a disappointing failure when first published. And the novel that initially won him fame, *Billy Budd*, was not published until 1924 – *33 years after his death!* Like so many others, Herman Melville's greatest achievements and impact took place long after his death. There is certainly a lesson in this: That none of us should judge his life a failure if he sees no fruit of his labor by life's end. Even from the vantage point of death, we cannot see that our greatest work is yet to come.

But there is another unforeseen aspect of our death. Very often, a person's death may be *the very catalyst* of his or her greatest work. The obscure missionaries John and Betty Stam labored for only one year in China before meeting their death at the hands of Communist revolutionaries in the 1930s. Initially it seemed like such a waste – years of ministry training and language study only to be beheaded after so short a time of service. Yet when their deaths were announced at Moody Bible Institute, more than a thousand students were inspired to enter missionary work. By their deaths John and Betty Stam multiplied their effect a thousand-fold.

Like the biblical strongman, Samson who killed more of the enemy by his death than by his life (Judges 16:31) and Jesus Christ who, according to the Gospels, raised more to life at the moment of his death (Matthew 27:50-53) than he did throughout his life on earth – many a man and woman has triggered their greatest and most enduring work by death rather than by life.

PRAYER: Dear Father in heaven, help me to live with eternity's values in mind and to grasp that fact that death, for a worthy cause, is neither tragic nor the end. Help me to understand that both by living and by dying I may glorify you and accomplish great things. Amen.

GOOD THINGS TAKE TIME

The amount of work it takes to generate a simple 16-ounce jar of honey is truly incredible. Tens of thousands of female bees have to fly about 112,000 miles to gather nectar from 4.5 million flowers. This nectar is "boiled down" to honey by an agonizingly long process performed by thousands of "receiver bees." The receiver bees fan it to remove its moisture, digest and regurgitate it over and over (up to 200 times) to rid it of all germs and bacteria, and then place it in hexagonal cells for safekeeping. Then another type of bees put a wax seal over the cell to allow the honey to ripen. All this work is behind every jar of honey. With all our technology, a less labor-intensive means has never been found. It's one product that requires a great deal of work by many of God's little creatures.

There is no way around it. Good things take time – by God's design. There are still many tasks in life that require large investments of our time and a long-term commitment to long-term goals. In the professional world, mentoring, teaching, counseling, and developing subordinates are such tasks. But the greatest of all these is that which takes place in the home: parenting and rearing children.

Our culture is not very supportive of such jobs. We demand instant results and the highest yield for our labor. We also demand recognition and appreciation for our efforts. But when it comes to developing other human beings and rearing children, results come very slow and we seldom receive praise and recognition for our work.

But as tough as these jobs may be, they are also the most important to the preservation and development of our society. God has ordained that a lot of work and time must go into the making of honey. He has also ordained that a lot of work and time must go into the making of men and women. So gear up for the long-term and don't get discouraged if the results are few and slow in coming. Don't be disappointed if your children or your students fail to appreciate your sacrifices and faithfulness. Remember, God is mindful of your patient faithfulness in what you do for others and he will reward at the end of the age. In the Scripture the Lord promises: "Be faithful unto death, and I will give you the crown of life." (Revelation 2:10)

PRAYER: Dear Father in heaven, I thank You that you invest you infinite love and patience in developing me, my character and my faith. And yet I show so little progress for all Your efforts in my life. Help me, therefore, to be patient and forgiving with others, especially with those whom You have placed in my charge. Amen.

January 28

DEFINED BY SUCCESS, NOT FAILURE

This patriot was court-martialed for cowardice and insubordination during the revolutionary war. He had been in command of a garrison of soldiers at Castle William, near Boston, from the beginning of the War until 1779 – when he participated in the ill-fated Penobscot Expedition, which amounted to an attempted invasion of a British stronghold in Maine. But he and the invasion failed miserably. But we do not remember Paul Revere for his failures or his alleged insubordination and cowardice. We remember him for his famous "Midnight Ride" in which he and William Dawes alerted the militias of Concord and Lexington of the approaching British force, so that they were able to repel them at Lexington and harass them with guerilla fire all the way back to Boston.

This Navy ensign was court-martialed for running his destroyer, the USS Decatur, aground in 1907, causing significant damage to the vessel. But we do not remember Admiral Chester Nimitz for his early blunders, but as the World War II Fleet Admiral who beat Japan's Imperial Navy into obliteration – consummately avenging America's defeat at Pearl Harbor.

We do not remember the former record-holder for the most strike outs at bat – a total of 1330 of them – for his failures! No, instead we remember Babe Ruth as the former record-holder for both the most homeruns in a season (60 home runs) and for the most career homeruns (714 home runs). Nor do we remember the *present* record-holder for the most strikeouts at bat for his failures at the plate – a staggering 2,597 strike outs! Instead, we remember the Yankees powerhouse hitter, Reggie Jackson, as "Mr. October" for incredible heroics on the field, usually when heroics counted most – hitting 10 homeruns in 27 World Series games – four of them in consecutive order, along with 24 RBIs and a World Series batting average of .351.

What's the point? The point is that we all have failures to our credit. Every one of us has stains on his record. But we do not define our lives by our failures, but by our successes.

Harold Kushner has the following advice in dealing with failure: *"Life is not a spelling bee, where no matter how many words you have gotten right, if you make one mistake you are disqualified. Life is more like a baseball season, where even the best team loses one third of its games and even the worst team has its days of brilliance. Our goal is not to go all year without ever losing a game. Our goal is to win more than we lose, and if we can do that consistently enough, then when the end comes, we will have won it all."*[vii]

Someone has wisely states: "Failure is a temporary detour, not a dead-end street," and "Failure should be our teacher, not our undertaker."

So if your record is blemished with failure, be assured that you have plenty of company. The Scripture reminds us that "though a righteous man falls seven times, he rises up again." (Proverbs 24:16).

PRAYER: Dear Father in heaven, when I stumble and fail, help me, Lord to learn from my failures, move on and to grow stronger and wiser. Amen.

January 29

WHO DOES HE THINK HE IS?

What's so great about Pluto? It's the smallest of the planets. In fact, the International Astronomical Union has declared that it is not a planet at all. Yet Pluto meets the classic requirements. It's spherical. It rotates. It revolves around the sun in its own orbit. It even has its own moon – Charon.

True, it's the smallest of the planets. It's even smaller than some of the moons in our solar system. Pluto is only 1,429 miles (2300 km) in diameter. This pales in comparison to Titan – one Saturn's moons – which (at 3,200 miles) is *twice the diamter* of Pluto. The same is true of Ganymede which (at 3,270 miles in diameter) is the largest known moon in our solar system. In fact, there are at least *seven moons* in the solar system (including Earth's) that are *larger than the "planet" Pluto.*

Can you imagine the members of the Big Moon Society convening and comparing themselves to little Pluto. There they stand – Ganymede, Titan, Callisto, Io, Europa, Triton, and our own Moon – staring disdainfully at the so-called planet Pluto.

"Who does he think he is? We've got more mass than he does. He's only half the size of some of us. What does he think he's doing – pretending he's a planet? What makes him so special?"

To this giant Jupiter would answer, "What makes him so special is this – while you guys hide out in the shelter of the "real planets," he's got the guts to venture out on his own. It's not how big you are that counts. It's how far you go with what you have."

Think about it. There are many gifted people in our world who cling to their comfort zones and run from life's challenges. Then they see weaker and less talented people doing what they only dreamed of doing. "Who do they think they are? I'm a better person than they are. What makes them so special?" Only this – they are willing face challenges, risk failure, and endure the criticism of "those cold and timid souls who know neither victory nor defeat."

Don't let difficulties, the fear of failure, or the fear of criticism immobilize you. Trying and failing is better than never trying at all. Robert Kennedy once said, "Only those who dare to fail greatly can ever achieve greatly." The Scripture says, "Be strong and courageous. Do not be afraid or terrified because of them, for the LORD your God goes with you; he will never leave you nor forsake you." (Deuteronomy 31:6)

PRAYER: Dear Father in heaven, though my heart is fearful and my faith is small, Help me to master my fears and face my challenges. Please hush the storm within my heart and fix my thoughts on You. In Your strength give me victory, I pray. Amen.

January 30

WE NEED CHALLENGES

People need challenges. They need responsibilities. They need a sense of purpose and significance. But they will not get it from lots of leisure time and a light workload. Believe it or not, the burdens we carry, day by day, provide a source of emotional and mental stability. Let me explain.

The famous 20th Century medical missionary, Dr. Thomas Lambie, served for 35-plus years in Ethiopia. While traveling thousands of miles on foot into the country's interior, he had to cross many raging streams and rivers. During these crossings, he saw many unsuspecting porters and missionaries swept off their feet and to their death by the swift river currents.

The Ethiopians understood the dangers of the strong river currents and had discovered a way to survive them. To keep a firm footing when crossing these rivers, the Ethiopians would pick up large rocks, the heavier the better, and carry them on their shoulders while crossing rivers and streams. This added weight stabilized their footing and planted their steps firmly on the river bottoms. The added weight on their backs stabilized them against the current and preserved their lives.

Dr. Lambie reflected often on what he'd seen and thought about the most difficult times of his life. His most depressing times – when he was losing his "emotional footing" - were when he had little to do and no clear direction. In contrast, his happiest times were when he had much to do and a sense of mission and purpose. Just as the Ethiopian stabilized his footing against the current by carrying a heavy rock, so the burdens and responsibilities we bear give us stability against self-pity, distractions, depression, and the noise of this life.

It should be no surprise to us, that when Jesus Christ calls people to come to Him for rest, he says "Take my yoke upon you and learn from Me … and you shall find rest for your souls." (Matthew 11:29) Rest of soul is not found in inactivity, but in service to God and to our fellow human beings. Happiness is not achieved by hoarding loads of leisure time, but in using time to serve others. As Winston Churchill said, "We make a living by what we get, but we make a life by what we give." And Saint Francis of Assisi wrote: "For it is in pardoning that we are pardoned, it is in giving that we receive, and it is in dying that we are born to eternal life."

PRAYER: Dear Father in heaven, Help me not to shirk responsibility nor shrink from challenges. Remind me how much I need them – to find stability of mind and rest of soul. Amen.

January 31

DON'T PASS JUDGMENT ON YOUR LIFE

His paintings have the distinction of drawing the highest price ever paid for a work of art - $82.5 million for a single painting! The painting? *The Portrait of Dr. Gachet.* Two other paintings of his are also among the top ten of the highest price ever paid. They are his *Self Portrait*, which sold for $65 million, and his *Irises*, which sold for $49 million.

Who was this artist? An extremely wealthy man? An artist recognized and appreciated as an artistic giant? Actually, no. The artist was Vincent Van Gogh. And although his paintings sell for tens of millions today, they barely sold for a few dollars in Van Gogh's lifetime. In fact, of his 900 paintings and 1100 drawings, only a handful sold at all. Van Gogh spent most his adult life in poverty and obscurity and was completely unappreciated for his genius. Combined with his chronic depression, Vincent Van Gogh's inability to find financial success or recognition as an artist brought him to the point of despair. On July 29, 1890, at the age of 37 - with his best works still in him, Vincent Van Gogh took his own life.

Even to our dying day we must withhold judgment on our lives. No one but God knows the ultimate effect our lives will have – and that effect may not be realized until many years after our death. Never judge your life a failure. The last chapter is yet to unfold and God is not finished with you yet.

At the end of his life, Samson could not possibly have known the stunning victory he won over the Lord's enemies – greater than any victory during his life (Judges 16:31). As he languished in prison, just days before he died, Paul the apostle could not possibly have understood that his letters, written to individuals and small churches, would endure for millennia after his martyrdom to inspire millions of believers. In the same way, none of us can know the good that God can bring forth from our efforts. Therefore, withhold judgment until God has had a chance to write the final chapter of your life.

PRAYER: Dear Father in heaven, help me to be faithful in the work to which you have called me and to leave the success of my efforts in your hands. Amen.

February

February 1

TREASURES OLD, BUT NEW

Military life involves constant moving. Families are uprooted again and again, moved from stateside assignments to overseas assignments – in Germany, South Korea, Japan, Okinawa, Italy, the UK, and Belgium – to name a few. When overseas assignments come, families will have most of the household goods – furniture, appliances, toys – put in storage. Then, when military families return to the States and get back their household goods, something pleasant and wonderful happens. They experience a "Christmas morning," re-discovering treasures that they had forgotten they owned. This is especially true for children, who receive back toys and electronic games they had long since forgotten. When they get them back it's like getting a bunch of birthday presents.

Foggy memories tend to put the blessings and joys of our lives "in storage." So many wonderful events, blessings, people, and things have been poured into our lives. But our lazy and under-worked memories have packed them all up "in storage" and we've forgotten what we have.

Get those things out of storage! Uncrate them all. Go through all those treasures. Count your blessings and have yourself a holiday – every day!

The Scripture says, "So then, just as you received Christ Jesus as Lord, continue to live in him, rooted and built up in him, strengthened in the faith as you were taught, and overflowing with thankfulness." (Colossians 2:6-7)

PRAYER: Dear Lord, Please jog my memory and help me recall all the blessings You've poured into my life. Help me to re-discover my treasures long forgotten. Amen.

February 2

NOBODY CAN DO-IT-ALL

Some of you will remember the popularity of those gadget commercials? I'm talking about those commercials that advertised gadgets that could replace a *whole set of tools* or *an entire set of cleaning utensils!* These commercials started with the same line: "Are you tired of using all these utensils? Then throw them all away! Now there's a single appliance that does the work of them all." Probably the most memorable parody of such commercials was that of the Honeymooner's Ralph Cramden's attempt to sell his 1000-in-One Chef's tool. That's the time he played the part of the "Chef of the Future" and gave a haughty "Ha-Ha," at the "Chef of the Present" (Ed Norton) who struggled with his array of chef's tools. Naturally Ralph Cramden's *live* TV commercial was a disaster. Not only was he overwhelmed with stage fright, but his "jack of all trades" tool was no match for specialized tools. It couldn't core an apple or peel a potato as well as the tools that were specifically designed for those purposes.

Or have you ever seen a Swiss Army Knife? It's a handy thing to have around. I have a cheap imitation of one. It's got an assortment of blades – including both a flathead and Philips-head screwdriver, a corkscrew, a tiny scissor attachment, a tiny saw blade, and a few others. But what about that set of Craftsman tools in my truck? Now that I have my Swiss Army knife, am I going to "throw them all away?" Naaah! That little knife is nice to have and may help in a pinch, but I'd hate to have to work on my car with it. It's simply no match for a good set of tools.

You know, many of us live with the idea that we have to "do-it all." We think there's something wrong if we're not a "Swiss Army knife" leader – the leader who can do everything. We might even feel threatened or up-staged by a subordinate who's better at something than we are. But a key task of leadership is discovering, developing and utilizing the gifts and abilities of others for the success of the organization and the mission. Each person is a specialized tool, created by God to do a few things very well, but not everything. Even the Bible reminds us that all of us together constitute a body that has many members, and all the members are different, each performing a different function. Not everyone is an eye or a hand or a foot. Otherwise we don't have a body but a collection of similar parts (1 Corinthians 12:12-31).

So what's the lesson? Let each of us find his specialized gift and learn to appreciate it. Learn also to appreciate the gifts and abilities of others, share the workload with them, and work together for the common good.

PRAYER: Dear Father in heaven, help me to understand and appreciate my own strengths and abilities. Help me to develop and use the gifts you've given me for the good of others. Help me also to appreciate and utilize the talents of other people. Amen.

February 3

WHEN LITTLE THINGS CAST A GIANT SHADOW

In 1933 RKO Pictures released the greatest adventure-fantasy film of all time: King Kong. It is difficult for modern audiences to grasp the immediate impact of this film. Watching on thirty-foot screens, viewers were overcome with fear and wonder as they saw a 40-foot ape and gigantic dinosaurs and monsters crush underfoot dozens of helpless humans. The drama was greatly enhanced by Max Steiner's stirring musical score and sound effects by Murray Spivack. The average moviegoer was shocked to see King Kong hold Fay Wray in his hand and close up shots of Kong chewing on some poor victim or crushing them beneath his feet. Kong was a terrifying spectacle, something out of their darkest nightmares.

Only years after the movie's release did producers Merrian C. Cooper and Ernest Schoedsack explain that the towering Kong was only about 18 inches tall. Using stop action animation, special effects artist Willis O'Brien used two 18-inch flexible models and one 24-inch model (along with innovative rear-projection and trick photography) to create the moving images of the 40-foot Kong.

Throughout the film's production, Merrian Cooper kept King Kong's true size a carefully guarded secret. He knew such a disclosure would greatly reduce the fear-effect King Kong would have. For no one would be afraid of an 18-inch model.

What Willis O'Brien did with special effects, our worries do with the problems that face us. Willis O'Brien convinced millions that an 18-inch model was actually a 40-foot gorilla. Worry does the same thing with our problems. It tricks us into believing that an 18-inch problem is a 40-foot monster. "Worry makes an anthill cast the shadow of a mountain," a wise man once said. This is why the Scripture says, "Don't worry about anything, but pray about everything (Philippians 4:5) and "Cast all your anxieties upon Him, for He cares to you." (1 Peter 5:7)

PRAYER: Dear Father in heaven help me to see things as they really are – to see that my problems aren't near as bad as I fear and that You are greater than the worst of my sins and the most hopeless of my problems. Amen.

February 4

CASTING OFF RESTRAINT LEADS TO SLAVERY

Dieting, Anger Management, Budget Counseling and Debt Reduction, Alcoholics Anonymous. What do these measures have in common? They are efforts that recognize the need for human beings to control their appetites.

The stunning success of programs like Weight Watchers, Jenny Craig, and NutriSystem are all the result of Americans who have failed to restrain their appetite for food. Anger management and anger control are endorsed by the American Psychological Association (as well as the Army) to help people gain control of their "fleeting annoyance to full-fledged rage." Financial Peace University, created by David Ramsey, is one among many popular programs that has risen from Americans' unbridled desire to consume and to live beyond their means. The 12-Step Program of Alcoholics Anonymous (and the host of other programs like Narcotics Anonymous), created by Bill Wilson and Dr. Bob Smith, was birthed from the ravages of uncontrolled consumption of alcohol.

The proof is before us. Human passions and appetites must be controlled. People who give free reign to their anger become murderers. People who will not control their appetite for food become obese.

People who use their credit cards to purchase all they desire become slaves to indebtedness.

Strange that we readily recognize the human need to exercise restraint in all of our appetites but one – our appetite for sex. Despite all the societal casualties of the Sexual Revolution, our popular culture still lives in a state of denial. It condemns any advocacy of sexual abstinence among teens with an almost phobic frenzy. In its place it endorses the distribution of contraceptives to school-aged children – with instructions on how to use them. Such failed policies not only enable self-destructive behavior, but clearly send the message that unrestrained sexual activity among teens is both expected and acceptable.

But God has a better way: Conquer the tyranny of our passions. God gives us both the guidance – through the Scriptures – and the inner strength to overcome this slavery to ourselves. "It is God's will that you should be sanctified: that you should avoid sexual immorality; that each of you should learn to control his own body in a way that is holy and honorable." (1 Thessalonians 4:3-4) This is the greatest victory and most pleasurable freedom.

PRAYER: Dear Father in heaven, in my pursuit to achieve great things and overcome all my challenges, please grant that I will not neglect the greatest battle and lose costliest war – the battle to overcome my own passions and self-centeredness. Guide my path, inspire my heart, and empower me to overcome the temptations of life. Amen.

February 5

UNAPPRECIATED

In a film documentary, "The Joy of Ireland: The Quiet Man," Irish-born actress Maureen O'Hara, expressed the frustration she and John Wayne (the film's leading man) endured under the film's tyrannical director – John Ford. In one climatic scene, a frustrated John Wayne is escorting his runaway bride (O'Hara) back to her brother's house to demand an unpaid dowry. At one point she loses her footing and falls to the ground in a sheep pasture, littered with dung. "Do you want me to clean up the sheep dung so Maureen doesn't have to get smeared in the stuff?" the film director asked Ford. "Let her get smeared," was Ford's reply.

Now behind the scenes Wayne and O'Hara had painstakingly rehearsed this scene and carefully choreographed a scuffle between the two stars. Maureen O'Hara fell to the ground. John Wayne grabbed her by the scruff of her collar and dragged her along the grass for twenty feet or so. Enraged, she rose to her feet and threw a looping left-hand punch at Wayne. Wayne ducked, causing O'Hara to spin around from the force of her own punch. Wayne countered with a swift kick to O'Hara's hind quarters who bellowed out an, "Ooop!"

When it came time for the scene, all their rehearsing paid off. Though covered with grass stains and spattered with sheep dung, O'Hara and Wayne pulled off the physical exchange with flawless precision.

"Cut," roared Ford. All eyes turned to the autocratic director. Ford grinned with rare pleasure. But he was mostly pleased with himself and blurted out, "Now, do you see how well things go when you do as I told you and just let the characters act spontaneously rather than rehearse?" O'Hara, soiled from head to toe, was furious. The pompous John Ford was oblivious to all the hard work, physical pain, and *dung* she'd endured to do that scene. And then Ford proceeded to credit himself for its success.

It behooves every leader and supervisor to be mindful of all the hard work and sacrifices of their subordinates. It's easy for leaders to get lost in the "Big Picture" as they stay focused on their vision. But they also need to keep an eye on those "worker bees" who must "flesh out" all their leader's great ideas, and lavish them with praise. Nothing can demoralize the soldiers in the trenches quicker than being unappreciated for all the hardships they suffer. "Give honor to whom honor is due," says the Scripture (Romans 13:7).

PRAYER: Dear Father in heaven, help me in my leadership skills to develop the essential art of giving praise and expressing appreciation to those who labor in obscurity to accomplish the mission. Grant that I may not only be driven by the task to be accomplished, but equally motivated by love for those I lead. Amen.

February 6

DON'T TAKE FAILURE TO HEART

Earl was a half-rate minor-league second baseman who couldn't hit to save his life and never made it to the Major Leagues. So, one could reason, if he couldn't make it as a minor league player, what made him think he could instruct others how to play in the Majors? If he failed at a smaller task, then why expect him to succeed at a greater one with increased responsibility?

Yet Earl Weaver, though a lackluster minor league player, proved to be a stunning Major League manager with the Baltimore Orioles – earning the fifth highest record for wins of any manager in Major League history. In his 17-year tenure he led the Orioles to 1480 wins and only 1060 losses, five one-hundred-win seasons, six American League East titles, three American League Championships, and one World Series Championship (1970).

Hyrum had failed in nearly every effort to feed his family – farming, selling insurance, selling firewood, running a leather goods store. He became so financially strapped that he was forced to hock his gold watch to buy Christmas presents for his children. Obviously, a man of such limitations, who failed at so many things, probably wouldn't amount to anything. Yet Hyrum Ulysses Grant, AKA Ulysses S. Grant, became immensely successful as the Union's greatest strategist and commander and is credited with saving the United States in its greatest crisis during the Civil War.

William Faulkner's shot at being a postal worker was a disaster. But that was no indicator of his potential for better things. He became one of America's most successful of the 20th Century. Nathaniel Hawthorne, was fired from his customs office job for incompetence. Yet he went on to much bigger and better things as America's foremost novelist of the 19th Century.

James Whistler was booted from the Corps of Cadets at West Point after failing mathematics. Yet he went on to become one of the most celebrated artists of the 1800s – in both America and Europe.

Phillips Brooks failed miserably in his first job after graduating from college – a teacher of Latin in Boston. In fact, his supervisor told him he'd never known anyone who failed at teaching Latin to be successful at any other job in life. Yet Phillips Brooks became the most prominent pastor in all of 19th Century America. But he best known today for the Christmas song he wrote – "O Little Town of Bethlehem."

When a tall, skinny, sickly and deeply discouraged young William Franklin told Dr. Bob Jones that he had to drop out of his Bible Institute, the elder Fundamentalist statesman had a somber prediction for him. Dr. Bob told him: "Billy, if you quit this school, you'll never amount to anything but a backwoods Baptist preacher." Too sick and discouraged to continue, the young man dropped out anyway. But God had a plan for young William Franklin Graham's life (AKA Billy Graham). After recovering his health, he attended Southeastern Bible Institute in Florida and Wheaton College in Illinois, and went on to preach the gospel to more people than anyone else in the history of the church. He is credited with well over one million converts to Christ and impacting the faith of several generations.

The point is this - just because you fail in a smaller task, does not mean you have reached your peak or that you cannot be successful in a tougher, more demanding task. Quite often early failures only indicate that we are on a quest of self-discovery – by trial and error we are determining what we are good at and what is our "niche" in life.

Unsatisfactory performance and failure at the workplace may only indicate that we are the right person in the wrong job. But there's one thing we can be sure of. God has not put a person on this planet for whom he does not also have a plan and whom he has not also endowed with the ability to succeed in that plan. In 2 Samuel 7:8 God told King David, "I took you from the pasture and from *following* the flock to *lead* My people Israel." Competent shepherds do not *follow* sheep – they *lead* them. But God took an incompetent shepherd and made him the greatest king Israel ever had. God does that. He makes zeros into heroes.

PRAYER: Almighty Father, please take the raw material of my life and fashion me into a child of your own image and a person after your own heart. Amen.

February 7

DON'T TAKE LIFE TOO HARD

When Chicago Cubs relief pitcher Bob Patterson described his pitch, which the Cincinnati Reds' Barry Larkin hit for a game-winning home run, he faced his failure in the best way – though grieving the loss of the game, he cushioned the pain with some humor.

A reporter interrogated him, *"You knew, of course, that Barry Larkin always hits screw balls out of the park. Yet it looked to me like you threw him a screw ball. Can you explain?"*

With every eye on him, Patterson replied by saying, *"Yeah, but it was a cross between a screwball and a change-up. I guess you'd call it a screw-up."* The room came apart in laughter and eased the tenseness and anger of the moment.

Humor, light-heartedness, and flexibility are survival skills in the face of life's troubles. Consider Thomas Edison's reply when he was sharply criticized for his inefficient methodology employed for inventing the electric light.

"Mr. Edison, you failed 2,500 times before you reached your goal. Isn't it discouraging to you and your workers to go through so many trial and errors?"

"Failed? I never failed once. Inventing the electric light turned out to be a 2500-step process and I too all 2500 steps."

Consider also the process stonecutters use for engraving granite, one of the hardest of stones. When engraving headstones, the stonecutter first covers the polished granite with a thin coating of rubber. He draws his design on the rubber surface and then cuts away the design, exposing the granite. He then sandblasts the front of the headstone. The stinging sand bounces right off the rubber because of its flexibility. But it easily grinds away the exposed granite, because of its obstinacy.

The same is true with our responses to the adversity of life, which comes at us with the fury of a sandblast. The same is true with our response to difficult and abrasive people. If we remain flexible, good humored, and roll with the punches, our resilience will preserve us. But if we become obstinate, hard and sour against the things and people we cannot change, then we'll be broken. The familiar prayer of serenity thus asks: "God grant me the serenity to accept the things I cannot change, the courage to change the things I can, and the wisdom to know the difference."

PRAYER: Dear Father in heaven, as my strength and patience are pushed to their limitations, please renew my strength and flood my heart with your power and love. Help me to bend, flex and adapt with every change and disappointment that comes. Amen.

February 8

WHEN LIFE FRUSTRATES US

"Oh God, why did this have to happen now?" Domingo muttered in disgust. "Can't you see I'm in a hurry? My mother's sick and I need to get to her right away."

Domingo Pacheco was in a big hurry. He was racing on the Palmetto Expressway across the Florida Everglades to catch a plane. Then it happened. On that steamy day on May 11, 1996, Pacheco's 1985 Cadillac blew a tire. He managed to change the tire, but by the time he was finished not only was he covered in tire soot and sweat, he was also too late for his flight.

With his dirty, sweaty hands he called his mother with his cell phone. "Hello, mom – I'm sorry, but I missed my plane."

A woman's voice on the other end screamed. "Domingo! You're alive! You're alive! Oh, thank God you're alive!" Puzzled, Domingo tried again to explain: "Mom, what are you talking about? Didn't you hear - I missed my plane?"

"Son, don't you know what happened? Turn your radio on. Your plane – *Valujet flight 592 – crashed in the Everglades thirty minutes ago!*"

The Scriptures remind us: "And we know that God works all things together for good, to those who love God, to those who are called according to His purpose." (Romans 8:28)

When life frustrates our efforts, it just might be that God is protecting us from something very bad. Trust God for his guidance and protection this day.

PRAYER: Dear Lord, guide and direct my steps this day and lead me in the path of peace. Amen.

February 9

WHEN YOU'RE SKEPTICAL ABOUT ASKING GOD FOR HELP

In his article, "Voyage of Faith," Thomas Fleming tells the true story of how a B-17 Flying Fortress crew survived a crash in October 1942 in the South Pacific Ocean. The crew and passengers quickly manned 3 small life rafts, but had almost no food (only 4 oranges), no water, and little equipment. Among these men were Eddie Rickenbacker, the WWI flying ace, and Colonel Hans Adamson.

The copilot was Jim Whittaker who, early in the ordeal, had been contemptuous of the prayers and Bible reading of the others as they sought divine help on the heaving, open sea. Whittaker equated prayer and religion with weakness. Only brains and nerve would get them out of this mess.

Yet Whittaker saw one prayer after another being answered. On one occasion, just after Rickenbacker had offered a prayer for food, a sea swallow landed on his head. Its raw flesh was quickly consumed and its intestines were used as bait to catch several more fish. After another prayer the pilot, Bill Cherry, fired his flare gun into the evening sky.

But the flare malfunctioned and plunged into the water, driving several fish into the raft. After another of Bill Cherry's prayers, this time for desperately needed water, the baffled crew watched as a fleecy white cloud turned darkish blue and proceeded to drench them with rain.

By the 13th day Whittaker and his companions were desperate from the scorching sun and from lack of water. Whittaker noticed rain falling about a mile from their rafts but the wind was driving it away. Whittaker prayed aloud, "God, you know what that water means to us. It's in your power to send back that rain." The bluish-black curtain of water began moving toward them-against the wind! Within minutes, it was drenching the rafts and quenching their thirst.

By the 20th day Whittaker and his companions spotted land. They made a vain attempt to paddle with their hands but did not have strength enough to sit up. Whittaker cried out to God for help. Feeling strengthened, he began to paddle and continued to do so for 7 1/2 hours.

Land was now within 250 feet, but an unexpected current suddenly carried their rafts about a mile away, outside a jagged coral reef, and into a swarm of encircling sharks. "God," Whittaker cried, "don't quit on me now!" He felt a new surge of energy to his arms and shoulders and invigorating rain fell on his back. Whittaker continued to paddle safely passed the sharks and a swell carried them over the reef. After they touched land friendly natives gave them shelter and food and notified the U.S. Navy. During those days of crisis, Whittaker said, "I found my God." He learned the lesson that all of us must learn - we all have limitations, but God can carry us beyond them if we turn to him for strength. The Scripture says, "Cast all your anxiety upon Him, for He cares for you." (1 Peter 5:7)

PRAYER: Dear Lord, through all the events of this day, remind me of Your abiding presence and love and help me to reach out to You for strength and help in my daily tasks. Amen.

IF I COULD ONLY ESCAPE

In December 1968, the crew of Apollo 8, Commander Frank Borman, James Lovell, and William Anders made space exploration history when they became the first people to ever break away from the earth's orbit and travel 240,000 miles to reach and circle the moon.

In a 1998 thirty-year reunion the three astronauts recalled their utter amazement at the precision with which the mathematicians and scientists could predict certain events on the incredible journey of half a million miles. Most notable, was when the moon, which for the first part of the journey appeared only as a black hole – being in the shadow of the earth – suddenly burst forth into the light and into their sight. The Scientists had told them at the exact minute this would happen.

James Lovell recalled how they became like kids in a candy store, as they spent twenty hours during their lunar orbit with their noses pressed against the windows of the Apollo 8 space craft, soaking up every bit of this close up view of the moon – which was a mere 60 miles away.

Absolute wonderment seized them as they traveled to the moon's far side – the first of humankind to do so - and witnessed the colorless and deeply scarred lunar surface.

Then something happened for which they were completely unprepared and which none of the NASA scientists had predicted. In this vast world of blackness and just beyond the moon's jagged landscape, a brilliantly beautiful, blue gem suddenly appeared – the only visible color in the universe. It was *the Earth!* This first "earth rise" ever witnessed by man was the most glorious thing the astronauts had ever seen. Immediately the moon, the whole focus of their trip, was forgotten. The earth – the world they had so ardently sought to escape-appeared to them as the most desirable jewel in the universe. Bill Anders recalled how he was deeply moved by the event and thought to himself: "We've come all this way to get to the moon and yet the most significant thing out there is the earth."

Appropriately, as the men were broadcasting live to the largest audience ever available to any speaker, the three astronauts read the Creation account from the Book of Genesis. It was Christmas Eve and Frank Borman closed the transmission with: *"And from the crew of Apollo 8, we close with Good Night, Good Luck, a Merry Christmas, and God bless all of you, all of you on the Good Earth."* Truly, the earth, seen as it really was, never looked better to any human being.

But isn't that true of everything in our lives. The things we seek to escape – our assignment, our job, our marriage, our family responsibilities – are really beautiful and desirable when seen from a distance. How often a deployed soldier looks longingly and yearns for the wife and children he has left behind. How often the person who looked forward to the day when he could retire and break loose from the Army and all its restrictions, will then find himself wishing for those days again. How often mothers with "empty nests" now wish they had relished those moments with their children a whole lot more. Looking from a distance, we can see things as they really are and appreciate and understand their true value.

Perhaps this is why the Scripture tells us: "This is the day which the Lord has made, let us rejoice and be glad in it." (Psalm 118:24) Relish the moment and count your blessings while you have them.

PRAYER: Dear Father in heaven, help me to slow down today and to appreciate my job, my family and my spouse. Most of all help me to appreciate your blessings in my life and to develop an attitude of gratitude. Amen.

February 11

DON'T PASS JUDGMENT ON YOUR LIFE TOO SOON

How is success measured in a person's life? Does it come when society recognizes him or her as a success? When he amasses material wealth? When he experiences family and marital bliss? When he achieves supreme job satisfaction?

There was a musical director and choirmaster of Saint Thomas' Church and School in Leipzig, Germany who never reached any of these criteria. His job left much to be desired and he squabbled continually with the town council, and neither the council nor the populace appreciated his musical genius. They said he was a stuffy old man who clung stubbornly to obsolete forms of music. Consequently, they paid him a miserable salary, and when he died they even schemed to defraud his widow of her meager inheritance.

His marriage was marked by profound tragedy. From the years 1723 through 1737, his wife Magdalena endured 12 full-term pregnancies and suffered the loss of eight of her children, varying in ages from one hour to six years old. Of her remaining four children, one was severely retarded.

Despite his personal tragedy, lack of recognition by his countrymen, and his meager income, this man found consolation in composing music. In fact, this humble man composed cantatas at the staggering rate of one each week – today a composer who writes a cantata a year is highly praised! 202 of these survive today.

But his work continued to be unappreciated - even after his death. Though he had managed to sell some of his works, his music was largely discarded and his compositions were even used to wrap up refuse. Clearly, Johann Sebastian Bach (1685-1750) was a flat failure. By every criterion for success, Bach had failed miserably.

For the next 80 years his music was neglected by the public, although a few musicians (Mozart and Beethoven, for example) admired it. Not until 1829, when German composer Felix Mendelssohn arranged a performance of "The Passion of St. Matthew" (which is widely recognized as "the supreme cultural achievement of Western civilization") did a larger audience appreciate Bach the composer. Today he is considered the consummate classical composer, the last great representative of the Baroque period, and one of the most successful and prolific composers of all time.

Sometimes we judge our lives prematurely and consider ourselves failures because success is not immediately apparent. But though the merit and value of our contributions are not always recognized immediately, this does not make us failures. Johann Sebastian Bach the composer, Herman Melville the author and Vincent van Gogh the artist all failed to be appreciated for their genius in their lifetime. The greater impact of their lives took place after their deaths. God and time are the final judges. We are called to use our talents to the best of our ability, leave the results with God and the ripple effects of our lives will go on forever. No one is a failure when he does his very best for God and his fellow human beings. The Scripture tells us, "Commit your way to the Lord, trust also in Him, and He shall bring it to pass. He shall bring forth your righteousness as the light and your justice as the noonday sun." (Psalm 37:5)

PRAYER: Dear Father in heaven, I entrust my life, my future and what I do into Your hands. Please bless the work of my hands, make me an instrument of Your peace, and grant that You and time shall judge me a success. Amen.

February 12

WHEN WE CRITICIZE OUR GOVERNMENT LEADERS

All of us have criticized our President, Congressmen, Chief Justices, Governors, and Mayors. As citizens we certainly have a moral obligation to vote. But as Christians we have an obligation to pray for our leaders. This need for prayer support was indirectly expressed by one of America's foremost Presidents – Abraham Lincoln.

It seems that a group of concerned citizens had gained an audience with the President and sharply criticized his policies and actions. Their words were painful and caustic. The President cut them off and pleaded for their help in the form of an anecdote.

"Gentlemen, suppose all the property you were worth was in gold, and this you had placed in the hands of a man to carry across the Niagara River on a rope. Would you shake the cable and keep shouting at him: 'Stand up a little straighter, stoop a little more, go a little faster, go a little slower, lean a little more to the south'? No, you would hold your breath as well as your tongue and keep your hands off until he got safely over.

"The government is carrying an enormous weight. Untold treasure is in our hands. Don't badger us. Keep silent and we will get you across."

On another such occasion, Abraham Lincoln dealt with criticism with this analogy.

"A traveler on the frontier became lost one night in one of the hostile regions. To make things worse, a terrible thunderstorm broke upon him. He prodded his horse onward until, exhausted, the horse collapsed beneath him. Now he was lost, on foot, soaked to the bone and scared. The brilliant flashes of lightening were the only light by which he could see his way, but the peals of thunder were frightful. One bolt, which seemed to crash beneath him, brought his to his knees. Now, he was certainly no praying man, but he made this short and desperate prayer to Heaven: 'O Lord, please, give us a little more light and a little less noise!'"[viii]

It is the same with our government leaders. They need God's light and direction through our prayers, not our noise. The Scripture says, "Seek the peace of the city where I have sent you into exile, and pray to the LORD on its behalf; for in its peace you will have peace." (Jeremiah 29:7) and again, "I urge, first of all, that prayers, petitions, entreaties, and thanksgivings be made to God on behalf of all … who are in authority, so that we may lead a tranquil life in all godliness and dignity." (1 Timothy 2:1-2)

PRAYER: Dear Father in heaven, please bless our President, his cabinet, the Congress, the Senate, the Chief Justices and all those who govern our land and determine its destiny. Please fill them with wisdom and courage. Grant that they may pursue that which is good and reject that which is evil. Cause them, O God, to lead our nation into the paths of peace and righteousness, that America may honor Your holy Name. Amen.

February 13

NOT EQUAL TO THE TASK

He held the record for winning the most Academy Awards for musical scores for motion pictures – a total of nine Oscars. He earned a staggering 45 Oscar Nominations, and from 1938 through 1957 he was nominated for Oscars in twenty consecutive years. He worked on the soundtracks for an incredible 400 films in a career that spanned 40 years, spending half of it as the Musical Director of 20th Century Fox Studios. Yet for all his vast achievements and experience, Composer and Conductor Alfred Newman approached every project with a terrible sense of inadequacy. "I'm terrified every time I take a new film score," he told an interviewer when accepting the task of scoring the film, *The Greatest Story Ever Told.* "I sit and stare at the blank manuscript paper, pondering the unfathomable depth of my own dry well. Finally, in pure desperation and before I can run and hide, I jab a quarter-note on the page. It is not that necessity is the mother of invention, but more like insecurity being the father of action."[ix]

Yet Alfred Newman rose to the occasion every time – he earned an Oscar nomination for "Greatest Story" as well (1965). Despite his fears and overwhelming sense of inadequacy, Newman always did the job and did it amazingly well. In fact, right up to his dying day Newman scored successes. In the last film he scored, "Airport" (1970), he won his ninth Academy Award – he died just after the film was completed.

And many men and women live with that same gnawing sense of inadequacy and impotency. They never feel equal to the task. They always sweat the challenges that confront them. Yet their records show an impressive tally of victories. They always get the job done. They always rise to the occasion. In the final analysis, their fear of failure drives them to success and their pain turns to gain.

People will sometimes tell you pain, insecurity, and discomfort have no place in your life. The "experts" may claim that we should be completely whole and self-confident in our personalities and fully satisfied in our hearts. But in reality our pain is the plow that breaks up the fallow ground and generates creativity in our lives. The very pain that vexes us becomes a blessing, which we turn into something pleasant and ultimately share with the world. "If we are afflicted," wrote Paul the apostle, "it is for your comfort and salvation." (2 Corinthians 1:6)

PRAYER: Dear Father in heaven, if I cannot fully rid myself of the insecurity, pain, and dysfunction in my life, please turn these curses into blessings and grant that they will make my life more fruitful. Amen.

February 14

THE HARDEST DISTANCE TO BRIDGE

The Transcontinental Railroad that connected California and the West Coast with the rest of the country had taken decades to plan and six years to construct (1863-69). It stretched nearly 1800 miles from Sacramento, California to Omaha, Nebraska. Overnight, once completed, this railroad reduced the time it normally took to travel to California from five months to five days. It was widely considered the greatest engineering feat of the 19th Century. The work was accomplished by two giant railroad companies: the Central Pacific Railroad, which built the rail from Sacramento eastward, and the Union Pacific Railroad, which built the railroad from Omaha westward.

These railroads had to overcome staggering obstacles in the process – towering mountain ranges, canyons, shortages of labor, shortages of money, shortages of supplies, Indian attacks, sweltering heat, bone-chilling cold, floods, droughts, and blizzards. This was especially true for the Central Pacific Railroad, which had to literally cut its way through the impassable Sierra Nevada Mountains. In the end the Central Pacific Railroad laid 690 hazard-filled miles of track and the Union Pacific laid 1,087 miles.

But something happened in early 1869 that almost killed this monumental effort. As the two railroads hurdled toward their link up in the desert of northern Utah, they actually passed each other. That's right, they passed each other and continued to lay *200 miles of parallel track within just 100 feet of each other.*

Because each company stood to make more money for each mile of track it laid, they refused to come to an agreement on where to link up – one railroad trying to push the link up further east, the other further west. They had come so far and overcome so many obstacles and now they could not bridge the short distance that separated them to unite the country and complete the longest journey and most hazardous undertaking. It took several months and pressure from Congress to get the two railroads to agree on a link up point – Promontory Summit on April 10, 1869.

I think of couples who, like the two railroads, weather all sorts of storms and come such a long way in their relationship and marriage. Then – because of mounting resentment and bitterness – they come to the place where they cannot so much as reach across the bed to their partner. They have traveled so far and overcome tremendous obstacles in their relationship. But after years and multitudes of little hurts, they become powerless to soften their hardened hearts and reach out emotionally to the person they swore to love for eternity.

But God can soften the human heart. He can rekindle the flame of love. He can fill an empty heart with his love and heal and breathe new life into old marriages. If your relationship needs healing, reach out to the God who reaches out to you.

PRAYER: Dear heavenly Father, please heal my wounded heart. Soften it and fill it with your love. Bless my spouse and help both of us to love each other, understand each other, appreciate each other, and meet each other's needs. Amen.

February 15

MILESTONES AND FINISH LINES

In December 2005 Roger Loughran, a horse-racing jockey, in a moment of triumph, stood tall in the saddle and held his whip high as he celebrated his first professional win atop his horse, *Central House*. But as he continued to exult with an outstretched right arm and looping underhand punches, the crowd did not seem to respond or share his joy. In fact, his audience stared in silence.

Much to Roger's great disbelief and disappointment, he had mistaken a milestone (the end of the running trail) for the actual finish line – which was another 80 meters beyond. Roger Loughran had quit too soon. Before he was able to return to reality, two other horses, *Hi Cloy* and *Fota Island*, galloped past him, leaving him to finish in third place. Loughran returned to the stables a sadder but wiser man.

Many of us do the same in life. We mistake a milestone for the finish line. In the military we attain a certain rank and feel we've arrived and subsequently decline in our performance and vision. We accomplish great things and proceed to coast along on the strength of past victories and laurels.

We forget that the finish line is not some great obstacle or achievement in this life. The real finish line is the Judgment Seat of Jesus Christ, hoping to hear from the Lord those words, "Well done, you good and faithful servant." Nothing else in all eternity will be as satisfying. "Therefore we have as our ambition," Paul said, "whether alive or dead, to be pleasing to God. For we must all appear before the judgment seat of Christ, so that each 0ne may be recompensed for his deeds in the body, according to what he has done, whether good or bad." (2 Corinthians 5:9-10)

PRAYER: Dear Father in heaven, help me to look beyond the challenges and rewards of this life and to focus on the eternal reward in heaven. Help me to look beyond my earthly master and to seek to please my Master in heaven. Help me never to quit before I'm finished running the race. Amen.

February 16

SEEING GOOD IN THE BAD

Can one person's problem be someone else's solution? Yes - if we only have eyes to see the "good" that resides in the "bad."

For example, soon after the advent of cyanoacrylate adhesives (superglue), critics warned that the glue was so dangerous that a person might easily glue his fingers together with it. This problem – a permanent skin bond – soon became a fabulous solution for doctors. Surgeons in Vietnam began to use superglue to glue wounds together.

The problem for another glue, this time a glue that was too weak, also proved to be a great solution. 3M chemists were experimenting with adhesives and accidentally came up with one that was so weak you could peel it right back off. Hold strength, shear strength, all were way below minimum standards for any self-respecting adhesive. A glue that won't hold? Quite a problem. But this problem was also a solution, as you now see in Post-It Notes.[x]

When miners searched for gold in 19th Century Nevada, they were often plagued by a nagging, sticky bluish mud that clung to their shovels and picks. So troublesome was this blue mud that they paid laborers to haul it away for them. The blue mud was certainly a nuisance – until a specimen was sent to a chemist who discovered the mud was silver ore. The tons of discarded blue mud had been worth millions!

May God open our blind eyes to the good and the blessings that he daily pours into our lives. The Scripture tells us: "Hope does not disappoint because the love of God has been poured out in our hearts." (Romans 5:5)

PRAYER: Dear Father in heaven, help me to see the blessings you pour into my life day by day. Amen.

February 17

HUMBLE BEGINNINGS

They were only gas station attendants. How could they ever amount to anything? Who were they? Johnny Carson, Michael Douglas, and Clint Eastwood. Evidently, though they started small, they had potential for bigger things.

Consider these other humble beginnings: He began as a grave and ditch digger, but went on to become a famous rock star – he was Rod Stewart. These two were once mediocre boxers, but went on to bigger things – they were Bob Hope and Billy Joel. Comedian Drew Carey, however, did begin working in Las Vegas – as a waiter in a Denny's restaurant. Famous explorer Amerigo Vespucci (for whom America is named), once worked as a pickle merchant. The great philosopher and teacher, Confucius, was once a grain inspector. King David was once a shepherd. Jesus Christ, the Son of God, once earned his living as a carpenter.

A humble beginning is not an indicator of a person's potential or limitations. Nor is it right to conclude that if we perform poorly at an unskilled job that we have no future hope succeeding in a skilled one. The fact is that God has gifted and equipped us all for some task in life. Discovering our gifts and abilities is the problem. We can only learn what our gifts are by trial and error, by "getting out there" and working. If we meet with failure or a lack of fulfillment in some job, don't sweat it. Trial and error is how we learn.

Edgar Rice Burroughs first failed as a student, a cowboy, a railroad policeman, a law clerk, a stenographer, a salesman, and a correspondence school president before he succeeded as a famous novel writer and author of the many Tarzan novels – 50 of which became bestsellers, translated into more than 20 languages.

Harlan Sanders failed as a soldier, a locomotive fireman, a streetcar conductor, an insurance salesman, a ferryboat pilot, a lawyer, and a gas station attendant – before he succeeded at his Kentucky Fried Chicken business, which he later sold for $15 million.

If you've failed and feel you have no future, don't lost heart or hope. You're learning what you're not good at on the journey of self-discovery. The Scripture assures us: "We all have different gifts according to the grace that God has given to us" (Romans 12:6) and we are told to use these gifts in serving others (Romans 12:6-8).

PRAYER: Dear Father, please take my hand and guide me into that job, profession and calling for which you have created me. If I meet with failure early on, help me not to lose heart, but to accept failure as part of the process of discovering who I am and what you've called me to do. Amen.

February 18

THE LESSON OF THE "DONKEY BOMBS"

The little-known Battle of Valverde, that took place in February 1862, presents one of the strangest incidents in American history. Near the town of Valverde, New Mexico Territory, two brigades, one Confederate and one Union, fought to gain control over areas of the Southwest that had not yet declared themselves slave or free.

The Union forces, numbering 3,200, were commanded by Lieutenant Colonel Edward Canby. The smaller Confederate force, commanded by General Henry Silby, numbered about 2,500.

On the eve of the battle one enterprising Union company commander devised a plan to destroy the Confederate supplies and force an early withdrawal of the enemy. Captain "Paddy" Grayson's plan called for two mules to be loaded down with twelve 24-pound explosive artillery shells and rigged with fuses. Captain Grayson and some volunteers would lead the mules to the edge of the Confederate camp by cover of darkness, light the fuses, turn the mules loose amidst the corralled horses of the enemy, and flee. The intent was to destroy the enemy's capacity for re-supply.

The plan had promise and all seemed to go well. Captain Grayson was able to stealthily lead the mules within "smelling distance" of the Confederate camp. He and his men lit the fuses, slapped the rumps of the mules, turned and fled. But then the plan fell apart.

When the mules looked back and saw their masters returning to the Union camp, they turned to follow. The men were horrified to see the "donkey bombs" heading straight for them. Grayson and his men began to run, but the mules easily gained on them. Unfortunately, the men had removed their boots to reduce noise and the risk of detection. As the mules got closer, the desperate Union soldiers had to run barefoot through prickly pear cactus and yucca patches to escape. Suddenly, a thunderous blast showered the men with artillery fragments and bits of the animals. However the men survived, but limped back to camp thoroughly footsore.

The image of those "donkey bombs" returning to their senders illustrates one of God's laws among humankind. It is the law of reciprocation. This law ensures that what we send forth to others will return to us. What deal out to others will be dealt out to us. "Whatsoever a man soweth, that shall he also reap." (Galatians 6:9) "Judge not, lest you be judged. For with what judgment you judge, you will be judged." (Matthew 7:1-2)

But this law also works for the good that we do to others. "Give and it shall be given unto you." (Luke 6:38) "Cast your bread upon the waters, and you shall find it after many days." (Ecclesiastes 11:1) "Blessed are the merciful, for they shall obtain mercy." (Matthew 5:7)

The way we treat our fellow human beings is a matter near and dear to God's heart. The Scripture tells us that we cannot hate our brothers and sisters whom we *have* seen and love God whom we *have not* (1 John 4:20-21). God will not even accept our worship when we are at odds with our brothers and sisters (Matthew 5:23-24).

Another religion may allow its adherents to have a scapegoat, an enemy upon which to vent their hatred. But the Gospel of Jesus Christ commands us to love our enemies, to bless those that curse us, to do good to those that hate us, and to pray for those who abuse us (Matthew 5:44).

But never fear. God assures us that loving and doing good to enemies is not the path to our own destruction. It is the only way of survival and happiness in this life, and glory in the life to come.

PRAYER: Dear Father in heaven, I am so quick to retaliate and return evil for evil. Remind me of the humility and love of Jesus Who endured much at the hands of those who hated Him. Remind me also that whatever I deal out to others, good or bad, will ultimately return to me. Amen.

February 19

THE IDEAL PERSON

In 2002 a Chilean agronomist named Luis Carrasco achieved something the world had never seen before. He produced the world's only five-fruited tree. That's right. Using a plum tree root stock, he successfully grafted into it branches of apricots, cherries, nectarines, and peaches. Each year his tree produces five different blossoms and fruits. But, just to bring us back to reality, Luis' "tree of many fruits" will only produce single-fruited trees – each one either a plum, apricot, cherry, nectarine, or peach. It seems that, by God's design, each tree will bear its own particular type of fruit.

Dr. Carrasco's desire to create a "child prodigy" of a tree is indicative of our concept of "the ideal person" as well as "the ideal tree." In our minds, the "ideal person" should be multi-talented and multi-gifted. And we tend to expect the same from ourselves, that we should be able to do it all, that we should be a one-man-band.

Consider our fascination with "do-it-all" utensils. Swiss Army Knives (and the many imitations), with their assortment blades and tool attachments, are perennial best sellers. We continue to be enamored with the gadgets as well as the people who seem to able to do it all.

But the reality is that no one can do it all. No sane person would trade a set of tools, each tool serving a specialized purpose, for a Swiss Army Knife? A Swiss Army Knife is nothing but a novelty that, at best, can only do a mediocre job of "real tools." The same is true of people. Jacks of all trades are masters of none. God has blessed each person on this planet with a certain mix of gifts and talents. But God also withholds some abilities from us and gives them to others. Why? He wants us to work together, to recognize the abilities and contributions of others, and to depend on each other to get the job done.

Consider Paul's words in Romans 12:3-5: *"Don't assess your abilities too highly, but think of yourself realistically. For God has only given you a measured amount of faith, not an unlimited supply. For just as one body has many members, each member performing a different function; so we are many members of a single body, each different, and each belonging to all the others."* It takes all the members, not just one, to do the work of the body.

There is a glorious freedom in this. You don't have to "do it all" or "be it all." There are no super saints in God's kingdom. There are no super-moms, super-dads, or super-pastors who single-handedly do the work of an entire household or church. God has given abilities to everyone, that everyone might lend a hand and help carry the burden.

PRAYER: Dear Father in heaven, too often I take too much on myself and become overwhelmed with my workload. Help me to look to You for strength and also to share the burden with others – others whom You have empowered to do the job as good as I can. Thank You for my brothers and sisters that You bring into my life. Please help me to appreciate them and work together with them. Amen.

February 20

**GOD DOESN'T DESTROY THE UNHOLY,
HE TRANSFORMS IT**

In the 2007 issue of the journal, *Assemblies of God Heritage*, author Glenn Gohr tells story of a church that recently celebrated its 100th birthday – the First Assembly of God of Findlay, Ohio. The church founder was a layperson, R. K. Leonard who, with the help of other Christians, purchased and renovated the church's first sanctuary in

1907 – a two story brick building. Nothing unusual about that, except that this brick building had been the town saloon.

The author explains that the saloon's transformation into a church used many of its old "sinful" features. A card table became the Communion table, the slot machine became the pulpit, and the bar rail became the altar rail where people knelt to pray, repent, and ask God's forgiveness.

The lesson from this transformation is that secular or "sinful" things, celebrations, and especially people can be wonderfully baptized into that which honors God. Consider also that such celebrations as Christmas and Easter, were once Pagan celebrations that were "baptized" and made holy celebrations of Christ's birth and resurrection. Does that disturb you – that the dates on which we celebrate the Lord's birth and resurrection were once high days on the Pagan calendar? It shouldn't, for the precedent for taking the unholy and making it holy was established centuries earlier.

Have you ever heard the words from this ancient hymn: "He makes the storm clouds his chariots and rides upon the wings of the wind"? Of course you've heard it, it comes from Psalm 104:3. But did you know that had been previously come from a hymn dedicated to the Canaanite god, Ba'al? The prophets of God took poetic words ascribed to a false god and simply applied them to the true God.

The prophets of God did the same in Psalm 48:2, where Mount Zion in Jerusalem is referred to as "the far north," or Zaphon (Mount Hermon in northern Palestine). In ancient Canaanite religion Zaphon or "the far north" was the Canaanite equivalent to Mount Olympus, the headquarters and home of the gods. In Psalm 48:2 the prophet was simply saying that the true home and headquarters of God, the only God, is atop Mount Zion, where the Temple rested. The prophets of God took what was Pagan and made it holy.

And God does the very same with people. Consider also, that every soldier in the Lord's army once served in Satan's ranks. Indeed, the only material from which God can make saints is sinners. Consider Paul the apostle's words in Ephesians 2:1-5: "As for you, you were dead in your transgressions and sins, in which you used to live … Like the rest, we were by nature objects of wrath. But because of his great love for us, God, who is rich in mercy, made us alive with Christ even when we were dead in transgressions—it is by grace you have been saved." Think you're not the right kind of person to serve the Lord? Think again. He can take the raw material of our lives, whatever it might be, and make us into people of value and destiny.

PRAYER: Dear Lord, I make no claims to spirituality or religiosity. I am a broken and empty person. But what there is left of me, I offer to You. Please take the broken pieces of my life and make me into something beautiful that will bless others and honor Your name. Amen.

February 21

REJECTION – SOMETIMES IT LEADS TO BETTER THINGS

"I'm fired? You can't fire me. I started this company!" Yet sure enough, the company Steve Jobs had begun ten years earlier with Steve Wozniak, was handing him his pink slip. How could it happen?

This is how. As their company, Apple Computers, mushroomed in its astounding growth, Jobs and Wozniak had hired someone to run the company and had established a board of directors. When he came in conflict with both his CEO and the board he was given the boot. And at the time it seemed like the end of the world. He had started that company in his parents' garage when he was 20 and in ten years it had become a $2 billion organization with 4,000 employees. In one day he lost it all. It was unquestionably the worst day of his life.

But in retrospect, Steve Jobs now sees things quite differently. "I didn't see it then, but it turned out that getting fired from Apple was the best thing that could have ever happened to me. The heaviness of being successful was replaced by the lightness of being a beginner again, less sure about everything. It freed me to enter one of the most creative periods of my life.

"During the next five years, I started a company named NeXT, (and then) another company named Pixar, and fell in love with an amazing woman who would become my wife. Pixar went on to create the world's first computer animated feature film, *Toy Story*, and is now the most successful animation studio in the world. In a remarkable turn of events, Apple bought NeXT, I returned to Apple, and the technology we developed at NeXT is at the heart of Apple's current renaissance. And (my wife) Laurene and I have a wonderful family together.

"I'm pretty sure none of this would have happened if I hadn't been fired from Apple. It was awful tasting medicine, but I guess the patient needed it."[xi]

Are you facing rejection and disappointment? It could be that God has allowed one door to slam shut because he has a better opportunity elsewhere. It could be that what you think is your worst nightmare will become your dream come true. God is able to take the sour and make it sweet. He is able to work all things (even the bad) together for good to those who love him and serve him. God is able to turn every curse into a blessing. The Scripture says: "The Lord your God turned the curse into a blessing for you because the Lord your God loves you." (Deuteronomy 23:5)

PRAYER: Dear Father in heaven, I know that I cannot always enjoy an unbroken string of successes and personal victories. Rejection and failure are inevitable. But, Lord, when rejection and failure do come into my life, help me to rise above them and to see your loving hand of providence opening other doors of opportunity and bringing good things into my life. Amen.

February 22

THE BEST IS YET TO COME

In 1940 Dwight David Eisenhower was a fifty-year-old lieutenant colonel serving as a regimental executive officer, and who seemed at the end of his career. He had spent sixteen years as a major and not until 1940, 25 years into his military career, did he finally attain the rank of colonel. But that would be the pinnacle of his career, so he thought. Too much time, he reasoned, had been spent in obscurity helping others succeed and making others look good – men like General Douglas Mac Arthur.

In a letter to his son, John, then graduating from high school, Eisenhower explained that he didn't expect to go much further in his own career. Though he still yearned for command and had spent his spare moments preparing for higher levels of leadership, he had little chance of ever reaching them. But he also explained that he was deeply content. The Army had provided him with a good life and had given him friends who respected him. "No man," Ike told his son, "could ask for more."

Yet within four years, this obscure Army officer was catapulted to the zenith of leadership, reaching the rank of a five-star general and Supreme Commander of Allied Forces during World War II. He could not have imagined the responsibilities, power and recognition that awaited him – not to mention that he would become the 34th President of the United States.

Consider another man whose long string of failures is represented in the following summary:

He failed in business in '31. He was defeated for the legislature in '32. Again in '32 he failed in a short military career, being reduced in rank from captain to private. He failed in business again in '33. He was sued for unpaid debts in '34. His sweetheart died in '35. He had a nervous breakdown in '36. He was defeated for speaker in '38. He was defeated for elector in '40. He was defeated for congress in '43. He was defeated for congress in '48. He was defeated for the senate in '50, defeated for vice president in '56, and for the senate in '58. Fortunately, he was elected president in 1860. His name was Abraham Lincoln.

Yet through all his ups and downs, Abraham Lincoln lived by the creed: "I shall prepare myself, and perhaps my time will come." Then, when his time came, he was ready. The same was true of Dwight Eisenhower – he prepared for levels of command he really had little prospect of ever reaching. But when his time came, he was ready.

Consider Moses at the age of 79, who must have believed that his best and greatest years were behind him – particularly those he enjoyed as the son of Pharaoh's daughter in the royal court of the King of Egypt. Yet within a year he would be called to deliver a people, become their lawgiver, and forge from them a nation. We just never know what great and glorious things God may have in store for us. Our responsibility is to devote ourselves to self-improvement and prepare ourselves for whatever future work God may have in store for us. The Scripture commands us: "Be diligent to present yourself to God as an approved workman, who will not be embarrassed by failure, but who accurately and effectively handles the word of truth." (2 Timothy 2:15)[xii]

PRAYER: Dear Father in heaven, though the prospects for greatness seem small, grant that I may apply myself and prepare myself for some greater responsibility in the future. Please guide my steps and open the right doors of opportunity for me. Amen.

February 23

DON'T DISMISS THE LITTLE THINGS

Little things can often spell survival or disaster in a critical situation. Consider these examples.

On April 10, 1963 the Navy's finest nuclear-powered attack submarine, the USS Thresher, was lost with all 129 officers and sailors while conducting its maximum depth dive tests. What happened? Was there a major malfunction with its nuclear reactor? Was there an undersea collision? No. Something much smaller took place. *First*, the tiniest cracks in its welds had been overlooked during its construction in 1960 and recent overhaul in 1962 – but at maximum depth, when there is 80,000 pounds of pressure *per square inch*, little things take on profound importance. Tiny ruptures in the sub's hull allowed water to shoot in with a force that could cut through concrete. The water shorted the sub's drive system. *Second*, when the ship's captain, LCDR John Wesley Harvey, ordered its ballast tanks to be filled with air – to cause the sub to rise to the surface – ice quickly formed on the little strainers that covered the air valves. This immediately stopped the flow of air and the sub sank deeper and deeper until it reached crush depth and imploded.

Tiny cracks and small metal strainers destroyed a multi-billion dollar submarine and snuffed out the lives of 129 brave men.

On July 26, 1956, the Italian luxury liner Andrea Doria was hit broadside by the Swedish ship, Stockholm, off the coast of Massachusetts. The 700-foot-long ship sank in 10 hours with the loss of 51 lives (1660 were rescued). What caused the terrible loss? Both ships were traveling in "pea soup" fog, but both had RADAR. Unfortunately, the range finder on the Stockholm's RADAR had no light – it was missing a *10-cent light bulb*. The lack of a simple light bulb made it impossible to determine how far away she was from the Andrea Doria. The ship's captain believed he was a safe distance from the Andrea Doria when in fact he was seconds away from a collision. The loss of a 10-cent light bulb caused the destruction of a $30 million (in 1956 dollars) vessel and the loss of 51 lives.

The great Northeast Blackout of 1965 (November 9-10) resulted in the loss of electrical power for 30 million people, covering an area of 80,000 square miles. How did it happen? There was no explosion or sabotage. A simple relay switch – only the size of *a shoebox* – had been improperly calibrated and shut down when a minor surge of power occurred on the line that ran from the Sir Adam Beck power station to

Toronto, Ontario. Once this relay switch shut off, power was diverted to other lines, creating a *real* overload and causing those relay switches to trip as well. This created a domino effect among the interconnected power stations.

Within minutes more and more relay switches shut down, unable to deal with the ever-increasing surge of power that was diverted to them, ultimately leaving parts of Canada, all of New York, and most of New England without power for about twelve hours. Tens of thousands of people were suddenly stranded in subways, on commuter trains, in elevators, in hospitals and office buildings. It was a nightmare. And it was all triggered by a small, shoebox-sized relay switch that failed to function properly. Yes, the loss or malfunction of little things can cause big problems.

How many of us feel as insignificant as a ten-cent light bulb? How many times do we feel our life's contribution could be fit into a shoebox? How many of us feel our place in this world is no bigger than the tiny weld in a mammoth vessel almost as long as a football field and weighing 3,700 tons?

But even if our feelings reflect reality, just look at how indispensable the little things proved to be in these examples? In the Scripture, the apostle Paul says that each of us is like a part of a body and all of us are members of each other. Take us away – regardless of how small or unsightly we are – and the body is maimed and ceases to function properly (1 Corinthians 12:14-22). Don't be fooled by negative thoughts or an inferior self-image. You and the contribution are indispensable. Therefore, whatever task God has given you, do it with all your might (Ecclesiastes 9:10).

PRAYER: Dear Father in heaven, open my eyes to the importance and significance of my life and work. Please help me to be faithful in the tasks with which you have honored me and to do it with all my might. Amen.

February 24

DOING MUCH WITH LITTLE

How do you measure success? By how much material wealth you acquire? By how high you climb the economic ladder? By how productive you are and how much work you accomplish? By how many mountains you climb? But there is another variable in measuring success – not merely how far you go, but how many obstacles you overcome in the process.

That's how Booker T. Washington explained it. He was born a slave in Franklin County, Virginia. But from these lowest of circumstances, Dr. Washington rose to become one of the greatest educators, reformers, and activists in America. He once said, "Success is measured not only by how much one achieves, but by how many obstacles one overcomes in the process."

Consider these great success stories from the halls of baseball stardom. Jim Abbott was born with no right hand, but managed to pitch for 10 successful years in the Major Leagues, even pitching a no-hitter while playing for the Yankees. Bert Shepard was a promising rookie when WWII broke out. But he left the game to serve his country by flying fighter missions over occupied Europe.

In 1944 his P-39 Airacobra was shot down and he suffered the loss of his right leg. But he recovered to play successfully in both the Major and Minor Leagues. Monty Stratton was one of the hottest pitchers in the American League in the 1930s. During his five years with the White Sox (1934-38) Monty compiled 36 wins against 23 losses. A tragic hunting accident resulted in the loss of his right leg. But he also rebounded to pitch professional baseball, inspiring the Hollywood motion picture, *The Stratton Story*.

But most amazing was Pete Gray. In 1945 Pete Gray was the sensational rookie of the St. Louis Browns. He had come up from the Minor Leagues where he batted .333, hit five homeruns, stole 68 bases and had won the Most Valuable Player Award. He accomplished all this – with only one arm. As an outfielder he had learned to catch, throw and bat with his one left arm. These men did much with little. They reached the Major Leagues and did so against all odds.

So the next time we're tempted to feel sorry for ourselves, or to feel inadequate and powerless to fulfill God's mission for us, remember these men and how they refused to let physical impairment hold them back. In the Scripture God encouraged Joshua with these words that apply to us all: "Be strong and courageous! Do not tremble or be dismayed, for the LORD our God is with you wherever you go." (Joshua 1:9)

PRAYER: Almighty and merciful Father, You do not call me where your grace cannot keep me. You do not task me to do anything for which You do not also equip me. I humbly acknowledge my need for your strength and wisdom and thank You for Your unfailing love. By Your grace, power, and love, make me all that You want me to be. Amen.

February 25

SLIM CHANCE

Jeopardy, the brain child of former TV talk show host and TV executive Merv Griffin, is the longest running game show in television history. It began in 1964 when it was hosted by Art Fleming, who continued with the show until 1979. Then in 1984, when *Jeopardy* was revived, Alex Trubek took the show's helm and has manned it ever since. It is unquestionably America's most popular game show.

A lot of work goes into every one of the nightly *Jeopardy* programs. Every question and answer is developed by a staff of twelve researchers, and then is checked and verified by another editorial staff. Prior to each show, host Alex Trubek studies the questions to ensure ease with the material. Over its long history, more than 300,000 questions and answers have been formulated and used on the show.

But the most interesting aspect of the show is the contestant selection process. Annually more than 250,000 people apply for their chance to play on Jeopardy. Of these only 15,000 are chosen for the initial screening exam and of these only 1,500 qualify. Yet, even most of these do not make it. In fact, only 500 of the original 250,000 applicants every get on the show – that's only *1 in 500*. In other words, your chances of ever competing on Jeopardy, no matter how smart you may be, are very slim.

What a contrast to your chances of getting an audience with your heavenly Father. In the Scripture our Lord assured us, "He who comes to Me I will *never* reject" (John 6:37). God's acceptance rate has never changed over the centuries – it's always been 100%. As an old gospel song says,

Did ever a saint find this Friend forsake him?
No, not one! No, not one!
Or sinner find that He would not take him?
No, not one! No, not one!

Jesus knows all about our struggles,
He will guide till the day is done;
There's not a friend like the lowly Jesus,
No, not one! No, not one!

PRAYER: Dear Father in heaven, thank you for your unconditional and unfailing love for me. Please keep me from the sin of neglect of this great love. Help me to understand and respond to your love. Amen.

February 26

GOOD FOR NOTHING?

Mubarak Abdullahi is a 24-year-old college student in northern Nigeria who works wonders with discarded junk. Mubarak takes the bodies and frames of old, discarded cars and motorcycles and he makes them fly! That's right. What is old, worthless, and useless to the rest of the world, Mubarak turns into *helicopters.* His most recent creation came from several different cars - including bucket seats from a Toyota Grand Saloon (a model not sold in the U.S.) and an engine from a Honda Civic. He even used pieces of a crashed Boeing 747.

And Mubarak's helicopters are not mere static displays. They really fly, as he has demonstrated numerous times and triggered interest from several aircraft manufacturers.

And as Mubarak is in the business of redeeming broken, discarded cars, God is in the business of redeeming broken and discarded people. Mubarak takes junked cars that cannot even creep along the ground and turns them into machines that can fly. And God is in the business of giving flight to the discarded and broken souls of humanity. What is refuse to the rest of the world, God sees as valuable and full of potential.

In the Old Testament, God spoke to the dying kingdom of Judah – about to be obliterated by Babylon – and said: "For I know the plans I have for you, says the LORD, plans for good and not for evil; plans to give you a hope and a future." (Jeremiah 29:11) In the New Testament we read of how God is in the business of taking "children of wrath" (Ephesians 2:2) and transforming them to "children of His love" (1 John 3:1). In fact, the hopeless, the worthless, and the damaged are the only raw material with which God has to work. Sinners are the only material from which He can make saints. So never lose hope for yourself, or for others, because you "don't work that well anymore." God does miracles with things that don't work at all.

PRAYER: Dear Father in heaven, please take the raw material and broken pieces of my life, and make me into the person You want me to be. Amen.

February 27

IN GOD'S LOVING CARE, NO ONE IS A VICTIM

In the early second millennium BC (1847 BC), King Erra-Imitti of Mesopotamia, chose his gardener, Enlil-Bani, to be king for a day. But this was no kind gesture. The King chose him to be his substitute during the Mesopotamian celebration of the New Year – the day on which the king was supposed to be sacrificed to the gods. The Mesopotamians believed that on the New Year, the gods would decide each person's fate for the coming year. To please them, the Mesopotamians would offer their king as a sacrifice. King Erra-Imitti had no intention of becoming such a sacrifice, so he selected his gardener to take his place.

But something went amiss. As the poor gardener-king nervously sat on the throne before his celebrating "subjects," with his gallows in full view, a servant dashed into the court, announcing that King Erra-Imitti had suddenly died. Immediately, the humble gardener was proclaimed king and he went on to successfully reign for the next 24 years, from 1847-1823 BC.

Although this story of a "stand-in turned ruler" bears a striking resemblance to the plot of the 1993 motion picture, "Dave," the theme of curses turning into blessings is also very biblical. The biblical character Joseph was the victim of his brothers' jealousy, the lies of a spurned woman, and the forgetfulness of a fellow prisoner. Yet God turned it all around and what others intended for evil, God intended for good (Genesis 50:20). In one day, Joseph rose from the prison to the throne of Egypt. The soothsayer, Balaam, was hired by King Balak to curse the Israelites. But every time Balaam opened his mouth he blessed Israel (Deuteronomy 23:4-5). Like the humble gardener, Enlil-Bani, people and circumstances may seem to conspire to make us a mere pawn, a sacrificial lamb, or someone else's stepping stone. But God will work behind the scenes to turn every evil intention into a blessing. God will work all things together for his glory and our ultimate good (Romans 8:28).

PRAYER: Dear Father in heaven, sometimes I feel so naïve and oblivious to the malicious intent of some who wish to use and abuse me. But I do not want to be paranoid – suspecting evil behind every corner. Instead, dear Lord, continue to open my eyes to the good in life and in others. Help me to count my blessings and to rest safely in Your love. For You have said, "The battle is not yours but God's." Amen.

February 28

THERE'S PAIN BEHIND THE POISON

If you love peace and calm then Jupiter is *not* the place for you. The gas giant Jupiter is the stormiest of all the planets. And its most prominent "blemish," the Great Red Spot, is a whirling storm of gases, 30,000 miles across, with winds of 250 miles per hour. And this nightmarish storm has been raging for more than 400 years.

But there's a good reason for Jupiter's storms. For although Jupiter has two and a half times more mass than all the other planets combined, it rotates faster than any of them. One day on Jupiter is less than ten Earth-hours long. This means that the speed of its rotation, at its equator, is nineteen times greater than that of Earth (more than 25,000 miles per hour vs. 1,000 miles per hour at Earth's equator). However, because Jupiter is mostly composed of gases in various physical states, it lacks the stability of solid planets like Earth. Therefore, its equator rotates faster than its northern or southern hemisphere. The extreme northern and southern surfaces of this planet cannot keep pace with its equatorial surface. This creates massive whirlpools and eddies – the biggest of which is the Great Red Spot.

Just as there is a reason for the storms that blemish the surface of Jupiter, there are reasons for the behavioral problems that surface in people's lives. We stand from a safe distance from people and critique their lives. "What an angry person he is!" "She is such a grouch!"

But what we fail to understand is that their stormy anger and their ugly grouchiness may be the result of the pain and turbulence of their lives. Like the surface of Jupiter, their lives are topsy-turvy and lack any foundation or stability. Painful childhoods, uprooted lives, and broken relationships send their lives spinning out of control while they struggle to keep some semblance of order. It's for a legitimate reason that they sometimes voice their pain and anger.

In his suffering Job explained his own angry words as due to the loathsomeness of his life: "Does a wild donkey bray when he has grass to eat? Does an ox low when he has fodder to chew? Can people tolerate food without salt? Or can anyone stomach the tasteless white of an egg? Therefore my soul is bitter and my words have been harsh." (Job 6:5-7) "Do not judge, lest you be judged," Christ told us (Matthew 7:1). For we have no idea of the burden our brother or sister is carrying. There's unseen pain behind the poison they spew.

PRAYER: Dear Father in heaven, please grant that I may not criticize my neighbor until I have walked a mile in his shoes. Amen.

February 29

BE FAITHFUL

60-year-old John Donovan was a retired social worker from Virginia when he set out on the 2600-mile Pacific Crest Trail. This trail stretches from California-Mexico border to the Washington-Canadian border. But somewhere in the San Jacinto Mountains of Southern California, Donovan became hopelessly lost in a freak snow storm. At the bottom of a narrow gorge, exhausted, out of food, and knowing that no one would be looking for him, John Donavan scribbled his last despairing thoughts in the margin of a trail map. Out of respect for the man's family, his final words have remained undisclosed – only to say that they expressed many regrets. His last entry was May 8, 2005.

One year later to the day, two other hikers, Gina Allen and Brandon Day, stumbled into the very same, deep and remote gorge. But unlike Donovan, they were poorly prepared for a lengthy hike, much less for survival in the wilderness. They had no backpacks, no food, no extra clothing, no cell phones, and nothing for shelter or for sleeping. Theirs was only supposed to be a day hike and they were only clad with light jackets and tennis shoes. But after three days and sleepless nights, unable to find their way back, they, too, began to despair. But on May 8, 2006, they found John Donovan's abandoned rucksack, still packed with desperately needed clothing and *matches*. With the warm clothing they averted hypothermia and with the matches they started a brush fire that helped rescue workers locate and save them. Day and Allen commented that, even a year after his death, John Donovan had saved their lives. Chris Cook, Donovan's longtime friend, explained, "Even in his death he was helping people."

John Donovan's example proves that our lives continue to influence others even after our death. This behooves us to be faithful in the task God has given us – that the legacy we leave behind will be one of blessing, not of a curse. But it also reminds us not to judge our lives as failures – because the positive effects of our labors may not materialize until after our death. Be faithful in the work God has given you and leave the results with God. The Scripture reminds us that throughout the ages God's people have had to walk by faith, and in many cases "die in faith" without seeing the tangible results of God's goodness or the fulfillment of His promises (Hebrews 11:13). Even if it appears you have left no lasting legacy, the seed you have sown will someday blossom into a harvest. Be faithful and have faith in God.

PRAYER: Dear Lord, into Your hands I commit my work, my future, and my life. Please bless my life and my work so that they will have eternal significance and will continue to benefit others even after I die. Amen.

March

March 1

WHAT IS OUR MISSION?

Viganella is a small northern Italian village of 197 inhabitants nestled in a deep valley among the Italian Alps. Sound like a great place to live? Maybe not. For a full three months (November through January) of the year this village sits in the shadow of the surrounding peaks and receives no direct sunlight at all. This makes for a bone-chilling winter and causes significant suffering among the village's elderly residents. But recently the Italian government installed a giant (16- by 26-foot), sun-tracking mirror on nearby Mount Scagiola (3400 feet above sea level) that reflects the sun's rays down onto the town's square, an area that comprises several acres. This allows residents to find warmth and light when they would otherwise dwell in the icy shadows.

This is not an isolated example. Recently, an Austrian manufacturer, Bartenbach Lichtlabor, in cooperation with the European Union, has embarked upon a series of similar projects. The goal is to install giant mirrors on mountainsides to bring sunlight to darkened towns throughout the Alps. These projects are costly. The price for each one ranges between $600,000 to well over $1 million. But the government simply recognizes the critical human need for light.

And isn't that the very heart of our mission to the community in which God has placed us – to reflect His light and the warmth of His love where it is needed most? However, we are not called to reflect God's light from a safe distance, from high above on a mountain, detached from the world's suffering. Jesus actually said: "You are the light of the world … Men do not light a lamp to hide it under a bowl or from under a peck measure, but to put it on a lampstand that it may give light to all in the house" (Matthew 5:14-15). It's nice and cozy and warm and safe under that bowl and under that peck measure. But that is not where we belong. We need to shine where it's darkest and where the light will not otherwise shine. This is the reason God often removes us from our comfort zones and puts us in those dark and difficult places. He wants us to brighten our world.

PRAYER: Dear Father in heaven, help me to shine the light and warmth of your love in the marriage, home, and workplace you have placed me. Amen.

March 2

DO WE HAVE THE WHOLE STORY?

Communication. It can be a perilous endeavor. When it's unaided by modern technology, communication only gets worse.

Communication can be too slow. It took five months for Queen Isabella to receive word about Columbus' discovery of the New World, two weeks for Europe to hear about Lincoln's assassination. Yet, with the help of technology it took only 1.3 seconds for the world to receive live telecasts of Neil Armstrong walking on the moon. Slow communication has resulted in some of our Nation's major conflicts. A full two weeks had passed after the War of 1812 officially ended with the Treaty of Ghent in December 1814, when its bloodiest battle occurred – the Battle of New Orleans on January 8, 1815. In fact, perhaps for the good, our Nation's own Revolution began because communication was too slow. Lord North, Prime Minister under King George III, had won approval from Parliament for numerous proposals intended to conciliate the American Colonies: proposals that allowed the Colonies to tax themselves and to provide for their own civil administration and defense. But word of this did not reach America until April 24, 1775 - five days after the Battle of Lexington had ignited the War.

And sometimes the message communicated can just get garbled. Consider the case of Judge Claudia Jordan. While attorneys were deliberating in her Denver courtroom she passed a note to the clerk that read, "Blind on right side. May be falling. Please call someone." Recognizing the seriousness of the situation, the concerned clerk immediately called 911, informing the dispatcher that Judge Jordan might be having a stroke, imploring them to come as quickly as possible. When the clerk stepped forward to Judge Jordan to assure her that the paramedics were on the way, the puzzled judge simply pointed to the court window and said: "I only wanted you to call someone from maintenance to fix those Venetian blinds."

So – before jumping to conclusions and rushing to judgment about the guilt of a soldier, a subordinate, a superior, a friend, or your spouse - get the facts. Things may not be what they seem. Wait it out until you understand both sides of the story. And if you must err, err on the side of mercy. Most of us cry out for justice until we remember that we all need mercy. As the Scripture says, "Judgment will be merciless to the one who has shown no mercy; mercy triumphs over judgment." (James 2:13)

PRAYER: Dear Father in heaven, I, myself, need your mercy and love – every day of my life. Yet there are times when justice must be administered and corrective action taken. Please give me wisdom to know when to show mercy and when to administer justice. Help me to wait out the storm, until I get all the facts and can rightly assess the situation. Amen.

March 3

WHEN OUR STRENGTH IS RUNNING LOW

It was called the blunder that cost a pennant. The day was September 23, 1908 and the New York Giants and the Chicago Cubs were locked in a close pennant race. The Giants had just slipped from their comfortable lead ahead of the Cubs when they lost both games of a double-header the day before. Now the two teams were tied for first place.

By the bottom of the ninth the score was tied, 1-1. The first two Giant players failed to get on base. Then, with two outs, Moose McCormick slammed a single – now there was a man on first. Then a nineteen-year-old rookie, Fred Merkle, got up to bat. Likewise, Merkle singled, sending McCormick to third base. Then Al Birdwell stepped up to the plate. He hit a line drive straight up the middle. This would normally have sent McCormick to home plate, scoring the winning run. He actually did race to home plate, but Fred Merkle failed to reach second base to complete the play. Giants fans had begun pouring onto the field to celebrate the pennant victory and Merkle opted to head straight for the dugout. He never touched second base

Cubs manager, Frank Chance noted this and filed a protest with the umpires, demanding that Merkle be called out. Umpire, Hank O'Day, called Fred Merkle out for not reaching second base. Then the Giants, who had won the game fair and square, protested this decision. The game was declared a draw, leaving both the Cubs and the Giants with identical records: 98 wins to 55 loses. To settle the matter the two teams met one more time with the Cubs winning with a score of 4-2. The New York Giants had gone from victory to defeat because one player failed to complete a play and finish strong.

The Scripture warns us, "He that endures to the end shall be saved." (Matthew 24:13) May God grant us power and strength to complete the race and to finish the course!

PRAYER: Dear Father in heaven, please empower me and fortify my spirit so that I can endure to the end and not die out before I finish my course. Amen.

March 4

BE FAITHFUL IN THE LITTLE THINGS

John and Doug were just Junior High School students. But they had caught the Rock n' Roll fever and decided to start their own band. With money earned from his paper route, John purchased a Sears Silvertone electric guitar and amp for $80 and proceeded to teach himself to play. Doug began with only a snare drum, which he balanced on top of a large flowerpot. Soon they invited Doug's friend Stu, a piano player, to join. The year was 1958. The name of their group was *The Blue Velvets*.

But the *Velvets* were hardly a success. They could only find a handful of bit jobs, playing at an occasional county fair, at local teen hangouts, or playing as a backup for more prominent vocalists. After John's older brother Tommy joined the group, the Velvets did cut a few records. Sadly, all of them bombed.

Yet the four young men worked on their skills and their sound. By the mid-60s the Blue Velvets changed their name to *The Visions*. But still success eluded them. They were all forced to work at other jobs – Tommy at a public utilities company, John as a shipping clerk at a recording studio, and Stu and Doug as students at San Jose State College.

Then Vietnam boiled over, and John and Doug were drafted. Both served out enlistments in the California National Guard. But even with the distractions, the lack of encouragement, and the meager opportunities, *The Visions* persisted in honing their skills and seeking every opportunity to play.

They again changed the name of the group – this time to *The Golliwogs*. Still they worked on their skills, not just as musicians, but also as song-writers, especially John and Tommy. Still they cut a handful of recordings. But still success and recognition did not come.

Then, in 1968, the group took on its fourth and final name. And, after ten years of struggling without success, recognition or any affirmation, these four men – John, Tommy, Doug and Stu – finally recorded a hit. The song was "Suzie-Q," a song previously recorded by Dale Hawkins. It was the first of dozens of hit songs that took America by storm over the next two years. The men? John Fogerty, Tom Fogerty, Doug Clifford and Stu Cook. The group? *Credence Clearwater Revival*. For a period of just over two years (1969-71) *Credence Clearwater Revival* burst forth on the musical scene with a torrent of super hits: *Proud Mary, Bad Moon Rising, Who'll Stop the Rain, Down on the Corner, Fortunate Son, Travelin'Band, Up Around the Bend*, and many others. The hits of *CCR* are considered American classics with an exceptional enduring quality that makes them just as popular today as when they were first released.

CCR's story is a reminder that life has its seasons. Not all of life's seasons are productive. In fact, most of them are not. Most seasons are formative and preparative. Just as a tree goes fruitless for three out of four seasons, all in preparation for the late summer-early fall season of fruit-bearing, so people tend to go through long periods of obscurity, periods of preparation, periods of spiritual formation long before we experience profound success in life. Our task is to *be faithful and diligent* in those seasons of obscurity, when the work is hard and rewards are few. In the Scripture our Lord taught that he who is faithful with little will be entrusted with much (Matthew 25:21-22). Be faithful in the small and menial tasks of life. For by doing *them* a greater work is being performed *in us* – the work of developing our character, determination and faith.

PRAYER: Heavenly Father, through times of adversity, obscurity, and tedium, help me to faithfully do my best. Remind me that, by my faithfulness in all of life's seasons, you are preparing me for future times of fruitfulness. Amen.

March 5

PROBLEMS, PROBLEMS

The creation of the indispensable *Post-It Note* has an interesting history. In 1964, 3-M chemist Spenser Silver developed a glue that he characterized as "tacky" but not "aggressively adhesive." That is, it was sticky, but not sticky enough to serve any useful purpose. He was intrigued by this new glue, but deeply frustrated that he couldn't seem to find a purpose for it. He would wander the halls of 3-M giving demonstrations of his "now it sticks, now it doesn't" adhesive. He would coat two sheets of paper with the glue and show how easily it could stick and peel. But no one seemed to care and only with great difficulty did he get 3-M to patent it.

Ten years passed. Then one fateful Sunday morning, Arthur Fry, another 3-M chemist, was preparing to direct the choir at the church he attended. Just as he stepped up to lead the choir in several hymns, he dropped his hymnal and all the bookmarks – marking the place of each hymn – fell to the floor. It took five embarrassing minutes for him to recover the bookmarks and his composure. But through the ordeal, he thought to himself, "If only I had bookmarks or notes that would stick in place, this sort of thing would never have happened." Upon reflection, his mind went back to one of Spenser Silver's demonstrations.

The next day, he tracked down some of Silver's adhesive, applied it to small pieces of scratch paper and Post-It Notes was born. Though 3-M remained unconvinced for several years and Arthur Fry had to do much research on his own – even building a "Post-It Note machine" in his own home - 3-M finally began to formally produce and market Post-It Notes in 1980 and they became one of the company's most stunning successes.[xiii]

Do you ever feel that, although you know you have gifts and talents, you're not sure just what purpose in life you could ever serve? I.e., do you ever feel like Spenser Silver's adhesive? "I know I'm good at something, but I just don't know what useful purpose I could ever fill in life." For many of us, life is like that. We must develop our gifts and talents and then our time will eventually come. A great need will arise. Our contribution will be recognized. And God will provide an opportunity for us to be used for the good of our fellow human beings and for his glory.

A fledgling young lawyer named Abraham Lincoln – once feeling all his efforts to study law and immerse himself in politics might be in vain – finally concluded, "I shall prepare myself and perhaps my time will come." After many frustrations, failures and a lifetime in obscurity, Abraham Lincoln's time finally came. The Scripture assures us that God has given each of us a special gift and endowment that we are to use for serving others (Romans 12:6-8). Our task is to discover that gift and develop it and to look for ways to employ it in serving. If we do our part, God will do his by opening doors of opportunity.

PRAYER: Dear Father, help me not to despise the periods of obscurity and seeming unfruitfulness, but help me to use those times to develop the gifts you given me that I may effectively serve you and others when the opportunity arises. Amen.

March 6

GOD CARES FOR THE "LITTLE THINGS"

The European eel represents an astounding example of God's care over his creation. This eel spawns in the Sargasso Sea, on the edge of the Gulf of Mexico, thousands of miles from its home in the freshwater rivers of Europe.

To reach the spawning grounds, this eel leaves the European rivers and streams, using any kind of waterway they can find, or even traveling short distances by land when obstacles such as dams force them to do so. When they reach the ocean, they set out on a compass course for their destination 3,000 to 6,000 miles away. The adult eels do not return from the spawning ground to Europe, so they cannot "teach" their young how to travel back home to Europe. Yet the larva, carried in part by the Gulf Stream, returns to, in many cases the very same river of its parents over a three-year journey.

Just as amazing is the migration of the monarch butterfly. According to Jules H. Poirier (One of the designers for the navigational systems aboard the Apollo spacecraft), the navigational feats performed by the monarch is nothing short of miraculous. "This tiny, yet beautiful, insect can perform a migration flight of thousands of kilometers, navigating unerringly to reach a place it has never seen. For instance, some monarchs fly from Nova Scotia, Canada to the mountains west of Mexico City, some 5,000 kilometers (3,000 miles) in all. Not just to the very same place to which their forefathers migrated, but each one often *to the very same tree!*

"Monarch butterflies can fly in still air at a speed of around 50 kilometers (30 miles) per hour, and considerably faster with a tail wind. They have been known to fly more than 600 kilometers (375 miles) over water non-stop in 16 hours. Their 5,000-kilometer migration takes them eight to ten weeks, traveling only in daylight.

"Monarchs can be taken hundreds of kilometers off course and still find their way to their destination. How do they perform this amazing feat? To this day, no scientist knows for certain.

"What makes it all the more sensational is that due to the short life cycle of the monarch butterfly, many have never before been to the place to which they are headed.

"Yet despite stopping many times on the way to drink nectar, and being blown off course, they unerringly make the necessary corrections to get back to the place from which their parent (or even grandparent) commenced the journey."

From his own experience with the Apollo space vehicle Jules Poirier concludes, "Designing navigation equipment to take men beyond the confines of this planet and safely back again took an enormous amount of intelligent effort. The fact that the monarch can do these unbelievable feats with such an amazingly miniaturized 'control center' reveals a level of design engineering which demands an overwhelmingly great intelligence."[xiv]

In the Scripture Saint Paul declared that God's invisible attributes and power are clearly seen through His creation (Romans 1:20). Jesus Christ reasoned that if God shows such care for the "little things" of his creation, then how much more will He care for his children? (Matthew 6:25-33)

Look around you. God is really there. He loves and cares for you. Seek Him and draw close to Him.

PRAYER: Dear Father, open my eyes to Your presence and love and help me to draw close to You. Amen.

March 7

DOES GOD LEAD US TO DEAD ENDS?

Stairways that lead to the ceiling. Doors that open to blank walls. Literally miles of secret passages that lead nowhere. In total, the Sara Winchester house is a seven-story, 160-room Victorian mansion that covers six acres – all built without a blueprint! Why? Sara Winchester, heiress to the Winchester Company, routinely consulted with spiritualists and mediums. One of these, upon whom she particularly depended, advised her that the she would not die as long as she continued building her home. So, beginning in 1884, Sara Winchester began her "life-saving" project and continued for thirty-eight years. But it didn't keep her from dying. By the time of her death came in 1922, at the age of eighty-five, she had spent $5.5 million on a hodge-podge of connected buildings with its 2,000 doors and 10,000 windows – many of which serve no purpose.

But that is not the way God designs our lives. God begins with a blueprint conceived in infinite love and wisdom. There may be times when it seems God has led us to a dead end. But "whenever God closes a door he somewhere opens a window." God has a plan for our lives and has already authored our life's novel. We do not yet know how the story will end. But God is the greatest writer and by the final chapter he will most certainly bring meaning to all those "dead ends" and "detours" we have experienced along the way. In the Scripture we read, "Oh, the depth of the riches of both the wisdom and knowledge of God! How unsearchable are His judgments and unfathomable His ways! For who has known the mind of the LORD, or who became His counselor? … For from Him and through Him and for Him are all things." (Romans 11:33-34, 36).

PRAYER: Dear Father in heaven, this day and always I entrust my life, my future and my destiny in your hands. Please guide and direct my steps and please bring meaning to all the parts of my life. Amen.

March 8

WHEN LIFE IS A CONTINUAL STRUGGLE

You've heard of the Beverly Hillbillies, but did you know the story of that rags-to-riches family is based on an actual incident? The place was not Tennessee, but Texas, in Pecos County. The man was not Jed Clampett, but Ira G. Yates, Jr.

Ira Yates was orphaned and forced to fend for himself at the age of twelve. He had tried his hand at ranching and shop keeping and was having a measure of success. Then he traded his store and $16,500 for a large 20,000-acre ranch. Friends had warned Ira about the land. One friend, Nub Pulliam, told him: "Buffalo know better than to cross that land and the crows won't even fly over it." But Ira Yates was eager to have a ranch of his own and he made the deal.

After five years it seemed clear Ira had made a mistake. Now impoverished and unable to break even, Ira was desperate, deeply in debt and unable to pay the principle on his mortgage. His days were filled with stress over the financial concerns of the family. They lived, dressed, and ate in poverty.

Then it happened. Against the conventional wisdom of the day, representatives from the Transcontinental and Ohio (later Marathon) Oil Companies agreed to drill four exploratory wells on the Yates' property. Most geologists were convinced there was no oil west of the Pecos. But in 1920, when the drillers reached 1,115 feet, they struck a huge oil reserve. The first well produced *80,000 barrels a day!* Ira Yates, the man who lived in poverty in an arid land, became an instant millionaire. Thirty years later one of his oil wells was still yielding 125,000 barrels a day.

This vast sea of wealth, known as the Yates Pool, had always belonged to Yates. He was a multimillionaire who had spent years in heart-wrenching poverty just because he didn't realize what he already possessed.

Many a child of God lives in the emotional and spiritual poverty of depression and gloom. All around is the inexhaustible God who can help us with every problem, bind up our broken hearts and fill them with hope and joy. Why then should we go on living like paupers? Experience his power and joy by putting your whole-hearted trust in him.

In the Scripture our Lord said, "Come to Me, all who are weary and heavy-laden, and I will give you rest. Take My yoke upon you and learn from Me, for I am gentle and humble in heart; and you shall find rest for your souls. For My yoke is easy and My burden is light." (Matthew 11:28-30)[xv]

PRAYER: Dear Lord, fill my poor heart with Your presence, Your power and Your joy. Forgive my failures and heal my broken heart. Help me to live a life pleasing to You. Amen.

March 9

LOOKING FOR WISDOM?

Faced with a problem? Wracking your brain for solutions? There's someone who might help with the answers. He's helped geniuses and inventors for millennia, giving them ideas and solutions to complex problems. Of course I'm talking about God. Dr. George Washington Carver, America's greatest agricultural scientist, often acknowledged God as the source of his genius. And science abounds with examples of inventions that borrowed their ideas from God's handiwork.

In Eighteenth Century Europe fine writing paper remained a precious commodity because the raw material from which it was made – rags and linen – were in short supply. Then, in 1719, the French scientist, Rene-Antoine Reaumur, observed wasps making a fine paper from the wood fibers they had consumed and digested. This ultimately led to the wide-spread use of wood pulp to manufacture paper.

The inventor of Velcro got his idea from the "gripping power" of cockleburs that clung to his clothing and his dog's fur after a walk in the woods. He reduplicated the very hooks of the burs he observed in a magnifying glass.

While watching a cat take swipes at a chicken and coming up with just a paw full of feathers, Eli Whitney got the inspiration for the "Cotton Gin." By replicating the "cat claws" on a tumbler, Whitney successfully removed cotton fibers from the seeds and made cotton production a profitable business.

A veteran logger, Joseph Buford Cox, got his idea for the C-shaped blades of the modern chain saw from observing beetle larva chomp away at wood with its C-shaped jaws.

Orville and Wilbur Wright developed the steering system for their air plane, the "Wright Flyer," from watching seagulls flex and alter the shape of their wings. They called the system "wing warping."

The inventors of sonar (SOund NAvigation and Ranging) did not consciously borrow ideas from nature, but could have. Bats use aerial echo-location and the duck-billed platypus uses underwater echo-location.

Scientists are even studying the double-helix DNA molecule for its merits as an information-storage system. According to Richard Dawkins, the DNA of one single cell is capable of storing four sets of the 30-volume *Encyclopedia Britannica*. Another physicist, Dr. Werner Gitt, claims that a pin head's worth of DNA can hold the information equivalent to a stack of books piled 500 times as high as the distance from the earth to the moon. He believes a study of the DNA's structure may yield important clues for improved data storage. This is barely the tip of the iceberg. In a recent article, "Ideas Stolen Right from Nature" (*Wired News*, November 9, 2004), science journalist Rowan Hooper, states that the possibilities of gleaning inventive ideas from nature are immense.

God obviously has the best ideas for making and fixing things. Is it any wonder that the scripture encourages us, "If anyone lacks wisdom let him ask of God who gives to everyone generously." (James 1:5) Take it from George Washington Carver, who said, "The secret of my success? It is simple – 'Trust in the Lord with all thine heart, and lean not upon thine own understanding; but in all thy ways acknowledge Him, and He shall direct thy paths.'" (Proverbs 3:5-6)

PRAYER: Dear Father in heaven, I humbly acknowledge You as the giver of wisdom and knowledge. Please enlighten me and give me the wisdom I need to resolve the challenges and problems I am facing today. Amen.

March 10

WHAT HAVE I DONE?

On February 20, 1943, a humble Mexican farmer committed a catastrophic and deadly sin – or, that's what he *thought*. He was merely plowing his field on this day. But when he turned and looked behind him, he noticed smoke rising from the furrow he had just made.

Within days, this "fracture in the earth" that *he* had created became a 1000-foot volcano that consumed his cornfield. Over the next nine years (1943 – 1952) the volcanic cone rose to 1500 feet and destroyed the town of San Juan. Of all the town's buildings, only the church steeple survived.

Of course, the farmer did *not* start this volcano. His plow did not rupture the earth and cause the destruction of the town. This was the famous Paricutin Volcano, and it is *just one* among 1400 in the Mexican state of Michoacan where such volcanoes dot the countryside. It was mere coincidence that his plow passed the very spot where the volcano was about to erupt.

As this farmer believed his actions triggered a series of horrific events, many of us may assume responsibility for things that are far beyond our control. We assume the responsibility for the unhappiness of a child, a parent, or a spouse. We blame ourselves for the death of a friend or family member and think to ourselves, "If I had only done more for this person, this wouldn't have happened." We go through life bearing a burden of guilt that does not belong to us. Each person is responsible for their own happiness or unhappiness. Death and tragedy are all part of the human experience and cannot be escaped. Put that burden of care on the shoulders that are big enough to bear it! The Scripture says, "Commit your burden to the Lord and he will sustain you. He will never allow the righteous to be shaken." (Psalm 55:22) Put that burden of guilt where it belongs – on the cross of Calvary. For as the Scripture says, "Christ, who knew no sin, became sin for us, that we might be made the righteousness of God in Him." (2 Corinthians 5:21)

PRAYER: Dear Father in heaven, You know that I only bear these burdens because I love those close to me who are suffering. But I am only dust, and I cannot do for my loved ones all I would like. Here and now, I place my loved ones in your care. I also place my shortcomings and failures – real and imagined – upon the cross. Bless and care for my loved ones. Forgive and strengthen me. This I ask in the Name and for the glory of Christ. Amen.

March 11

STAY FOCUSED

His name is Erik Weihermayer. This 32-year-old middle school teacher is a marathon runner, scuba diver, down-hill skier, long-distance bicyclist, and performs acrobatic skydiving stunts. To this list of activities Erik has added mountaineering. And, yes, he has done the ultimate. Erik Weihermayer has climbed to the roof of the world, that bleak and hostile place where the air pressure is only a third of what it is at sea level, where there is so little oxygen that every step is an agonizing effort, where dozens have perished on its forbidding slopes, that place that is more than five miles high (29,028 feet to be exact) – Mount Everest! You might say that Erik lives and enjoys life to the fullest, that he doesn't let fear get him down.

Nor does Erik let his handicap keep him back. For Erik Weihermayer is totally blind! At the age of 13 a degenerative eye disease robbed him of his sight. Many others would have been distracted by what they lost and destroyed themselves with self-pity and bitterness. But Erik's secret to survival, and success, is to stay focused – to stay focused on life's blessings, life's opportunities, life's goals.

That's how he made it to the top of the world. Without the benefit of inspiring vistas, without the satisfaction of being able to look back and savor the heights he had gained, and with fears bombarding him and pain racking his body – Erik stayed focused on the goal. "I just kept telling myself: 'Stay focused. Be full of energy. Keep relaxed. Don't let all those distractions – the fear and the doubt – creep into your brain, because that's what will destroy you up there."[xvi]

That's great advice for facing all the mountains of our lives. Erik's words also echo something recorded in Scripture long ago: "Be strong and courageous! Do not fear or be dismayed, for the LORD your God is with you wherever you go." (Joshua 1:9)

PRAYER: Dear Father in heaven, so many things cry out for my attention and seek to distract me from what is most important in life: Your unfailing love, Your call upon my life to live righteously, the blessings You have poured into my life, the family and friends You have given me, and the work to which You have called me. Help me, O God, to stay focused on these things that matter most. Amen.

March 12

DON'T EVER GIVE UP ON YOURSELF

John Toole was like any of us. He pursued success, but feared rejection and failure. However, success always seemed to elude him. Rejection and failure did not.

Like any of us John began to lose hope. After an unbroken string of failures, he began to despair that he would never find success or happiness. Have you ever felt that way? Then one lesson you must learn from John Toole's life is this: Success is sure to come – just make sure you're there to enjoy it.

John Toole began writing a novel in his early teens. He finished it in the 1960s, while he was still serving in the Army. Already given to self-doubt, John was reluctant to send his manuscript to the publishers lest they reject it and confirm his fears. They did confirm his fears. After leaving the Army he sent his life-long project to no less than eight publishers. They all rejected it.

But John's mother, Thelma, believed in John even when John did not. "It's a great book!" she insisted. So John would send his manuscript out again and again, until one day in 1969 he gave up on life altogether. That same year John took his life.

Mrs. Toole took her late son's manuscript and submitted it to the Louisiana State University Press. They published it. It was entitled, *Confederacy of Dunces*. It sold tens of thousands of hardback copies, became a best-seller on dozens of books lists and was acclaimed by many critics as the year's best book.

Another publisher bid for and was awarded paperback rights. The manuscript that nobody wanted, the sensitive writing by an author whose genius was appreciated only by his mother, that book, in April of 1981, was awarded the prestigious Pulitzer Prize for fiction. With that distinction goes the fame, fortune, and recognition which the author had sought, yet had failed to find. How sad and tragic John Toole wasn't there to enjoy it.[xvii]

How sad, too, John Toole forgot or was not aware that success is almost always preceded by repeated failure. English novelist John Creasy got 753 rejection slips before he published 564 books. Publishers refused George Bernard Shaw's first five novels. Far from being wasted, however, the effort taught him valuable writing skills. Once he became famous, one of those novels was published and became a bestseller.

Failure is a necessary stepping stone to success. Soichiro Honda, founder of the Honda Motor Corporation, once said, "Success is 99 percent failure." The Scripture says, "Though a righteous man falls seven times, he rises again." (Proverbs 24:16) Don't give up on yourself or life.

PRAYER: Dear Father in heaven, failure and rejection are so painful, but inevitable. Help me to remember that failure is a teacher, not an undertaker, and that You will lead me to eventual success and consummate victory. Amen.

March 13

NOTHING IS IMPOSSIBLE

Can you imagine anything as frightening as being captured in the jaws of a crocodile? Crocodiles are powerful and heavily armed creatures. They can out-swim and (for short distances) out run any human alive. Once their jaws clamp on an arm or leg there is no escape. The bite-strength of a crocodile is more than 5,000 pounds per square inch (psi) – which far exceeds that of any other land animal (Compare to the bite-strength of a Rottweiler – 335 psi, a great white shark – 690 psi, or a hyena – 800 psi).

The Estuarine Crocodile of Australia is a particularly successful killer. And when one attacked 11-year-old Hannah Thompson, grabbing her arm with its deadly jaws and dragging her in the water, everyone around her gave her up for dead and fled - everyone except Ray Turner. Ray Turner was a retired crocodile hunter and he knew that crocodiles, as well as all the world's deadly predators, have weaknesses and will back away when hurt.

Ray Turner leaped upon the back of the 500-pound, ten-foot crocodile and jabbed his fingers into its eyes. The croc immediately let the girl go and crawled away. Hannah Thompson was rushed to a Queensland hospital where her arm was treated for puncture wounds and released.

Now no one is suggesting that a person should pick a fight with a crocodile. The point is this: like the dreadful croc that fled when poked in the eyes, so the biggest and baddest of your problems will flee when we put our faith in God. Nothing will be impossible. Every monster of the night, every specter that strikes fear in the heart, and shadowy figure is laughable when we turn on the light. And it is faith in God turns on the light. If fear knocks on the door, let faith answer. No one will be there.

In the Scripture David wrote, "The LORD is my light and my salvation—whom shall I fear? The LORD is the stronghold of my life—of whom shall I be afraid? … For in the day of trouble he will keep me safe in his dwelling; he will hide me in the shelter of his tabernacle and set me high upon a rock." (Psalm 27:1, 5)

PRAYER: Dear Father in heaven, when the problems and challenges of this life threaten to overwhelm me, help me to trust in you. Empower me by Your Spirit. Make me equal to every task and help me overcome every problem. Amen.

March 14

THE ESSENSE OF LEADERSHIP

The town of High Wycombe in Buckinghamshire, England, carries on a centuries old custom every year. Since 1678, in the month of May, the town's people require its mayor, his wife, the deputy town mayor and wife, and the district councilors to be weighed on a large scale. The purpose of this ceremony is to determine if the town's public servants have grown fat at the tax-payers' expense.

The mayor and other "weighees" sit on a velvet covered seat that hangs below the scale and the traditional macebearer calls out the weight in stones and pounds, followed by the pronouncement "and no more," or "and some more." If the mayor or other public servants have gained weight, they are met with jeers, though in decades past the town's people would have pelted them with tomatoes and eggs.

The custom was banned when Oliver Cromwell and the Puritans came to power in the Seventeenth Century, but was revived again in the early Nineteenth Century.

This custom may seem harsh and antiquated. However, it reinforces the truth that those who fill the ranks of leadership in government and in the military are essentially servants of those in their charge. It also serves as a reminder that public servants and elected officials are accountable to their people. While leaders may find a great sense of satisfaction in their work, they must remember that they were not entrusted with their position for their own personal fulfillment or gain.

Jesus Christ explained, "Among the heathen, kings are tyrants and each minor official lords it over those beneath him. But among you it is quite different. Anyone wanting to be a leader among you must be your servant. And if you want to be right at the top, you must serve like the slave. Your attitude must be like my own, for I, the Messiah, did not come to be served, but to serve, and to give my life as a ransom for many" (Matthew 20:25-28, *The Living Bible*)

PRAYER: Dear Father in heaven, remind me that my leadership position is a sacred trust and that I am a servant of those in my charge. Give me a wise and understanding heart so that I may be successful in my work and may more effectively serve those in my care and put their needs before my own. Amen.

March 15

SUPPORT YOUR LEADERS

Your brain makes up a mere 2 percent of your body weight (2 ½ - 3 pounds) but it uses 20 to 30 percent of your calorie intake and 20 percent of your blood.

Does that seem unfair? That such a small part of the body uses so much of its resources? Shouldn't the brain receive the same treatment, resources, and care as the feet or the toes? But, also consider that the "three-pound brain is the most complex and orderly arrangement of matter known in the universe." The brain has an incredible 1,000 trillion connections that conduct electrical impulses for everything from creative thoughts to involuntary body functions. And since the brain irretrievably loses 1,000 brain cells each day – each cell taking with it 10,000 connections to other brain cells – we probably shouldn't be too eager to cut down our blood supply to the brain, so as to make it equal to all the other parts of the body. Why? Because it runs the whole body and we cannot function or survive without it.[xviii]

What? Dare I say that all parts of the body are NOT equal? Well, no offense intended against the feet and toes, but could we survive the loss of a foot or some toes? Or a leg, or an arm? Yes, we could. But can we survive without the brain? No – though the actions of some people make us wonder if they've even got a brain.

Yesterday's devotional thought indicated that leaders are essentially servants. It stated that leaders exist for the benefit of the body, the organization and its mission and that they should put the needs of their subordinates before their own. But the other side of the coin is that leaders carry a much larger burden than the other members of the organization and expend a greater amount of energy. They therefore require more support and resources in order to function - just as the brain uses up an inordinate measure of the body's resources. In the Bible the apostle Paul admonished church members to "appreciate those who diligently labor among you and lead you in the things of the Lord and instruct you. ...esteem them very highly in love because of their work." (1 Thessalonians 5:12-13)

So the next time we're tempted to gripe against our leaders, because they live so comfortably, consider the heavy burden they bear and give them your whole-hearted support and pray for them.

PRAYER: Dear Father in heaven, please bless those entrusted with the leadership of my unit, the care of its soldiers and the success of its mission. Please empower them by your divine spirit and make them more than equal to the task. Help me to give them my whole-hearted support and to serve You by faithfully serving them. Amen.

March 16

LEAVE THE RESULTS OF YOUR WORK IN GOD'S HANDS

In the early 1850s Elisha Otis worked as a master mechanic for the Bedstead Manufacturing Company in Yonkers, New York. But he didn't make bedsteads. He fixed machinery. There was one piece of machinery that he wanted to fix at all costs – the cargo and passenger hoist. Elisha was horrified at the accidents that frequently occurred with hoists when ropes broke and cargo was destroyed and people were killed. Elisha resolved to do something about it – to develop a safety device that would prevent these grizzly accidents.

Using springs from a wagon, Elisha rigged a device at the top of the lifting platform that would allow up and down motion only if the rope was taunt. But should the rope break, the sudden lack of pressure on the rope caused hooks to spring out sideways and stop platform in its tracks. The year was 1852 and Elisha Otis had just invented the "safety elevator."

A year later Elisha started his own company to manufacture his "Life and Labor Saving Machinery." But sales were barely modest. Elisha gave public demonstrations of his safety elevator at the Crystal Palace Exhibition, in which he'd raise himself in one of his elevators to a height of thirty feet and have someone cut the *lifting rope*. Crowds would gasp. But, again and again, his elevator dropped just a few inches, stop, and Elisha Otis would call out, *"All safe!"* Elisha Otis continued to refine his product. But sales for the safety elevators remained poor and by the time of his death in 1861 (at the age of 49) Elisha's company barely showed a profit.

His two sons carried on the business and steadily improved his invention. But there just wasn't much demand for safety elevators – not much demand until an American phenomenon broke onto the scene: *the Skyscraper*. That's right, once the very first skyscraper – Chicago's ten-story Home Insurance Building was built in 1885, the demand for the Otis Elevator sky-rocketed with it. In fact, historians attribute the advent of high-rise buildings to *two inventions*: steel frame construction and the *Otis Elevator*. And today the Otis Elevator Corporation remains the largest elevator company in the world, employing 60,000 people and earning $12 billion annually.

Elisha Otis went to his grave believing he had not achieved any significant success. He had only envisioned a safe way of lifting cargo and people from one floor to the next. Yet he had no idea of the new heights his efforts would bring people. But Elisha Otis would probably be more gratified by a different statistic: not that there are more of his elevators in more skyscrapers than any other kind, but that his invention – of which there are 600,000 that transport 120 billion people every year – *remains the safest mode of transportation in the world!*

Friend, perhaps you cannot see any fruit from your labors. Perhaps you have sown much and reaped little. Do not lose heart. Be faithful in the work to which God has called you. Perhaps, like the saints of old "who died in faith without seeing the fulfillment of the promises" (Hebrews 11:13), you may never see the consummation of your work in this life. Faithfully do God's will and leave the results with Him. God is mindful of your labors and He will take the seeds you have sown, make them grow, and produce a great harvest.

PRAYER: Dear Father in heaven, sometimes I question the value and validity of my work. Help me to faithfully do all I do to Your honor and glory and to trust You with the results. Amen.

ARE YOU TIRED OF THE LITANY OF DOOM?

"Conditions in America and in the world have never been worse. Surely the end of civilization is at hand!" Ever think that? You're not alone. Throughout history the world's greatest leaders have predicted doom for their world.

In 1706, William Penn, the founder of Pennsylvania, said, *"There is scarcely anything around us but ruin and despair."*

In 1801, William Wilberforce, the British statesman who rooted slavery out of Great Britain, said that he dared not marry because the future of the world was too unsettled.

In 1848, Lord Anthony Ashley Shaftsbury, British philanthropist and statesman, stated, *"Nothing can save the British Empire from shipwreck."*

In 1849, Benjamin Disraeli, Britain's Prime Minister, said, *"There is no hope for our industry, commerce, and agriculture."*

In 1852, the Duke of Wellington, Arthur Wellesly, said on his deathbed, *"I thank God that I shall be spared from seeing the consummation of ruin that is settling around us."*

And in 1914, Lord Edward Grey, British statesman, despaired, saying, *"The lamps are going out all over Europe; we shall not see the light again in our lifetime."*

Prophesies of doom are certainly nothing new. Isaac Asimov notes that an ancient clay tablet, dating from *2800 B.C.,* has been found that states: *"Our earth is degenerate in these latter days. There are signs that the world is speedily coming to an end. Bribery and corruption are common."* 2500 years ago, the Greek philosopher, Socrates, wrote, *"Children are now tyrants ... They no longer rise when an elders enter the room. They contradict their parents, and tyrannize over their teachers."* His chief disciple, Plato, concurred, *"What is happening to our young people? They disrespect their elders. They disobey their parents. They ignore the law. They riot in the streets inflamed with wild notions. Their morals are decaying. What is to become of them?"*[xix]

The media and those around us will often predict doom for our world. But do not lose heart. God has a future for our nation and our world. Someone once said, *"With every newborn baby comes a divine message that God isn't finished with us yet."* And don't be too quick to judge the younger generations. The very generation that many of us condemned as "the MTV-Generation, that's only good for playing video games" is now fighting and winning the Global War on Terrorism and securing our freedoms. God is planning good things for the world and for all who place their future into His hands. The Scripture says, "For I know the plans I have for you," says the Lord; "Plans for good and not for evil; plans to give you a hope and a future" (Jeremiah 29:11).

PRAYER: Dear Lord, with every other person of faith, I join in praying, 'Our Father, who art in heaven, hallowed be your name. May your kingdom come. May your will be done, on earth as it is in heaven. Give us this day our daily bread. And forgive us our sins, as we forgive those who've sinned against us. And lead us not into temptation, but deliver us from evil. For yours is the kingdom, and the power and the glory forever. Amen.

March 18

WASTED KINDNESS?

Ever feel that your kindness and courtesy are wasted on some people? That's how it seems many times. That's how it seemed to Melina Salazar.

For seven years Melina Salazar, a waitress at Luby's Cafeteria in Brownsville, Texas, did her best to show kindness to an old, sour, complaining customer. Day after day she overlooked his swearing and made his every meal a happy experience.

The cantankerous customer was an 89-year-old WWII veteran named Walter Swords. And though he rarely displayed any appreciation, Melina returned his scowls with smiles and his swearing with pleasant words.

Then Walter stopped coming and she never heard from him again. But just before Christmas 2007 attorneys contacted Melina. They informed her that Walter had indeed died, and he had willed her $50,000 and his 2000 Buick. Though he didn't show it, Walter was deeply touched by the kindness of this waitress.

In the Scripture we are encouraged to bless when cursed and return love for hatred. At times this may seem like a wasted investment, but nothing we do in Christ's name is ever a waste – and we have no idea the profound effects our kind words and deeds may have in another's life.

"But I say to you, love your enemies, do good to those who hate you, bless those who curse you, pray for those who mistreat you ... and your reward in heaven shall be great, and you will be sons of the Most High, for He Himself is kind to ungrateful and evil men." (Luke 6:27-28, 36)

PRAYER: Dear Father in heaven, Please fill me with Your Spirit and empower me to show Your love to those who deserve it least, but who need it most. Amen.

March 19

WHY WE FEEL PAIN

Most people are hedonists – they believe in the pursuit of pleasure and the avoidance of pain. Most people view pain as an evil and cannot understand how a God of love would ever create his children with the capacity to feel pain, then allow them to suffer so badly. And being a parent does not always help us understand, since parents invariably seek to shelter their children from pain. But one mother, Tara Blocker, thinks differently. She has learned the value and necessity of pain in our lives.

Tara Blocker describes her daughter, Ashlyn, as utterly fearless. Her school teachers would all agree. But little Ashlyn is fearless because she can feel no pain.

In the school cafeteria, teachers put ice in 5-year-old Ashlyn's chili, because even though her lunch is scalding hot, she'll gulp it down anyway.

Ashlyn has chewed through her tongue while eating, and once tore the flesh off her finger after putting the finger into her mouth.

Ashlyn is among a tiny number of people in the world known to have congenital insensitivity to pain with anhidrosis, or CIPA—a rare genetic disorder that makes her unable to feel pain.

Family photos reveal a series of these self-inflicted injuries. One picture shows Ashlyn in her Christmas dress, hair neatly done, with a swollen lip, missing teeth, puffy eye, and athletic tape wrapped around her hands to protect them. She smiles like a little boxer who won a prize bout.

Tara Blocker, Ashlyn's mother, concludes, "Pain is there for a reason. It lets your body know something's wrong and it needs to be fixed. *I'd give anything for her to feel pain.*"[xx]

In the Scripture, the Psalmist wrote: "Before I was afflicted I went astray, but now I keep your word." (Psalm 119:67) and "It is good for me that I was afflicted, that I may learn your laws." (Psalm 119:71)

PRAYER: Dear Father in heaven, the storms of life have left me with so many questions. I still do not understand why you have allowed such painful events to invade my life. But even in my darkness, help me to walk by faith, to believe, and to rejoice in your love. Amen.

March 20

GETTING IN THE WAY OF GROWTH

In the early spring of 1883, the great artist of the Impressionist Period, Claude Monet, was painting an unusual portrait – a leafless oak tree that stood out vividly against the red-colored cliffs on the Creuse River near his home in Giverny. But before he could complete his painting, three weeks of torrential rains brought his efforts to a halt.

When Monet returned to the site, he was disturbed to find that the tree had burst forth with buds and tens of thousands of lush, green leaves. The tree was in full bloom. "How dare that tree change before my painting is complete," Monet thought to himself. And in a rather selfish act, Monet recruited the help of Giverny's Mayor to muster the town's people to strip every bit of foliage off the oak tree so he could complete the picture of a leafless, lifeless tree. Monet kept his painting, but destroyed a magnificent tree in the process.

In a way, Monet's portrait of the tree is analogous to the pictures of people we paint in our own minds – negative pictures and bad images we develop – like the image of a leafless, lifeless tree. But let those same people break out from the confines of that negative image, let them set their feet on a prosperous course, become fruitful and redeem themselves – and our cherished negative view is challenged. Tragically, we might even wish such people to fail – for the sake of the image of them we've already developed.

God help us not to become dependent upon someone else's failure to boost our own ego. God help us never to strip other people of dignity and hope, in a vain effort to satisfy our own insecurities. The Scripture says, "Let no unwholesome word proceed from your mouth, but only such words that are good for building others up, according to the need of the moment, that our words may bless those who hear." (Ephesians 4:29)

PRAYER: Dear Father in heaven, grant that I may never get in the way of other people's growth and that I may not secretly wish others to fail lest my cherished negative view of them crumble. Please help me with my own problems and grant that I may build others up and bless them with my words and actions. Amen.

March 21

WHEN YOUR JOB SEEMS NEVER-ENDING

Are you faced with a task that appears overwhelming, a task with no end in sight? Consider the towering job that faced those who compiled the major dictionaries of the world.

The first great French dictionary, that of the *Academie Francaise*, took 56 years to complete, the *Oxford English Dictionary* 71 years. The basic German dictionary was published in 1960, 106 years after it had been launched by the Grimm brothers, who relieved tedium along the way by collecting fairy tales. The standard Italian dictionary, begun in 1863, *is still unfinished!* Indeed, editing a dictionary is not a job for people with short attention spans - or short lives!

James Augustus Henry Murray is credited with compiling and editing the massive *Oxford English Dictionary*, a multi-volume work that defined 414,825 words. He was only the son of a poor tailor and never got past the eighth grade. Yet Murray was a gifted linguist and so impressed England with his scholarly publications that he was honored with the task of writing a new dictionary. He inherited a project that had begun 22 years earlier, but was now abandoned and in disarray.

But by working 80-hours a week and enlisting the help of his 11 children, Murray plowed ahead with the project. After toiling for five years he produced his first volume of 352 pages - and it only covered "A" though "Ant"! In a later volume the single word "Do" required six months to complete. For thirty-six years James Murray battled tirelessly to complete the *Oxford English Dictionary*. The final volume was not completed until 1928 - 13 years after his death! Though Murray died with his task unfinished (He had reached the letter "T"), he had been knighted by the Queen, had received many honorary degrees, and had striven faithfully in a never-ending task, always rising above discouragement.[xxi]

What great task are you facing? Don't be discouraged. Others have done great things - so can you.

Consider the words of this verse by Longfellow:

We have not wings, we cannot soar;
But we have feet to scale and climb
By slow degrees, by more and more,
The lofty summits of our times.

The mighty pyramids of stone
That wedge-like cleave the desert airs,
When nearer seen, and better known,
Are but gigantic flights of stairs.

The distant mountains, that uprear
Their solid bastions to the skies,
Are crossed by pathways, that appear
As we to higher levels rise.

The heights by great men gained and kept
Were not attained by sudden flight,
But they, while their companions slept,
Were toiling upward in the night.

Step by step we can make any journey. The Scripture says, "Do you not know? Have you not heard? The LORD is the Everlasting God, the Creator of the ends of the earth. He will not grow tired and weary, and his understanding no one can fathom. He gives strength to the weary and increases the power of the weak. ... And those who hope in the LORD will renew their strength. They will soar on wings like eagles; they will run and not grow weary, they will walk and not faint." (Isaiah 40:28-31)

PRAYER: Dear Father in heaven, help me to place my trust in You, to spend time in Your presence, to draw strength from Your infinite power, and to absorb light from Your transforming glory. Then my strength will be renewed and I will have power to run the last mile of the race and to walk to the last step of the journey. Amen.

March 22

PAST SAVING

The motion picture, *Sound of Music* – widely acknowledged as the most popular Hollywood musical ever made - is the screen adaptation of the Broadway play based on the true story of Georg and Maria von Trapp, and their seven children. The von Trapps fled their homeland Austria in 1938 after it was annexed to Nazi Germany.

But, unknown to the general public, before leaving Austria, Georg von Trapp deeded the von Trapp Villa over to the religious order, the Missionaries of the Precious Blood. This Roman Catholic order originated in Italy and spread throughout Europe and the Americas.

But in 1939 the Nazis confiscated the mansion before the religious order would take possession of it. Then, much to the horror of the von Trapp family and the Missionaries, the diabolical figure Heinrich Himmler - the Reichfuhrer, architect of the Final Solution, and head of the infamous SS - used this very house as his headquarters. In fact, Himmler set up his personal office in Georg von Trapp's own study, from which he directed the most hideous crimes against humanity.

After Germany capitulated to the Allies, the American military returned the house to the von Trapp family, who gave it back to the Missionaries of the Precious Blood in 1948. Today the old von Trapp Villa serves to train seminarians who are studying for the priesthood. Visitors, however, are sometimes puzzled to find that Heinrich Himmler's personal office, the very center of evil, has been converted into – a chapel! "How could you use such an evil place for religious purposes?" is the question many visitors ask. "Certainly that room has been defiled beyond all hope of redemption" is the logic many express.

But isn't the very heart of the Gospel the message that no one is "past saving"? God is not in the business of merely taking the good and making them better. Jesus said, "I did not come to call the righteous, but sinners." (Matthew 9:13) "Blessed are the spiritually destitute," Jesus said, "for to them belongs the Kingdom of Heaven." (Matthew 5:3)

Everyone that serves in the Lord's Army once served in Satan's. And the only material God has from which to make saints is sinners. Yes, it is perfectly appropriate and in keeping with the Gospel message that good take possession of evil. This is the ultimate triumph – not the eradication of evil, but its transformation into good.

PRAYER: Dear Father in heaven, sometimes I feel so broken and beyond the point of redemption. Please take my sin-sick soul, cleanse it, and transform it into your throne room. Amen.

March 23

EVER FEEL INVISIBLE?

Something extraordinary happened at the L'Enfant Plaza Metro station in Washington, DC, on January 12, 2006. On that day a man who seemed to be just another busker – a musician who entertains in public places for donations – stopped, opened his violin case, placed it on the pavement, and began playing. He was a white man in his thirties, dressed in jeans, a long-sleeved t-shirt, and a ball cap. For 45 minutes he played Mozart, Schubert, and other classical composers. But hardly any of the 1,097 people who rushed by even noticed him. A few did stop to listen. Impressed by his music, they gave a few donations – totaling $32 dollars. But of the nearly 1,100 people who passed by that day, only one actually recognized the violinist and his instrument.

Who was this busker? He was none other than Joshua Bell, the greatest violinist in America, who has played in every major orchestra in the world and who, just three days earlier, had sold out the Boston Symphony Hall where listeners had paid $100 for the cheapest seats. And Bell's violin? It was the famous Gibson ex Huberman Stradivarius - hand made by Antonio Stradivari in 1713 - which Bell had purchased for more than $3 million.

This event, sponsored as an experiment by the Washington Post, was a vivid reminder that people of inestimable talent and importance may go completely unrecognized and unappreciated by the majority. The fact that almost no one valued Josh Bell's playing was no indicator of the quality of his music. The fact that almost no one recognized him was no indicator of his true importance and worth.

Compare this to Jesus Christ, whose sojourn upon this planet was summed up in the words: "He was in the world, and the world was made by him and the world knew him not." (John 1:10) Even so, we may go through periods in which we feel invisible – virtually unnoticed and unappreciated. Based upon the praise and recognition we fail to receive, we might even consider our contribution, and ourselves, as worthless. But don't give in to those thoughts and feelings.

Like the great violinist who, convinced of his own worth and ability, continued to play even when others did not seem to notice or care, so we must continue to live and to labor at the task God has given us. Though the majority may not notice – God notices and will reward us. Therefore, we are encouraged in Scripture: "Always give yourselves fully to the work of the Lord, because you know that your labor for the Lord is not in vain." (1 Corinthians 15:58)

PRAYER: Dear Father in heaven, at times I feel virtually invisible – both my work and myself unnoticed and unappreciated. When I go through these long valleys of obscurity, please remind me that you are watching and that you are mindful of my struggles. Remind me that you take delight in me and rejoice when I am faithful. Amen.

March 24

DON'T HATE YOURSELF

There are two ways to buy a new car. One way, that most of us use, is to look around the lots of many car dealers. We may begin our search with a certain vehicle in mind, but we've got to be realistic. As we head out to the Ford, Chevy, or Honda dealers, we check the lot to see what's available and what's within our budget. We might hope for a certain color, a certain engine size, and certain accessories. But, in the end, we'll have to settle for what we can afford. Maybe we hoped for a beautiful, silver BMW with a big engine and lots of frills. But we will most likely come away with a plain white, Hyundai Excel with a tiny 4-cylinder motor. It's not what we wanted, but – it's new!

The other way of buying a car is far different. Money is no object. The buyer doesn't go to the lot at all. He knows exactly what he wants and he's willing to pay for it and to wait for it. So he *orders* precisely what he wants: a certain color, make, model, with a certain engine size, and specific accessories. And on the day he picks it up from the dealer it's exactly what he ordered. It's the very car he envisioned. It reflects his personality. It is the car of his dreams.

You know, most of us view ourselves as one of those "plain-Jane," "box with four wheels" – the leftover car that nobody else wanted. We conclude that we're a disappointment to God – nothing of what He hoped for, but only what was left on the lot.

Yet little do we ever comprehend that we are, in truth, the very high-speed model that is made to God the Father's exact specifications. The God who has loved us from all eternity has made us "to order," with just the right skin color, just the right hair color, just the right eye color, just the right gender, just the right size, just the right build, just the right personality, with just the right gifts, talents and abilities.

There are no mistakes. There are no disappointments or surprises with God. Who cares if others do not like us? Who cares if the rest of the world does not value us? We were made by God and for God. And if He's pleased with us, it doesn't matter if the rest of the world rejects us.

You are exactly what God your heavenly Father ordered. And only when you realize this and experience his unconditional acceptance, realize He delights in you, and rest in his loving arms will you ever find healing for your wounded soul.

In the Psalms David wrote, *"I praise you, for I am fearfully and wonderfully made. Wonderful are your works, my soul knows this very well."* (Psalm 139:14) There, you have it from God's own word - "You are wonderful." God said it and He does not lie.

PRAYER: Dear Father in heaven, I praise You as my Creator and as the lover of my soul. Thank You for making me who I am. Please continue Your work of renewal and renovation in my life that I may become all You created me to be. Amen.

March 25

FORGETTING OUR PURPOSE

According to a recent article in the *London Telegraph*, a chunk of dark gray slate, topped by a bone-shaped piece of wood, won the right to compete against other art exhibits in the prestigious Royal Academy's art gallery. To the surprise of the Royal Academy's art officials and judges, they had mistakenly selected what was only a mere *pedestal* for the actual work of art – the sculpture of a human head. It seems that both items, the sculpture and its stand, were shipped separately and the art judges mistook them for separate submissions to the art exhibit.

What is even *more* interesting is that, while the art experts accepted and praised the chunk of slate and piece of wood, they rejected the sculpture. The "stand" for the sculpture was accepted and the sculpture *itself* was rejected.

Ministers of the gospel need to always remind themselves of their God-given purpose – to bring glory to Christ, not to themselves. For a minister to seek the praise of men and bask in the limelight is as perverted as the mere stand for a work of art getting praise while the work of art itself is ignored and rejected. Consider the words of John the Baptist, when his disciples expressed the concern that more were following Jesus than were following him. "He must increase," John said, "and I must decrease." That should be the attitude of every servant of Christ.

PRAYER: Dear Father in heaven, please touch my heart and set me free from pride and the love men's praise. May my heart's desire be to exalt Jesus Christ and may he be my only true love. Amen.

March 26

GIVE YOURSELF CREDIT

Irina Sendler. You may have never heard of her. She was a Polish social worker who from 1940 to 1943 repeatedly risked her life to save Jewish children from the Warsaw Ghetto.

How did she do it? First, Irina developed a list of willing accomplices: sympathetic families, convents, churches, and orphanages who were willing to house, and even adopt, Jewish children. Then she went to work forging documents, like phony IDs and phony passes from the Warsaw Epidemic Control Department, to get children past the German guards. Of course, she had to ask their Jewish parents to do the unthinkable – to allow their children to leave them and entrust the children into her care. But the Warsaw Ghetto was no place for anyone, especially a child. In 1940, the Nazis had crowded over 400,000 Jews into this one-square mile, disease infested area. By 1942, more than 80,000 of these had died.

So Irina continued to rescue the children. When her forged passes no longer worked, she would smuggle the children out of the ghetto in crates and wheel barrels. And all the while she was keeping records, lists of the children's true identities and the names of their parents – in hopes of reuniting them after the War. Irina kept these lists sealed in jars that were carefully hidden beneath an apple tree in a neighbor's yard.

Unfortunately, the Gestapo discovered Irina's rescue efforts. They arrested and tortured her, breaking the bones in both her feet and legs, in an effort to get her to reveal the location of her lists, as well as to identify her accomplices. But she revealed nothing. And after spending three months in prison while awaiting execution, she was rescued by the Polish resistance.

In the end Irina had saved the lives of more than 2,500 Jewish children. After the war Irina successfully reunited hundreds of the Jewish children with their parents. Sadly, however, she would learn that most of the parents had died in Nazi death camps.

Irina Sendler's accomplishments during the war were nothing short of heroic. She saved more than twice as many lives as the more celebrated Oskar Schindler saved from the same ghetto.

Perhaps Irina's work may seem small in the face of the six million Jews who perished at the hands of the Nazis. But we must never judge our life's work based on what we've left undone.

There is a story of a child walking down the beach after an ocean-churning storm had cast thousands of starfish upon the shore. The little would-be-rescuer went along, grabbing starfish after starfish, and tossing them back into the sea.

An old man watched the boy from a distance, then approached and stopped him. "What do you think you're doing," asked the old man. "There are hundreds of thousands of starfish on the sand, all destined to die. You can't possibly save them all. What you're doing isn't going to make any difference."

With that, the little boy picked up another starfish, tossed it back into the life-giving water, and remarked, "Well, it made a difference for that one."

Even so, never measure the significance of your contribution based of what is left undone. Measure your work based upon those you help, *not* upon those you cannot help. For ripple effects of your smallest deeds will go on forever and will never be forgotten by God. In the Scripture we read the promise, "If anyone gives so much as a cup of cold water to one of the very least of my brothers … I tell you the truth, he will certainly not lose his reward." (Matthew 10:42)

PRAYER: Dear Father in heaven, though I cannot do all that I'd like to do, help me to faithfully do what I can. Though there is still so much evil in the world, help me to faithfully do the work you've given me and to leave the results in your hands. Amen

March 27

THE ROOT OF OUR PROBLEM

It has been called the worst political crime of humanity – the result of bigotry, pride, arrogance, lies, and a frightening abandonment of scientific achievement. Where did this take place? Nazi Germany? The American deep South? The "Bible Belt?" No. The crime took place in the Soviet Union under Joseph Stalin and in Communist China under Mao Tse Tung. And in the end the crime resulted in the deaths of tens of millions of people.

The crime began when Joseph Stalin named Trofim Denisovich Lysenko to the Supreme Soviet and placed him in charge of agriculture in the Soviet Union in the late 1930s. Lysenko found favor with Stalin because he had fused Communist and Marxist ideas to agricultural science. For instance, Lysenko totally rejected Mendel's universally accepted theories of genetics, and embraced in their place discredited Lamarkian theories of acquired characteristics due to environment.

Lysenko believed that refrigerating wheat seeds prior to planting them would cause them to produce plants with characteristics of winter wheat. He had a long history of fabricating positive results of his experiments and making incredible claims. Stalin believed him because he rejected the stunning agricultural advances made by the United States. Anything that smacked of Capitalism or the West was rejected, no matter how successful it had been.

Once in control of Russia's agriculture, Lysenko suppressed and eliminated all opposition. He arranged for the imprisonment and execution of most of Russia's legitimate agricultural scientists and proceeded to destroy his country's farming capacity. Productivity plummeted. Thousands starved. Lysenko maintained a massive cover up. Not until Stalin's death was criticism of Lysenko even permitted. By the late 1950s it was finally acknowledged that Lysenko's policies had been a catastrophic failure and had sent Soviet agriculture back to the Middle Ages. But the worst was yet to come.

Undeterred by Lysenko's failures, in 1958 Mao Tse Tung, Chairman of the Red China, implemented these same policies in his own country. The disastrous track record of "Lysenkoism" didn't matter. All that mattered was that it was Marxist, not Capitalist, and completely at odds with Western technology. Blinded by his hatred of the West, especially of America, Mao imposed an agricultural reform in his country that resulted in massive and prolonged crop failures and the starvation of 30 to 40 million of his own people. But the cover up continued. Anyone who so much as admitted there was a famine was arrested and disappeared. In fact, Mao insisted the entire famine was part of a political subversion and he ordered the execution of thousands of starving Chinese for "hiding food." But the crime only continued as Lysenko's "Marxist agriculture" was subsequently implemented in Vietnam, Cambodia and by other Communist regimes.

How is it that a belief system that promised to free people from humanity's evils only succeeded in multiplying them (and this is just one small chapter of Communism's dark history)? Russia had identified the "evil" of mankind to be in the Czar, in Capitalism, and in religion. It failed to identify the true source of evil – the human soul, man's ego-centric, selfish, sinful heart. Under Communism, people remained people. They were still prone to bigotry, narrow-mindedness, pride, and greed (if not for money, then for power).

The ancient Scripture reminds us of the root of our problems: "The heart is deceitful above all things and desperately sick; who can understand it? I, the LORD, search the heart, I test the mind, and give to each man according to his deeds." (Jeremiah 17:9-10) But God not only gives the diagnosis, but also prescribes the cure: "I will give you a new heart and put a new spirit within you …and I will put My Spirit within you and move you to walk in my statutes and be careful to observe My ordinances." (Ezekiel 36:26-27)

Let your prayer be like King David's, who prayed: "Create in me a clean heart, O God, and renew a steadfast spirit within me." (Psalm 51:10) God can do it. He can cleanse and re-create the person on the inside. He can fix the root of our problems – the human heart.[xxii]

PRAYER: Dear Lord, help me to realize that neither things, nor ideas, nor governments, nor my neighbor are the enemy. I am my own enemy and I humbly pray for deliverance from myself. Please create in me a new heart. Cleanse and change me within – by the power of the Risen Christ. Amen.

March 28

FIT FOR SUCCESS

It's a fabulous building material, tool, and weapon. It comes in strands, each one only about *one ten thousandth* of an *inch* thick, yet it is stronger than steel, more elastic than nylon, and much harder to break than rubber. It needs to be so strong – for it is used to capture and imprison the most powerful (pound for pound) animals on earth. Plus it's resistant to degrading by bacteria and fungus. Who makes this fabulous material? *Spiders.* And the fabulous stuff they make is their spider's silk.

But there's more to tell. This silk is not all the same. Spiders can have up to six different spinning glands with which they can produce specialized silk for different purposes. For instance, spiders make one kind of silk for making egg sacks, another for rappelling, another for making webs and catching prey, and another for tying them up for a meal later on.

The spider silk is a liquid until it comes in contact with the air and hardens. It is pumped out of pores called spinnerets. The spider further specializes its silk for specific purposes by regulating the speed by which it exudes the liquid.

Think of it. Here we have a creature of nature that, without any tools or the benefits of scientific technology, effortlessly produces a high-tech material that even human beings cannot duplicate. Clearly, spiders are creatures designed by a loving Creator for survival in the wild.

But God prepares all of his creatures for the role to which he calls them. He does not send us packing, without first giving us what we need to succeed. Whatever he calls us to do, he equips us to do. God calls spiders to catch flies and other annoying critters. But he calls people to some form of service to his or her fellow human beings. But many people are tempted to fear that they are not adequate, that they are not equal to the task in life with which God has honored them. Quell this fear by thanking God for the gifts and talents he has already blessed you with, by asking him for strength and wisdom, and by facing the challenges he's called you to overcome. He has made you fit for success.

The Scripture tells us, "Do you not know? Have your not heard? The Lord is the everlasting God, the Creator of the ends of the earth. …He gives strength to the weary and increases the power of the weak. Those who trust in the Lord will renew their strength. They soar on wings like eagles; they will run and not grow weary, they will walk and not faint." (Isaiah 40:28-31)

PRAYER: Dear Father in heaven, empower me by your divine Spirit, make me greater than myself and more than equal to every challenge. Amen.

March 29

WHEN YOU FEEL ABANDONED

Sports Illustrated reported on six enthusiastic basketball players from Livermore Falls (Maine) High School concluded that their school spirit and support for their athletics teams was far too low. So they thought up an idea to inspire school support for their next game. They decided to dribble a couple of basketballs *twenty-two miles* to the location of their next game – Farmington High School – where they were scheduled to play that night. These dedicated players braved the long distance and bone-chilling, freezing rain to lead the way and rally the school behind them. Weary, wet, chilled – but dedicated – the six arrived at the Farmington gym, only to learn that school officials from both high schools had postponed the game because of adverse traveling conditions.

Do you ever feel like those basketball players? As though no one around you (your subordinates, peers, or even your supervisors) shares your level of commitment? If so, it might help to remember these simple truths.

1. You're not alone. Every leader has had those who have let him or her down. During the Revolutionary War, George Washington endured a lack of support from Congress, criticism from his fellow generals (e.g. Charles Lee, Thomas Conway, Horatio Gates, Thomas Mifflin), and the painful betrayal of a key subordinate – Benedict Arnold. The Apostle Paul had to endure the desertion of his assistant John Mark. Jesus Christ, at his most critical moment, was abandoned by those in whom he had invested most of his time and energy – the twelve apostles. The Lord knows how you feel.

2. Though the mission suffers because others fail, don't forget that you and your development as a man and as a leader are God's major interest. God will use the painful experiences of abandonment and being let-down by others to strengthen and fortify you.

3. The failures and lack of commitment of others should never dictate what our level of commitment and motivation should be. Successful people are self-starters and do not allow the apathy or laziness of others to stop them.

4. Be the person God created you to be. Don't let others dampen your enthusiasm. Continue to share your vision and be committed and enthusiastic about the mission. Enthusiasm is contagious and others will catch the vision and follow. Eventually, because of your perseverance, the mission will succeed. But the greater mission, your development as the person God created you to be, will also succeed. Phillips Brooks once admonished, "Do not pray for easier lives, pray to be stronger men. Do not pray for tasks equal to your powers, pray for powers equal to your tasks. In doing so, not only will the accomplishment of your task be a miracle – you will be the miracle. Every day you will wonder at the grace and power that has come into your life because you trusted God, faced the challenges of life, overcame them and were transformed in the process."

PRAYER: Dear Father in heaven, as you breathed into man the breath of life, breathe into me the motivation, inspiration and commitment I need to fulfill your mission for my life. Help me to be the person you created me to be. Amen.

March 30
PUT THE WORLD AND ITS PROBLEMS IN GOD'S HANDS

Author and pastor, Craig Brian Larsen, once presented an illustration for living a life of faith in God. Consider this: in front of Rockefeller Center's International Building, in Manhattan, NYC, stands a mammoth bronze statue of the Greek god Atlas, who was condemned by Zeus to carry the weight of the world on his shoulders. This 15-foot-tall statue presents Atlas straining every muscle to bear up the burden of the whole world.

Across the street is Saint Patrick's Cathedral. There, in front of the high altar of the great cathedral is a statue of the Christ child, just a boy of ten to twelve years, with crown and scepter and effortlessly holding the entire world *in his hand.*

These two statues depict the two ways people can to deal with life. Most people live like Atlas, as if they are bearing the weight of the world and all its problems on their backs. They are distressed about things in their own personal lives, in their work places, and in the world.

But the other statue, that of Christ holding the world in his hand, offers a better way. Instead of bearing the world and its problems on your own heart and shoulders, put it all in the Lord's hand. For, the fate of the world and the solution to its problems rests not with us, but with Him. Instead of becoming agitated and upset over the gloomy state of our world, pray. The Scripture admonishes us, "Cast all your anxiety on him, for he cares for you" (1 Peter 5:7) and "Cast your burden upon the Lord and He will sustain you – He will never allow the righteous to be shaken" (Psalm 55:22).

PRAYER: Our Father, who art in heaven, hallowed be thy name. Thy kingdom come, they will be done on earth as it is in heaven. Give us this day our daily bread. And forgive us our trespasses as we forgive those who have trespassed against us. And lead us not into temptation, but deliver us from evil. For thine is the kingdom, and the power and the glory forever. Amen.

March 31

THE HUMAN PARADOX

There is an old Chinese tale of five brothers, all of whom looked exactly alike, but each endowed with a different power. For instance, one brother could not be burned. Another could hold his breath indefinitely. Another brother had an iron neck, i.e. neither executioner's axe nor hangman's noose could harm him. Another brother could stretch his legs extremely long, so as to stand very tall. But another brother had the strangest power of all - *he could hold the entire sea in his mouth!* That's right – this one could swallow the water of the sea. In her children's book, *The Five Chinese Brothers*, Claire Huchet Bishop illustrates this feat by representing the brother with a bulging head and cheeks.

Now even as a child I understood that there was no way that the water of the entire sea could squeeze into a person's mouth. Even though a first-grader, I understood that the capacity of the brother's head and bulging cheeks, though stretched to enormous proportions, could not contain the water of the sea.

But as I reflect on life, I think there was more truth in that story than I first understood. What I mean is this: that, with human beings, the inside is bigger than the outside. Sound crazy? A pagan philosopher once said, "Fate has given man the soul of a god in the body of a worm." What the philosopher meant was this, that the human capacity for genius, for creativity, for inexpressible joy and for sorrow as deep as the sea, far exceeds the small physical frame of our body. The biblical patriarch Job – who suffered the loss of all ten of his children and all his wealth – expressed this same idea when he cried: "Oh, that my grief could be weighed in a balance – it would outweigh the sand of the seashore." (Job 6:2-3)

As ministers in uniform, we chaplains have witnessed time and again the vast measure of sorrow of a mother for her dead child, of a wife for her dead husband, and of a soldier for his fallen brother-in-arms. One time I held a soldier in my arms for two straight hours and he wept inconsolably for his murdered two-year-old son. Another time I tried ineffectually to ease the pain of a young mother whose one-year-old daughter was pronounced dead. This poor mother erupted in frightful surges of grief, repeatedly crying out, "No! No! No!" As I reflect on the grieving, I cannot help but wonder how such small little creatures as we can experience and bear virtual oceans of emotion.

As ministers in uniform, we chaplains have also witnessed love and courage displayed by frail human beings – love and courage that drives them to confront danger and disregard the instinct for self-preservation. How is it that such small creatures can have such large hearts?

And we have also witnessed faith and the universal thirst that all people have for God. Though we are so small the soul within us hungers for a Great Being who is infinite in power, love, and wisdom.

This hunger is evidence in and of itself for the existence of God. For why else would we thirst and hunger for that which does not exist? The fact that our tongues thirst for water is evidence that water exists to satisfy it. The fact that our stomach's hunger for food is evidence that food exists to satisfy it. And since people appear to be incurably religious – from the most primitive tribes to the most sophisticated societies – hungering for a great transcendent Being, doesn't this indicate that there is such a Being who can fill the cavernous void locked away in our misleadingly small bodies?

I've seen the evidence and I believe there is more to human beings than meets the eye. I believe the inside is greater than the outside. I believe God has left his mark, his nature, and his divine imprint upon our souls. We are his children. And I also believe that there is too much of us for God to discard us after death. For what artist would spend a lifetime creating a masterpiece only to throw it away once it's completed? What sculptor would spend his life carving a marble statue only to smash it when he is done? God has invested his love and patience and the blood of his own Son in our lives. Why would he do so except to prepare us for eternity with him?

PRAYER: Dear Father in heaven, open my eyes to my worth and preciousness in your sight and help me to have a hope befitting and to live a life worthy of a child of God. Amen.

April

April 1

HISTORY'S SHORTEST AND MOST POWERFUL MESSAGES

Throughout history some of the shortest messages have also been the most powerful. For instance, during the largest German offensive on the Western Front of WWII, known as the Battle of the Bulge, an ultimatum was handed to the 101st Airborne Division Commander under siege at Bastogne, BG Anthony McAuliffe, demanding his immediate surrender. The general's short, but defiant reply to the Germans: *"Nuts!"*

Another brief but heavy message was that which Dr. Edward Teller, nuclear physicist, telegrammed to his colleagues in Los Alamos in 1954, that the H-Bomb had been successfully detonated in Bikini Atoll. The message: *"It's a boy!"*

Another famous message was both brief and heartbreaking. Attorney and businessman Horatio Spafford had suffered the loss of his only son to rheumatic fever and his business to the great Chicago fire of 1871. Then he received word that the very ship his wife and four daughters had boarded in route to France had sunk in the Mid Atlantic. For ten anxious days Spafford waited to learn the fate of his family. Finally, he received this two-word telegram from his wife that revealed the fate of his children: *"Saved Alone!"*

History also records the short, defiant response of the Spartans to King Philip II of Macedonia (382-336 BC) when the king warned of what he would do to them, "If I conquer Laconia" (their capital city). Their reply: *"If."*

Perhaps the shortest significant message in American history came at the end of one of the most costly and courageous ventures – that of building America's Transcontinental Railroad, which spanned nearly 1,800 miles from Sacramento, California to Omaha, Nebraska. After decades of planning and six years of construction, after cutting through the granite sentinels of the Sierra Nevada and Rocky Mountains, the final spike (a gold one) was driven into place at Promontory Summit, Utah on May 10, 1869. With a telegraph line hooked up to both the maul and the spike, each pound of the hammer was registered and sent by telegraph in directions east and west. Then, when the final blow was laid, this one-word message was simultaneously sent to San Francisco and New York City: *"Done!"*

But the greatest message of all, also one of the shortest, came from a dying man being executed on trumped up charges. The dying man was the Redeemer of mankind. He was the Lamb of God who was bearing both the sins of the world – piled higher than the heavens - and the unquenchable fire of God's wrath. His short message: *"It is finished!"* (John 19:30) Never underestimate the power and finality of that message. Never feel that you must, or even can, add to it. It is finished. It is done. Jesus has bridged the greatest distance in the universe – the distance between a holy God and sinful humanity.

PRAYER: Dear Father in heaven, I thank you that you have done something for me that I could never do for myself. You have spanned the great gulf that separated me from you and reconciled me to yourself by the sacrifice of your Son. Help me to turn to you with all my heart and put my faith in you. Amen.

April 2

WHEN WE FEAR THE JUDGMENT OF GOD

Fires that used to sweep the Great Plains of North America were among the most terrifying of all events. Few realize that the native grasses of such plains states as Kansas, Nebraska, and the Dakotas would grow six to seven feet tall – virtual forests of grass. Through the hot dry summers the grasses would dry out. By the following spring the Great Plains had stored up vast amounts of dry tinder that the smallest spark would ignite. All it would take was the lightning strike of an isolated thunderstorm and the plains would become a sea of flames – a fire storm that no man or animal could hope to outrun.

How then could the Plains Indians hope to escape? They used a simple, but ingenious method. They set their own fires – controlled fires - over large sections of low ground. Then they would move their families, their possessions and themselves onto this "scorched earth." And there – where the fire had already fallen – they would be safe from the fury of the coming flames. The great fires of the plains could not harm them.

And how can we escape the coming fury of the flames of God's terrifying wrath? We cannot outrun or hope to hide from the wrath to come. But what we can do is to flee to the scorched earth of the Cross – the place where the fire of God has already fallen upon the Son, Jesus Christ. The Scripture says that Jesus is the Lamb of God who bore the full fury of God's fiery wrath. He is the propitiation, i.e. the sacrifice that fully satisfies God's holy justice (John 1:29, 35; Romans 3:25-26; 1 John 2:1-2). Those who believe in Him, who flee to Him, the Scripture says, "do not come into judgment, but pass from death to life." (John 5:24)

Do you fear God's anger, God's judgment? Flee to the scorched earth of the cross. Run to Jesus Christ who already bore the judgment of God for us all. When we cling to Christ by faith, judgment becomes a thing of the past, forever passed, and we can forever live in the eternal sunshine of God's love.

PRAYER: Dear Father Almighty, I confess my sins and shortcomings to You. I also confess that I have no hope of ever escaping your divine judgments. By faith I cling to your Son Jesus Christ, who bore my sins and your judgments. Please, for Christ's sake, forgive my sins, cleanse my heart and let me enjoy the sunshine of your love forever. Amen.

April 3

ARE WE GETTING THE RIGHT MESSAGE?

Are we getting the right message from life? Consider the following story that illustrates how we can easily misread the painful events of our lives.

South of the town of Waterloo, near Brussels, Belgium, the allied forces of England, Holland, and Prussia under General Arthur Wellesly (recently made the 1st Duke of Wellington) confronted and crushed Napoleon Bonaparte's forces on June 16-18, 1815. This battle, which cost France 40,000 casualties (to the Allies' 22,000 casualties), was the last and most decisive of the Napoleonic Wars and forced the final abdication and exile of the French Emperor.

However, when news of the battle's outcome reached England *the message got garbled.* The glorious news of Wellington's victory was signaled from hilltop to hilltop by means of semaphore (i.e. signal flags): *"Wellington defeated Napoleon at Waterloo."* Early in the transmission, however, a heavy fog rolled in, allowing only the words *"Wellington Defeated"* to get through. Those words, *"Wellington Defeated,"* continued to be relayed throughout England. Thus the message most people received was that Napoleon had won and would rise again to terrorize Europe. Despair and panic ensued throughout the land.

On the following morning, when the fog gave way to clear skies, the whole message was transmitted - *"Wellington Defeated Napoleon at Waterloo! "Wellington Defeated Napoleon at Waterloo!* What England thought was a horrifying defeat turned out to be a glorious victory. England's hero had conquered.

Tomorrow, the Orthodox Church celebrates the day when, 2000 years ago, Jesus of Nazareth rose from the dead – victorious over death. Yet, just as the true message became garbled at Waterloo, so the message became garbled at Jesus' crucifixion. Shocked and horrified at the murder of their beloved master, Jesus' followers only received the message: *"Jesus Defeated!"* But on the third day the fog cleared and the glory of an empty tomb gave the whole message: *"**Jesus Defeated Death** at the Cross!"*

As we weather the storms of life there are times when tragedy and sorrows break into our lives. Personal failure and disappointment send us the message: *"Defeated, Defeated!"* But God turns our curses into blessing (Deuteronomy 23:5), changes the bitter into sweet (Exodus 15:23-25), and causes all the pain and adversity of life to work out for our ultimate good (Romans 8:28). When the day of the Lord breaks we will read the true message of our lives: *"Victorious, Victorious!*

PRAYER: Dear Father in heaven, in every sorrow, trial and disappointment, remind me that You in the business of turning tragedy into triumph and turning night into day. Amen.

April 4

WHY BRILLIANT PEOPLE BLUNDER

The Christmas Bullet. The name probably evokes all the wrong ideas, since the Christmas Bullet has nothing to do with the Christian holy day or with a projectile from a gun. The Christmas Bullet was an airplane – designed by a Dr. William W. Christmas, a medical doctor turned aviator. His airplane was also known as the Christmas Strutless Biplane and it was built on the principle that a plane's wings should be allowed to flap in the wind like a bird's. And flap they did. On its only flight the first Christmas biplane crashed after its wings contorted and came apart resulting in the death of its pilot.

Undeterred, Dr. Christmas, convinced of the validity of his theory, built a second "Bullet" on the flapping wing principle. The results were the same. It crashed on its only flight, also killing its pilot.

But Dr. Christmas was utterly unrepentant. He lied about the crashes and, instead, claimed his Bullet had attained a record-breaking speed of 222 miles per hour. Not only was his flapping wing idea such an obvious flop, but his boasts that the plane was capable of 200 miles per hour (in 1918 when the fastest fighters reached only 125 miles per hour) were as unfounded as they were unrealistic. Instead of admitting his failures, Dr. Christmas plunged deeper and deeper into his claims of greatness: that the U.S. government had paid handsomely for his wing-design, "that he had 'hundreds' of aeronautical patents and that he was swamped by orders for Bullets from Europe and by million-dollar offers to rebuild Germany's air forces."*

How is it that a man of Dr. Christmas' education and enlightenment could be so hardheaded and blind in the face of facts? The answer is in our fallen human nature. Human nature, with its selfishness, pride, and prejudice, can turn our reasoning powers into mush and cloud our judgment. All of us are susceptible. And what is the cure? Consider the sound advice from one of America's greatest agricultural scientists, George Washington Carver. He wrote: "What is the secret to my success? It is this: 'Trust in the Lord with all thine heart, and lean not on thine own understanding; in all thy ways acknowledge Him, and He shall direct thy paths.'" (G.W. Carver quoting Proverbs 3:5-6)

PRAYER: Dear Father in heaven, deliver me from bigotry, pride and prejudice. Quicken my mind and fill my heart with wisdom. Grant me insight for living that I may choose the path that leads to your glory and my happiness and salvation. Amen.

April 5

THE LIVING STUMP

In southwest Oregon, as you travel State Highway 62 beside the turbulent Rogue River, the motorist will come upon an amazing feat of nature – a living tree stump! This 3-foot stump is all that is left of a Douglas Fir that was cut down. But it still lives – without foliage, air, or photosynthesis!

How does it survive? Just a few feet from this stump is an interpretive sign which explains: Before it was cut down, its roots had intertwined and become joined with the roots an adjacent tree (see attached photo). Consequently, the two trees now share the same root system. The standing Douglas Fir supplies nutrients gained from light and air to the stump. But the stump also contributes to the standing tree. For the soil in which they both live is very shallow and has nothing but impenetrable volcanic basalt beneath. This stump uses its extensive roots to draw nutrients from the soil for both itself and its neighbor. Thus the two trees depend upon each other for survival.

Like these two trees, none of us was meant to stand alone. God intended us to strengthen others and to draw strength from them as well. God has created us in such a way that we are parts of a greater whole and are stronger as a team than as the mere sum of the parts. Consider the words of King Solomon:

"Two people are better off than one, for they can help each other succeed. If one person falls, the other can reach out and help. But someone who falls alone is in real trouble. Likewise, two people lying close together can keep each other warm. But how can one keep warm alone? A person standing alone can be attacked and defeated, but two can stand back-to-back and conquer. Three are even better, for a triple-braided cord is not easily broken." (Ecclesiastes 4:9-12, New Living Translation)

PRAYER: Dear Lord, give me the compassion to help others and the humility to reach out to others for help. Amen.

April 6

GET THE FACTS

Suetonius Tranquillis reported in his *Life of Augustus* that the great Roman poet Virgil once held a funeral for a dead fly, complete with pallbearers and lengthy eulogies. "Sacrilegious," you say. "Irreverent." "Totally insensitive to the dying and the grieving." "Deliberately trying to undercut society's values."

Well, not entirely. Maybe there was irreverence, insensitivity, and a little sacrilege involved. But Virgil's motivation was actually quite pragmatic. Believe it or not Virgil had a practical reason for holding a funeral for a dead fly.

It seems that, in ancient Rome, cemetery land was not taxable. By interring a fly on the land surrounding his private villa, the wily poet turned his home into a burial ground and thus made it tax-exempt. Virgil was merely trying to avoid paying taxes. He was not trying to undercut traditional values. It's unwise to rush to judgment. It's best to withhold judgment, listen, and get the facts. The Scripture tells us, "Let everyone be quick to hear and slow to speak and slow to anger" (James 1:19)

PRAYER: Dear Father in heaven, help me not to judge another person until I have walked a mile in his shoes. Amen.

April 7

JUDGE NOT

In *Isaac Asimov's Book of Facts*, the famed author explains that the carpenter who constructed the first wooden stocks in North America also became their first victim. They were made to order for the Puritan legislature of Boston in the late 1600s. But when the carpenter charged it 1.5 English pounds, the government thought the fee excessive and punished the carpenter by putting him in his own stocks.

With similar irony John Coffee built the jail in Dundalk, Ireland, only to become its first inmate in 1853 for bankruptcy. And, according to Robert Ripley (*Ripley's Believe It or Not*), I. N. Terrill, state legislature for Oklahoma, drew up the criminal law statutes for murder and also became the first person tried and convicted under them.

In none of these cases did the carpenter, the jail-builder or the legislator ever intend for their own implements of judgment to be applied to them. But that is exactly what happened. Nor do any of us ever intend that the judgment and criticism that we levy against others should be used against us. Yet Jesus assures us that this very thing will occur.

"Do not judge, or you too will be judged. For in the same way you judge others, you will be judged, and with the measure you use, it will be measured to you. Why do you look at the speck of sawdust in your brother's eye and pay no attention to the plank in your own eye? How can you say to your brother, 'Let me take the speck out of your eye,' when all the time there is a plank in your own eye? You hypocrite, first take the plank out of your own eye, and then you will see clearly to remove the speck from your brother's eye." (Matthew 7:1-5) Everyone cries out for justice, until they remember that they also, like the rest of humanity, needs mercy.

PRAYER: Dear Father in heaven, when I am tempted to look for faults, please help me to use a mirror and not a telescope. Grant that I may never criticize my fellow human beings until I have walked a mile in their shoes. Amen.

April 8

SEE THROUGH THE MIST OF SORROW

Kenneth Baldwin, of Tracy, California, is one lucky man. He didn't always think so. In fact, one day in 1985, after a long period of despondency, he decided to do the unthinkable – to end his life. Ken called his wife to tell her he'd be working late. Instead he drove out to Old Fort Point beneath San Francisco's Golden Gate Bridge. He was so sure he had nothing to live for and so walked far out on the bridge's magnificent span. And there, 249 feet above the Pacific's chilling waters, Kenneth Baldwin jumped to what he thought was his only escape from the pain of life.

But as soon as he jumped, a veil seemed to be lifted from his mind. He immediately thought of his wife Ellen and their daughter Katherine and of the life with them he was throwing away. I said to myself. "Oh my God, this was a bad idea."

But Kenneth was one of the lucky ones. In fact, he was one of only twenty-six persons (of the 1300 who have leaped from the Golden Gate to commit suicide in the last 68 years) *who survived!*

And his testimony is the same as the other twenty-five. After they jumped, they all, without exception, felt as though "the lights went on" and they suddenly realized what they were throwing away and regretted their mistake.

Like Kenneth, they also realized something about their depression and despair. *It passes!* Sure, Kenneth still has bouts with depression. But he's learned that the waves of sadness that engulf him are only temporary. He knows he will feel much better at another time and has learned to "wait out the storm" until the sun breaks through again.

There is a profound lesson in Kenneth Baldwin's example – we should never trust out negative feelings: our depression, despair and our fears. These negative emotions cloud our view of life and distort our sense of reality. Plus, these negative feelings will pass. Kenneth has adopted the approach that we find in the Psalms: *"Why are you cast down, O my soul, and why so disturbed within me. Put your hope in God, for I shall yet praise him, my Savior and my God"* (Psalm 42:5, 11; 43:5) and, *"God's anger is just for a moment, but his favor lasts a lifetime; weeping may remain for a night, but joy comes in the morning"* (Psalm 30:5).[xxiii]

PRAYER: Dear Father in heaven, when sorrow and despair come in like a flood, help me to endure the night and to experience your joy in the morning. When a mist of depression hangs over my heart and my mind, help me to see with eyes of faith the brighter day that you will bring. Amen.

April 9

DON'T MISS THE REAL BEAUTY

The Northwest Passage. It was the ultimate goal of Meriwether Lewis and William Clark's Corps of Discovery from 1804-1806. It had been Canadian explorer Alexander MacKenzie's objective more than a decade earlier. For the previous three centuries Spain, France and Great Britain had pursued the Northwest Passage through men like Hernan Cortez, Henry Hudson and Martin Frobisher. In the years to come, it would be the goal of the ill-fated Franklin Expedition of 1845 in which all of its 128 members perished. Dozens of other attempts were made.

But not until 1906 did anyone successfully navigate the Northwest Passage by water - Norwegian explorer Roald Amundsen. Today, this famed passage – through the perpetually frozen waters north of Canada – remains a difficult and impractical route, even for the most formidable of ships.

But this was not the "passage" that men of history had in mind. For President Thomas Jefferson, the Northwest Passage was what he believed to be an easy water-route across the North American continent via the Missouri and Columbia Rivers. Finding it became the whole justification and impetus for funding and commissioning the Corps of Discovery.

But to Lewis and Clark's profound disappointment, there was no easy and continuous water route across North America. The headwaters of the Missouri and Columbia Rivers were separated by 200 miles of towering mountains. The chief objective of the Lewis and Clark Expedition had ended in utter failure.

But no one today considers the Lewis and Clark Expedition a failure. Begun shortly after the Louisiana Purchase, which more than doubled the size of the United States, the Corps of Discovery charted more than 4,000 miles of waterways. They mapped thousands of square miles of unknown territories and established friendly relations with important Indian nations like the Hidatsas, Mandans, and the Nez Pearce – almost 50 such Indian tribes.

From a naturalist's perspective, the expedition was the greatest adventure of all time. For Captain Lewis carefully catalogued and illustrated 122 new species of animals and 178 new varieties of plants. Lewis and Clark opened up a whole new world of unanticipated scenic beauty and wildlife. Somehow, along the path of scenic enchantment and discovery, the quest for the Northwest Passage became unimportant. The people, the wildlife and the land itself took on inestimable value.

Life is like that. We often find our primary mission frustrated again and again. We curse our circumstances, pound our fist on the desk, and vent our rage. But all along the journey for our "Northwest Passage" we find a beauty of people and a divine Providence that graces our lives. If we would only stop staring at the horizon, straining after that frustrated goal, to consider the blessings that God daily brings into our lives, we would see the real beauty.

The Scripture admonishes us: "Bless the Lord, O my soul, and forget *none* of His benefits." (Psalm 103:2)

PRAYER: Dear Lord, when circumstances frustrate my goals and keep me from reaching my objectives, help me not to lose heart. Give me wisdom and insight to make a necessary change of direction and help me not to overlook the blessings along the way. Help me to enjoy the journey. Amen.

April 10

WHEN WE LOSE SIGHT OF LIFE'S GREATER MISSION

In 1993 a white South African photojournalist named Kevin Carter was on mission to the Sudan. There he was to photograph the famine victims at a UN feeding center in that drought-stricken part of the world. Overcome by the misery around him, he sought relief by walking outside the camp into the open bush. There he overheard the faint crying of a little child. Upon investigation, he found a starving little girl, on her hands and knees, struggling to make her way to the feeding center. "What a picture," Carter thought to himself. So he positioned himself in front of the little girl and began snapping away. Suddenly, an enormous and well-fed vulture landed just a few feet behind the girl, ready to claim his next meal.

Did the journalist drive the bird away and save the little girl? No. Instead, Carter stood by waiting for the vulture to spread its wings or make some dramatic move toward the girl so he could capture the picture of a lifetime. After expending several rolls of film, Carter walked back to the camp, leaving the little girl to struggle on her own.

Kevin Carter published his work but was criticized for not helping the girl. His defense: "I'm a journalist, not a rescue worker. I was on a different mission." Then, almost as a vindication, Kevin Carter received the 1994 Pulitzer Prize for photojournalism. But his fulfillment was short-lived. Two months after receiving the coveted award, Carter committed suicide.

How is it possible for someone to become so distracted by such a minor task that he neglected his greater calling to help his fellow human beings? It happens all the time. Even Jesus told the story of how a man in his day was robbed and beaten by bandits, and then ignored by several passing clergymen who were in a hurry to get to church on time (Luke 10:30-37). God help us all not to lose sight of life's greater mission.

PRAYER: Dear Lord, open my eyes and my ears to those around me who are suffering and use me to bring healing to their lives. Amen.

April 11

WHOM WILL YOU SERVE?

Following the death of the Roman Emperor Nero in AD 68, Rome experienced a period of turbulence known as the "Year of the four Emperors." In fairly rapid succession Nero was followed by Galba (June 68 – January 69), Otho (January 69 – April 69), Vitellius (April 69 – December 69) and finally Vespasian (July 69 – June 79).

With each new Emperor old loyalties became incriminating and fates turned from day into night. A dramatic example of this occurred with the assassination of the Galba. After his death on AD January 16, 69, about 120 people stepped forward, claiming to be the assassin in an effort to gain favor with his successor – the Emperor Otho. Unfortunately for them, Otho's reign was very short. He died by his own hand after losing the Battle of Bedriacum in April 69. Once his successor assumed command of the empire the status of the 120 changed from hero to villain. To make things worse, a list of their names soon fell into the hands of Vitellius, who proceeded to execute all 120.[xxiv]

In the Scripture we read Joshua's cry to Israel: "Choose you this day whom you will serve ... as for me and my house we will serve the Lord." (Joshua 24:15) Loyalty to God and to the cause of righteousness may not seem like the most profitable path in this life. Our popular culture has certainly made America a hostile place for those who profess faith in Jesus Christ and who espouse biblical and family values. But ridicule from the world will someday turn into praise from God – whose kingdom shall have no end. Remember this well when choosing your loyalties. The Scripture reminds us that "the world is passing away and all its lusts; but he who does the will of God shall abide forever." (1 John 2:17)

PRAYER: Dear Father in heaven, to You and Your eternal kingdom I pledge myself and my life. Help me to never become short-sighted so as abandon my loyalties to You for the sake of friendship with the world. Amen.

April 12

EVERYONE'S GOOD FOR SOMETHING

"You don't throw a whole life away just because it's banged up a bit." That is the theme of Gary Ross' screen adaptation of Laura Hillenbrand's best-selling book, *Seabiscuit: An American Legend.* In one of the movie's most profound scenes, an emotionally broken businessman, Charles Howard, talks with a down-on-his-luck cowboy, Tom Smith, over a campfire. Tom Smith had been nurturing a discarded horse back to health. Charles Howard asks the old cowboy why he wastes his time on the horse, since it will never be strong enough to race again. *"Every horse is good for something,"* Tom Replies. *"You don't throw a whole life away just because it's banged up a bit."*

Those words resonate deeply in Howard's heart, for his life had been dealt some terrible blows – the death of his son, the breakup of his marriage, and some horrendous financial reverses. In fact, the movie is filled with "banged up" and "broken" figures. Among them was the desperate jockey, Red Pollard, whose hard times had driven him to alcoholism.

Also among life's "damaged goods" were the millions of unemployed and demoralized Americans, whose world had crumbled in the grip of the Great Depression. But foremost among failures was the "lazy, worthless, and hopeless" horse, Seabiscuit.

This undersized, knobby-kneed Seabiscuit had been judged "incorrigible" by the finest horse-trainer in America – James Fitzsimmons, who discarded him for the rock-bottom price of $2,000.

Yet, in the loving care of Tom Smith, Seabiscuit was brought back to life, and became the highest-earning, fastest, and greatest racehorse in American History. Through the love and unconditional acceptance of Charles Howard, Red Pollard also finds redemption. In one memorable scene, an enraged Tom Smith wants to fire Pollard for concealing blindness in his left eye. Charles Howard repeats Smith's own words back to him: *"It's all right. It doesn't matter. You don't throw a whole life away just because it's banged up a bit."*

By the way, that is essentially the message of the Gospel of Jesus Christ. "But God, who is so rich in mercy, loved us so much that, even while we were dead in our trespasses and sins, he brought us back to life and seated us with Christ in the heavenly realms." (Ephesians 2:4). God tells us, "It's all right. No matter what you've done, no matter how you've failed, no matter how messed up your life is – I don't throw away anyone just because their life is banged a bit or banged up beyond repair."

PRAYER: Dear Father in heaven, please take the broken pieces of my life and make me into something beautiful that blesses other people and brings honor to your name. Amen.

April 13

WHEN WE GIVE UP TOO SOON

The ancient Greek Olympic game of *pankration* (meaning a game of "all strength") was a combination boxing-wrestling match between two opponents. Virtually anything was legal. No holds were barred. And it was brutal. In fact, deaths in this game were quite common.

The ancient historian Pausanius records one contest that is particularly interesting. It involved a man named Arrachion in the Greek Olympic Games of 564 B.C. Pausanius doesn't record the other man's name. That's too bad. Because it's the other man with whom we have so much in common.

You see the other man was doing well, so it seemed. He had a choke-hold around Arrachion's neck and a powerful scissor-grip around Arrachion's midsection. He clearly had the advantage. He was squeezing the life-breath out of Arrachon. All Arrachion had was the other man's foot. So with all his remaining strength – which wasn't much - Arrachion began to twist the other man's foot. As his life was ebbed away he continued to twist and twist until the other man cried out in pain. In fact, so great was the momentary pain that the other man wailed, "I give up, I give up. I concede the bout to my opponent."

Too bad we don't know the other man's name. We know Arrachion because he holds a certain distinction. You see, he is the only man in the history of the Olympics who won the victor's crown *while he was dead*. That's right. The other man, that nameless individual in whom we all see a little of ourselves, accepted defeat in contest with a man who was already defeated. In fact, he was stone dead.

And how many times do we accept defeat in life and toss in the towel when victory is already in our grasp. General George S. Patton defined courage as "fear holding on five minutes longer." That's why the Scripture admonishes us: "Be strong and courageous! Do not tremble or be dismayed, for the LORD your God is with you wherever you go." (Joshua 1:9)

PRAYER: Dear Lord, remind me that all my problems have limited life spans and that there is nothing in my life that You and I cannot overcome. Amen.

April 14

THE IMPORTANCE OF FAMILY

Mount Everest, 29,035 feet above sea level, is the "roof of the world." It is also the most inhospitable place on earth. At its summit the air pressure is only one third that of sea level. The effects of this near-airless environment are so severe that if someone were transported there by plane or helicopter, without first taking the usual months to adapt, they would die within three to four minutes. Close to the top of Everest, 100-mile per hour winds rip into climbers creating triple-digit wind chills. Even at its lowest base camps, 18,000 feet high, the air is so dry so as to create coughs that can fracture ribs. Above this height wounds do not heal, delirium afflicts the mind, and agony comes with every step.

On Friday, May 10, 1996, 31 climbers from five expeditions launched from their camps to reach Everest's summit. Without warning, a vicious storm descended upon the long string of climbers, blinding and confusing them in a cloud of frozen mist and snow. One of these climbers was Doug Hanson, a postal worker from Renton, Washington. When the storm hit, Hanson laid down – something very dangerous to do on the descent, when the temptation to yield to fatigue is almost irresistible and always lethal. He never got up again.

Another climber was Beck Weathers. He also fell to the ground and lay unconscious for hours. When rescue workers from the base camp found his body, they determined he was past saving. It was too dark, the trail too treacherous and his body too frozen.

Yet a few hours later, Weathers awakened from his stupor and found inspiration to rise up and stagger back to his base camp. According to *Newsweek*, Weathers reported, "I was on my back on the ice. It was colder than anything you can believe. My right glove was gone and my hand looked like it was molded in plastic. …yet I could see the faces of my wife and children. I figured I had three or four hours to live, so I started walking." Although his wife had initially received word that her husband had died on the mountain, the love of family pushed Beck Weathers on to survive that dreadful night that took the lives of so many others.

The love of a spouse and children is one of God's greatest blessings – a blessing that we so often take for granted. Sometimes only the most painful adversity can awaken us to their importance and how their love can help us survive. Dwight L. Moody once said, "I believe the family was established long before the church, and my duty is to my family first."[xxv]

The Scripture reminds us, "He who finds a wife, finds a good thing and obtains favor from the Lord" (Proverbs 18:22) and "children are a gift from the Lord." (Psalm 127:3)

PRAYER: Dear Father in heaven, open my eyes to the blessing I have in my family. Help me to cherish, to love and to care for them. Amen.

LET FAITH ANSWER FEAR

Halley's Comet. Today we do not fully appreciate the apprehension and abject terror this celestial visitor has inspired through the ages. Roughly, every 76 years (since it was first observed in 468 B.C.) Halley's Comet passes by the earth to spread fear among humanity. One reason people dreaded the comet was that it is often associated with catastrophe. The Roman war against Judea in AD 66 that brought about the destruction of Jerusalem was preceded by the comet's visit. The same is true for the devastation of Rome by the Huns in AD 373, the Battle of Hastings in 1066 – Halley's Comet "announced" the death of King Harold in the famous Bayeux Tapestry - and many other tragic events.

Consequently, when the comet's return in 1910 was announced, panic ensued throughout Europe. Above all people feared the "poisonous gases" of the comet's tail would poison the earth and bring about famine, disease and death of cataclysmic proportions. However, advancements in science have brought to light some very comforting facts about Halley's comet.

First, its size – the body Halley's Comet, described as a "dirty snow ball" of ice, frozen gases, and other solids, measures a mere 10 miles long by 5 miles wide – which is comparable to some of earth's largest icebergs.

Second, there is the size of its dreaded tail. Although the dust tail of Halley's Comet can extend 60,000 miles as it nears the sun, the amount of particles in its tail will only fill a small Dixie cup! In the final analysis, Halley's Comet put on a good light show but is too small to pose any danger to the earth.

The tail of Halley's Comet reminds us of how those things we fear appear to us – blown way out of proportion from their actual size. The things we fear seem so large that they fill the universe. But upon examination, the "sum of all our fears" will barely fill a Dixie cup.[xxvi]

In the Scripture we find dozens of commands to "Fear not." It must be for a good reason. Someone said, "Fear knocked on the door. Faith answered. No one was there." The Scripture says, "Fear thou not, for I am with thee; be not dismayed, for I am thy God. I will strengthen thee; yea, I will help thee; yea, I will uphold thee with the right hand of my righteousness." (Isaiah 41:10)

PRAYER: Dear Father in heaven, please help me to face those things I fear so that I may unmask them for the tiny midgets they are. Help me to face all my fears with faith in you. Amen.

April 16

WHEN WE CANNOT ESCAPE TROUBLE

Can you imagine having your honeymoon spoiled by a pesky bird? That's what happened to Walt and Gracie. While honeymooning in a rustic log cabin on the lake, Walt and Gracie were awakened at dawn day after day by an annoying woodpecker. The steady and unnerving "rat-a-tat" on the cabin walls, kept the newlyweds awake all morning.

What did they do? Shoot the bird? Whine and complain that their honeymoon was ruined? Cut their honeymoon short? They did none of the above.

This incident with the woodpecker happened to Gracie and Walter Lantz on their honeymoon, but they were determined to get something good and positive out of this annoying experience. Gracie and Walt were a happy, playful couple and they discovered an opportunity. By the time they had returned from their honeymoon, they were inspired to create the cartoon character "Woody the Woodpecker." Walter was the illustrator, Gracie the voice. Many years later, when interviewed on their 50th wedding anniversary, Gracie said, "It was the best thing that ever happened to us."

And isn't God able to do that with all the troubles in our lives? He can turn them into something good and positive. He can turn our hurts into halos and our scars into stars.

The Scripture says, "God works all things together for good, to those who love God, to those called according to his purpose." (Romans 8:28) But in order for this to happen, we must conquer our moods and maintain a positive attitude so we can be on the lookout for the opportunities that God will bring to us.

PRAYER: Dear Father in heaven, open my eyes to your love and the possibilities for good that present themselves every day. Amen.

April 17

WHEN SOMEONE HAS WRONGED YOU

Bernie vowed revenge. He was wounded, angry and determined to get even with his nemesis – Sanford "Sandy" Sigoloff.

Bernie had been the corporate manager of the Handy Dan Home Improvement Center – a chain of sixty-six stores and the only *successful* sub-division of the Daylin Corporation. Under Bernie's leadership, Handy Dan had grown and flourished while the rest of Daylin was filing Chapter 11 for bankruptcy.

In a desperate effort to save Daylin, its board of executives hired Sandy Sigoloff to do the dirty work of "trimming the fat," and sometimes the muscle, from its workforce and to send thousands of people packing their bags. The problem was that Sandy enjoyed his "gunslinger" role too much. He prided himself on being ruthless and relished in his nickname, "Ming the Merciless." But the success of Handy Dan kept Bernie out of Sandy Sigoloff's reach. So Sigoloff filed suit against Bernie on trumped up charges. Bernie was fired, physically thrown out of his office and his reputation tarnished. He states, "I had never been fired in my life and never experienced anything like this … It was the lowest point of my life."

Nothing but hatred filled his heart and schemes of revenge filled his mind. But when visiting his friend, Sol Price, one of the founders of Costco, he was confronted with a startling revelation. At his home Sol took Bernie into a room with no furniture, but with dozens of stacks of paper, piled five to six feet high. "Here, Bernie, are three years of my life," Sol explained. "They are all depositions from law suits in my own personal quest for revenge." Then he turned to Bernie and said, "For God's sake don't waste your life on revenge. Go out there and be successful at the things you really love. Otherwise you'll end up with a room like this."

On the two-and-a-half-hour ride home Bernie couldn't get that image out of his mind. By the time he pulled into his driveway he had decided Sol was right. He fired his attorneys and abandoned his quest to get even.

Instead Bernie Marcus pursued his dream – the creation of the giant retail hardware store – The Home Depot. Bestselling author, Harvey Mackay writes, "For years, Home Depot has been the hottest specialty retailer – a Wall Street darling. A $60-plus-billion-dollar business today, it consistently ranks in the top echelon of the *Fortune* and *Forbes* lists. It now has around 1,700 stores."

That's a far better legacy than a room filled with legal depositions. And what was Sandy Sigoloff's legacy? He presided over Handy Dan's "Going out of Business Sale."

The Scripture says, "Never pay back evil for evil to anyone. ...Never take your own revenge, beloved, but leave room for the wrath of God, for it is written, 'Vengeance is mine, I will repay,' says the Lord. ...Do not be overcome with evil, but overcome evil with good." (Romans 12:17, 19, 21)

PRAYER: Dear Father in heaven, please help me in my time of pain and anger. Heal my wounded heart. Speak peace to the storm that rages in my soul. Set me free from the chains of bitterness and release me to pursue your glorious plan for my life. Amen.

April 18

WHEN LIFE GETS YOU DOWN

Sick and stuck in a rut. That's how Truett felt. He had weathered the Great Depression and survived the Second World War. With his two brothers he had struggled to get his own restaurant started in Atlanta – the Dwarf Grill. They opened a second restaurant. His horizon finally began to brighten. Then life hit him hard. Both brothers were killed in a plane crash. One of the restaurants burned to the ground – without insurance to cover the loss. And before Truett could begin to rebuild, this energetic businessman became laid up for months while surgeons performed multiple operations to remove polyps from his colon. Yes, Truett was sick and stuck in a rut.

Yet God has ways of slowing us down. Sometimes he brings life to a screeching halt to get our attention. Sometimes he simply wants to tell us something that we'd never be able to hear in the furious pace of life. For during those longs months that Truett lay face-down on his hospital bed, it seemed that God dropped an idea in him mind. This idea germinated and grew so that when he was finally was released from the hospital, Truett had a fabulous idea for preparing and marketing seasoned chicken. Instead of rebuilding old ideas, Truett Cathy launched out in a new direction and began the 1000-store and billion-dollar enterprise we know as *Chick-fil-A*.

But Truett's success goes far beyond his entrepreneurship. Truett Cathy has donated countless millions from his earnings in college scholarships. He has established ten foster-care homes and numerous other charitable works to help the poor and to train young people to be successful in life. Among his many awards for his humanitarian efforts, Mr. Cathy was recognized as one of "The Ten Most Caring People" in the world by the Caring Institute of Washington, D.C. and was admitted to the Hall of Fame for Caring Americans. And to think all his success and all his humanitarian efforts began with a sickness and a long stay in the hospital!

The Scripture reminds us, "God works all things together for good, for those who love God, for those called according to his purpose." (Romans 8:28) The next time illness or misfortune frustrates our efforts to succeed, remember Truett Cathy. Maybe God is slowing us down or trying to get our attention. As the old adage goes: "Disappointment is His appointment."

PRAYER: Dear Father in heaven, please guide and direct my steps. Cause the delays, roadblocks, and detours of my life to bring about good in my life. Amen.

April 19

ABANDONED

Back in 1973, the 16-year-year-old grandson of billionaire John Paul Getty was kidnapped by the Italian Red Brigade, who kept him chained to a post in a cave in the Calabrian Mountains. The kidnappers demanded a ransom of $17 million. The father, Paul Getty, did not have the money, so he pleaded with his father for help.

The grandfather stiffly refused to pay any ransom. He claimed that he had other grandchildren and if he gave into the demands of these kidnappers, all of his grandchildren would be kidnapped and ransoms would be demanded of all. Not until the kidnappers sent an envelope to a Rome newspaper, containing a lock of the grandson's hair and *his severed right ear*, did the grandfather finally budge. But, even then, the grandfather only gave in to the kidnappers after bargaining for a deal of $2 million for a ransom. All the while the grandson, J. Paul Getty III, languished chained in a cave for five long months while his grandfather haggled for a lower ransom. This is the same J. Paul Getty who, in his will, left his son, J. Paul, Jr.: "the sum of $500, and nothing else."

And there are many times when we feel just as abandoned, considered not worth the time and effort of other people. But God is not like that. The Scripture says, "For there is one God and one Mediator between God and man, the man Christ Jesus, who gave himself a ransom for all" (1 Timothy 3:15) and again, "He who did not spare his own son, but delivered him up for us all, how shall he not with him freely give us all things." (Romans 8:32) God did not bargain with the devil for a cheaper price or hold out for a lower rate. God gave everything he had to ransom us from Satan's grasp – even gave his one and only Son, Jesus Christ.

PRAYER: Dear Father in heaven, thank you for considering me worth the effort and worth the price of your only Son. Help me to live a life that pleases you and honors the name of him who redeemed me. Amen.

April 20

GOD HAS A PLAN FOR YOUR LIFE

From the smallest of seeds, weighing only 1/6000th of an ounce, this tiny plant rose to become a towering monarch among trees. It is believed to have been nearly 2000 years old and over 250 feet tall. But all that remains today is the "Centennial Stump."

Its tragic end began in 1875, when two brothers, William and Thomas Vivian, sought to make a fortune by providing a crosscut of a massive Giant Sequoia tree for the Centennial Exhibition in Philadelphia that same year. They sought out a perfect specimen, a massive tree that bore none of the burn marks or scars that tainted so many of the other trees. The Sequoia they found exceeded all their expectations. It had a massive truck, 26 feet wide and towered above all the surrounding trees.

It took the brothers more than a week to cut the giant down, saw off a cross-section, cut it into manageable pieces, and haul it by wagon to the train depot for shipment to Philadelphia. But the whole plan backfired. When officials at the Philadelphia World's Fair saw the incredibly-wide cross-section and observed the many dissecting cuts, they concluded that the whole thing was a fabrication and condemned it as "the California Hoax." The "perfect specimen" was laughed out of town. It had all been a waste. Its cross-section was discarded and its great trunk lay shattered on the ground – unfit even for use as lumber. And what compensation did the brothers receive for all their efforts? A measly $50! What an ignoble and tragic end to such a king of trees that took nearly two millennia to grow.

Like this awesome tree, God has destined us for greatness and glory. As God built into that tiny seed the blueprint for a towering giant, God had a plan for our lives – for our good and God's ultimate glory. But like the tree, we also may have found ourselves sold cheaply and considered useless. We may have even concluded that our life has been a total waste. But unlike the fallen tree, God is able to raise us up and rebuild our lives. As the Scripture says, "For I know the plans I have for you, says the Lord, plans for good and not for evil, plans to give you a hope and a future" (Jeremiah 29:11). What our unwise choices and life's events have destroyed, God is able to resurrect and rebuild.

PRAYER: Dear Father in heaven, you have destined me for greatness. Grant that I may not sell myself cheaply nor abandon hope for myself if I fail. Remind me that I can never fall beyond the reach of your love nor be broken beyond your ability to repair and redeem. Amen.

April 21

WHEN THERE SEEMS TO BE NO WAY

In 1991 I took a trip across the Pennsylvania Turnpike that cuts across the state from East to West. There is a problem, however, with highway traffic that seeks to go across Pennsylvania in an East-West direction. The long ridges of the Allegheny Mountains tend to run in a North-South direction. Ridge after ridge presents what appears to be an impenetrable barrier.

On a journey traveling the Turnpike I recall the highway leading me head-on into the one such ridge. This ridge was far too long to go around. It extended as far north and as far south as the eye could see. The ridge was far too high and steep to go over. I scanned the ridge further to see if there was some hidden gap that was imperceptible from a distance. But no such gap existed. There was simply no way through the mountain, no way around it, and no way over it. Yet the highway was hurdling me along, straight toward the mountain. I actually became a little concerned. "Where is this highway taking me," I thought.

Then, when it seemed I was up against the very face of the towering ridge, I saw the answer – *a tunnel*, more than a mile long, had been cut right through the mountain.

Now since that time I've reflected on that experience and I've identified several mistakes I made that caused me needless worry.

First, finding a way past the mountain is **not the motorist's concern** or responsibility. It's **the engineer's responsibility**. In the same way it's not the believer's responsibility to overcome the impossible or to find a way through the Red Sea. The responsibility is God's. As God parted the waters of the Red Sea to allow Israel to cross, so God will make a way for us to get through our difficulties – through them, around them, or out of them.

Second, I forgot that I was not alone in this problem, many other motorists were speeding along on the same highway that I was. Remember the word of the Lord: "No temptation has overtaken you except that which is common to man." (1 Corinthians 10:13)

Third, there was traffic coming from the opposing lane – surely they had made it past the mountain from the opposite side. Sometimes we forget that millions of other people have already gone through the trial we are now facing and have survived. And they are no greater, stronger, or better equipped than we are.

Fourth, just because *I* cannot see a possible way through the problem is meaningless. The human five senses are pathetically inadequate and cannot but begin to discern the means at God's disposal to bring about a solution to our problems. The "answer" and the "way *out*" may be imperceptible to us, but God will bring it to light.

Finally, roads are not built haphazardly. They are the result of careful planning, immense expertise, and extensive work. God already has a plan and a blueprint to take care of the mountain in your life.

Consider the Gospel story where Jesus fed the 5,000. When faced with this huge hungry crowd, Jesus turned to one of his disciples and asked, "Philip, where are we to get food that all of these may eat?" But the Scripture reminds us that, "Jesus only said this to test him, for He Himself knew what He was intending to do." (John 6:5-6). Jesus never intended for Philip to embrace the problem, make it his own, and rack his brains to find a solution. But that's what Philip did. Overwhelmed, Philip blurted out: "Eight month's wages could not buy enough to give everyone a bite."

Then Andrew stepped forward and said, "There is a boy here with five loaves and two fish, but what are these among so many?" (John 6:8-9) Andrew effectively handed the problem back to the Lord. And that's what all of us need to do when a huge problem is dumped in our lap. Hand it back to God. "Cast all your care upon Him for he cares for you." (1 Peter 5:7) "Cast your burden upon the LORD and He will sustain you; He will never allow the righteous to be shaken." (Psalm 55:22)

God has already prepared a way through the obstacles of our lives. When the challenges of life loom on the horizon like great towering ridges, when they stretch so far to either side that it is apparent we cannot go *around* them when they tower so high that we cannot go *over* them, don't worry. God has already provided a way. He sees the end all the way from the beginning (Isaiah 46:10). He already knows what He is intending to do. God will either help us over them, around them, or he'll tunnel a way through them.

PRAYER: Dear Father in heaven, give me courage and faith to face the challenges and seemingly un-solvable problems of my life. Remind me that you have foreseen these problems and have made provision to help me overcome them. Amen.

April 22

A GOOD EVIL

By 1889 Civil war had been brewing in Samoa for several years. This was largely the result of heavy-handed tactics by the Germans who had exiled the old Samoan king Malietoa Laupepa and had installed their own choice for king, Tamasese. Resentment rose even higher when a German gunboat shelled a Samoan village for not paying taxes.

The world was outraged, especially America, who was determined to limit German influence in the area. The United States quickly dispatched three gunboats to match the three German warships in harbor. Demands and threats were hurled by both sides. Things came to a flashpoint in March of 1889 and open war seemed inevitable.

But something happened – Samoa was struck by a devastating typhoon. On March 17, 1889, a typhoon of great magnitude hit Samoa, damaging or destroying all six warships and killing about 150 of the sailors.

But the typhoon had an undeniable "bright side" as well. It prevented a war between Germany and America. In fact, the storm hit the two powers so hard that the opposing commanders reconciled and joined together in rescue and recovery efforts. And, after the storm had passed, they conducted joint memorial services on the Samoan Islands for those sailors on both sides who had perished. All talk of war ended and the two countries agreed to a joint protectorate for the Samoan Islands. Something as evil and destructive as a typhoon had brought about peace when man was incapable of doing so.

Many times the adversity that we condemn as evil is "heaven sent." Tragedy, disappointment and failure hit us like a knockout punch. But as much as the pain hurts us, it protects us from a greater evil.

Consider the story of Joseph. Joseph was rejected and sold as a slave by his brothers, unjustly imprisoned, and abandoned in prison by friends. A terrible evil, you say? But Joseph came to understand that all which others had done to him with evil intent, God had blessed and turned around to bring about good (Genesis 50:20). God turned Joseph's curses into blessings (Deuteronomy 23:5). He can do the same for us all.

PRAYER: Dear Lord, please guide and direct my life and help me to yield to your holy will. By your love, wisdom, and power, please turn my curses into blessings, my hurts into halos, and my scars into stars. Amen.

April 23

WHEN EVERYTHING SEEMS AGAINST YOU

His real name was Rembrandt Harmenszoon van Rijn. He was born on July 16, 1606 in Leiden, Netherlands. He became the greatest of the Dutch Masters and one of the most towering figures in the history of art. His stunning use of shadow, light and color created a never-before-seen depth in paintings of any kind from any previous period. The most puzzling thing about Rembrandt, however, is that he should not have been a painter at all. For Rembrandt suffered from an eye condition called *extropia*, where one eye (Rembrandt's left eye) was lazy and drifted outward, destroying his capacity for binocular vision. Yet both art historians and medical professionals have become convinced that the handicap of his eye-condition may have been the driving force behind his extensive use of shadow and light – to help him overcome the flat look of the canvas.

Added to this difficulty was the measure of tragedy in Rembrandt's life. By 1636 Rembrandt had entered a quieter, less imaginative period of his life. Then a series of heart-rending events broke upon him. In the next few years three of his four children died in infancy, culminating with his beloved wife's own death in 1642. Both Rembrandt and his friends believed he would not recover from his grief. But he did. And somehow his suffering precipitated a new era in his life wherein he painted with a far greater passion, power, and purpose, resulting in his most productive years.

God is able to use our handicaps, our pain, even our tragedy to make us greater than we otherwise could be. Psychiatrist Gerald May once explained, "We have this idea that everyone should be totally independent, that everyone should be totally together spiritually, totally fulfilled. That is a myth. In reality our lack of fulfillment is the most precious gift we have. It is the source of our passion, our creativity, our search for God. All the best of life comes out of our human yearning, our 'not being satisfied.'" The testimony of Scripture is this: "God works all things (even the most painful things) together for good, to those who love God, to those who are called according to his purpose." (Romans 8:28)

PRAYER: Father in heaven, please produce good in my life out of the pain I suffer. In my suffering, disappointment and heart-break, help me to have faith, to endure and to rejoice in the glory that you will ultimately bring about on my behalf. Amen.

April 24

WHEN WE FEEL INADEQUATE

He was a 'round-the-world' traveler in the early Nineteenth Century, before the days of the steamship, the railroad, or the balloon. The only 'public transportation' available in his day was by horse, stagecoach, or sailing ship. Yet despite these barriers, James Holman, became one of the greatest world travelers and geographers of his day.

But Holman didn't merely trod the path others had trod. When he visited Rome he climbed atop Saint Peter's Basilica. When he visited Naples Holman climbed the steep slopes of Mount Vesuvius' smoking crater, smoldering cinders filling his shoes as he made his way to the summit. On one occasion he took the helm and piloted his ship to safety after it had collided with another vessel (he was only a passenger). Decades before the Trans-Siberian Railroad Holman braved the vast expanse of Russian wasteland only to be arrested by the Czar's secret police and face charges of being a spy. Yet against all adversity James Holman traveled every continent on the globe and wrote a four-volume work that chronicled his five-year adventure, *Voyage Round the World*. To this day, Holman's literary works remain some of the most informative and fascinating geographical studies.

There were a few other handicaps James Holman had to overcome in his travels. One was a lack of resources in personnel and finances. James Holman traveled alone and relied entirely on what crude public transportation was available. He had no organizational support-base back home in England. His only income came from a half-pay pension from the Royal Navy.

Yet the greatest handicap that James Holman had to grapple with was not technological, financial, or logistical. It was physical. For James Holman, one of the greatest geographers of the Nineteenth Century, traveled around the world, to every continent, *in total darkness*. He was completely *blind!*[xxvii]

What limitations do you have? Rather than using them as an excuse, lean upon God to turn your weakness into strength. In the Scripture Paul the apostle explained that he was plagued with "a thorn in the flesh," perhaps some physical limitation or perhaps something too personal to discuss without cryptic language. But rather than bemoan his plight, Paul stood upon God's promise: "My grace is sufficient for you, for My power is perfected in weakness." (2 Corinthians 12:9) Thus Paul concluded, "Most gladly, therefore, will I boast about my weaknesses, so that the power of Christ may dwell in me. Therefore, I am well content with weaknesses … for when I am weak, then I am strong." (2 Corinthians 12:9-10)

Here's how the 19th Century clergyman and abolitionist, Phillips Brooks, put it: "Do not pray for easier lives, pray to be stronger men. Do not ask for tasks equal to your powers, but ask for powers equal to your task. Then, not only shall the doing of your work be a miracle, but you shall be a miracle. Every day you shall wonder at yourself at the richness of life which has come in you by the grace of God."

PRAYER: Dear Father in heaven, please strengthen me and lift me above all human weakness. Transform me by Your power and grace and make me into the person You created me to be. Amen.

PUBLIC OPINION: HOW IMPORTANT IS IT
IN MORAL CRISES?

A well-known story from baseball sensation Babe Ruth's heyday relates how umpire Babe Pinelli called "the Bambino" out on strikes. When a storm of disapproving "boos" erupted from the stands, an irate Babe Ruth shouted at the umpire, "There's 40,000 people up there who know that last call should have been a ball." Pinelli answered, "Maybe so, Ruth, but mine is the only opinion that counts."

Like Babe Ruth, many voices today proclaim the sheer weight of public opinion is the final determining factor of what is right and what is wrong. Politicians constantly hold their finger in the wind, determine which direction the crowd is moving, then get out in front and pretend to be leading it. The media constantly reminds us of the President's approval rating or of popular support for the war in Iraq.

But does the loudest voice determine right and wrong? Should the ever-shifting wind of public opinion direct our course as a nation?

Before we abandon principle to popular opinion, consider how following public opinion in the past would have been ruinous to our nation.

What was popular opinion during the American Revolution? Historians acknowledge that only one third of American colonists wanted independence from Great Britain. Another third tenaciously maintained their loyalty to King George III of England – in fact, no less than 25,000 Americans fought on the side of the British against their own countrymen. Another third of Americans were wholly indifferent, and most of these felt they benefited from British protection in some way or another. Consequently, if popular opinion was allowed to decide America's fate, we would have never become a nation.

And what did popular opinion say about the slavery question in the 1860 election. Had the Democratic vote not been divided between the southern and northern Democrats (represented by Stephen Douglas and John C. Breckenridge – neither of whom opposed slavery), Abraham Lincoln would not have been elected President. He received only 40% of the popular vote – 1,866,452 votes against 2,226,738 for Douglas and Breckinridge. Another 588,879 votes went to John Bell of Tennessee who maintained that America should remain as it was – both slave and free. So, again, if popular opinion was allowed to decide America's future, slavery would have endured much longer than it did.

Some cite how popular opinion sides against the President and against the war. But historically, it has always been the courage and determination of the minority, and sometimes only of a few, who has accomplished the good and great things in our nation's history.

In the Scripture our Lord said, "Whoever is ashamed of me and my words in this evil and adulterous generation, of him will he Son of Man be ashamed when he returns in the glory of his Father and with the holy angels" (Mark 8:38).

PRAYER: Almighty Father, empower me to stand and be counted for what is right – regardless of the opposition I face. Fill me with divine boldness and power, I pray. Amen.

April 26

BLAZING "DEAD END" TRAILS

We only intended it to be a simple day trip to scout out some hiking trails in preparation for a youth camping trip. But it turned into a nightmare.

One West Texas summer day in 1982 Joe Paiz, a boy from our church youth group, and I traveled to Caprock Canyon State Park, near the town of Quitaque, Texas. This park encompasses a portion of the labyrinth of canyons that make up what is known as the Caprock Escarpment, located in the Panhandle of Texas. The red sandstone cliffs of this escarpment plunge 1200 feet in elevation from 3700 feet above sea level in the West Texas High Plains, down to the East Plains which are about 2500 feet above sea level.

The park had only opened the year before and portions of it were still undeveloped – including the hiking trails. The park offered a "hiking trail map," but it proved worthless. The trails on the map did not exist. But that did not stop Joe and I from trying to find and follow what we thought were the trails that would lead from the canyon floor and climb over 1000 feet to the canyon rim. But before long the "trail" we were following thinned out and disappeared. We had to blaze our own trail. But we risked our lives in the process as we inched our way along tiny ledges of cliffs and climbed up steep hills. But finally, exhausted and thirsty, we made it to the rim of the canyon.

But there was little time for sightseeing. We had to figure out a better way to get back down – better than the way we used to climb to the top. But finding a way down proved even harder than going up. The trails recorded on the map were nothing but draws and dry wadis. We would follow one down through a ravine only to be stopped when we came to a cliff and have to turn around and climb back to the top. We repeated this painful procedure four or five times until we were both weak from fatigue and frustration. We just couldn't find a way down to the bottom of the canyon.

As the sun began to hang low in the sky, I became very concerned that we'd be spending the night on top of the canyon – no way down and thirty miles from the nearest town. So Joe and I did the only thing we knew to do – we prayed and asked God to help us find our way back.

Within minutes I noticed a car a few hundred yards away, driving along what appeared to be a paved road. Joe and I ran up to the road – the first sign of civilization we had seen all day. And as we approached the road, a large black Cadillac pulled up to us – I couldn't believe it. The driver asked if he could help us.

"Oh, yes, Sir. We need some help – can you show us the way to the bottom of the canyon?"

"Sure. Just follow this road. It goes down to the Boy Scout Camp at the bottom of the canyon. From there you can easily hike to your car before it gets dark."

I was shocked. "Are you saying that there is a paved road that leads down to the bottom of the canyon? And all this time I've been trying to blaze my own trail?"

"Yes, this road will take you down to where you need to go. In fact, hop in the car and I'll drive you down."

So into his big, air conditioned car we climbed as he served us Cokes and drove us down to the bottom of the canyon. For the entire day I had wasted time trying to blaze my own trail and all my efforts ended in frustration and failure. And all the while engineers had already paved a road that reached from the canyon floor to the canyon rim.

I have never forgotten that event. It reminds me of the efforts people make to reach God, to make themselves acceptable to Him, to find forgiveness, and to obtain the hope of heaven. We try so hard to claw our way to God and to please Him. But it is like an unassailable cliff. For God's standards are beyond our reach: "You must be perfect, even as your heavenly Father is perfect," Jesus said in Matthew 5:48. All our efforts to meet God's demands and please Him end in failure and frustration.

But then we realize God has already paved a way to Himself. The "way" is Jesus Christ Himself. "I am the way, and the truth and the life," said Jesus. "No one comes to the Father except through Me." (John 14:6) We don't have to blaze our own trail to God. Christ has already bridged the gap between us and God. He has already borne our sins (1 Peter 2:24), blotted them out in His blood (Hebrews 9:14, 24-26), and clothed us with the robe of His righteousness (Isaiah 61:10). You cannot improve upon what Christ has done. You can only receive it in humility and faith.

PRAYER: Dear Father in heaven, here and now I put my faith in Your Son, Jesus Christ. Here and now I cease to go my own way – trying to blaze a trail to happiness, fulfillment, and peace with You. Here and now I commit myself to following Jesus Christ. Amen.

April 27

WHEN YOUR RECORD IS FAR FROM PERFECT

Can a person have many failures and still be a success? Yes – it happens all the time. Consider the world of baseball. Baseball players routinely take risks, make staggering mistakes, and yet win again and again. Here are a few examples.

In 1942 Joe Gordon led the major leagues in most errors, strike outs, and hitting into the most double plays. Yet that same year he was voted American League *Most Valuable Player*.

Can you imagine a major league baseball player setting the record for striking out at bat and yet still being voted into the Baseball Hall of Fame? The player was Yankee powerhouse, Reggie Jackson, whose record of 2,597 strikeouts still stands. Jackson once admitted that this was the equivalent to doing nothing but striking out for four consecutive seasons.[xxviii]

Rabbi Harold Kushner has the following advice in dealing with failure: "Life is not a spelling bee, where no matter how many words you have gotten right, if you make one mistake you are disqualified. Life is more like a baseball season, where even the best team loses one third of its games and even the worst team has its days of brilliance. Our goal is not to go all year without ever losing a game. Our goal is to win more than we lose, and if we can do that consistently enough, then when the end comes, we will have won it all."[xxix]

Someone has wisely stated: "Failure is a temporary detour, not a dead-end street," and, "Failure should be our teacher, not our undertaker."

So if your record is blemished with failure, be assured that you have plenty of company. The Scripture reminds us that "though a righteous man falls seven times, he rises up again." (Proverbs 24:16).

PRAYER: Dear Father in heaven, when I stumble and fail, help me, Lord to learn from my failures, move on and to grow stronger and wiser. Amen.

April 28

JUDGING A BOOK BY ITS COVER

Physiognamy. Not exactly a household word, is it? It refers to the art and "science" of determining the temperament and character of a person from his or her outward appearance, particularly from the facial features. Is it accurate? Hardly. Consider this famous quote by the award-winning French writer, Alphonse de Chateaubriant in 1939.

"The physiognomic analysis of ... his face reveals ... his immense kindness. Yes, [he] is kind. Look at him in the midst of children, bending over the graves of those he loved; he is immensely kind, I repeat it."

Of whom was the French writer speaking? None other than Adolf Hitler. So much for judging a book by its cover.

Consider also the judgment passed upon this actor when he auditioned for the part of the President of the United States in the movie, *The Best Man.* With one look, this United Artist executive declared: "[He] doesn't have the presidential look." Who was the actor? None other than Ronald Reagan.[xxx]

The truth is, only God can see a person's true character and potential for good and for evil. Just consider how misleading the size of *a seed* may be. For instance, to judge the potential of the tree *Lodoicea seychellarum* based on its seed might lead you to believe the tree will grow 500 feet tall. For its single seed can weigh up to *40 pounds!* Yet, the huge seed of *Lodoicea seychellarum* becomes a slender palm tree, sixty to ninety feet tall. On the other hand, to judge the potential growth of the tree *Sequoia sempervirens,* or its cousin *Sequoiadendron giganteum,* based on the size of their seeds, might lead you to predict that they will be no more than tiny shrubs. For their seeds are among the smallest of any tree – as small as 1/7000th of an ounce!   Yet these tiny seeds will grow into towering giants, *40-feet across at their base and 300-feet tall!*

Truly, only God, our Creator, can see what potential for goodness and greatness lies within us. As George Washington Carver once said, "Anyone can count the seeds in an apple; but only God can count the apples in a seed." The Scripture says, "For the Lord sees not as man sees. For man looks at the outward appearance, but God looks at the heart." (1 Samuel 16:6)

PRAYER: Dear Father in heaven, in faith I place myself, my future, and the raw material of my life in your hands. I trust that you alone know what potential for good and evil lies within me. Please, dear Lord, bring out and multiply the good in me and remove the evil. Make me into the person you created me to be. Amen.

April 29

A CRUTCH OR A CROSS

A classic Peanuts cartoon presents Charlie Brown shooting arrows at a wooden fence. Each time the arrow flew from his bow and landed in the fence, he ran to the fence and drew concentric circles around the arrow – his way of guaranteeing a bulls eye every time. Lucy entered the scene and protested, *"You're doing it all backwards. You're supposed to draw the target first. Then shoot the arrow at it."* Charlie replied, *"I know what I'm supposed to do, but when I do it my way I never miss."*

In a way Charlie Brown's actions are analogous to the religious faith of most Americans – it is a religion of convenience. We shoot the arrow first, then draw a bull's eye around it, i.e. we live a certain lifestyle first, then we build our faith around it. Hence, our faith never calls us to live differently, does not call us to be accountable to others, does not require us to love our neighbor much less our enemy, or to be more holy. In this sense our religion is a crutch – only to lean on and not to call us to greater responsibility. But that is not the faith which Christ, the prophets and the sages ever spoke of. The prophet Micah declared: "He has told you, O man, what is good; And what does the LORD require of you but to do justice, and to love kindness, and to walk humbly with your God?" (Micah 6:8)

Bishop Fulton Sheen once explained: *"Religion is not a crutch; it is a cross. It is not an escape, it is a burden; not a flight, but a response. We speak here of a religion with teeth in it, the kind that demands self-sacrifice and surrender. One leans on a crutch, but it takes a hero to embrace a cross."*

PRAYER: Search me, O God, and know my heart. Try me and know my anxious thoughts; and see if there be any hurtful way in me, and lead in the way everlasting. Amen.

April 30

DON'T WITHHOLD PRAISE

He has been called the greatest homerun hitter and baseball slugger of all time. He batted a phenomenal .461 in his rookie year. In his fifth year of professional baseball he batted .467 and hit an astounding 55 homeruns. The following year he blew that benchmark away with an incredible 69 homeruns. His lifetime accumulation of homeruns is disputed because of poor record keeping, but estimates run in excess of 900. Who was this towering figure? Why is it likely that you've never heard of him? The man was the immortal Negro League baseball hero, Josh Gibson. Despite his stellar performance at bat and in the field, he was denied the chance to ever play in the Major Leagues because of his color.

Perhaps the most heart-rending aspect of his story was that this sensitive man, who yearned for recognition for his sporting feats, went unnoticed by the vast majority of Americans. Throughout his professional career he would only hear the praise of *other* baseball players – Babe Ruth, Ty Cobb, Lou Gehrig, Joe DiMaggio, and a host of other white Major League players. An unsung hero, forced to dwell in endless obscurity and endure meager pay and sub-standard living conditions, Josh Gibson's emotional and physical health began to deteriorate.

In his last few years in the game he was racked with terrible knee pain and suffered from high blood pressure. But the lack of recognition did most of the damage – damage to his heart and soul. He drank heavily to self-medicate and numb his emotional pain. On January 20, 1947 he died from a stroke at the age of 35 – just three months before Jackie Robinson breached the color barrier in baseball - without even enough money for a funeral or gravestone.

Those who knew him were convinced Josh Gibson had died from a broken heart. The Editor for the Pittsburgh Courier spoke for many when he wrote: "I know the real reason Josh Gibson died. I don't need a doctor's report for confirmation either. He was murdered by big league baseball."

Every human being shares the need for recognition and praise for achievement and hard work. We hunger for approval from parents, peers and other important people in our lives. Psychologist William James once said, "The deepest principle in the human heart is the craving to be appreciated." Psychologist Cecil Osborne said, "Perhaps once in a hundred years a person may be ruined by excessive praise, but surely once every minute someone dies inside for lack of it."

Therefore be generous with your praise to others, especially to your children, spouse, co-workers and subordinates. The Scripture says, "Pleasant words are a honeycomb, sweet to the soul and healing to the bones." (Proverbs 16:24)

PRAYER: Dear Father in Heaven, help me to bring healing and encouragement with my words, and help me to inspire increased devotion and performance by my praise to others. Make me an instrument of Your peace. Amen.

May

May 1

WHEN IT SEEMS WE'LL NEVER BOUNCE BACK

Sometimes we can fall so far that it seems we'll never rise again. As Hugh Herr, a man who lived and breathed rock climbing, looked down at the ghastly, bloody stumps of what were once his legs – he was sure he'd never rise again.

Hugh Herr scaled one stony sentinel after another, up and down the Appalachian Mountain range. Climbing the sheer granite cliffs of the Catskills, the Adirondacks, the Alleghenies, and the White Mountains consumed all his waking moments. One of the most challenging cliffs on the East Coast, reserved only for the most proficient climbers, was a route in New Hampshire's White Mountains named *Stage Fright*. Conquering this giant was Hugh Herr's goal.

Then it happened. In January 1982, while ascending the sheer face of Mount Washington, the site of some of North America's most severe weather, Hugh Herr and a companion became hopelessly lost in a storm. Three days later they were rescued, but only after frostbite had done its wicked work on Hugh's feet. Gangrene set in and doctors had to amputate both his legs below the knees.

What followed was sheer hell. Hugh Herr descended into an abyss of rage and despair. His body was tortured by phantom pains in the legs that were not there anymore. He agonized through the period of withdrawal from the morphine doctors had used to quell the fierce pain. But slowly he began to climb out of his pit of despair. Slowly he began to imagine himself back on his "feet" – if only prosthetic feet. And eventually he even grasped the hope that he might one day walk again, and climb again!

"Rock climbing? Look, Hugh, with prosthetic devices you might walk again, even drive a car - but there is no way possible you can ever climb again." Doctors saw his scars but not his heart. Hugh Herr steadily trod the agonizing path of rehabilitation and recovery. He pushed himself through brutal workouts and improved his walking skills with newer, less painful artificial limbs.

Finally the day came in 1985. He stood at the base of a towering stone giant and began to climb. Upward Hugh went, probing the tiniest cracks and ledges with fingers and the pointed "toes" of his prostheses. Finally Hugh Herr reached the summit of one of the most technically challenging climbing routes in North America – *Stage Fright!*

But Hugh Herr was not finished with this ascent. He was determined to turn his pain into gain. Hugh graduated *Summa cum Laude* from Millersville University, near Lancaster Pennsylvania. Then he earned his Master's degree from the Massachusetts Institute of Technology (MIT). Finally, Hugh Herr received his Ph.D. after graduating Harvard University in 1998. His field of study? Hugh Herr works in the leg laboratory at MIT in the field of physical medicine and rehabilitation – helping others who feel they'll never bounce back after an amputation. Hugh Herr has truly turned his scars into stars.[xxxi]

In the Scriptures a deeply discouraged psalmist wrote: "Why are you in despair, O my soul? And why have you become disturbed within me? Hope in God, for I shall again praise Him for the help of His presence." (Psalm 42:5) "Hope in God, for I shall again praise Him." "I'll get through this." "I'll see the light of day again." "This is only a valley – this is not the destination." "Thousands before have passed through these deep waters and they survived – with Gods help I'll get through this too – and when I do I'll be stronger than ever before." That's what we need to tell ourselves. Then, one day, when we have recovered, we will meet another broken, despairing soul. And the very hope that has got us through the hard times, we will use to help them. We will turn our pain into their gain.

PRAYER: Dear Lord, in my times of anger and despair I need You most. But that's when I turn against You and vent my pain on You. Thank You that You are big enough to bare my pain, my anger, and the poison in my soul. Please remember that I love You and hunger for You and will never be satisfied without You. Please use this pain for good – to deepen my walk with You and to draw my heart closer to Yours. Amen.

May 2

IT ALL ADDS UP

It is amazing how the time we devote to little things piles up over a lifetime. For instance, the average American office worker will spend fifty minutes every day (almost nine months of his or her life, in a 30-year career) looking for lost files or other items. The average American will also wait six months of his/her life waiting at red lights, two years waiting for restaurant dinners to be served, and a staggering *six years* stuck in traffic. The average person's eyes will be closed for about 18 months of his life just from the time he spends blinking and the average man will spend more than four months shaving. And, in an average lifespan, six months will be spent sitting on the toilet.[xxxii]

It all adds up, doesn't it? Time devoted to the commonplace things adds up. The time we devote to the good and profitable deeds, and to the useless and the bad deeds, adds up as well. How will you want to have spent your days and years by life's end?

* The famous University of Alabama coach Paul "Bear" Bryant used to quote this poem authored by W. Heartsill Wilson:

* *This is the beginning of a new day.*

* *God has given me this day to use in such a way that it will count for eternity.*

* *I can waste this day or use it for good, but what I do today is important, because I am exchanging a day of my life for it.*

* *When tomorrow comes, this day will be gone forever, leaving in its place something that I have traded for it.*

* *I want it to be gain, and not loss; good, and not evil; success, and not failure, in order that I shall not regret the price I have paid for it.*

* *This day is all we have. Is there someone to whom an act of kindness – not tomorrow, but today – could make a world of difference?*

* *Today, whether we spend it well or throw it away, will be gone tomorrow. What is there to do that is worth our effort?*

Moses prayed in Psalm 90:12 "Lord teach us to number our days that we may gain a heart of wisdom." God help us to make the most of our days. Someone once said, "Only one life, so soon it will pass; only what's done for Christ will last."

PRAYER: Dear Father in heaven, please teach me to number my days and to weigh the ultimate outcome of my actions. Grant me wisdom to spend my life for the best possible purpose and to exchange my life for what endures for all eternity. Amen.

May 3

POOR JOE

Adria Bryan of Rhyl, Wales, was racing to get to work on time, when she noticed that nearly every passing car was flashing their headlights at her. At first she thought she left her handbag on the roof, but it sat right beside her in the passenger seat. Finally, one motorist pulled up close to her car, rolled down his window and pointed to her roof. After pulling off the road, Adria was shocked to find her fourteen-year-old cat, Joe, clinging to the roof.

"Joe is a heavy sleeper," she explained and evidently didn't wake up until the car was moving too fast for him to leap safely. "I must have been going 60, but Joe clung on for dear life."

But Joe's troubles weren't over yet. Two days later poor Joe the cat was attacked by a Bull Terrier and suffered three broken ribs and a punctured lung. He survived and recovered, perhaps not sleeping again as soundly as before.

You know, the majority of people seek to live uneventful lives of tranquility and predictability. But, like old Joe whose peaceful slumber was shattered, they find themselves carried away by circumstances beyond their control. Life takes them on a hair-raising journey they never bargained for. They may feel like they are hanging on for dear life – life that resembles a cat clawing to survive the twists and turns.

But God is sovereign. And if He is your shepherd He promises to make you rest in lush green pastures, to nurture you by still waters, and to restore your wounded soul (Psalm 23:1-3). Even when we're living life on the rooftop of a speeding car, God remains our refuge and strength, a very present help in trouble (Psalm 46:1) who will sustain us by His peace (Philippians 4:7).

PRAYER: Dear Lord Jesus, as You ruled the wind and waves while You dwelt below, please speak peace to the storm that rages in my heart. Upon Your strong shoulders and Your caring heart I cast my cares – please bear them for me and give me Your peace. Amen.

May 4

"IT'S THE STORY OF MY LIFE"

Among some of the worst maritime disasters comes the story, perhaps more legend than fact, of a ship's stoker named Frank Towers. Frank Towers was one of the 706 survivors of the *RMS Titanic's* 2,223 passengers and crew after it hit an iceberg and sank on April 14, 1912.

Two years later Frank Towers was again working as a stoker, this time aboard the Canadian steamship, the *Empress of Ireland*. In the early morning hours of May 29, 1914, as the *Empress* steamed down the St. Lawrence River on its way to Liverpool, England from Quebec City, it collided with the Norwegian coal freighter, the *Storstad*. Although the freighter survived the accident, the *Empress* rolled onto its side and sank within fourteen minutes. Of its 1,477 passengers and crew, only 473 survived. Incredibly, one of them was Frank Towers.

But there is one more chilling chapter in Mr. Tower's life. A year later, Frank Towers was still working at his profession – as a stoker, firing the ship's boilers. His next job took him aboard the *RMS Lusitania* – which, on May 5, 1915 was torpedoed by a German U-boat and sank in less than twenty minute, taking he lives of 1,195 of its 1,907 passengers and crew. Amazingly, Frank Towers again escaped death, swearing with every stroke as he swam from the sinking vessel to a lifeboat, that he would take up farming. His incredible string of tragic coincidental events inspired author Rod Serling to write the *Twilight Zone* episode, "Lone Survivor." According to accounts, when the torpedo struck the *Lusitania*, a frustrated Frank Towers cried out to the heavens, "Now what?"

Like the story of Frank Towers, we often feel there are problems that have hounded us throughout our years. "It's the story of my life – I'll never be free of this problem – It will hound me to my dying day."

But what is impossible with people *is* possible with God. After 400 years of servitude to the Egyptians, the Israelites of Moses' day doubted they would ever be fee of them. The Egyptians were the "story of their lives." But Moses assured them that, by God's deliverance – "Do not fear! Stand by and see the salvation of the Lord which He will accomplish for you today; for the Egyptians you see this day, you will never see again." (Exodus 14:13)

God can break the cycle of failure, sin and tragedy in our lives, if we turn to him in faith and whole-hearted sincerity and commitment.

PRAYER: Dear Father in heaven, please break the cycle of sin and failure in my life by your divine power. Please help me to overcome all the adversities and problems of my life. Amen.

May 5

HIDDEN TREASURE

It seemed like a worthless find. Antique dealer Robert Webber discovered it among a large collection of books for which he had just paid $500. It was old, for sure – dated 1827. But it was ugly and bore a ring stain from a drinking glass on its dark brown cover. The book was a collection of poems entitled *Tamerlane*, its author only identified as "A Bostonian." Robert's wife wanted to keep it, but his first inclination was to discard or sell it cheap. So he placed it in his shop among some old pamphlets on farm machinery and fertilizer, with a price tag of $18. But when a customer came in and offered $15 for the old, ugly book, Robert Webber promptly took the money.

Too bad for Robert. The customer (whose identity is a closely guarded secret) checked with Sotheby's and found the ugly, old volume, a self-published book, to be the very first book by a famous author. The "Bostonian" turned out to be Edgar Allen Poe and this serendipitous find, considered to be the rarest and most valuable book in American literature, was eventually auctioned for $198,000.

In a way each of us is like that ugly, old book. We're so convinced of our own worthlessness. Unfortunately, our immense value remains obscured to most people, but it is particularly hidden from us. Consequently, we all too often sell ourselves cheap to the lowest bidder. But God knows our true worth and he paid the highest possible price for us – the life of His own Son. And so the Scripture tells us, "He who did not spare his own Son, but delivered Him up for us all, how shall he not with him also freely give us all things?" (Romans 8:31) and "I pray … that you may understand how gloriously rich God has become by inheriting you." (*The Living Bible*, Ephesians 1:18)

PRAYER: Dear Father in heaven, open my eyes that I may understand the value You place upon me and the vast price You paid for me. Grant this, dear Lord, that I may live a life worthy of a true child of God. Amen.

May 6

MAKING MISTAKES IS PART OF BEING HUMAN

The term "typo," short for typographical error has been around for a long time. It dates from 1892 and is as nearly old as the typewriter itself (first marketed in 1873) – although "typo" refers to both errors of typeset material as well as of the typewriter. But everyone makes them and everyone hates them – especially when they undergo mass duplication so as to publicize our errors. And if you've made one recently, take comfort, some very bad ones have preceded yours.

One of the worst was in an authorized edition of the Bible, printed in London in 1631, which mistakenly printed the seventh of the Ten Commandments: "Thou *shalt* commit adultery!" It raised a storm of criticism from church leaders and was condemned as the "Wicked Bible." Its printers, Robert Barker and Martin Lucas, were fined 3,000 pounds.

In 1978 Random House issued a cookbook that contained directions for a harmless batch of caramel slices. The problem was that the directions called for ingredients that were potentially explosive and lethal. Random House had to recall all 10,000 copies of the cookbook.

Some typographical errors are born out of faulty information, as in the *New York Times* erroneous report of Mark Twain's death in response to a cable from London. The famed author reassured the public with this update: "The reports of my death are greatly exaggerated."

And some errors are due to a lack of foresight and very poor timing. The same *New York Times*, on December 10, 1903, condemned Samuel Langley's efforts to develop an airplane were hopelessly futile. On that very day, Orville and Wilbur Wright made their first successful flight at Kitty Hawk, North Carolina.

Errors and typos even come from such venerated sources as the *Encyclopedia Britannica*.   After a five-year study of the 1958 and 1963 editions of the encyclopedia, Dr. Henry Einbinder uncovered hundreds of articles that contained serious flaws and erroneous information. He cited 666 articles of half a page or larger that had not been updated in more than fifty years. "The *Britannica* offered as true or without qualification long-discredited legends about John Smith's being saved by Pocahontas, the Black Hole of Calcutta, the exploits of Paul Bunyan, the ride of Paul Revere, Robinson Crusoe's island, the existence of William Tell, even the tale of George Washington and the cherry tree."

Even famed authors as Shakespeare have been flawed in their depiction of history. For instance, in *Julius Caesar*, Shakespeare refers to a clock that strikes the hour – 1,400 years before the invention of such a clock. The fact that he never traveled from England is evident in his description of Bohemia, a land-locked country, as having a coast in *The Winter's Tale*. And he mentions billiards being played by the characters in *Anthony and Cleopatra*, he mentions cannon in *King John*, and turkeys in *1 Henry IV* – all before their time of invention or discovery.[xxxiii]

The point is not to poke fun at others' mistakes, but to make it easier for us all to accept our own imperfections and to take our place with the rest of flawed, sinful humanity. God accepts us as we are, loves us even with all our dark secrets, but loves us too much to leave us that way. The Scripture says, "For while we were still helpless, at the right time Christ died for the ungodly. For one will hardly die for a righteous man; though perhaps for the good man someone would dare even to die. But God demonstrates His own love toward us, in that while we were yet sinners, Christ died for us." (Romans 5:6-8)

PRAYER: Dear Father in heaven, help me to grasp your unconditional love for me. Help me to accept myself with all my flaws and imperfections and to accept your redeeming love. Amen.

May 7

IS MILITARY LIFE TAKING ITS TOLL?

Admiral Lord Horatio Nelson rates as one of the most formidable naval commanders in history. His stunning victories at Cape Saint Vincent, Battle of the Nile, Battle of Copenhagen, and finally his decisive victory at Trafalgar, immortalized him in the hearts and history of Great Britain.

But by the time he was killed by enemy fire on the quarterdeck of his flagship *Victory* at Trafalgar on October 21, 1805, Admiral Nelson – who barely stood five feet two inches – had already lost his health to malaria, the sight of one eye while fighting in Corsica, and his right arm in the battle at Tenerife. He had truly spent himself in the service of his country.

There is something noble and glorious in spending your life, health and resources in a worthy cause. Conversely, the person who wastes his days by risking nothing and sacrificing nothing is a pitiful creature indeed. The great tragedy of life is not in dying but in having never truly lived. Jim Elliott who perished for his faith at the hands of the Auca Indians in Ecuador – just one year into his mission - used to say, "He is no fool, who gives what he cannot keep to gain what he cannot lose." Jesus Christ said, "He who seeks to save his life shall lose it, but whoever loses his life for my sake, shall find it." (Matthew 16:25)

PRAYER: Almighty and merciful Father, help me to spend my energy, my days and my life on a worthy cause, for a purpose greater than myself, for your kingdom that the positive significance of my life will last for all eternity. Amen.

May 8

IS YOUR WORK "BENEATH YOU"?

Jane Addams (1860-1935), social worker, reformer, champion of the poor, women, and minorities, and co-founder of such organizations as the NAACP and ACLU, was awarded the Nobel Peace prize in 1931. She founded the Hull House, a converted mansion, in Chicago's slums, which among many other activities, fed 2,000 people weekly, provided education for children and adults, and assisted immigrants. As a reformer she fought for the protection of Chicago's lower classes and minorities.

But when she wrote her entry for *Who's Who*, she proudly listed "Garbage Collector" among her most outstanding achievements. Garbage collector? Yes, because a corrupt Chicago bureaucracy was refusing to fund or enforce the collection of refuse from the city's slums and was creating a health crisis. Frustrated, angry and appalled at lazy politicians who were endangering the health and lives of thousands and offering only excuses why they couldn't do their jobs, Jane Addams did the job herself. She organized a massive clean-up of the city's slums – chipping in and getting her own hands dirty in the process.[xxxiv]

There is something profoundly admirable about this woman. Jane Addams not only recognized that the most despised jobs are often the most essential. She also was willing to soil her own hands for the sake and safety of others. She was willing to do the job that had to be done and that no one else was willing to do – and she did it proudly. This was not unlike Jesus Christ washing the feet of his own disciples – a task his disciples would not lower themselves to do (John 13:5-17). Dr. Martin Luther King, Jr. once wrote: "If a man is called to be a street sweeper, he should sweep streets as Michelangelo painted, or Beethoven composed music, or Shakespeare wrote poetry. He should sweep streets so well that all the hosts of heaven and earth will pause to say, here lived a great street sweeper who did his job well." The Scriptures say that, at the end of the age, the Lord will say to those who are faithful: "Well done, you good and faithful servant. Because you have been faithful in the little things, I will put you in charge of the greater things. Come and share your Master's happiness." (Matthew 25:23)

PRAYER: Dear God, whether my life's tasks are great or small, help me to be faithful in my work and sign all my work with excellence. Amen.

May 9

LESSONS FROM A ONE-DOLLAR-BILL

Of the $12 billion of paper currency that the U.S. Government prints every year, $8 billion of it is $1 bills. The $1 bill costs the government a mere 2 ½ cents to print. Yet its value is not based upon the materials that go into it – a combination of rag bond, cotton, and linen – but its value comes from the Government that mints it. And in its short lifespan of one and a half years, it is exchanged more than 400 times.

Thus, it fulfills its purpose when it performs the work of $400 – not by remaining in "mint condition," merely on display in a numismatic collection. Now, of course, such use - after passing through hundreds of grimy hands - the one-dollar-bill gets quite soiled and frail. It becomes nothing but a withered rag of its former state. Yet, no matter how soiled it becomes, not one penny of its value is ever lost.

There is a lesson in this for human beings. First, our value is not based upon our physical attributes or upon the handful of chemicals and several gallons of water that make up our bodies. Nor is our value based upon embellishments like academic degrees or upon positions or titles. Our value comes from the God who created us and breathed into us the breath of life. Second, we do not find fulfillment or experience our destiny by avoiding service and commitment. On the contrary, like the one-dollar-bill, we fulfill our purpose by being used – over and over. "For he who seeks to save his life," Jesus said, "shall lose it, and he who loses his life for My sake and for the gospel's sake, shall find it." (Mark 8:35) Third, no matter how soiled or stained our lives become, not one bit of our value in God's sight is lost.

PRAYER: Dear Father in heaven, I acknowledge you as my Creator and Lord, and ask that You will fulfill your plan for my life. Grant that my energies, resources and time may be spent for Your great purpose, that my life will have eternal significance. Amen.

May 10

DO YOU WANT YOUR LIFE TO COUNT?

Norman Borlaug wanted to do something significant, something that would benefit humanity. Against many obstacles, including the ravages of the Great Depression, Norman finally worked his way through college and graduated from the University of Minnesota in 1942 with a Ph.D. in plant pathology.

He seemed on his way to helping humanity when the Rockefeller Foundation recruited him for a mission in Mexico: to save that country's crops from the ravages of stem rust, a parasitic fungus that saps the life from plants. Norman had witnessed first-hand the evil effects of hunger and starvation. During his years working in the Civilian Conservation Corps (CCC) in America during the Great Depression, he had seen young men reduced to animals as a result of prolonged hunger. Now he wanted to devote his life to stopping it.

But after he arrived in Mexico in 1944, Dr. Borlaug became disillusioned and increasingly convinced he had made a big mistake. In his book, Norman Borlaug on World Hunger, he wrote, "It often appeared to me that I had made a dreadful mistake in accepting the position in Mexico." Mexican farmers, desperate from repeated crop failures, were uncooperative, even hostile. Borlaug lacked the large staff of scientists and equipment he needed to conduct the thousands of "trial and error" experiments that would be required to develop a disease-resistant form of wheat. He clashed with his superiors when he sought to accelerate the pace of his research. And the prospect of spending his life in a Third World country, laboring in total obscurity, was hardly inspiring.

Yet, despite the obstacles, the obscurity, and the lack of recognition and reward, Borlaug remained faithful to the task and overcame the difficulties. After more than 6,000 crossings of wheat and after devoting 16 years to this project, Borlaug developed a disease-resistant form, then a high-yield form. But these successes ran into a roadblock: the tall stem of his wheat could not support the added weight of the larger head of grain. So, after many more experiments, Borlaug introduced a dwarf, high-yield, disease-resistant form of wheat. The result: by 1963 Mexico became self-sufficient in its grain production and, for the first time in its history, exported grain. As a result of Borlaug's painstaking and relentless work, Mexico's grain production had increased to six times what it had been when he arrived. But these successes were eclipsed by what was to come.

In 1963 Norman Borlaug organized two massive shipments of his grain (Pitic 62 and Penjamo 62) from Mexico to India and Pakistan. Borlaug's introduction of these "semi-dwarf" varieties of grain turned the agricultures of those countries around. Initial crop yields from Borlaug's wheat were so high that these countries did not have the resources to harvest, transport and store the grain. By 1970 the crop yields of both countries had doubled. By the year 2000 Pakistan's wheat production was five times higher than what it had been in 1965. In India its crop yields had increased to six times larger. During that period, and to this day, Norman Borlaug's work has been imported to scores of countries (including China) with similarly spectacular results.

Norman Borlaug's work is all the more notable when contrasted with the Apocalyptic vision that many experts had of the world in the 1960s and 1970s. In 1968, Dr. Paul Erlich, professor of entomology at Stanford University, published the best-selling book, The Population Bomb, in which he predicted massive famine and starvation. With irrefutable evidence to back his claims, Dr. Erlich demonstrated that the world's population growth was outpacing its capacity to produce food. As a result billions would perish from hunger.

But something unexpected happened that prevented the billions from dying. A lowly research scientist, laboring on for two decades in obscurity, without recognition or reward in a Third World country, developed simple seeds that would save the lives of more than a billion people – for which he was awarded the Nobel Prize for peace in 1970.

It's true, Norman Borlaug remains virtually unknown in America, though he is beloved abroad. But notoriety is not the measure of success. Success is measured by our faithfulness to the task to which God has called us, by our love for our fellow human beings, and by how we have made the world a better place by living in it.

"When the Son of Man comes in his glory, and all the angels with him, he will sit on his throne in heavenly glory. ...Then the King will say to those on his right, 'Come, you who are blessed by my Father; take your inheritance, the kingdom prepared for you since the creation of the world. For I was hungry and you gave me something to eat, I was thirsty and you gave me something to drink, I was a stranger and you invited me in, I needed clothes and you clothed me, I was sick and you looked after me, I was in prison and you came to visit me.' Then the righteous will answer him, 'Lord, when did we see you hungry and feed you, or thirsty and give you something to drink? When did we see you a stranger and invite you in, or needing clothes and clothe you? When did we see you sick or in prison and go to visit you?' The King will reply, 'I tell you the truth, whatever you did for one of the least of these brothers of mine, you did for me.'" (Matthew 25:31-40, NIV)

PRAYER: Dear Father in heaven, help me to be faithful to the task you have given me, though it be small, unseen, and unrewarded. Remind me that there is coming a day when I must stand before you and be recompensed for all I have done in this life. Amen.

WHEN WE THINK OUR LIFE'S BEEN A FAILURE

Nancy Hanks was born in Mineral County, West Virginia, in 1784, in a humble log cabin near a place called Mike's Run. While Nancy was still a girl, her mother Lucy (probably an unwed mother) took her along the Wilderness Road through the Cumberland Gap into Kentucky. In 1806 she married Thomas Lincoln, who was a carpenter and itinerant farmer. The couple settled on the Sinking Springs Farm near Hodgenville, Kentucky. There she gave birth to her only surviving son, Abraham, on February 12, 1809.

In 1818, while the family was living near Pigeon Creek, Indiana, Nancy Hanks became seriously ill from a disease called "milk sickness" – contracted from drinking milk from cows that had grazed on poisonous white snakeroot. She died on October 5, 1818, leaving behind her husband Thomas, and her children, Sarah and Abraham. According to her cousin, Dennis Hanks, in her last moments Nancy called her children to her side and begged them to be good and kind to others.

What went through this poor mother's mind in her dying moments? Worries over her children? A prayer to God that they would be safe? A dying hope that they might rise above her poverty and be successful? Painful regret that she had not done better for them? Perhaps she died believing she had failed.

The poet, Rosemary Benet, imagined a grieving and concerned Nancy Hanks coming back to the community she left behind and trying to find out what became of her son, Abraham.

If Nancy Hanks came back as a ghost,
Seeking news of what she loved most,
She'd ask first, "Where's my son?
What's happened to Abe? What's he done?"

"Poor little Abe, left all alone
Except for Tom, who's a rolling stone;
He was only nine, the year I died.
I remember still how hard he cried."

"Scraping along in a little shack,
With hardly a shirt to cover his back,
And a prairie wind to blow him down,
Or pinching times if he went to town."

"You wouldn't know about my son?
Did he grow tall? Did he have fun?
Did he learn to read? Did he get to town?
Do you know his name? Did he get on?"

Certainly Nancy Hanks could not have imagined the profound impact her little boy would have upon America and the entire world. Like her, we forget that God has a plan for us and our children. When we place them, ourselves and our life's work in his loving and able hands – and do our best – then we can leave the results with God.

Another poet, Julius Silberger, felt Rosemary Benet's poem had to have a proper reply and wrote:

Yes, Nancy Hanks, the news we will tell
Of your Abe whom you loved so well.
You asked first, "Where's my son?"
He lives in the heart of everyone.

Too often we judge our life a failure before its final impact can be assessed. The Scripture tells us not to pass judgment on our own lives or on someone else's prematurely, for not until the day of eternity will God bring to light the quality of our life's work and the hidden impact it has had on others (1 Corinthians 4:5).

PRAYER: Dear Father in heaven, help me to do my best to do my duty and to leave failure and success in your hands. Amen.

May 12

THE HEART OF THE MATTER

The South African film director Jamie Uys' 1980 movie hit, *The Gods Must Be Crazy*, portrays a dramatic clash of cultures as the Bushman Xi's peaceful co-existence with the harsh Kalahari Desert is interrupted by a small, but profound object – a virtual icon of Western Culture. This small object seems to bring untold evil upon Xi and his family. Before Xi and his family enjoyed peace and harmony. Then "the evil thing" came. Suddenly everyone became selfish, thoughtless, angry and hostile toward one another. The family became filled with strife. What was this evil icon of western civilization, this source of demonic power? *A Coke bottle!*

Obviously, whatever the filmmaker's intent, there is nothing inherently evil about a *Coca Cola* bottle. It was just a passive object that everyone wanted, but did not want to share. The true source of evil among Xi and his family of Bushmen is the same source of evil among us all. The Scripture explains the true source of evil in society: It's not lack of education, not the type of government we have or don't have. The evil is not Capitalism, it's not gender, and it's not even poverty. The evil is sin in the human heart: "The heart of man is deceitful above all things and desperately wicked, who can know it. I the Lord search the heart, I try the mind; to render to everyone according to his deeds." (Jeremiah 17:9-10) Thomas Paine once said, "Power corrupts and absolute power corrupts absolutely." The reality, however, is that power merely gives free rein to the corruption that already exists in the human heart and it must be restrained – either by a moral voice and self-controlling spirit within, or by a written code and the threat of force from without.

Humankind's problem is a heart problem, a spiritual problem. And God's remedy? Radical (spiritual) heart surgery. After his own moral failures, King David cried out to God: "Cleanse me from my sin. … Against Thee, Thee only have I sinned and done what is evil in thy sight. …Behold I was brought forth in iniquity and in sin my mother conceived me. …Create in me a clean heart, O God, and renew a steadfast spirit within me." (Psalm 51:2, 5, 10) That prayer is appropriate for us all and it is a prayer that God will answer. Don't blame circumstances, others, your parents or your spouse for the misery of your soul. The root of the problem is in you and you must allow God to confront it with the cure.

PRAYER: Almighty and merciful Father, here and now I confess to you my own sinfulness and imperfections. Please forgive and heal my sin-sick soul. Create in me a new heart, a clean heart and make me a brand new person by the power of the risen Son of God, Jesus Christ. Amen.

May 13

HOW FAR CAN YOU GO?

The massive granite sentinels of Yosemite National Park, California, provide an important spiritual lesson in the believer's life. Consider the spectacular Half Dome – a granite monolith (8,836 feet high) that rises more than 4,700 feet above the Yosemite Valley floor.

The Dome's curved top can be deceptively dangerous, leading those atop it to believe they can inch further and further forward to look below. Before one realizes it, he can easily step to a point where he loses his balance or cannot stop himself and plunges headlong to his death. Far safer is the Dome's face – a crest that marks a sheer 4,000-foot cliff. The Dome's crest has no gradual descending grade, but a distinct edge that marks a point across which no one may pass without perishing.

Another such granite monolith is Moro Rock (6,725 feet high), in California's Sequoia National Park. This granite outcrop also has a rounded top that leads to sheer drops on all sides, in excess of 1000 feet. But at the top of this granite dome are parallel rails that mark a place of safety between them. Obviously, if a climber steps just outside the rail, he will not die. In fact, if he steps several feet away from the rails, lightening will not strike from heaven. But somewhere beyond the rails – unknown to the climber – is an unmarked point, past which the climber will lose his balance and plummet to his death.

All of us would prefer temptations that can be marked by distinct lines – boundaries that mark the difference between life and death. We'd like to know exactly how far we can go without perishing. But no such temptations exist. Our entrapment in sin is subtle, a gradual descending grade that, if we proceed in it, leads to enslavement and death. Where is the point of no return? The Scripture does not tell us – it may be different for each person. But what Scripture does provide are rules, boundaries that mark places of safety in our lives. These rules, like the Ten Commandments (Exodus 20), are not meant to deprive of us of pleasure, but to keep us from passing too far off the gradual decline of sin and from plummeting to eternal destruction. They mark out for us the path of safe passage through this life. The Scripture says, "Those who love thy law have great peace, and nothing will make them stumble." (Psalm 119:165)

PRAYER: Dear Father in heaven, help me to realize that your commandments are not meant to harm me or make me unhappy, but to do me good. Open my eyes to the dangers of disregarding them and help me to follow the straight path they mark out for me. Amen.

May 14

GOD IS MINDFUL OF YOUR CONTRIBUTION

Can you imagine a world without Shakespeare? No *Romeo and Juliet*, no *Macbeth*, no *Hamlet*, no *King Lear*, no *Otello* no *Henry IV*, *Midsummer Night's Dream*, nor any of the other 38 plays or 154 sonnets attributed to the greatest writer of the English language? The fact is, these literary masterpieces of Shakespeare nearly perished with him, were it not for two of his devoted friends.

Like so many other artists and literary geniuses, William Shakespeare was never fully appreciated in his own lifetime. It took subsequent generations to grasp the stellar quality of his work. But those generations would never have ever heard the name Shakespeare were it not for two men, John Heminge and Henry Condell. John and Henry had been actors under Shakespeare's direction and sometimes alongside – for Shakespeare acted as well. After Shakespeare's death in 1616, they wanted to keep his memory alive and share his plays with the rest of the world. So for seven years Heminge and Condell rooted through theaters to search for copies of Shakespeare's plays. Fortunately, as actors they themselves had memorized the lines of most of his plays. From their memories and from what they recovered in the dusty cabinets of theaters, John Heminge and Henry Condell compiled and published *Mr. William Shakespeares Comedies, Histories, & Tragedies* in 1623. Though they have since been forgotten, they succeeded in their mission: "to keep the memory of so worthy a Friend & Fellow alive, as was our Shakespeare."

In a way, these two unsung heroes had a share in all the subsequent success and acclaim that was lavished upon Shakespeare. Indeed, all those who serve in a support role and who work behind the scenes to ensure the success of others share in that success.

A famous clergyman was traveling from New York City to Los Angeles on a certain Veterans Day. At John F. Kennedy Airport a veteran approached him, soliciting donations in exchange for a poppy. But the man was late for his plane and had to dash to the gate: "I'm so sorry," he told the veteran, "I have to run to catch a plane." The pastor also had to catch connecting flights in Chicago and Denver, and in both places was also approached by veterans selling poppies for a donation. In his haste, the pastor had to turn them down, feeling increasingly guilty. When the pastor finally reached LA, his first act (even before picking up his baggage) was to hunt down a veteran, give a hefty donation, and get a poppy, which he proudly placed on the lapel of his jacket.

To his audience that night at a religious gathering, the pastor shared his experience and then asked the question: "Who sold me the poppy?" His answer: they had all sold him the poppy, though only the last veteran, who did the least but made the sale, got the credit.

Even so, there are many unsung heroes out there – unseen by people, but known by God – who are always supporting the success of others. But the success of those they support is their success as well. They may feel like the farmer who faithfully tills the soil, plants the seed, and nurtures the growth only to see someone else reap the harvest and receive the credit. But God sees everything and he will reward us for our faithfulness to him. "Your heavenly Father who sees in secret, will reward you openly." (Matthew 6:4, 6, 18)

PRAYER: Dear Father in heaven, I thank you that you see the small and humble deeds that are done in secret. Help me to be faithful in the tasks you have given me. And even if I never enjoy the limelight, may I be content to make my contribution to the cause of justice, freedom and truth, that my life may be spent in a worthy endeavor. Grant that, when I stand before your throne, you will be pleased with my life and accept me into your heavenly kingdom. Amen.

May 15

HOW DO YOU MEASURE SUCCESS?

He was one of America's greatest agricultural scientists and one of America's foremost educators. He is credited with saving the economy of the South. His innovations in crop rotations and his introduction of sweet potatoes, cabbage, soybeans, peanuts, and many other beneficial crops, to supplement the South's dependency on tobacco and cotton, virtually saved southern agriculture. At a time when the self-proclaimed "agricultural genius" of the Soviet Union, Trofim Denisovich Lysenko, was destroying the Soviet economy and setting science decades behind the times, this true scientist had turned the peanut industry into a $200 million-a-year business.

But this humble farmer was also a man of profound faith who credited God for his seemingly magical power and insight into botany and agriculture. He believed that God opened his mind to discover manifold uses for the simplest crops: more than 100 uses for the sweet potato and more than 300 uses for the peanut.

We are talking, of course, about Dr. George Washington Carver. But what most Americans don't know is that his life began in slavery in 1864 – the year after the slaves were supposedly "emancipated." Back then his name was simply "George." And life for George was fraught with peril. His father died before his birth and he and his mother were kidnapped by slave catchers when he was just an infant. Though his owner rescued him in exchange for a horse, his mother was never heard from again. George himself was a sickly child and frequently ill. What future could such a child have with everything against him?

It seemed as if life had begun to shine on him when he found lodging with a German immigrant couple, Moses and Susan Carver, who ran a farm in Missouri. But his insatiable thirst for knowledge drove him to leave home at the age of ten and travel ten miles away and live in a *barn* in order to attend school. Somehow, against all odds, George made it through high school. He earned his bachelor's and master's degrees, and, in 1894, obtained a high-paying faculty position in the agricultural department of Iowa State University – the very first African-American on the Iowa State faculty. He had finally made it, right?

But George Washington Carver didn't measure success in the size of his paycheck or in the accolades he received from people or in the prestige of the college in which he taught. When Booker T. Washington invited him to take a huge salary cut by accepting the task of teaching at the Tuskegee Normal and Industrial Institute for Negroes in poverty-ravaged Alabama in 1897, *he accepted!* And throughout his illustrious career, Dr. Carver turned down multiple offers for better-paying jobs – one of them from Thomas Edison in 1917 for $100,000 a year – in order to make a positive difference where his help was needed most. And what a difference he made! Near the end of his life he handed over his life-savings, $33,000, to establish the George Washington Carver Foundation at Tuskegee Institute. In accordance to his final wishes, at his death, the remainder of his estate – nearly $30,000 – was also donated to the school. President Calvin Coolidge once said, "A man is not honored for what he receives, but for what he gives." For that reason we honor the man who turned down so much to benefit so many. Truly a stunningly successful man!

Our Lord once admonished us: "Do not lay up for yourselves treasure upon earth, where moths and rust destroy and where thieves break in and steal; but lay up for yourselves treasure in heaven." He also said, what shall it profit a man if he gains the whole world and loses his own soul." In the light of eternity's values, success cannot be equated in money, but in doing God's will for our lives and being a blessing to our fellow human beings.

PRAYER: Dear Father in heaven, help me to live and pursue goals with eternity's values in mind. Amen.

May 16

WHOSE OPINION REALLY MATTERS?

Robert Heft was a 17-year-old high school student in Alaska. When Congress began deliberation in 1958 on admitting Alaska and Hawaii as the 49th and 50th States, his teacher gave him, and the rest of the class, this assignment. Design a new flag from the current 48-star flag.

In 1958, the U.S. Flag had an arrangement of 6 horizontal rows of 8 stars. Robert's design arranged staggered rows of stars – At the top, a horizontal row of 6, then a staggered horizontal row of 5: A total of five horizontal rows of 6 stars and 4 horizontal rows of 5 stars, totaling 50 stars. Robert's arrangement had surprising symmetry. If you counted the rows diagonally, they used only odd numbers: 1-3-5-7-9-9-7-5-3-1. One diagonal row of 9 stars reached the lower left corner of the field of blue, while the other diagonal row of 9 stars reached the upper right corner of the field of blue. Robert was quite pleased with this design.

But Robert Heft's excitement received a dousing from his teacher. She critiqued his work as "unimaginative" and gave him a B-. Robert refused to accept her judgment. He rejected the rejection and sent his design to his Congressman in Washington, D.C. The Congressman was impressed with Robert's idea and submitted it as a proposal in the event that both Hawaii and Alaska became States. They did - in 1959. And Robert Heft's "unimaginative" design for a new National Flag won unanimous approval from those whose opinions really mattered.

God has blessed every human being with an assortment of gifts, talents and special qualities. He entrusted every one of us with some power - in our heads, in our hearts, and in our hands - and He wants us to use this power to bless those around us. Certainly there will always be people who will not appreciate our gifts or the contribution we can make.

Forget them and focus on your Creator, Who designed you to the most precise specifications and Whose opinion of you is very high. Believe in the God Who believes in you and fulfill His plan for your life. In the Psalms David wrote: "I praise you, O Lord, for I am fearfully and wonderfully made," and "All the days ordained for me were written in Your book before one of them came to be" (Psalm 139:14, 16).

PRAYER: Dear heavenly Father, I acknowledge you as my Creator and as the source of all that is good within me. Please help me to rise above the criticism of others, who wish to limit me, that I may use my God-given talents to bless Your people. Amen.

May 17

GETTING THROUGH THE TOUGH TIMES

It is one of the most underestimated, least utilized, and yet most powerful tools we have for survival in the tough times. What is it? Our memory. In a *Science Digest* article entitled "The Magic of Memory," Laurence Cherry says: "Our memories are probably our most cherished possessions. More than anything else we own, they belong uniquely to us, defining our personalities and our views of the world. Each of us can summon thousands of memories at will: our first day at school, a favorite family pet, a summer house we loved." Oscar Wilde had all this in mind when he said, "Memory is the diary that we all carry about in us." And the German writer Jean Paul Richter said, "Our memory is the only paradise out of which we cannot be driven."

Happy memories can be a paradise for us in difficult times, which is why it is so important to build happy memories with our families and loved ones when we have the opportunity – on mid-tour leave, in-between deployments, on four-day weekends (when we get to observe them). Too often we opt for more "practical and profitable" uses of our time or we dismiss such family fun times as unnecessary. But having a treasury of pleasant experiences stashed away in our memories will sustain us and our marriages through the grinding tough times. James Matthew Barrie once explained: "God gives us memory so that we may have roses in December." The Scripture says, "Whatever is true, whatever is honorable, whatever is right, whatever is pure, whatever is lovely, whatever is of good repute, if there is any excellence and if anything is praiseworthy, think on these things." (Philippians 4:8)

PRAYER: Dear Father in heaven, grant me the wisdom to build a storehouse of happy memories with my family and friends that my memory may serve as a paradise into which I may find relief. Amen.

May 18

DO YOU KNOW ANY SUPERHEROES?

It's not all that fun being a superhero. Being a superhero has serious drawbacks. That was the theme of the 2004 computer-animated movie sensation, "The Incredibles."

For one thing, the work of a superhero is never done and it is agonizingly repetitious. The mess you clean up today, reappears tomorrow. That's what Mr. Incredible said: "No matter how many times you save the world, it always manages to get in jeopardy again. Sometimes I just want it to "stay saved" – you know - for a little bit. I feel like the maid sometimes. "I just cleaned up this mess, can we keep it clean – for ten minutes?""

Another dilemma that superheroes face is that the person they save today may become an enemy tomorrow. Remember Buddy, aka "Incrediboy" – that obnoxious kid whose life Mr. Incredible saved? Years later he became the superhero's arch-nemesis.

Another reason why being a superhero is difficult is that the public does not always appreciate their contribution. In fact, many citizens didn't even consider their calling a valid one. That's what Mr. Incredible found out. Who would have ever thought that a superhero would be sued for saving people? But it happened. And what followed was a virtual feeding frenzy of greedy lawyers, an irresponsible media, and ungrateful citizens. To add insult to injury, politicians in the nation's capital began to vilify the superheroes and identify them (not criminals) as the "real problem" in our society. As one smug politician put it: "It is time for their 'secret identity' to become their only identity, time for them to join us, or go away."

But "going away" proved difficult for the superheroes. They had a very difficult time adjusting to civilian life. This was the case for Frozone, for Gaserbeam, and especially for Mr. Incredible.

Do you see a parallel here, between these computer-animated superheroes and the real superheroes of America? You know who I'm talking about. I'm speaking of those superheroes that do the never-ending job of keeping the peace or putting out wars that seem to spring up everywhere, that are forced to fight enemies whom they once helped, the superheroes that go unappreciated – even vilified – by the citizens whose lives they save, and whose contribution is dismissed and whose existence is considered unnecessary. Yeah, you know the superheroes I'm talking about. Chances are that you're one of them yourself – or you're married to one.

True, it's not easy being a superhero. But it's the calling God's placed on your life. Sure, you'll rarely have the popular support of your fellow citizens. But neither the fate of our country, nor of freedom, nor of civilization itself is ever secured by those who wait for public support to back them up. Our freedoms and our way of life are secured by those men and women of action who confront and conquer evil. It's always been that way. It always will be. As one American put it, "America will only be the land of the free as long as it is the home of the brave."

The Scripture also speaks of superheroes. "And what more shall I say? For time will fail me if I tell of Gideon, Barak, Samson, Jephthah, or David (all soldiers)... who by faith conquered kingdoms, performed acts of righteousness (interesting – war and righteousness are grouped together) ... escaped the edge of the sword, from weakness were made strong, became mighty in war, and put foreign armies to flight." (Hebrews 11:32-34) They did all this by faith in God – God who is more than your greatest fan. He's your greatest friend.

PRAYER: Dear Father in heaven, I confess to You my faults, my frailty, my sin and my humanity. Forgive my shortcomings, O God. Please empower me and help me to serve faithfully and honorably in the calling You have placed on my life – the calling to be a soldier in the cause of freedom, justice and truth. Amen.

May 19

THE HYPOCRISY IN PACIFISM

Janette Rankin, a Republican from Montana, had the distinction of being the first woman elected to the United States House of Representatives. She took office on April 2, 1917 – three years before women in America were allowed to vote.

But Congresswoman Rankin has another distinction. On December 8, 1941 she was the only member of Congress to vote against a declaration of war after the attack on Pearl Harbor. This was not the first time she had voted against war. In 1917 she had also opposed America's involvement in WWI – a decision that so displeased her voters that she lost the following election.

But on the day after the attack on Pearl Harbor, December 7, 1941, things were different. America was shaken out of its isolationism and realized the two oceans were no longer a defense. An enemy could now "reach out and touch us" with malicious intent.

The public and the press were outraged at the Congresswoman and believed her actions were treasonous. When she left the chambers of Congress after the vote, Rankin had to barricade herself in a phone booth against an angry mob of protesters. Meanwhile from the phone booth she called security and requested the police come and escort her out of the Capitol Building.

As armed guards fought their way through the crowds and brought the Congresswoman to safety, few took notice of the apparent display of hypocrisy on Ms. Rankin's part – hypocrisy that many professed pacifists exhibit, hypocrisy that condemns the use of force under all and any circumstances, and then seeks it for one's own protection.

But the Congresswoman's own dependence on the use of force went unnoticed, unfortunately, by Ms. Rankin herself. Janette Rankin remained rigidly fixed in her pacifism – even though she briefly abandoned it when her own safety was threatened.

Those who cite the Bible to condemn the men and women who defend our Nation tend to overlook one important biblical truth: That the military is an arm of divinely authorized government. "Submit to the governing authorities," wrote the Apostle Paul, "for those powers that exist have been ordained by God" and they serve as his messengers that He sends forth to deliver the oppressed and punish the wicked. Paul wrote that God places a sword (the armed forces) in the hand of government to execute his divine justice among men (Romans 13:1-7).

Obviously not everyone is called, or even capable, of serving in the military. But we should support those who do. The worst hypocrisy is to condemn those assigned the grizzly and daunting task of confronting and conquering the enemies of civilization, and then partake of the freedoms, equality, and way of life those men and women in uniform have secured. John Stuart Mill, the British philosopher and statesman, eloquently stated:

"War is an ugly thing, but not the ugliest of things. The decayed and degraded state of moral and patriotic feeling which thinks that nothing is worth war is much worse. The person who has nothing for which he is willing to fight, nothing which is more important than his own personal safety, is a miserable creature and has no chance of being free unless made and kept so by the exertions of better men than himself."

PRAYER: Almighty and merciful Father, we humbly confess our frailty and failures and plead your forgiveness and mercy. Please bless our nation. Make it morally straight and spiritually strong. Guide America on the path of righteousness – for righteousness exalts a nation, but sin is a reproach on any people. Bless also our men and women of the Armed Forces. Please grant them success in their mission, safety in conflict, and a joyous reunion with their families and loved ones. Above all, may Your rule and reign come quickly to our world and may the knowledge of the Lord cover the earth as the waters cover the sea. Amen.

May 20

OUR NECESSARY DEFENSE

Minutes after David Vetter was born on September 21, 1971, he was placed in a sterile cocoon. Everything that came in contact with his world - food, water, diapers, clothing – had to be sterilized with special cleaning agents. Why such extreme measures? David was born with a rare genetic disorder called *Severe Combined Immune Deficiency Syndrome.* As a result, David would be confined for the rest of his life to a plastic germ-free environment, becoming well-known as "The Boy in the Plastic Bubble." Only after NASA donated a $50,000-protective "space suit" for David to wear, could he venture to the outside world. But he only made seven such trips in his lifetime.

As hopes for a cure diminished, doctors considered removing David from the protective bubble and placing him on a regimen of antibiotics and gamma globulin. But his parents resisted the idea, convinced it would condemn David to certain death. Finally, when David became desperately in need of a bone marrow transplant, he was removed from his bubble. Unfortunately, the bone marrow donated by his sister Katherine contained traces of a dormant virus.

If there was ever any doubt as to the reality of deadly germs or of David's inability to fight them off, it was quickly dispelled. Once exposed, the virus (and a host of other germs) spread throughout his body producing hundreds of cancerous tumors. He immediately developed a fever, with vomiting and diarrhea. On February 22, 1984, just fifteen days after stepping out of his protective world, David Vetter died at the age of twelve.

The ability of our bodies to fight off continual invasions of outside organisms is truly amazing. But it is also taken for granted. Our immunity system is so efficient in maintaining our health that it's easy to dismiss its importance or to acknowledge the threat of disease, virus and bacteria – that is, until we get sick.

In a similar way, America has gone *so long* without any serious threat to its freedoms and way of life that it often fails to appreciate its own defenses or even to acknowledge the existence of its real and potential enemies. Like rich children who have never known poverty and who fail to appreciate the sacrifices that secured their wealth, Americans are rich with freedom and too often take their freedom for granted.

May God help us all to support America's defenses – our men and women in uniform – and to pray for our nation that it may ever remain vigilant, righteous, and free! The Scripture says, "If my people, who are called by my name, shall humble themselves and pray, and seek my face and turn from their wicked ways; then will I hear from heaven and will forgive their sins and will heal their land." (2 Chronicles 7:14)

PRAYER: Dear Father in heaven, *please bless America.* Heal our nation of its many divisions and mend its every flaw. Turn the hearts of Americans to you in faith and repentance and to each other in love and reconciliation. Raise up godly men and women to fill the ranks of leadership in our government, that they may lead our nation on the path of righteousness. Please bless and protect the men and women of our Armed Forces. Grant them success in their mission and bring them safely home to their families. Keep our nation strong and free, dear Father, and lead our nation from victory to victory as your instrument of freedom, justice, and peace. Amen.

May 21

WHEN IT'S EASY TO MAKE EXCUSES

If anybody could have made excuses it was Francesca. If anyone had reason to call it quits, it was she.

Francesca was the proverbial runt of the litter – born two months premature in 1850, when Italy's infant mortality rate was horrifying. Even though she survived infancy, she remained frail and sickly throughout childhood and early adulthood.

At six years old, however, Francesca believed God was calling her to bring the gospel to China. Everyone, including her family mocked her idea. At twelve she took a vow of chastity and planned to become a nun. Everyone made fun of that idea too. When she reached the minimum age of eighteen, she applied to join the Daughters of the Sacred Heart, but was rejected for being too sickly. For six years she continued to apply, and for six years she was repeatedly rejected. Rather than brood and be bitter, Francesca filled her hours with good deeds, teaching children and ministering to the sick.

Finally, six years later Francesca gained acceptance into the order. But did she find support to take the gospel to China? No. No one took the request of a pint-sized sickly nun serious and she was given menial tasks with the local populace. Finally, a superior advised her that if she wanted to be part of a missionary order she should form one herself – something not likely to happen. Yet that's what Francesca did. In 1880, she and a half-dozen other nuns formed the Missionary Sisters of the Sacred Heart. Then after establishing foundations in Milan, Rome and other Italian cities, she again sought approval to take the gospel to China. But her dreams finally were crushed when Pope Leo XIII sent her instead to – New York City, where he wanted her to help run an orphanage, school and convent.

Yet when she arrived in the strange land of America, she found that the plans to establish those facilities had fallen through and was told to go back from where she came. At this point Francesca had received nothing but opposition to the dreams God had placed in her heart. How easy it would have been to conclude she was never meant to serve God and to make excuses for not doing God's will.

Yet Francesca had come as a missionary to America and in America she would stay. She quickly solved the problems with those failing plans for the school, orphanage, and convent and established those facilities. And over the next twenty-eight years Sister Francesca Cabrini – better known as Mother Cabrini - established more than seventy hospitals, schools, and orphanages in the United States, Spain, France, England, and South America. The impact of this little dynamo of a woman was immense. All because she refused to make excuses or give up in the face of adversity.[xxxv]

All of us will face opposition to our dreams and plans. And we, too, will have plenty of opportunities to make excuses for doing nothing. But the Scripture admonishes us: "Have I not commanded you? Be strong and courageous! Do not tremble or be dismayed, for the LORD your God is with you wherever you go." (Joshua 1:9)

PRAYER: Dear Father in heaven, help me to persevere in the face of adversity, opposition and discouragement. Motivate me, energize me, and inspire me to press onward to the dream you've placed in my heart. Amen.

WE CAN SIT BY AND WATCH
OR STAND UP AND HELP

She saved the lives of everyone aboard a Greyhound bus –
packed with 38 passengers, most of them children. 16-year old Laura
Simpson of Queensland, Australia was on an all-night bus trip to her
home from St. Margaret's Anglican Girls School in Brisbane.

At 3 AM, while most of the students and passengers were asleep,
the bus was traveling on a remote highway between two distant towns.
Suddenly the bus veered off the road, ran over a sign, bounced through a
dry creek bed, then headed straight for a river. Laura, saw the driver
was having a seizure. His body had stiffened and his foot was braced
against the gas pedal, causing the bus to accelerate to its doom.

Laura raced to the front, grabbed the wheel and steered the wild
bus away from the river, while she screamed at the driver to wake up.
He awoke enough to take his foot off the gas – but Laura continued to
drive. She steered the bus back to the road, brought it to a halt. Using
her flashlight Laura then directed all the passengers to disembark and
then phoned the police for help and Greyhound for a replacement driver.

Authorities notified parents of the event and that their children
were safe, though delayed. And Laura Simpson? She had used her
phone to make so many emergency calls that, when it was all over and
she wanted to speak with her parents, her phone battery was dead. She
had to wait four hours on the roadside for a replacement driver and an
eight-hour journey to arrive home.

Laura Simpson's quick thinking and desire to help averted a
horrific disaster. But what if she had chosen to be a mere spectator?
What if she had sat passively and watched the bus drive to its
destruction? What if she had been content to criticize the terrible
driving, but offered no help?

Absurd questions? Yet people do just that every day. They
passively watch their communities, churches, and organizations struggle.
But they choose to find fault rather than to help. May God help us to put
our hands to work instead of our tongues, and to support our overworked
leadership carry the load.

The Scripture tells us, "Obey your leaders and submit to their
authority. They keep watch over you as men who must give an account.
Obey them so that their work will be a joy, not a burden, for that would
be of no advantage to you." (Hebrews 13:17)

PRAYER: Dear Father in heaven, open my eyes and help me to be sensitive to the needs of those who lead me. I don't want to be a thorn in their side, but a joy to their heart. Please, Lord, may it be so. Amen.

May 23

IS FAILURE NECESSARY?

Jonas Salk attempted 200 unsuccessful vaccines for polio before he came up with one that worked. Somebody once asked him: *"How did it feel to fail 200 times trying to invent a vaccine for polio?"* His response: *"I never failed 200 times at anything in my life. My family taught me never to use that word. I simply discovered 200 ways how not to make a vaccine for polio."* (John Ortberg)

Consider how Thomas Edison looked at failure. In his single invention of the incandescent light, Edison amassed more than 2,500 failures in the process. This was largely due to his painstaking "trial and error" process. At times he was criticized over his "inefficient" methodology: *"How can you justify so many failures for a single invention?"* Edison's reply: *"Failures? I never failed once. Inventing the light bulb turned out to be a 2,500-step process and I was persistent enough to take all 2,500 steps."* And look at the results – Thomas Edison still holds the record for the most patented inventions – 1,093! And Jonas Salk saved millions of lives!

It's all about reframing failure and seeing it as a necessary component of success and growth. Consider the solemn caution of J. Wallace Hamilton in Leadership magazine: "The increase of suicides, alcoholics, and even some forms of nervous breakdowns is evidence that many people are training for success when they should be training for failure. Failure is far more common than success; poverty is more prevalent than wealth, and disappointment more normal than arrival."

We need to see that failure, even spiritual and moral failure, does not constitute "the end." In fact, God can incorporate our failures into his plan for our lives and into his molding of a Christ-like character within us. Why else did Peter's denial of the Lord ultimately make him a more compassionate and effective apostle? Why else did Paul's reflection on his own persecution and murder of Christians drive him to consider himself the least of the apostles (1 Corinthians 15:9), the least of the believers (Ephesians 3:8), and ultimately, the worst of sinners (1 Timothy 1:15) – developing within him a profound sense of humility. Only then, could Paul forgive and believe in others (like John Mark) who had wronged him (2 Timothy 4:11). It's a fact, God *can* and *does* use failure in our lives for our growth and ultimate good. If you fail, it's not the end. Rise from failure and allow God to bring out an ultimate good in your life.

PRAYER: God of Hope, no matter how dark my path and how checkered my record becomes, please help me to rise up, march on and grow more and more into the image of your Son, Jesus Christ. Amen.

May 24

JOIN THE HUMAN RACE

The opening credits of modern movies reveal a great deal about human nature. For instance, star actors often jockey vigorously for "above title" credits (i.e. for their names to appear before the title of the movie appears), or for "separate cards" (i.e. for their name to appear on the screen by itself rather than to be one among many names), or even for how long their name remains on the screen.

Directors are more subtle. Thinking that the best is saved for last, they elect to place their names at the very end of the credits. However, if they sense that the movie they themselves directed is going to be a dud, they do something different. When directors believe their movie will fail, they sometimes appeal to the Directors Guild of America that a pseudonym be used in place of their own name.

One of the most frequent pseudonyms to have appeared in movies was Alan Smithie. Alan Smithie was named as director for about 50 bombs, whose directors abandoned them and wanted no credit for a failure. Movies like *Death of a Gunfighter* (1969), *Burn, Hollywood, Burn* (1997), and *American History X* (1998) were all critical and financial failures that became children of the imaginary director Alan Smithie. John F. Kennedy was correct when he said, "Success has many fathers, only failure is an orphan." Maybe he had the Bay of Pigs disaster in mind, but his words accurately describe the human tendency to take credit for success but shirk responsibility for failure.

But that puts us in a dilemma. For just as we tend to avoid accepting blame and responsibility for failure, it is just as true that failure and sin are part of human nature. And according to the Scripture, the first step into the Kingdom of God is to acknowledge our humanness, that we are sinners. "For all have sinned and fall short of the glory of God," the scripture tells us (Romans 3:23), and "Whoever conceals his sin shall not prosper, but whoever confesses and forsakes it shall find mercy." (Proverbs 28:13) Then why not do as God says? Join the human race and admit your humanity. Admit your propensity for greed, for racism, for bigotry, and for everything else that you profess to despise. We do not overcome evil by denying its existence in our lives. The first step to victory is to admit our weakness and to seek God's help and forgiveness.

PRAYER: Dear Father in heaven, here and now I take my place with the rest of sinful humanity. I admit my sins, my racism, my sexism, my bigotry, and my complete humanity. Please forgive me, please cleanse me, and please transform and strengthen me to live a life pleasing to You. Amen.

May 25

KEEP THE BIG PICTURE IN VIEW

How do we handle the most painful events of life? How do we make sense out of tragedy of every fallen Soldier? Does the promise of Romans 8:28 even apply: "And we know that God works all things together for the good of those who love him, who have been called according to his purpose?" In the light of life's tragedies and or the dreadful reckoning of casualties since September 11, 2001, how can such a promise be valid?

The secret is to view life's most painful events as components of a greater purpose and as parts of a bigger picture. Let me explain.

Consider the miracle that takes place in a shipyard. Almost every part of our great oceangoing vessels is made of steel. If you take any single part—be it a steel plate out of the hull or the huge rudder or the propeller—and throw it into the ocean, it will sink. Steel doesn't float! But when the shipbuilders are finished, when the last plate has been riveted in place, then that massive steel ship is virtually unsinkable.

Taken by themselves, life's most painful events are senseless. Throw any individual tragedy into the sea of Romans 8:28, and it will sink. Yet we have the promise that the Eternal Shipbuilder will put all the pieces together, according to his perfect design, and will somehow work it all out for our eternal good.

This is true of every event of our lives. Life's individual events are mere components of an entire life and their meaning cannot be understood except in relation to the whole. Neither the single piece of a jigsaw puzzle, the single stroke of an artist's brush, or the single dark thread of a tapestry has any meaning by itself. Yet they are all necessary and each can only be understood in relation to the "big picture."

The same is also true of painful and tragic events on a national and global level. The American Civil War, from 1861-1865, was our most costly war - 600,000 men died on both sides. Examined all by itself, out of its context of the American struggle to rid itself of slavery and to forge the individual states into a nation, yes, the Civil War seems not worth the cost. The 3000 casualties that V Corps suffered in just two hours of fighting on Omaha Beach on June 6, 1944, may seem like a meaningless tragedy. But it was an essential, though painful, part of the great crusade in Europe to free the world of Nazi domination and secure a future free of its evils. In the words inscribed on a Normandy Monument: "They gave up all their tomorrows for your today."

Many would rather forget the painful struggles in Korea (33,000 American lives lost from 1950-1953) and Vietnam (58,000 lives lost from 1961-1973). But the true meaning of those conflicts lies in their relation to the greater Cold War. For without taking those stands against Communist aggression, America would not have been victorious in the Cold War - which was once condemned as un-winnable!

And so it is in our present struggle in the Global War on Terrorism. Most Americans would rather forget the terrorist attacks against us on September 11, 2001 and the evil that inspired them. But this enemy will not simply go away if we ignore him. We must confront and conquer terrorism. And when facing the cost of the present conflicts in Iraq and Afghanistan we need to keep in sight the bigger picture – the future of America and the free world, which only belongs to those willing to pay the price of vigilance and sacrifice to secure it.

May God grant us patience, strength and wisdom not to lose heart in the midst of the conflict, nor to lose sight of the glorious freedom that will follow if we remain faithful and united!

PRAYER: Almighty and merciful Father, please bless America in the midst of its struggles against terrorism from without and dissension from within. Mend it's every flaw. Turn the hearts of Americans to You in faith and repentance and to each other in love and reconciliation. Bless our brothers and sisters in arms who are deployed to war. Protect them and grant them success in their hazardous mission. Raise up godly men and women to fill the ranks of leadership in our government that they may lead our country in the paths of peace and progress. Raise America to true greatness and lead us from victory to victory as Your instrument of peace and your torch of freedom – in Iraq and throughout the world. Amen.

May 26

LIFE HAS ITS SEASONS

The giant sequoia tree does not produce cones until it is 175-200 years old – the most delayed sexual maturity in all nature. And when it finally does spout cones, they are tiny – not much bigger than a marble – and carry seeds weighing only 1/3000th of an ounce. In its long life, up to 200 of the sequoia's years are fruitless.

There is a variety of bamboo, *Phyllostachys bambusoides*, which only flowers every 120 years! And it does so in unison with all other plants of the same species, regardless of when each individual plant was seeded or transplanted.

Mayflies, after hatching, will spend one to three years developing as naiads. But as adults they live only one day – in which time they molt twice, mate, and lay eggs in water.

The periodical cicada (*Magicicada septendecim* and *Magicicada cassini*) are known respectively as the 17-year and 13-year locusts. They spend many years (98% of their life) as grubs burrowing in the ground before they finally burst upon the scene to sing their shrill calls, mate and lay eggs in the few weeks they live as adults.

So what's the point? The point is that many living things, most in fact, go through long periods of fruitlessness and obscurity – by God's design – before they encounter shorts bursts of fruitfulness. The same is true for people.

There once was a Persian king who wanted to teach his four sons not to pass judgment too quickly. At his command, the eldest son made a winter journey to see a pear tree across the valley. When spring came, the next oldest was sent on the same journey.

Summer followed, and the king sent his third son. After the youngest made his visit to the pear tree in the autumn, the king called them together and asked each son to describe the tree.

The first son said it looked like an ugly, old stump. The second disagreed, describing its blossoms were as beautiful as roses. The third son declared it as lovely – large and green. The fourth son said that they were all wrong. To him it was a tree filled with fruit – luscious, juicy fruit.

"Well, each of you is right," the old king said. Seeing the puzzled look in their eyes, the king went on to explain. "Each of you saw the pear tree in a different season; thus you all correctly described what you saw. The lesson," said the king, "is to withhold your judgment about your life, or anyone else's, until you have seen it in all its seasons."[xxxvi]

And so it is with us. Not every season of our lives is going to be productive and fruitful. And those seasons of fruitlessness do not indicate that our lives are failures or that something is wrong with us. Have patience with yourself and others. Seek God's plan for your life. Do the good that you can. Then leave all the results with God.

PRAYER: Dear Father in heaven, help me to be faithful, even when I cannot see the effects or fruit of my labors. Help me to do the good that I can and to leave the results with you. Amen.

May 27

WHEN WE ARE BROKEN BEYOND REPAIR

God equips his creatures for survival in some absolutely amazing ways. Some of the most remarkable examples are those creatures equipped for regeneration after suffering some traumatic loss. For instance, although all species of starfish can grow back limbs ("rays") that have been lost, some (like the *Asterias vulgaris*) can be torn apart, suffering the loss of more than half its body mass, and still rebuild itself and grow back whatever of its body has been lost. Another species (*Linckia*), can grow back an entire starfish from a single detached limb ("ray").

Perhaps more remarkable is a species of sponge, the Caribbean Red Sponge, that can be pushed through a piece of fabric so that it is broken into thousands of tiny pieces. Instead of perishing, the thousands of pieces reassemble themselves back to its original, whole self and it continues with its life.[xxxvii]

Maybe you and your family feel a little "fragmented," as though you've been broken into pieces or torn asunder by the ravages of life and the upheavals of deployment. To the devastated land of Israel, "I will restore to you the years that the locust and cankerworm have devoured" (Joel 2:25) and "See now that I, I am He, and there is no god besides Me; it is I who put to death and restore to life; it is I who wound, and it is I who heal." (Deuteronomy 32:39) What deployment and the Lord's discipline has broken, God will bind back together and make stronger than ever.

PRAYER: Dear Father in heaven, I feel as though I am broken beyond repair, shattered beyond recognition and that I will never be the same again. Please pick up the shattered fragments of my heart and life and put them back together. Please bind up my broken heart. Amen.

May 28

CLEAN UP YOUR OWN BACKYARD

The *Rainbow Warrior II*, flagship of the Green Peace party, travels the seven seas on a crusade against all those who would dare harm the environment. *Rainbow Warrior II* is always on the lookout for those who slaughter whales or murder baby seals or dump raw sewage into the ocean or litter the earth's waterways. On one 2006 mission to study the effects of global warming upon the coral reefs off the coast of the Philippines, the Rainbow warrior II ran aground on the reef, inflicting significant and irreparable damage on the eco-zone.

This was no isolated incident. In August 1994 the *Columbus Iselin*, was doing environmental work in the Looe Key National Marine Sanctuary, off the Florida Keys. Its mission was to determine the harmful effects of oil spills on the Florida coastal ecosystem, particularly upon its delicate coral reefs. Unfortunately, the *Columbus Iselin* ran aground on the reef, punctured its fuel tanks and spilled two hundred gallons of diesel fuel. Efforts to free the ship from the reef only exacerbated the problem. Huge chunks of living coral were broken off as the ship was pulled free of the reef and large plumes of sand, generated by the ship's propellers, buried portions of the reef.

The Shimohetsugi Fire Department, in southern Japan, was celebrating the final day of its "Fire Awareness Week" observance with a barbeque when disaster struck. The fuel tank for the gas grill was improperly connected and triggered a fire – in the fire station! There were no fatalities, but the two-story fire station was destroyed.

There is nothing wrong with crusading against evil, so long as we begin the crusade in our own backyards, in our own lives, and in our own hearts. Paul the apostle stressed that, in his preaching to others, he was careful to discipline himself and walk circumspectly lest, "while preaching to others, I myself may be disqualified." (1 Corinthians 9:24-27)

PRAYER: Dear Father in heaven, please grant that my sermon to this world will begin in my own heart, lifestyle, and actions. Help me to glorify you, O Lord, in my thoughts, words and deeds. Amen.

May 29

SNARLS VS SMILES

Many have forgotten or never heard of baseball pitcher, Clarence Blethen. He was the mean-spirited, 30-year-old rookie who had the habit of removing his false teeth to make himself look scary and to intimidate his batters. One day, on September 21, 1923, Blethen went to bat, but forgot to take his teeth from his pocket and put them in his mouth. He hit a line drive up centerfield, passed first and slid into second. Although the umpire called him "safe," Clarence cried out in pain. The teeth he had stuck in his pocket were deeply embedded in his "fourth point of contact." In his effort to scare others, Clarence Blethen had quite literally "bitten himself in the butt."

A smile will do far more than a snarl. A kind word is more effective than a cutting remark. Consider the following anonymous bit of wisdom: *"A smile costs nothing, but gives much. It enriches those who receive, without making poorer those who give. It takes but a moment, but the memory of it sometimes lasts forever. None is so rich or mighty that he can get along without it, and none is so poor but that he can be made rich by it. A smile creates happiness in the home, fosters good will in business, and is the outward sign of friendship. It brings rest to the weary, cheer to the discouraged, sunshine to the sad, and it is nature's best antidote for trouble. Yet it cannot be bought, begged, borrowed, or stolen, for it is something that is always given. Some people are too tired to give you a smile. Give them one of yours, as none needs a smile as much as he who has no more to give."*

Shine the light of your life into someone else's darkness - give them a smile! Proverbs 15:30 tells us, "A cheerful look brings joy to the heart, and good news gives health to the bones."

PRAYER: Dear God, help me to brighten and enrich the lives of others with my smile. Amen.

May 30

WHEN ALL SEEMS TO BE LOST

Out of work in Philadelphia during the Depression, Charles Darrow supported his family by fixing electric appliances, patching concrete, and walking dogs. He also invented things: puzzles and beach toys and a new bridge score pad, while musing about old times like vacations in Atlantic City.

One night in 1931 Darrow sat down at the kitchen table and sketched the names of various Atlantic City streets on the oilcloth. He colored the name spaces and cut tiny houses and hotels from bits of wooden molding. He typed out title deeds, and added dice and buttons for play money. The family played night after night.

Friends soon joined in. Nothing, it seemed, was better for Depression-battered spirits than an hour or two of buying real estate, even the make-believe kind. Enthusiasts wanted their own sets, and Darrow accommodated them, making games (while a friend of his printed the title cards) and selling them for $2.50.

In the beginning he made six sets a day. But Philadelphia stores demanded more sets. So Darrow took his game to Parker Brothers in Salem, Massachusetts. Parker rejected Darrow's game, stating the game was too complicated and contained 52 errors.

But Darrow rejected their rejection and persevered on with his dreams of mass-producing his game. At his own expense he ordered his printer to make up 5,000 copies of the game, which he sold to Wanamaker's and F.A.O. Schwartz. In no time customers bought up his games. So impressed was Parker Brothers, that in 1935 they relented and gave Darrow a contract with royalties on all sets sold. Soon he became a millionaire, gentleman, farmer, world traveler, and collector of exotic orchids. Monopoly became Parker's biggest seller and America's favorite game. Since 1935 more than 200 million sets have been sold world-wide and it is estimated that that more than half a billion people have played Monopoly.[xxxviii]

All people reach a low point in their lives. Maybe some of us will be tempted to believe all is lost. But our mission in life is to live it, to persevere and to keep pursuing our God-given dreams. The Scripture reminds us: "In all labor there is profit, but mere talk leads only to poverty." (Proverbs 14:27)

PRAYER: Dear Lord, when adversity, disappointment and rejection come, grant me staying power and faith so that I will never give into my doubts and fears, but pursue the dreams you've placed in my heart. Amen.

May 31

GETTING GOOD OUT OF EVIL

In 1879 Lewis Waterman was a New York insurance broker who was about to close the hottest deal of his career. The contract lay on the table and the client was ready to sign. Lewis chose an ornate fountain pen that befit the occasion. But the pen didn't write. The customer tapped it on the paper and out spilled the pen's contents of black ink all over the contract. The customer was annoyed and Lewis was horrified. He apologized profusely and dashed to get another contract drawn up. But when he returned to his office, the client was gone – he had signed with a competitor who was prepared to do business.

Though angry and frustrated, Lewis Waterman vowed to never let that happen again. If he couldn't find a reliable fountain pen, he'd invent one himself. Working in his brother's workshop, within a year Lewis Waterman developed and patented a capillary-fed fountain pen that proved perfectly reliable. Though his sales began rather modestly, first selling hand-made pens in a cigar shop and later in a popular magazine, his new-found business began to boom. By the time of his death in 1901, Lewis Waterman's Montreal factory was selling 350,000 pens a year. In 1919, his pens were chosen for the signing of the Treaty of Versailles that formally ended WWI. The family-owned company he started in 1894 continues to thrive to this day. And it all began with a moment of frustration and humiliation.

Our setbacks and disappointments can become the impetus for our greatest achievements. Remember the old adage: "If life only hands you lemons, make lemonade?" It's the best way to turn our curses into blessings, our stumbling blocks into stepping stones, our hurts into halos, and our defeats into victories. Believe God when he says, He works all things together for good for those who love him and who serve him (Romans 8:28).

PRAYER: Dear Father in heaven, please help me to keep a positive attitude in adversity, so I can turn my pain into gain. Amen.

June

June 1

BLESSING OR CURSING OURSELVES

The hurt you intend for someone else just might come around to hurt you. It's happened before, many times, in the most unusual ways.

For instance, May 22, 1968, the nuclear submarine, the USS Scorpion was destroyed after it released one of its conventional torpedoes. The torpedo was fired for the safety of the ship when its propeller activated while still in the torpedo tube. Once released, the torpedo became fully armed and engaged its nearest target – the Scorpion itself. The Scorpion and all hands perished by its own weapon.

During WWII, a British ship, the HMS Trinidad, almost destroyed itself after it fired on a German destroyer while patrolling the Arctic Ocean. The icy Arctic waters caused the torpedo's steering mechanism to malfunction. As a result, the torpedo's path looped around the struck the Trinidad in its stern, disabling it for the duration of the war.

In 1979, a Spanish Air Force jet crashed after some of its own practice rounds were fired and then ricocheted off the ground back at the plane that fired them.

Another author cites the destruction of a U.S. Navy jet fighter that shot itself down over the deserts of Nevada while testing a new cannon mounted on its wing. The plane was flying at supersonic speeds, faster than the high-caliber rounds it had fired. The ill-fated jet overtook and flew into its own cannon fire. Its own rounds, intended for another aircraft, destroyed itself.

Author Zig Ziglar once wrote about one of the most unusual boxing matches ever to take place. In this 1930s-era match, C.D. Blalock knocked himself out when he hurled a round-house right that missed and struck himself in the jaw.

Again, in 1959, boxer Henry Wallitsch threw and missed a looping left hook at his opponent's head. The punch intended to take out his opponent, led to his own demise. When Henry missed the shot he threw himself off-balance, fell out of the ring, crashed onto the floor on his head just next to the timekeeper, and who promptly counted him out.[xxxix]

There is a parallel in these true stories with the "rounds" and "punches" we fire at others; our criticism. The Lord warns us that criticism will lead to our own judgment: "Do not judge or you will be judged. For in the same way you judge others you will be judged, and with the measure you use, it will be measured to you" (Matthew 7:1-2). But this divine law of "reaping what you sow" goes the other way as well. The good that we speak and the good that we do to others will come back to bless us.

PRAYER: Dear Father in heaven, grant that I may never criticize my fellow soldier until I have marched a mile in his boots. Amen.

June 2

ONE STEP AT A TIME

Aspiring author, Kyle MacDonald of Montreal, Canada, became a celebrity in 2006 after his much-publicized success in gaining a two-story home in Kipling, Saskatchewan for a red paperclip. Yes, you heard it right. Kyle got a house for a paperclip.

How'd he do it? On numerous television show appearances, Kyle MacDonald explained that this was no pipe dream and no quantum leap. It was a step-by-step process of moving from something very small to something a little bigger. He based this venture on a game he played with his family as a child, "Bigger and Better." Kyle began with a red paperclip, which he traded for a fish-shaped pen, which he traded for a ceramic doorknob, which he traded for a Coleman camp stove. On and on he went and, with the help and kindness of others, he later obtained more considerable things. He bartered for a used moving van, then a recording contract, then a year's free rent in a Phoenix, Arizona house, then an afternoon with rock star and TV/radio personality Alice Cooper, and then a movie contract, which he finally traded for the home.

In television interviews Kyle used his long string of deals as a metaphor for life. He stated that we all progress and grow, not in giant leaps, but in small incremental steps and we don't do it alone. We get to where we want to go with the help of others.

The Bible also teaches this truth about life. When God directed an apprehensive Israel to conquer the land of Canaan, He assured them they only had to accomplish this "little by little" and not in a single year (Exodus 23:29-30). To Christian believers the apostle Paul said that they will be slowly transformed "from glory to glory" by believing in Christ and beholding His glory (2 Corinthians 3:18). But we ultimately accomplish God's will and grow spiritually by God's power and in the company of other people, who stretch us, challenge us, and encourage us to better things.

PRAYER: Dear Father in heaven, sometimes I get overwhelmed when I see what I am today and where I need to go in my spiritual and moral development. Please take me and lead me on this faith journey and make me, step by step, into the person You want me to be. Amen.

June 3

DECISIONS THAT DETERMINE OUR DESTINY

Yellowstone National Park, established March 1, 1872, is the oldest of America's National Parks. With its famous geysers, geothermal springs, waterfalls, grizzly bears, and free-roaming herds of buffalo, Yellowstone is a natural treasure of scenic wonders. It is also the location of a strange, but less-famous creek: Two Ocean Creek.

Actually, its name is North Two Ocean Creek. It derives its name from a peculiarity. When the creek reaches Two Ocean Pass, which is located on the Continental Divide in Yellowstone, it divides into two distributaries: Pacific Creek and Atlantic Creek.

Pacific Creek flows into the Snake River, then into the Columbia River, then into the Pacific Ocean. Atlantic Creek flows into the Yellowstone River, then into the Missouri, which flows into the Mississippi, which flows into the Gulf of Mexico and then into the Atlantic Ocean. This may be the only stream in the United States that sends its waters to two different oceans.

The point at which North Two Ocean Creek divides is called The Parting of the Waters. It is marked by a sign that points to the right and left: Atlantic Ocean – 3,488 Miles, Pacific Ocean – 1,353 Miles.

In a way this point, The Parting of the Waters, where the waters of Two Ocean Creek divide to the right and to the left, is like the decisions we make in our lives – decisions that determine the direction our lives will take, decisions that will ultimately determine our destiny. Consider the words of Moses when he called Israel to choose a life of faith and obedience to God. "I call Heaven and Earth to witness against you today: I place before you Life and Death, Blessing and Curse. Choose life so that you and your children will live." (Deuteronomy 30:19-20, *The Message*)

PRAYER: Dear Father in heaven, please guide me in the decisions I make. Day by day, grant that may I choose the path that leads to honor and eternal life. Lead me in the paths of righteousness for Your name's sake. Amen.

June 4

REDEEMING OURSELVES

Many called him the original Dr. Evil. Who was he? A Swedish inventor who amassed millions of dollars devising weapons of warfare: Torpedoes, mines, explosives and other means of mass destruction. While working on one of these inventions his own brother and four other people were killed. But no price was too great to achieve his ends – even if the price was human life. And the most famous of his inventions? Dynamite – invented in 1866. Yet as he neared the end of his life, this "Dr. Evil" became disturbed about his public image and about the fact that so much of his work had been dedicated to war. So he decided that he did not want to go down in history as a war monger, but as a beneficiary of mankind and as a lover of peace.

Who was this Dr. Evil? He was none other than Dr. Alfred Nobel, who left his millions to be distributed as prizes for those who have made significant contributions in physics, chemistry, medicine, literature, economics and (of all things) peace. How is it that a name that has become synonymous with goodness and greatness had such a shady, dark past? The fact is that Dr. Alfred Nobel redeemed his name by noble deeds. In fact, to this day, people mistake the name Nobel Peace Prize for *noble* peace prize.

Some may tell you there is no going back. Once the stain of sin has left its mark on your character, there's no point in trying. They tell you, people will always remember, will always associate your name with evil. You can never redeem yourself or your reputation.

But Dr. Alfred Nobel did. So did the men of Jabesh-Gilead. Never heard of them? You should have, for their story is worth telling. They represent one of the greatest examples of self-redemption. Their names are immortalized in Scripture as the supreme example of courage and loyalty. They were the brave and valiant souls who risked their lives to steal away King Saul's desecrated body from the Philistines (1 Samuel 31:11-13). Saul's successor, King David, was so deeply touched by this loyalty to a dead hero that he praised them and highlighted their heroism in the biblical record (2 Samuel 2:4-7). Henceforth, through all generations, loyalty and bravery would be synonymous with the men of one city – Jabesh-Gilead.

But what makes this story so appealing is that these very same men from the very same city once had the very worst reputation. Judges 21:8-12 tells the sad story of how when Israel was in its greatest crisis and needed the help of its countrymen more than at any other time, the men of Jabesh-Gilead sat idly by and failed to help. For this they were severely punished. But worse than any punishment was the reputation for faithlessness and cowardice that haunted them for years. The men of Jabesh-Gilead lived in shame and alienation from their brother Israelites. And when they were attacked by the wicked Ammonite King Nahash, they despaired of ever being rescued. After all, they did not answer the call for help, so why should anyone answer theirs? But someone did answer their cry and come to their rescue and save them from death – King Saul! (1 Samuel 11:1-15) And the redeeming love of King Saul forever won the hearts of these outcasts, these faithless cowards. Even when Saul's mind and spirit deteriorated, the men of Jabesh-Gilead did not waver in their love and loyalty for the man to whom they owed their lives. And finally, when their loyalty had no hope of being rewarded, the men of Jabesh-Gilead retrieved the body of their master at the risk of their own lives. The redeeming love of a king had forever changed these faithless cowards into valiant warriors.

And so, if our reputation seems stained past saving, remember the example of Jabesh-Gilead, men whose name and destiny were changed for the good by the power of God's redeeming love.

PRAYER: Dear Father in heaven, God of hope and all comfort, fill my poor heart with hope for myself. Redeem me and make me an instrument of your peace. Amen.

June 5

IS IT REALLY BAD LUCK?

Tom Dixton, of Los Angeles, California, was just cleaning up after changing the oil in his car when he heard the garbage truck coming down the road. So he quickly gathered the soiled rags, old oil filter, and the other bagged trash and ran after the garbage truck. Tom made it - just in the nick of time.

Tom was feeling pretty lucky *not* to have missed the garbage collectors until, while washing his hands, he realized his wedding ring was gone! In his rush to get rid of the trash, the wedding band had slipped off his oily hand into the garbage truck.

Tom was in a panic. He phoned the sanitation department to trace his wedding ring to the correct city dump – but it took him six hours of sifting through maggot and rat infested refuse before he saw the first sign that he was searching in the right area - he spotted some of his own junk mail. But for all his dirty work – there was no sign of his wedding ring.

Deeply discouraged, Tom was about to give up when he noticed a $20 bill next to a paper bag that "smelled like dirty diapers." He opened the bag and was amazed to see a stash of large figure bills - $63,000.00 worth! But, being an honest man, Tom turned the money over to the police.

Over the next four days of rooting through 15 tons of foul-smelling refuse, Tom never found his wedding ring. But what he did find was truly amazing: a collection of 2,000 vintage baseball cards (including one of Babe Ruth that was valued at $9,000.00), a box containing 23 prized gold coins valued at $12,000.00, and most amazing – Tom found the perfectly preserved and previously missing Fender Stratocaster guitar (the famed "Hatchet") of guitarist Jimmi Hendrix – which was later auctioned for more than $15,000.00. And remember that $63,000? No one claimed it, so the police returned it (along with everything else – minus the two kilos of Cocaine that Tom had also turned into the police) back to Tom Dixton. The total sum of Tom's treasure – almost $170,000! With all the treasure he stumbled upon, Tom bought himself a "new" wedding ring – and also a new car for his wife! Tom Dixton's bad luck certainly turned out to be good.

A classic Chinese legend tells of an elderly man whose stallion broke loose from the corral. "What bad luck," his neighbors concluded. Wisely, the old man replied, "How do you know it was bad luck?"

The next day the stallion returned, leading twelve more stallions with it into the old man's corral. "What good luck," his neighbors concluded. "How do you know it was good luck?" the old man replied.

Then, while breaking the stallions, the old man's son was thrown and broke his leg. "Oh, what bad luck," the neighbors again prematurely concluded. "How do you know it was bad luck?" the wise old sage questioned.

And sure enough, just a few days later, while the old man's son was just beginning to recover from his broken leg, a local warlord came through the village, recruiting every able bodied young man to fight in a war. None of the young men ever returned. As the old man suggested, his son's "bad break" wasn't so bad after all.

The Scripture assures us that, for those who put their trust in Him, God is continually causing all the events of our lives to work for an ultimately good purpose. He is turning our bad luck into good. The Scripture says: "And we know that God works all things together for good, to those who love God, for those who are called according to his purpose." (Romans 8:28)

PRAYER: Dear Father in heaven, help me not to judge the events of my life too rashly – until I have given you time enough to turn my curses into blessings, my hurts into halos, and my scar into stars. Amen.

June 6

HAPPY ONLY WHEN WE'RE BUSY?

Ever hear of "Wahlstrom's Wonder"? Wahlstrom was a mechanically minded man who spent his time exploring Army surplus stores and buying various electrical and engineering gadgets. He'd disassemble them then put them back together in unique and different combinations. After a while he filled an entire room in his home with a long chain of interconnected cogwheels, ringing bells, and lights. His many visitors would simply press a button to set the whole marvelous machine in motion. First a small wheel would start spinning. This would set another in motion, then another. In a matter of minutes, 3000 whirring wheels of assorted sizes would be buzzing, countless lights flashing, and dozens of bells ringing.

One day a visitor, impressed by the intricate mechanical responses to the push of a single button, said to Mr. Wahlstrom, "The is really fascinating, but what does it do?" Mr. Wahlstrom explained, "Well, you push a button, the wheels turn, the lights flash, and bells ring." The man replied, "Yes, I can see that, but what does it do?" Then

Mr. Wahlstrom admitted, "Well, I guess it doesn't do anything, it just runs."

Sadly, "Wahlstrom's Wonder," with all its purposeless activity, illustrates many of our lives. How many of us confuse activity with purpose, effectiveness or usefulness? How many of us fill our lives with ceaseless tasks and take comfort from the false notion, "If I'm busy, my life must count, I must be important." The wheels turn, the lights flash and the bells ring in our lives, but at the end of it all we have accomplished little of lasting value. We should be investing time in the things that matter most: our relationships with God, our spouse, children, families and friends. Instead, we waste our efforts on work, activities and busyness. And if we continue we'll reach the twilight of life empty-hearted. When U.S. Senator, Paul Tsongas, recovered from cancer, he remarked: "Spend time with your family. Nobody on his deathbed ever said, 'I wish I'd spent more time at the office.'" Jesus Christ once asked the question, "What shall it profit a man if he gains the whole world and loses his own soul?" (Mark 8:36)

PRAYER: Dear Lord, open my eyes to the blessings of this life that really count and that deserve my time and energy. Help me to pursue the things that matter most. Amen.

June 7

MISGUIDANCE

In the 1840s Lansford Hastings was an ambitious lawyer who had dreams of ceding California from Mexico and establishing it as a republic with himself as head of state. To lure more white settlers to California, Hastings published a book in 1845, *The Emigrant's Guide to California and Oregon*, in which he described an easy short cut to California. He claimed that his new route, later referred to the "Hastings Cutoff," would save travelers 350 – 400 miles on their journey, and would avoid many of the dangers of the old California Trail.

Naturally, Lansford Hastings' blissful descriptions of California wetted the appetites of many who yearned for a better life. But above all the idea of a short cut, a way of saving time and avoiding adversity, appealed to every west-bound American.

But there were some serious flaws in Hastings' description of his new route. First, he had never seen or traveled the route he described. His "short cut" existed only in his mind and was based on his own guess-work from the crude maps of the time. Unfortunately, he led unsuspecting travelers through some of the worst terrain for wagons – especially through the Wasatch Mountains and across the Great Salt Lake Desert. In reality, Hastings' Cut Off proved to be far more treacherous than the old California Trail – and 125 miles longer. Lansford Hastings had given tragically misleading guidance.

Among those that followed Lansford Hastings' Cut Off in 1846 was a group of 87 persons from Springfield, Illinois. The Hastings' Cut Off succeeded in destroying many of their wagons, most of their oxen and cattle, and the precious time that remained before the snow fell on the Sierra Nevada Mountains. Delayed by the infamous "Cut Off," they ran out of time and became entrapped near the summit of the trail through the Sierra Nevada. This was the tragic Donner Party and only 46 of the 87 survived, most resorting to cannibalism to stay alive. They paid a horrific price for heeding the guidance from a man who didn't know what he was talking about.

Our culture is saturated with conflicting moral voices that hit us from every side. With an air of authority and a self-righteous attitude, they proclaim to us, "This is the way you should live, think, and feel!" Some of these voices are certainly suspect because their message seems to change with the season. Other voices are questionable because of their self-serving and self-promoting motives. Others are suspect, because their message is wholly untried and demands a departure from the traditional faith and values of the past. They promise short cuts to happiness, holiness, and prosperity – defining prosperity in exclusively materialistic terms. These voices are the Lansford Hastings of our time. But 3000 years ago, King Solomon warned those who wish to blaze new trails of morality rather than adhere to the path prescribed in Holy Scripture. He wrote: "There is a way that seems right to a man, but in the end it leads to death." (Proverbs 14:12) May God help us not to stray from the path He has called us to follow!

PRAYER: Almighty Father, please guide and direct my steps and help me to follow the life-saving guidance of your Word. Amen.

June 8

ARE YOU WORTH THE EFFORT?

Sea World in Orlando, Florida, is a virtual hospital for many forms of ill or injured wildlife. For instance, Sea World operates a recovery ward for manatees that have been wounded by the blades of outboard motors. It also runs a nursery for dolphins and shelters a multitude of assorted injured wildlife. But most abundant among its "patients" are more than 100 crested penguins.

Why are there so many of these birds at Sea World? It's because of a behavior peculiar to crested penguins. They throw away their young. That's right. Every female crested penguin lays two eggs, the first much smaller than the second. The mother usually abandons the first egg or, if it is allowed to hatch, neglects it and allows it to starve. The parents sense that the smaller chick is not worth the investment of their time and energy and they devote everything to raising the larger chick. By rescuing these discarded, smaller chicks Sea World has built its own flock.

This heartless behavior by the crested penguin may seem disturbing to humans, that parents should choose one of their offspring to perish – the one that needs their help the most. Perhaps it is most unsettling to us because, deep within us, we may feel a little like that abandoned chick. Maybe, because of our own failures and frailty, we feel we're not worth the investment of God's time and energy.

But God will never abandon us. It is against God's nature to feed the strong and leave the weak to starve. Our heavenly Father doesn't look at the weak and the poor as "not worth the effort." The Scripture specifically tells us that God chooses the weak (1 Corinthians 1:27) and the poor (James 2:5). God is surely the wisest investor in the universe and yet He has chosen us and invested all of heaven in us. Surely he sees a brighter future for us than we see for ourselves. Take heart. God loves you and believes in you.

PRAYER: Dear heavenly Father, I love You and thank You that You have not written me off as "a waste of time," "not worth the effort," or "destined for failure." Thank You for loving me and investing everything in me. Please help me not to disappoint You. Amen.

June 9

WHEN YOUR LIFE SEEMS TO BE GOING NOWHERE

Botanists and Dendrologists marvel at the phases of the bamboo tree's life cycle. The bamboo seed will be planted and then fertilized and watered for four consecutive years without any visible progress. Suddenly, in its fifth year, the bamboo shoot begins to grow – very fast, up to two to three feet *per day!* Within six weeks it can easily reach *more than ninety feet in height!* Why such sudden astonishing growth after so much dormancy?

Actually the bamboo is not dormant during its first four years in the soil. During this period it generates, quite literally, miles of roots that will support its explosive growth in the fifth year.

Maybe there is a lesson for our own lives in the bamboo. Our lives go through periods of apparent dormancy without any productivity or visible progress. Yet God may be working behind the scenes in our lives, developing our character and preparing us for future responsibilities. Think of Joseph in the Bible, whose childhood dreams seemed derailed by a series of personal tragedies and who for years languished in obscurity. Yet those years as a slave and later as a prisoner prepared him for the pressures he would face as second-in-command of Egypt.

To Joseph we could add the lives of Moses, David, Saint Paul, and many others – all of whom suffered long periods of obscurity and fruitlessness as they prepared for opportunities that had not yet availed themselves.

Such periods of apparent dormancy are *not* indicators of human error, but of divine design. It is also God who designed the 13-year and 17-year locust (*Magicicada*) to remain burrowed in the ground as a nymph, merely sucking roots for more than 90% of its life, only to burst upon the earth to sing its shrill songs, mate, lay eggs and perish within a few weeks.

So, if your dreams and ambitions are on indefinite hold, if you feel like an exile in obscurity because of besetting responsibilities (parenthood, military obligations, or long deployments), do not lose heart. Nothing is necessarily wrong. God may be working behind the scenes, preparing you for something great yet to come.

PRAYER: Divine Master, help me to submit to your leading, to do my part in self-preparation through my periods of dormancy, and be ready and responsive for opportunities that appear. Amen.

June 10

LET CURSES BECOME BLESSINGS

Laura had traveled a hard, weary road. Draught, famines, diphtheria (which left her husband partially paralyzed for life), the death of her son, the destruction of her farm by fire, the stock market crash of 1929, the Great Depression, financial ruin, and an assortment of other tragedies had darkened her path.

Laura's family moved extensively when she was young. Her parents would only live for short periods in some of the most isolated places on earth – all in a desperate quest to eek out a living. Because of this she seldom attended school. Laura also had to forego School in order to help support her family. The family eventually settled in De Smet, Dakota Territory. But the Dakota Territory proved too cold and severe for young Laura. After she married, she and her husband, Almonzo, moved first to Minnesota, then to Mansfield, Missouri where the couple finally were able to make a life for themselves. Then came the Depression and they lost everything. And in the 1930s, in the depths of economic depression, 63-year-old women did not "start over." Life had passed Laura and Almonzo by and they had nothing to show for their labors.

But there was one thing the couple still had plenty of - memories. Then her daughter Rose got an idea. For years Laura and Almonzo had run a rural newspaper. So why not, Rose asked, write those memories down in a book. This, then, was the beginning of Laura Ingalls Wilder's stunning career as an author. Her first book, *Little House in the Big Woods*, first published in 1932, was a fabulous success. Ten more books followed, including *Little House on the Prairie* (1935) which became the basis for the highly successful 1970s TV show starring Michael Landon. Laura Ingalls Wilder had turned the pain of her life into a source of inspiration for generations to come. Her books also brought her and Almonzo the first financial security they had known in fifty years of marriage. At 63 Laura had believed that her life was over. But God had other plans. Laura lived to be ninety, enjoying both fame and fortune. She died in her sleep in 1957 in her Mansfield, Missouri farm.

We read of the oyster, which turns those sharp, painful grains of sand into pearls. People are capable of doing the same with the painful events of their lives. God gives us the grace to turn our hurts into halos, our stumbling blocks into stepping stones, and our scars into stars. The old adage is worth heeding: "If life only hands you lemons, then make lemonade. In the Scripture we read how God is able to turn our curses into blessings (Deuteronomy 23:5) and to change the evil that others intend for us into something good (Genesis 50:20).

PRAYER: Dear Father in heaven, through all the adversity and pain of life, please keep my spirit sweet and my heart young. Please work all things in my life together for my ultimate good and for your ultimate glory. Amen.

June 11

STRIP MAPS: THEY DON'T TELL THE WHOLE STORY

Strip maps. We've all used them. They are those simplified "line directions" that show the way to get somewhere. But that's all they show. They show only the correct way to go – and nothing else. Their value is that they simplify the route of travel.

But strip maps have a serious drawback. For the poor soul who makes a wrong turn and gets lost, the strip map does nothing. "Where am I?" the lost soul cries. The strip map is silent. "How do I find my way back?" The strip map is powerless to help. The lost person looks at the strip map to figure out his location, and all he sees is a blank. According to the strip map, the lost person is hopelessly lost. The lost soul realizes that although the strip map tells him how not to get lost, it offers no help if he *does* become lost. Although it tells him the way he should go, it offers no hope if he makes a mistake. The strip map is only meant for the person who hasn't yet made a mistake, not for the person who has.

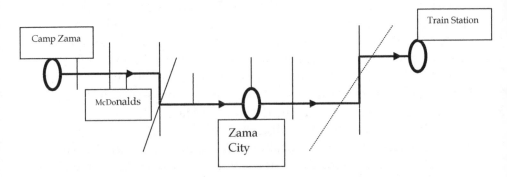

Note: This map is only hypothetical and does not represent reality.

In a similar way the commands of Scripture tell us "this is the way, walk ye in it." But they don't always tell us what happens if we fail or disobey God's commands. Is there hope for us if we disobey? Is there life after failure? To answer these questions, God gave us the life-stories of flawed men and women.

God not only said, "Thou shalt not commit adultery" and "Thou shalt not kill." He gave us the life story of King David, who broke both commandments. From David's experience of horrific failure, we realize that we can still find our way back to God and enjoy his forgiveness and salvation. In the Gospels Jesus had said, "Whoever denies me before men, I will deny before my Father in heaven." What, then, was to become of one of his apostles- Peter - who denied the Lord? We have the life-story of this flawed man to give us hope, that even when we do the unthinkable, we are not hopelessly lost, nor out of the reach of God's love. The lives of the saints – all of whom were once sinners – are like a complete roadmap, that tells us both where to go, and also (if we become lost) how to find our way home.

The apostle Paul wrote, "For whatever was written in earlier times was written for our instruction, that through perseverance and the encouragement of the Scriptures we might have hope." (Romans 15:4) Don't just keep a list of the Ten Commandments. Read the whole Bible to get the whole picture – of where you should go, and, should you fail, how to find your way home.

PRAYER: Open my eyes, that I may behold wonderful things from Thy law. Amen. (Psalm 119:18)

June 12

HOW TO INHIBIT YOUR CHILD'S GROWTH

As he expounded on the imitative nature of birds, Isaac Asimov, presents us with a powerful analogy to parenting. He explains: "Many songbirds learn to sing by listening to adult birds of the same species. If separated from the adults, they develop unintelligible warbles rather than normal song patterns. But if taught the song of another species, a bird often can pass the foreign language on to its offspring. In one experiment, a male bullfinch raised by a female canary learned a canary's song to perfection. When it was later mated to a female bullfinch, its children and later its grandchildren could sing like a canary."

What is true of song birds is true of humans regarding our imitative nature and our tendency to learn from our parents – or from those who "fill in" for parents – the television, Rap or Rock and Roll artists, or icons of our popular culture. Children need guidance on how to live and in the absence of good guidance will follow bad guidance.

The great English poet, critic, and philosopher, Samuel Taylor Coleridge was visited by a man who had a pet theory about raising children. He stated, "I believe children should be given a free rein to think and act and thus learn at an early age to make their own decisions. This is the only way they can grow into their full potential." Coleridge made no comment but simply led the man to his garden. "Come see my flower garden," he said. The opinionated visitor took one look at the over grown garden and remarked, "Why, that's nothing but a yard full of weeds." The wise poet declared, "It used to be filled with roses, but this year I thought I'd let the garden grow as it willed without tending to it. I let it have free rein to let it reach its full potential. This is the result."[xl]

Children, like gardens, will not automatically flourish. They need our love, attention, and discipline daily. And, like song birds, children can only learn what is taught and exemplified before them. The Scriptures tell us, "Train up a child in the way he should go, and when he is old he will not depart from it" (Proverbs 22:6).

PRAYER: Dear Father in heaven, give me the courage, strength, and love to train and nurture my children as I should. Amen.

June 13

JUST THINK OF WHAT MIGHT HAVE BEEN

It could have been the end of all civilization, the end of every living thing on earth. The date was December 27, 2004. On that fateful day a star known only as SGR 1806-20 exploded with an incredible release of gamma rays. *In one tenth of a second* the explosion released the energy equivalent to what our sun *generates in 100,000 years!* This type of star is called a magnetar – a very small neutron star (only 12 miles in diameter) that rotates rapidly (once every 7 ½ seconds) and gives off immense amounts of energy. It was the largest explosion witnessed by human beings since the supernova in 1604 – witnessed by Johannes Kepler. If this star had been as close as 10 light years away

(58,656,960,000,000 miles *or* fifty-eight trillion, six-hundred fifty-six billion, nine hundred and sixty million miles), its gamma rays would have destroyed our planet's protective ozone layer, thus dooming all life on earth. Fortunately, it occurred at more than 50,000 light years away. The next nearest magnetar is 13,000 light years away – so we're relatively safe. Clearly, our earth enjoys a rather sheltered existence.

Life is truly good on Planet Earth. Yet we rarely appreciate the comfort of this world in contrast to the nightmarish conditions on other worlds. For instance, the surface temperature of Venus averages 867 degrees Fahrenheit and experiences constant winds that rage at supersonic speed, accompanied by showers of sulfuric acid that hit with the force of bullets and incessant lightening that pulsates throughout the Venetian skies.

Mercury, which has the fastest orbit - only 88 earth-days long and travels at almost thirty miles per second, remains baked on one side and eternally dark on the other.

Mars is the most hospitable planet in the solar system besides earth, yet its average surface temperature is only minus 40 degrees. And its air pressure is only 1/150 of that on earth and mostly consists of carbon dioxide. This low atmospheric pressure makes it impossible for liquid water to exist on Mars. Frozen water immediately turns to vapor when it melts.

Jupiter is the largest and stormiest of the planets. Its great Red Spot, 30,000 miles across, is a storm of 25,000-mile-per-hour winds that has been raging for more than 300 years. With its rapid rotation (Jupiter rotates every ten hours) and no solid surface or terrain features to slow winds down, Jupiter's angry storms of poisonous gases are continually out of control. Conditions on Saturn are much the same.

And don't expect life to get easier on Uranus, Neptune or Pluto. Uranus, the seventh planet, is nineteen times more distant from the sun than earth and has an average surface temperature of minus 350 degrees. And it just keeps getting colder as you move on to Neptune and finally on to Pluto. Because of its tiny size (less than half the size of Jupiter's moon, Ganymede) and strange orbit, many do not even consider Pluto to be a planet. Pluto is so distant from the sun (3.7 billion miles) that the sun appears as no more than a distant star from the planet's surface, which has an average temperature of minus 400 degrees.

Yes, life is pretty good on Planet Earth. Our Creator has provided a rare oasis of beauty, comfort, and protection in a vast and hostile universe. And I strongly suspect that every day God shelters us from hostile events and dangers that would otherwise destroy us. If fear and worry are getting the best of you, remind yourself that God is a guardian who is always on duty and never sleeps or gets distracted. In the Psalms we read: *"My help comes from the LORD who made heaven and earth. He will not allow your foot to slip; He who protects you will not slumber. Behold, he who protects Israel will neither slumber nor sleep. ...The LORD will protect you from all evil; He will guard your soul. The LORD will guard your going out and your coming in, from this time forth and forever."* (Psalm 121:2-4, 7-8)

PRAYER: Dear Father in heaven, thank you for watching over me continually and for saving me from dangers of which I am blissfully ignorant. May your unfailing protection keep me from all danger. Amen.

June 14

TAKE CARE OF YOURSELF

In December 1998 the Bureau for At-Risk Youth of Plainview (New York) had a big problem on its hands. It had ordered thousands of pencils and distributed them to dozens of schools throughout New York State. Imprinted on the pencils were the words "Too Cool to Do Drugs" – a good message for "at-risk youth."

Unfortunately, no one at the pencil company foresaw that, when the pencils were sharpened down, their message would be seriously altered. 10-year-old Kodi Mosier of Ticonderoga Elementary School was one of the first to spot the problem. As she sharpened down her pencil the message changed to *"Cool to Do Drugs"* and then simply *"Do Drugs."* As the pencil was whittled down, it preached a message opposite to the one intended.

The embarrassed Bureau re-called the pencils and ordered new ones – this time with the message written in the other direction, so that it ended with the words "Too Cool."

Like these pencils, people can get "whittled down" with repeated use. This is especially true of those in leadership positions, who can be reduced to "a nub" from overwork, lack of rest, and burn-out. When this happens, their message can be changed to the very opposite of what they stand for. People in the helping professions can become sour, abusive, and hurtful. Ministers can discredit the very Gospel they preach.

It then behooves every caregiver to take care of oneself – to get adequate rest, to nurture and feed one's soul, and to find healthy diversions. In the Scriptures Jesus explained, "No good tree bears bad fruit, nor does a bad tree bear good fruit. … The good man brings good things out of the good stored up in his heart, and the evil man brings evil things out of the evil stored up in his heart. For out of the overflow of his heart his mouth speaks." (Luke 6:43, 45)

PRAYER: Dear Lord, help me to do those things and exercise those disciplines that feed and nurture my heart and soul, and make me spiritually fit. Amen.

June 15

GIVE A WORD OF ENCOURAGEMENT

As a boy Herbert labored 14-hours a day, rising at 0500 each morning and working well into the evening as a draper's apprentice in a London shop. But he fared poorly. Herbert not only hated the long hours, he hated the work itself. But what could he do? His father's business had failed and he had fallen ill and died while Herbert was still a boy. And Herbert had been less than a promising student, having failed in school. So Herbert and his brother were forced into apprenticeships in hope of supporting themselves and their mother. But after two years as an apprentice, he became deeply depressed and began to consider suicide as his only way of escape.

But before Herbert took his life, he made one last cry for help. In a letter to his former teacher, Herbert poured out his heart and soul, describing his pain and unwillingness to live any longer.

The teacher wrote Herbert a deeply personal letter in return. It was filled with encouragement, affirmation, and genuine love. The letter lifted the young man's spirits and gave him hope for his future. That word of encouragement changed Herbert's life and set him in a new direction. In fact, Herbert became one of England's most influential authors of the 19th and 20th Centuries. Who was he? The noted novelist, journalist, socialist and historian – Herbert George (H.G.) Wells, known best for the classic novels *The War of the Worlds*, *The Time Machine*, *The Invisible Man*, and *The First Men on the Moon*. Just think of what H. G. Wells, and the whole world, would have missed if a sympathetic teacher had not taken the time to write a kind word.

The Scripture reminds us, "Kind words bring life, but cruel words crush the spirit" (Proverbs 15:4) and "What you say can give life or destroy it" (Proverbs 18:21). May our words be the seeds for success and blessing in the lives of our families, friends, and fellow soldiers.

PRAYER: Lord, make me an instrument of your peace;
Where there is hatred, let me sow love;
   Where there is injury, pardon;
   Where there is doubt, faith;
   Where there is despair, hope;
   Where there is darkness, light;
   Where there is sadness, joy.
Divine Master, grant that I may not so much seek
   To be consoled as to console;
   To be understood as to understand;
   To be loved as to love.
For it is in giving that we receive;
It is in pardoning that we are pardoned;
And it is in dying that we are born to eternal life. Amen.

June 16

BORN FOR ADVERSITY

"So the work on the Temple of God in Jerusalem had stopped, and it remained at a standstill until the second year of the reign of King Darius of Persia. At that time the prophets Haggai and Zechariah ... prophesied to the Jews in Judah and Jerusalem. They prophesied in the name of the God of Israel who was over them. Zerubbabel (the Jewish governor) responded by starting again to rebuild the Temple of God in Jerusalem. And the prophets of God were with them and helped them." (Ezra 4:24 – 5:2, *New Living Translation*)

   This was a bad time to be a prophet. And it was a most unfavorable time to exhort the returning exiles to spend what little resources they had to rebuild the Temple in Jerusalem. For one thing, the Kings of Persia (Darius and Xerxes) had ordered construction to cease. In addition to this, the surrounding nations opposed the project.

And finally, the returning exiles were having a difficult time just surviving. They did not have the resources to risk life and limb on a project that offered no material gain. Yet, in the face of all opposition and the poverty of the people, the prophets Zachariah and Haggai urged the people, "Rebuild God's Temple!" What an inappropriate time for such a message. What a terrible time to be a prophet!

But in reality, the very worst of times are the best for such a message. The worst of times are the most appropriate times to be a prophet – in times of adversity and hopelessness, when God's people need encouragement the most.

God doesn't call prophets to merely state the obvious or to second the motions of others. They are called to preach the impossible and to say what no one else dares to say.

In Acts 27 the apostle Paul found himself on a doomed voyage, sailing on a ship that would never make it to harbor. Did he complain, "What a time to be an apostle! Why did this storm have to come on my watch? Why does my ship have to run into a hurricane?" No Paul realized he was born for adversity. He didn't spend his life trying to escape adverse circumstances. He realized God had called him to that situation for such a crisis – to bring hope to the despairing.

You could also say that this is the worst time to be a soldier – in a time of war, war that is ugly and seemingly without end. Has there ever been a time when so few are willing to stand at freedom's frontier to safeguard the lives and freedoms of so many? Then isn't this actually the best time, the most critical time to be a soldier. For soldiers are not born for tranquility and security.   Soldiers, as well as prophets, are born for adversity and conflict. They fulfill their mission in the most perilous times.

The same is true of the disciples of Jesus. God will deliberately set the believer in the midst of calamity – to bring relief and blessing where it is needed most. God places the "children of light" in some of the darkest circumstances – to brighten their world with the light of God's love and the light of the gospel. Certainly children of light will feel most comfortable bathed in the sunlight, but the darkest night is where they shine brightest. If the humble candle had feelings and thought, would it not yearn for bright places? Wouldn't it consider the midday sun to be its most natural element? Wouldn't it feel a special kinship with the light of day and feel "out of place" in darkness? Yet darkness is where it is needed most and shines brightest. "You are the light of the world. No one lights a lamp and then puts it under a basket. Instead, a lamp is placed on a stand, where it gives light to everyone in the house." (Matthew 5:14-15)

Has God brought you to a dark and troubled station in life? Do you find yourself in adversity and despair? This is what you were born for – that you might bring light to the dark places, bring peace to the troubled, and joy to the despairing. Stop bemoaning your circumstances and start fulfilling your mission.

PRAYER: Almighty and merciful Father, open my eyes to those around me who are hurting and use me to bring healing and help into their lives. Amen.

June 17

LIFE FROM ADVERSITY AND DEATH

The Knobcone Pine grows all along the West Coast of the United States and Baja California. It thrives best in the poor, sandy soils located in northern California and southern Oregon, where its greatest concentrations are located.

At first glance, there is nothing amazing about this tree, which bares resemblance to a large bush. Yet its very survival is amazing. For the seeds of the Knobcone are locked away in the toughest, hardest pinecones in the world. Neither seed-hungry critters nor all the ravages of the weather can pry those cones apart to release their seeds. As a result, Knobcone Pines go decades without giving forth a single seed or producing any offspring. There is, in fact, only one force of nature that can bring about a new generation of Knobcones, guarantee its future, and ensure its survival – *fire*. Only after fire has charred the pinecones do they begin to open and release their seeds on the ash-enriched soil.

However, the very forest fires that give freedom to the seeds of the Knobcone Pine, also destroy it. The Knobcone Pine is considered a "fire-climax" tree. This means it must be destroyed in a fire in order to give life to its progeny. Yet despite the tree's destruction, hundreds of seedlings rise up in its place.

This fiery destruction of the Knobcone pine is reminiscent of another conflagration – the fiery ordeal of the God's people throughout the ages. The emperors Caligula, Nero, Domitian, Diocletian and others all waged war of varying degrees against the church. Even before the time of Christ, the Hellenist King, Antiochus Epiphanes (175-167 BC), tried to eradicate Judaism and impose upon God's people the pagan religion and customs of Greece.

Throughout the centuries many have sought to annihilate God's people and burn their sacred writings. More recently, under Stalinism, Leninism, and Fundamentalist Islam, the church has undergone its most painful tribulations. Yet, all the fires of hell have not been able to incinerate and erase the church. Like the Knobcone Pine, the fires of persecution have only served to facilitate the church's growth. Time and again, tyrants have sought to stamp out the last vestige of Christianity. Yet for every martyred witness, dozens have sprung up in his place. Truly, as Jesus prophesied: "I will build my church and the gates of hell shall not prevail against it." (Matthew 16:18)

PRAYER: Our Father, Who art in heaven, hallowed be Thy name. Thy kingdom come. Thy will be done, on earth as it is in heaven. Give us this day our daily bread, and forgive us our debts, as we forgive our debtors. And lead us not into temptation, but deliver us from evil. For Thine is the kingdom, and the power, and the glory forever. Amen.

June 18

WHEN WE MAKE EXCUSES FOR NOT ACHIEVING

Legson Kayira was born and raised in an impoverished village in the African country of Malawi. He was resigned to his circumstances until he read a book about Abraham Lincoln and his rise from abject poverty and illiteracy to becoming President of the United States. Lincoln, a determined man who refused to let adversity stand in his way, became a role model for Kayira.

In 1958, at the tender age of 16, Kayira set off on foot from his family and his village – hoping to obtain a formal education in America and make something more of his life. He took with him only a Bible, an extra shirt, a small ax, a blanket, the book *Pilgrim's Progress*, food for five days, and a motto he'd learned in school, "I will try."

Three thousand miles lay between his village and Egypt, where he hoped to catch a boat for America. The journey was daunting. He encountered many tribes he knew nothing about and, unable to bridge their differences through a common language, quickly discovered their intolerance of outsiders. Quite alone, he foraged for food and took shelter wherever he could find it. When he grew discouraged, he read his books, thought of Lincoln, and repeated to himself, "I will try."

In a library in Uganda, he found a listing for Skagit Community College in the state of Washington and wrote to them. The dean of the school was quite impressed by the young man's determination and offered Kayira a scholarship and a job. All the prospective student had to do was get there. Inspired by this news, Kayira continued on his journey.

When at last he reached Sudan, Kayira learned that the students at Skagit and the local residents near the school had raised enough money for his plane ticket to America. They had even secured housing for him in Washington. It had been two years since Kayira set off barefoot from the only home he'd ever known, and now his biggest dream was on the horizon.

After graduating from Skagit, Kayira continued his education and earned a doctorate from Cambridge. This time, though, he didn't have to walk thousands of miles to get there.

What excuses do we make for ourselves for not achieving or even trying? Proverbs 13:4 tells us: "The sluggard craves and gets nothing, but the desires of the diligent are fully satisfied."

PRAYER: Dear Father in heaven, as you breathed into the first man the breath of life, breathe into me the drive and motivation to pursue the path you've chosen for me and to fulfill the dreams you've placed in my heart. Amen.

June 19

THE SAFEST PLACE ON EARTH

July 27, 1953 began a sixty-year cease fire to one of the bloodiest conflicts in human history, a war that claimed the lives of more than 3 million people – the Korean War. But after the guns were silenced, the border between North and South Korea returned to precisely where it was before the war began on June 25, 1950 – with this one difference. The terms of the cease fire required the creation of the demilitarized zone or DMZ. The DMZ is a 155-mile long and 2 ½-mile wide stretch of land that separates the two countries along what is the most heavily fortified border on earth.

The DMZ is, hands down, one of the most undesirable places in the world for people to live. This blood-stained earth was the site of humanity's most desperate conflicts and lies between thousands of artillery and machinegun positions.

Yet, there is something else you should know about the DMZ. It is also an environmental paradise and a safe haven for hundreds of endangered species. In fact, there are animals that live in the DMZ – like the Siberian tiger, the Asiatic black bear, the white-naped crane and the red-crowned crane – that no longer live anywhere else in the whole of the Korean Peninsula. This is because the DMZ is free of human beings and hundreds of endangered animals are therefore safe from their most deadly enemy – humankind. How strange that the site of such a terrible conflict should become the place of safety and salvation for so many of God's creatures.

But there is another place of supreme safety and this was also the site of a terrific and bloody conflict. This safe haven is the blood-stained ground of the cross – the place where Christ, by his death, defeated Satan and the forces of darkness (Colossians 2:15; Hebrews 2:18; 1 John 3:8). This refuge is the scorched earth of the cross where the full fury of God's wrath fell upon Jesus Christ (2 Corinthians 5:21). And those who cling to the cross for refuge are forever free from Satan's accusations and forever safe from God's fiery wrath and judgments.

PRAYER: Dear Father in heaven, forgive my sins and protect me from the spiritual forces of wickedness. But most of all save me from your wrath. To Your cross, O Jesus Christ, I cling for protection and safety – both in this life and in the age to come. Amen.

June 20

GOOD OR BAD LUCK?

Was he the unluckiest man alive, or the luckiest? You be the judge.

The story begins in September 1914, during the early days of World War I. The "man" was a fourteen-year-old midshipman named W. H. "Kit" Wykeham-Musgrave. He was serving aboard the British cruiser, HMS Aboukir, which was patrolling off the Dutch coast with two other cruisers, the HMS Hogue and HMS Cressy.

Then, on the fateful day of September 22, Captain Otto Weddigen, commanding the German submarine U-9, sighted the three cruisers. The U-9 fired a single torpedo at the Aboukir and sank the ship in minutes. Musgrave went over the side into the North Sea and barely escaped with his life.

The Hogue rescued a handful of Aboukir's survivors. Kit Musgrave was among them. But no sooner did the sailors bring Musgrave safely aboard before the Hogue itself was hit with a torpedo from the U-9. The Hogue sank in 3 minutes. And again Kit Musgrave jumped into the chilling waters of the North Sea.

This time sailors from the Cressy saved Musgrave. But within minutes after his rescue, the U-9 torpedoed and sank the Cressy.

It was a heartbreaking day for the British Navy. Three cruisers and 1400 sailors were lost – all at the hands of one German U-Boat.

However, 700 British sailors *did* survive. One of them was Midshipman Musgrave. And throughout the war he would have the distinction of being the only man ever to be sunk three times *in a single hour!*

But Kit Musgrave's experience is not only one of misfortune, but of miraculous deliverance. For he was also the only man during the war to *survive* being sunk three times in one hour. We can conclude his luck was terrible – or incredibly good.

And we can do the same with our own experience. At times we are hit with one catastrophe after another. No sooner do we recover from one battering before we are "sunk" all over again.

But amidst all the adversity, don't lose sight of God's rescues and deliverances. True, you've had a rough time. But you've survived by the grace of God. True, you came so close to destruction and feel greatly shaken. But God helped you and pulled you through. And God will continue to do so. "Many are the afflictions of the righteous," the Scripture says, "but the Lord delivers him *out of them all.*" (Psalm 34:19) We have the choice of focusing on the affliction or on the wonderful ways God comes to our rescue.

PRAYER: Dear Father in heaven, Please keep my spirit fresh and my attitude soaring. Help me to remember the many times You've answered my prayers, delivered me from all my fears, and saved me out of all my troubles. Amen.

June 21

GET YOUR KICKS ON ROUTE 66

Route 66. It wasn't the first U.S. Highway. Nor was it the longest U.S. highway – that distinction goes to U.S. Highway 20 – which stretches 3,365 miles coast-to-coast. In fact, U.S. Highway 66 didn't even extend across the entire country. It only traveled from Chicago to Santa Monica, California, just north of Los Angeles – a total of 2,347 miles. To be honest, Route 66 doesn't officially exist anymore. It was decommissioned in 1985 and has since been replaced by a five different Interstate Highways – I-55, I-44, I-40, I-10 and I-15. Only fragments of this highway are still used – mostly as service roads and "Historic Highways," especially in Oklahoma and Arizona.

Why then such a mystique about an abandoned highway? Why were songs written about it, like Nat King Cole's "Get Your Kicks on Route 66?" Why was a 1960s TV show named for this highway? Even Phillips Petroleum's *Phillip's 66* bore its image. To this day one can find the *Route 66* logo emblazed on sign replicas, mugs, key chains, belt buckles, clothing, and a host of other items. Even cologne is named after this highway. Annually thousands travel from as far away as Europe for a chance to travel on "Old Route 66." Why?

Route 66 certainly has historical significance. During the 1930s it became the exodus route for hundreds of thousands of desperate farmers fleeing the dust bowl of Oklahoma, Kansas and Texas. This was highlighted by John Steinbeck in his book on the depression era, *The Grapes of Wrath*, in which he referred to Route 66 as "the Mother Road." Route 66 also had great commercial significance, providing a main thoroughfare between America's 2nd and 3rd largest cities. Not to mention that Route 66 served as a vacation route to the Grand Canyon, Las Vegas, Merrimac Caverns, the Painted Desert, Hoover Dam, and sunny California. Thus it earned the name, "America's Main Street."

But Route 66's greatest significance for Americans is that it represents a time when *the journey was as important as the destination.* In the heyday of Route 66, vacation began as soon as mom and dad backed out of the driveway. The entire journey all along Route 66 was an adventure. "The destination" was only part of the fun. The journey was the real joy.

In contrast, the faceless and colorless Interstates that replaced Route 66 all represent the obsession with getting through the journey, racing through life, wishing our days away in the quest for the destination. That is no way to enjoy life or to appreciate God's day-to-day blessings. The Scripture reminds us that *"This* – today, with all its troubles, challenges, opportunities and blessings - is the day which the Lord has made. Let us rejoice and be glad in it." (Psalm 118:24)

PRAYER: Dear father in heaven, help me to slow down and take time to count and enjoy the blessings you pour into my life. Show me that there is no "final destination" in this life – no place of final bliss and happiness. Remind me that the journey itself is your gift and is to be enjoyed. Amen.

June 22

THE GRASS IS NOT GREENER ON ANOTHER PLANET

In order to evoke interest in space travel, officials at the Hayden Planetarium in New York City ran a news ad about a pending trip to Mars. "Who would be interested in leaving the confines of this world on a quest to find new worlds?" The response was overwhelming. More than 18,000 people submitted applications for this hypothetical flight. When a team of psychologists reviewed the applications a recurring attitude surfaced among the thousands of applicants. The reason they wanted to seek out new worlds was because they were completely dissatisfied with life on this one.

Is planet Earth such a terrible place to live? Would another planet be far more hospitable?

Consider the other choices in our solar system. Mercury is a hot, cratered world, devoid of any atmosphere. It's diameter is less than half that of Earth (only about 3,000 miles), and is only 36 million miles from the sun (compared to the Earth's 93 million miles) and it rotates so slowly that one day lasts 58 Earth days - causing one side of Mercury to bake while the other side freezes.

Venus is the closest to Earth in size (7,518 miles in diameter for Venus compared to 7,923 miles for Earth) and in distance (only 23 million miles from Earth. That's as far as the similarities go. Venus has the hottest surface temperature of any planet - 900 degrees Fahrenheit! This is because its atmosphere of carbon dioxide traps heat from the sun. Its atmosphere pulsates with flashes of lightning and is clouded with whirling droplets of sulfuric acid blown by winds hundreds of miles per hour – hardly a Garden of Eden.

Mars is by far the most hospitable planet outside of Earth, yet its average surface temperature is a frigid minus 40 degrees Fahrenheit. There is no liquid water on Mars, nor can there be. The atmospheric pressure on Mars is so small (only 1/150 of the atmospheric on earth at sea level) that melted ice simply turns to vapor. This incredibly thin atmosphere consists primarily of carbon dioxide with only the smallest trace of oxygen.

Jupiter, 1,000 times the size of Earth, is the largest and stormiest of all the planets. In fact, Jupiter's "Great Red Spot" is a whirling eddy of poisonous gases (ammonia, methane, hydrogen and helium) 30,000 miles across. Astronomers speculate that Jupiter's storms last hundreds of years.

Saturn, like Jupiter, rotates at an incredibly high speed - one day is only about ten Earth *hours* long. Though its rings present an inviting picture, Saturn's atmosphere consists of poisonous gases like ammonia, methane, hydrogen and oxides of nitrogen and its winds rage at a staggering speed of 1,000 miles per hour.

Beyond Saturn lie Uranus, Neptune and Pluto. Life does not get any easier on these planets. Uranus is nineteen times more distant from the sun as the Earth (a distance of 1.8 billion miles) and has an average surface temperature of minus 350 degrees Fahrenheit. Pluto, the smallest and most distant of the planets, is nearly forty times more distant from the sun than the Earth (a distance of 3.7 billion miles). From the surface of Pluto our sun appears as little more than a point of light, like a distant star. Consequently, its surface temperatures are the coldest of any planet – minus 400 degrees Fahrenheit!

It certainly appears that Earth is the most pleasant spot in the solar system for living things. But what about other stars and galaxies?

The closest star to earth is our own sun – 93 million miles. The next closest star (Proxima Centauri) is 26 million million miles or 4.3 light years away (about 300,000 times farther away than our own sun). That's the *closest!* We'd better stick with the sun we have. Besides being too far away, the vast majority of stars are far less suitable than our sun.

Most stars are "variable stars," i.e. their energy outputs fluctuates so drastically, spewing gases and solar flares hundreds of millions of miles from their surfaces, that they would make life in this solar system impossible. Our sun is rare in this respect – its energy output varies only a few tenths of one percent.

Then there is surface temperature of our sun – 11,000 degrees Fahrenheit – perfect for life on the third planet. Other stars range from red stars (with a cool surface temperature of 5,500 degrees) to blue-white stars (with surface temperatures of 55,000 degrees).

Then there is the size of our sun – 860,000 miles in diameter. If our sun was as large an Alpha Orinis (known a Betelgeuse), which is one million times the size of our sun, it would envelop the orbits of Mercury, Venus, and Earth. Antares is even larger and would reach beyond the orbit of Mars.

Then there is the isolation of our sun. Most stars are part of multiple-star systems, which would greatly disturb the delicate balance of heat and energy in our solar system.

It appears this planet Earth is the best habitat we'll ever find. Certainly a caring and considerate Creator provided our place in this hostile universe. We should be thankful to our Maker and protective of the home he has given us. We must also guard and protect the only home this side of heaven that He has prepared for us. God has charged us with the care of the Earth and all its creatures, not its exploitation (Genesis 2:15; 6:19-21)

PRAYER: Dear Lord, please help us, your creation, to act as responsible children of God toward each other and toward the world in which you have placed us. Help us to be far-sighted enough not to pursue temporal gratification at the expense of destroying this planet. Please grant, O Lord, that we will never betray future generations of Your children, now powerless to effect good or evil but who will have to inherit the world we safeguard or destroy. Amen.

June 23

LEFT ON THE SHELF

A recent documentary on the squirrels of North America highlighted some peculiar behavior of these animals that aids in the germination of acorns.

Squirrels are discriminating eaters. When they find the mature, reddish brown acorns of the white oak tree they quickly consume them. But the green acorns of this tree are stored away in caches, buried in the ground. Many of these "shelved" acorns never get eaten. They are forgotten by the squirrel or the squirrel dies and they are abandoned. So, instead of providing a meal to the squirrel, the abandoned green acorns mature in the ground, germinate, and sprout into seedlings.

Now consider this from the acorn's perspective. The acorn is the main food staple of many birds and mammals, particularly jays and squirrels. If an acorn provides food for these animals, it has fulfilled its purpose. It has provided a useful service to creation.

But consider also the "neglected" green acorns that are buried in the ground and often forgotten. If this acorn had a mind and feelings wouldn't it believe its destiny was a dead end? Wouldn't it feel forgotten, shelved, and a failure in its primary mission.

But although it will never serve as food for hungry animals, it would do something far more significant. It would become a mighty oak tree that would produce literally millions of acorns that would feed animals by the thousands. And it would reproduce itself a hundredfold.

Sometimes we feel "shelved," "benched," out of commission, left in the dark, and a failure in our primary mission. Maybe we read and hear about others getting instant results and rapidly meeting with success, while we are left to languish in obscurity. But perhaps God's plan is to reserve us for something greater. Consider Joseph in the Old Testament – a man who was forgotten in prison, believing his life had reached a dead end. Yet God was using those humiliating circumstances to mature that man into a world leader (Genesis 37-50).

Surely we cannot interpret the ways of the Lord and his dealings with us in the midst of our trials. For "His judgments are unsearchable and his paths are beyond tracing out. Who has known the mind of the Lord? Or who has been his counselor?" (Romans 11:33-34) Most times we are no more perceptive of what God is doing behind the scenes than an acorn is about why it is buried and abandoned in the ground. But if God has such a stupendous plan for the forgotten acorn, isn't it reasonable to believe he has something wonderful in store for us?

"Rest in the Lord, and wait patiently for Him; do not fret when others succeed in their ways." (Psalm 37:7) That's good advice. Place yourself in God's hands. Commit your whole course of life to the all-powerful, all-loving, and all-wise God. He will execute His plan for your life and make sense out of all your adversity.

PRAYER: Dear Father in heaven, Help me to grow in the grace and knowledge of Jesus Christ that I might be prepared for the work that You have in store for me. Amen.

June 24

WHAT A FAILURE!

He was born Cornelius Alexander Mc Gillicuddy in 1862 to Irish immigrant parents in East Brookfield, Massachusetts. Although he performed decently as a catcher in the National League for eleven years, he went on to earn the most *infamous* reputation in all baseball history. For instance, as a manager he led his team to *last place* no fewer than *seventeen times!* In 1951 he was forced to sell his team because of financial mismanagement. To top it off, as manager he racked up a staggering total of *3,814 losses* – a shameful record that endures to this day!

But we do not remember Cornelius Mc Gillicuddy, a.k.a. Connie Mack, for his failures. We remember him for taking the "white elephant" Philadelphia Athletics, a rock bottom club that no one wanted, and for leading them to nine Major League Pennants and five world championships – even stopping the irresistible Yankees in their heydays of 1929 and 1930. In those years Connie Mack had assembled and trained what many believed was the greatest baseball team ever to play. We also remember him for his history making all-time record for most wins by any Major League manager – 3,753 – another record that stands to this day. We remember Connie Mack for his incredible longevity – a baseball manager's career that spanned fifty years and in which led his team through 7,755 games. For these achievements Connie Mack is remembered and was inducted into the Baseball Hall of Fame. Yes, baseball historians acknowledge Connie Mack's list of shortcomings. But they simply choose to define his life by his contributions rather than his failures.

God does the same with those who put their faith in him – he remembers their sins no more and remembers them for good, not evil. Read the record of Scripture - particularly the Book of Hebrews, chapter 11. There the apostle reviews the lives of Noah, Abraham, Sarah, Moses, David, and many others. Certainly they all lived flawed lives. But the Scripture remembers them for their faith and sacrifice, not for their failures. By their faith and trust in God, these everyday people, with all their shortcomings, found forgiveness, approval, and overcoming strength.

PRAYER: Dear Father in heaven, I confess my sins and failures to you. Please forgive me – failures and all – and make me into the person you created me to be. Amen.

June 25

OUT OF CHARACTER?

Yosemite Valley in California's Yosemite National Park is widely recognized as having the largest concentration of scenic beauty in one location. Characteristic of Yosemite Valley are its lush meadows bordered on all sides by towering granite walls that rise 3,500 feet above the valley. These cathedral-like granite sentinels offer sanctuary to the abundant wildlife of the valley, which are also nourished by the sparkling Merced River and its many tributaries. But for many visitors, the one feature of this shrine of scenic enchantment, that makes it truly Yosemite Valley, is its waterfalls.

The waterfalls of Yosemite are among the most beautiful and highest on earth. Bridalveil Fall plummets 620 feet to the valley floor, Ribbon Fall plunges 1,612 feet from top to bottom. The combined height of Vernal and Nevada Falls is more than 900 feet and Sentinel Fall drops a staggering 2,000 feet. But highest of all are the Yosemite Falls which, in three successive cascades, plunge 2,425 feet. These scenic treasures adorn Yosemite Valley on every side and make it the most adored spot on the planet.

But should you visit Yosemite Valley in late summer and early fall, you will find it quite "out of character." In the late summer and fall months all but one of these spectacular cascades (Bridalveil Fall) disappears! Only a damp streak on the valley wall remains in their place. No silvery streaks, no thunder from their frenzied descent, no billowing mist, no rainbows. They're all gone. The late summer visitor might mournfully ask, "Where are the waterfalls that Yosemite boasts of? What's wrong with this valley? Yosemite is not its true self."

But return again in the spring and you will find the valley its "true self" again – with its water falls in all their glory, at peak performance.

In truth, Yosemite Valley is always its true self. It simply goes through different seasons and each season offers a beauty all its own. Diminished waterfalls are characteristic of Yosemite Valley in the summer. The valley is not sick, it's not failing, and is not out of character. It is simply not the optimum time for waterfalls.

People have seasons too. They go through seasons of ebb and flow, of productivity and of mere preparation, of fruitfulness and seeming futility, of painful obscurity and mountain tops of recognition. But they are all valid experiences and are all necessary to our growth and survival. Most important, they are all characteristic of human experience. Sure, we all hope for a steady, unbroken stream of fruitfulness and success. But dry spells, failure and fruitlessness, do us more good than we know. They drive us to study more, to dig deeper and to pray harder. In the Scripture the psalmist confessed: "Before I was afflicted, I went astray; but now I keep your law" and "It was good for me that I was afflicted, that I might learn your statutes." (Psalm 119:67, 71)

PRAYER: Dear Father in heaven, help me to patiently endure the troublesome times of obscurity, fruitlessness and failure. Through it all, may my affliction drive me into your arms and make me more like you. Amen.

June 26

WHEN WE THINK IT CAN'T BE DONE

It was an impenetrable barrier that no man could breach. Athletes had tried for centuries, even earlier, since time was being measured by the minute. The barrier in fact was the four-minute-mile, and both athletes and trainers became convinced that human beings were incapable of running a mile in four minutes. The early Greeks had tried. They tried using wild animals to chase runners. They tried feeding their runners tiger's milk – real tiger's milk. Nothing worked. Men, they concluded, were not designed for such speeds. Wind resistance was too great. Our lung capacity was inadequate. There were a million reasons.

Then on May 6, 1954, Roger Bannister, a British medical student, did the impossible. He ran the mile in 3 minutes and 59.4 seconds. What's more amazing is that within just a month Australian John Landy beat Bannister's record, setting his own at 3 minutes and 57.9 seconds. Within that same year 37 others ran the mile in less than four minutes. And the next year more than 300 runners did the impossible, all of them running sub-four-minute-miles.

Why, after so long a time without success, did one man seem to open the door and allow the impossible to become commonplace? Though breaking the four-minute barrier was truly a great physical hurdle, the greater hurdle was in the human mind. People had for so long believed it impossible that for them it became impossible – but only in their minds. But once someone led the way and destroyed the illusion of impossibility, others followed.

And how many other "insurmountable" hurdles and barriers in life are also within our grasp if we will only have faith in ourselves and in God? In the Scripture Jesus said, "If you have the size of a mustard seed, you shall say to this mountain, 'Move from here to there,' and it will move; and nothing shall be impossible to you." (Matthew 17:20)

PRAYER: Dear Father in heaven, when I tread through unexplored territory and see obstacles beyond my ability to overcome, please empower me, make me greater than myself, and help me to have confidence in you and in my God-given abilities so that I may do the impossible. Amen.

June 27

TOO MUCH OF A GOOD THING?

Who said it? "We're more popular than Jesus Christ." - The Beatles. "I'm a pretty big star, folks. 'Superstar,' I guess you could say." – Bruce Willis. "All the women on *The Apprentice* flirted with me – consciously or unconsciously. That's to be expected." – Donald Trump. "Every decade has an iconic blonde – and right now, I'm that blonde." – Paris Hilton. "I am one of the greatest entrepreneurs and entertainers the world has ever encountered." – Sean Combs. Had enough?

Every time I hear someone say that "God never gives us more than we can handle," I think about athletes who know only victory and never defeat, or music celebrities who feed daily on national fame and never taste obscurity, or entrepreneurs who enjoy unbroken financial success and never suffer the humiliation of poverty.

I don't want to sound irreverent, but it *does* seem at times that God gives people more than they can handle – when it comes to fame, success, money, and power. Whether the person is a pugilist or a preacher, the effects of public adoration, success, power, and wealth are the same. They can create a monster. They tend to make a person boastful, arrogant, and heartless.

We need failure. We need physical limitations. We need disappointment. We need to go unrecognized. We need the very things we seek to avoid and the things we typically call evil.

Physical limitations teach us to depend on God. Sickness not only makes us thankful for health. It teaches us compassion for the weak. Failure teaches us humility. Obscurity and a lack of recognition purify our motives for serving. Disappointment turns our sights heavenward to our eternal reward. Can you see, then, why God cannot give us all that we desire?

In the book of 2 Chronicles 23 we read of King Uzziah. While he humbly sought the Lord he enjoyed great success and his kingdom flourished. But with unbroken success and power he became powerful, then very proud – and this led to his downfall (2 Chronicles 26:15-22).

But, if our deprivation is a greater teacher and causes us to make greater spiritual strides than in always getting what we want, should we then inflict this pain of poverty, obscurity, or failure on ourselves? Absolutely not! That would be the equivalent of playing the role of our own doctor, of prescribing medication or surgery for ourselves. We leave the diagnosis, prognosis, and the prescription for recovery in the hands of the Lord. We must trust ourselves to the skill and the scalpel of the Great Physician. But should He administer these painful things for our good, then we trust His love, wisdom, and sovereignty, and say like Christ, "Not my will, but Thine be done."

PRAYER: Dear Father in heaven, When the earthly things I seek are withheld, help me to resign myself to life and to Your will and trust in Your love and wisdom. Amen.

June 28

DISTRACTIONS

The *London Independent* (May 25, 2002) reported the escape of 31 prisoners from a Ugandan jail, one of them a convicted murderer. How did it happen? The prisoners were on a work detail digging a garden when a rabbit sprang from a bush. All five of the detail's guards turned and pursued the rabbit. Seeing the guards were distracted, the prisoners bolted and escaped in 31 different directions. Not only did the guards fail to recapture any of the convicts. They didn't even catch the rabbit.

What keeps us from finishing projects? What derails worthy pursuits? What robs us of precious family time? What constantly crowds God out of our lives? Distractions!

In the Scripture we read how the apostle Peter was able to walk upon the water as long as he kept his focus on the Savior. But once distracted by the wind and waves, he began to sink (Matthew 14:25-31). Like the good seeds that fell among thorns that choked the crops into fruitlessness (Matthew 13:7, 22), so the distractions of life will weigh us down and pull us away from the things that matter most – our calling, our families, and our God.

But the resounding command in Scripture is to "stay focused." We are told to "fix our eyes on Jesus" and to "run the race that is set before us" (Hebrews 12:2). Throughout the Bible we read that we should "be careful to do what the Lord has commanded and *not turn aside to the right or to the left*" (Deuteronomy 5:32; 17:11; 28:14; Joshua 1:7; etc.).

Like rabbits springing from bushes, 100 pointless pursuits will try to catch your eye and distract you. Don't let this happen. Fulfill the mission God has given you. Safeguard time with your family against intruders. Make a daily date with the Lord and keep it. Stay focused.

PRAYER: Dear Lord, as the compass needle returns to magnetic north again and again, help my soul and my sights to come back to you. Amen.

June 29

BECOMING WHAT WE HATE

It might surprise some to know that Japan, which has the third largest economy in the world and is the world's bastion of technology, has a whaling industry. Whaling, as well as fishing, is still considered an important part of Japan's food culture. This has made Japan the target of criticism from animal rights and environmental activists.

In November 2007 two animal rights activists, John Gravois and Karl Neilsen, planned an attack upon a Japanese whaling ship, the Nisshin Maru, in the chilling waters of the Ross Sea near Antarctica. They intended to hurl bottles of acid and smoke bombs at the whaler – regardless of the injury they might inflict on the sailors.

But their attack was foiled when they became hopelessly lost in the frozen fog. Desperate, the two men radioed a cry for help. For seven hours they hunkered down in their small Zodiac dingy, trying to survive the fog and drizzle. Then a ship came to their rescue. It was the Japanese whaler, the Nisshin Maru - the very same ship they had planned to attack!

The Japanese took the two aboard, fed them, and gave them shelter as they towed their boat to safer waters. But, once out of danger, the activists remarked, "I guess we're back on schedule," and resumed their attack. Gravois and Neilsen hurled a smoke bomb and a 1 ½ gallon-bottle of acid on the deck of the Japanese ship, injuring two of the sailors.

Whalers and activists, liberals and conservatives, the pious and the profane – are all made of the same material: frail and flawed humanity. But sometimes they can be so blinded by their own self-righteousness and hypocrisy that they become the very thing they profess to hate. May God help us not deny by our deeds what we profess with our mouths! Our Lord said, "Why do you look at the speck of sawdust in your brother's eye and pay no attention to the plank in your own eye? How can you say to your brother, 'Let me take the speck out of your eye,' when all the time there is a plank in your own eye? You hypocrite, first take the plank out of your own eye, and then you will see clearly to remove the speck from your brother's eye" (Matthew 7:3-5, NIV).

PRAYER: Dear Father in heaven, open my eyes to my own flaws and frailties before I seek to correct others. Grant that I will not criticize my brother until I have walked a mile in his shoes. Amen.

June 30

LET GOD BE THE JUDGE

At twenty-three F. Scott Fitzgerald enjoyed national fame as author of the runaway bestselling book, *This Side of Paradise*. That was in 1920. Two decades later he was a washed up, alcoholic, has-been who couldn't find anyone to hire him as a writer. His death at the age of 44 came as the final sigh of a broken life. His body was ravaged by years of alcohol abuse. His wife deranged with schizophrenia.

The last two of his four novels, *The Great Gatsby* and *Tender is the Night*, were regarded by the critics as disappointments and sold poorly. Only a handful of friends attended his funeral. F. Scott Fitzgerald, who as a child had vowed *not* to become a failure like his father, seemed to give new meaning to the word.

But that's not the end of his story. For later generations "discovered" the works of F. Scott Fitzgerald. All his novels were republished and remain in print to this day. They were made into Hollywood motion pictures. *The Great Gatsby*, which the critics once condemned, is possibly the best-selling American novel of all time. And the very man who died a failure, is today regarded, along with Ernest Hemmingway, as the consummate American author of the Twentieth Century.

Even at the twilight of our lives we should not judge ourselves as failures. The ripple effects of our life may not be known and appreciated until long after our death. Be faithful in the work to which God's called you and let Him be the judge. Let Him take the good seeds you have sown and cause them to grow into something beautiful, something that blesses mankind. In the Scripture Paul reminds us that only the Judgment Seat of Christ will reveal the true quality of every person's labors (1 Corinthians 3:13). Until then, be faithful and leave the results to God.

PRAYER: Dear Father in heaven, as I look back on my life and my work, I wonder if I have helped as many as I have hurt. I wonder if I've accomplished any lasting good. Please help me to be faithful and make me a blessing to others. Amen.

July

July 1

WHY CAN'T I LEARN AS FAST AS I USED TO?

One disturbing reality that comes with age is the increased difficulty absorbing and recalling new information. People that live past fifty years, or even thirty and forty, must routinely work harder to learn new skills. Is this a sign of deteriorating intellect? Do people get dumber with age? Hardly. Let me explain.

Thirty years ago, when I began my first year of college, I had a small library of twelve to fifteen books – mostly texts for my freshman semester. One of those fifteen books was an obscure volume, *Knowing the Doctrines of the Bible*, by Myer Pearlman. If you asked me to find it on the shelf, it would take no more than a second. It was only one of a dozen books.

Today my library consists of several thousand books. I've read most of them. But many of them are waiting to be read. And, to be honest, some of them I've forgotten about and will occasionally purchase a book I subsequently realize I already had. Now, today, if you asked me to find for you my volume of *Knowing the Doctrines of the Bible*, it will take me a few minutes to find a book it used to only take a second. Why does it now take so long? Because I must scan the titles of hundreds of books – so many books that fill twelve large shelves. Plus I have books stacked on top of the shelves and more books scattered through the house. The fact that it takes so long to recall the location of a book does not indicate I'm getting dumber. It's simply because I have so much more on the shelves than I used to. There's so much more information to manage and sift through.

The same is true with our minds. The older we get the more information, data, and life experience gets recorded and stored away in the library of our brains. At a young age *recall* is easy – there's not that much to sift through. The library is small. But for the person who's lived many years, *recall* becomes more difficult – for he's got volumes and volumes of information to search through. His many shelves are filled with books of memories, learning, skills, and life experiences.

Add to this reality, the fact that each successive generation stands on the shoulders of all preceding generations, benefiting from the accumulated knowledge of the past. All previous generations pass on the fruit of their research and the lessons they have learned to the youngest generation – causing it to stand intellectually higher than any previous generation. But this appearance of intellectual superiority is only an illusion. We are no smarter that our parents or grandparents. We are higher because we stand on their shoulders.

So stop beating yourself up if you're not learning as fast as your younger counterparts. Nor be arrogant toward those "older and slower" members of society. We are all made out of the same stuff and all share the same weaknesses and the same need for God's wisdom and guidance. To all of us, young and old, the admonition is valid: "If anyone lacks wisdom, let him ask of God, who gives to all people generously" (James 1:4) and "Trust in the Lord with all your heart, and do not lean on your own understanding. If all your ways acknowledge Him, and He shall direct your paths." (Proverbs 3:5-6)

PRAYER: Dear father in Heaven, deliver me from self-deception and the blind arrogance of believing that I am morally and intellectually superior to my forbearers. I, like everyone else, am a member of humanity with all its capacity for goodness and greatness, or for depravity and evil. Help me to learn from the examples of the past that I may gain insight for living. Amen.

July 2

LEARNING TO LIVE TOGETHER

Charles Vance Millar (1853-1926) was a famous Canadian lawyer and financier. But he is probably best known for the "last will and testament" that he left behind – a will that consisted mainly of practical jokes guaranteeing him "the last laugh."

For instance, he bequeathed all his shares in the Ontario Jockey Club to the country's foremost crusaders against gambling. Shares in other gambling establishments were willed to every minister in Toronto. Most controversial was his granting of part of his estate to the mother who had the most children in the decade after his death – which precipitated the famous "Stork Derby."

But one interesting clause of the will dictated that equal shares of his house in Jamaica would be granted to three of the city's lawyers who hated each other intensely. The intent was to force the three to come to an agreement on the sale price and equal distribution of the proceeds, or – far more interesting – *to learn to live together in the same home.*

In a way, God has bequeathed to his children the same gift – one house for many people who seem to naturally hate each other. But God's intent is by no means to have "a good" laugh in heaven. Our heavenly Father wants us to learn a valuable lesson – to learn to live together: to appreciate each other's contribution and to pull together for the common good.

In our country there are competing ideas of how to run our government and what the role of government *is.* Could it be that *each* of these opposing views has value and an essential contribution to make?

Which is more important in a family, the father's firmness and discipline or the mother's nurturing and love? The failed social experiments of the last 40 years have demonstrated both are critical to the health and development of children. It's not "one or the other." It's both.

The same is true for the "National Family." Instead of viewing America as a battleground for the quest for power, we should see our nation as a family that needs the good from each political party – whose respective facet of the truth should complement all the others.

The bottom line is this: no one person and no one political party has all the truth and all the answers for solving our nation's ills. It takes all of us – with a whole lot of help from God – to lead and care for our nation.

Remember the promise, "If my people, who are called by my name, shall humble themselves and pray, and seek my face, and turn from their wicked ways, then will I hear from heaven, and will forgive their sins and heal their land." (2 Chronicles 7:14)

PRAYER: Dear Father in heaven, please bless our nation. Mend its every flaw and heal its many divisions. Grant wisdom from above to our leaders that they may lead us on the path of goodness and greatness. Remove the pain and poison from our hearts and fill us with your love. Bind us together in that love and turn our hearts toward you in faith and repentance, Amen.

WHEN WE FEEL ALL IS LOST

On November 7, 1872, Captain Benjamin Briggs set sail aboard
the 103-foot sailing ship, the *Mary Celeste*, with his wife and daughter,
and crew of eight. The *Mary Celeste* (which displaced 280 tons) was
loaded with 1700 barrels of raw alcohol bound for Genoa, Italy.
Mysteriously, the captain, his family and crew were never seen again.
They vanished.

But the ship was found – about a month later, on December 4,
1872. Sailors aboard the *Dei Gratia* found the *Mary Celeste* in perfect
condition, perfectly seaworthy, perfectly intact, but abandoned!

Where were the captain and his crew? The sailors who found
her saw no signs of forcible boarding. No signs of piracy. No evidence
of a fire. However, they did find the captain's log and his (and his
family's) half-eaten dinner. They and the crew had left the ship in haste.
But where did they go? Did they vanish into thin air? Were they
abducted by UFOs? Did a giant squid pull all eleven people overboard
to their deaths? What happened?

The best explanation resulted from an inquiry by British and
American authorities determined that the 1700 barrels of alcohol on
board had probably given off a cloud of vapor (from either a change in
temperature or barometric pressure). Captain Briggs and the crew
(unaccustomed to this cargo) interpreted this vapor as smoke from a fire
and fled from what they believed to be a doomed ship in the ship's
lifeboat.

The most painful reality about the mysterious disappearance of
the Mary Celeste crew was that there was never any danger to the ship.
The captain and crew had abandoned a perfectly good ship and were
consequently lost at sea.

In a way, the abandonment of the Mary Celeste is somewhat
similar to those things we hold most dear, things we fear are doomed to
destruction – our families, our marriages, and our nation. We see the
signs and symptoms of disaster and we're convinced that "all is lost"
with America, with our families, and our jobs. We're tempted to believe
that we're on a sinking ship and we must escape.

But instead of worrying about America and abandoning our
responsibilities, the Scripture has a better idea: "Do not be anxious about
anything, but in everything by prayer and petition, with thanksgiving,
present your requests to God. And the peace of God, which transcends

all understanding, will guard your hearts and minds in Christ Jesus."
(Philippians 4:6-7)

PRAYER: Dear Lord, please bless my marriage, my family, and my
country. Heal America of its spiritual and moral depravity. Bind up our
many divisions and mend our every flaw. Breathe a revival across our
land and turn our hearts to you in faith and repentance and to one
another in love and reconciliation. O God of our fathers, raise up godly
men and women to fill the ranks of leadership in our government, our
universities, our media, and our corporations and lead us on the path of
righteousness. Amen.

July 4

WHEN WE THINK AMERICA IS A TERRIBLE PLACE TO LIVE

In the last thirty years, with the rise of Postmodern thought,
American history has been increasingly depicted as a story of
intolerance, evil, and oppression. Sometimes it takes an "outsider,"
however, to bring us back to the reality that America is really not so bad.

Author and Catholic priest, William Bausch, tells the story of a
rabbi from Russia who was visiting an American family in Texas. At
one point in the visit the family brought the rabbi to a Chinese restaurant
– a culinary treat he had never known in Russia. Throughout the meal,
the rabbi extolled the freedoms, prosperity, and opportunities of
America, in contrast to the bleak conditions he had known in Russia.
Then the waiter brought the bill and presented each of the family and the
rabbi with a brass Christmas ornament. Laughter erupted when they
noticed that all the brass ornaments had "Made in India" stamped on
them. The rabbi's eyes then filled with tears. The father then offered an
apology, asking if the rabbi had been offended by the presentation of a
Christmas gift. "No," said the smiling rabbi. "I was shedding tears of
joy to be in a wonderful country in which a Buddhist gives a Jew a
Christmas gift made by a Hindu."[xli]

Many years ago another "outsider," the famed French statesman, philosopher, and historian Alexis de Tocqueville traveled the breadth and width of America and marveled at its success at being a self-governing people. He had reason to marvel. History had proved that human beings were incapable of ruling themselves. It took the will of a king or dictator to enforce law. Since the American Revolution France itself has gone through seven forms of government. In the same period Italy has been through 52 different governments. Yet for more than 200 years America has thrived under the same Constitution.

The Scripture says, "Righteousness exalts a nation, but sin is a reproach to any people." (Proverbs 14:34) Teacher and songwriter, Katherine Lee Bates, wrote these words that make an appropriate prayer: *America, America, God mend thine every flaw, Confirm thy soul in self-control, thy liberty in law!*

PRAYER: Dear God in heaven, please bless our nation; forgive its sins; heal its moral and spiritual sickness; and turn the hearts of its people to You and toward each other in love. Amen.

July 5

THE THINGS WE THROW AWAY

The famous "Liberty Bell" has quite a history. It was originally cast in 1751 to commemorate the 50th anniversary (jubilee) of William Penn's Charter of Privileges, a radical document for its time, which spoke of universally recognized rights for all people, including Indians, and of religious freedom for all people. The bell contained on its hulls the words from Leviticus 25:10 in the Bible, *"Proclaim liberty throughout the land unto all the inhabitants thereof."*

Unfortunately, this original Liberty Bell was found to be flawed and was recast by its manufacturers, John Pass and John Stow, not once, but twice, before the final 2080-pound bell was raised on June 11, 1753 to the steeple of the Philadelphia Statehouse.

There the great bell labored for many years. It was rung again and again to herald critical moments in our nation's history. It rang to announce the ascendancy of George III to the throne in 1761. It tolled to assemble the people of Philadelphia to discuss the Sugar Act of 1764 And the Stamp Act of 1765.

It rang to assemble the First and Second Continental Congresses of 1774 and 1775, and to announce the outcome of the Battles of Lexington and Concord in 1775. On July 8, 1776 the great bell again tolled to assemble people for the first public reading of the Declaration of Independence. However, when British troops occupied Philadelphia, the bell was removed and hid for its own safe-keeping – lest it be melted down to make British cannon. After being restored to its proper place, the Liberty Bell continued rendering service by calling sessions of congress, summoning voters, and announcing National holidays like Washington's Birthday and the Fourth of July.

Certainly, veneration was high for this national heirloom, right? Hardly. Most Americans are appalled when they find out that the Liberty Bell was almost sold as scrap in 1828 by the Philadelphia city fathers. They had contracted with bell-maker, John Wilbank of Germantown, PA, for a new replacement. Wilbank agreed to reduce the cost by $400 in exchange for the old Liberty Bell. However, he realized that towing "the beast" back to Germantown would have been too troublesome, so he gave it back to the city. This enraged the city fathers, who even tried to sue Mr. Wilbank to *force* him "to remove *his junk* from our city." It didn't work and fortunately the city of Philadelphia *re-thought* its effort to discard the greatest relic of the Revolutionary War and symbol of our Independence.

But don't be too harsh with those old city fathers. All of us tend *not* to place adequate value on things when we have them – and later regret throwing them away. That's why all of us have only memories of "now" vintage toys, Barbie dolls, baseball card collections, and perhaps even *people* – all of which we failed to acknowledge and value in their day. Think of how many marriages would still be alive and thriving if husbands and wives had only valued each other and acknowledged each other's needs. Think of how much more successful we would have been at parenting if we had only valued those times with our children a little more, instead of racing them along and escorting our children out of the home as quickly as possible in our quest for personal independence.

The Scripture admonishes us to "Bless the Lord and to forget none of his benefits (spouse, children, jobs, possessions)." (Psalm 103:2)

PRAYER: Dear Father in heaven, please help me to escape the common fate of so many – to fail to know what I've got until it's gone. Dear Lord, open my blind eyes to see the blessings with which you've surrounded me in my spouse, my children, my friends, my job and my possessions. Help me to get out of the complaining business and to develop an attitude of gratitude. Amen.

July 6

TURN PAIN INTO GAIN

Al was the victim of a racket. In 1891 Almon Brown Strowger was an undertaker in Kansas City. But he was a frustrated undertaker. Time and again his competitor in the undertaking business was receiving almost all the business calls. It just didn't make sense. Even when a close friend died Al was certain he'd receive a call from the family to provide funeral services. Again, the call went to his competitor. Then he found out why. His competitor's wife ran the local switch board and, although he couldn't prove it, he was certain she was diverting business calls to her husband.

What could he do in such a situation? Seek revenge? Pursue legal action against the switchboard operator?

Al did something different. He decided to channel his anger into something productive. Almon Brown Strowger invented the world's first telephone switch system that eliminated the need for a person to connect local phone calls. He also invented first the dial telephone system, allowing callers to phone direct without the assistance of an operator. Although Strowger only made thousands of dollars from his inventions when he sold them and his shares in the Strowger Automatic Telephone Exchange Service, they went on to net millions and revolutionize telephone service across America.

As the old adage goes, "If the world only gives you lemons, make lemonade." That's what Almon Brown Strowger did. He turned his frustration and anger into profit for himself and blessing to others. He transformed his curses into blessings and his pain into gain.

The Scripture tells us "Do not repay evil for evil," "Do not take revenge," and "Do not be overcome by evil, but overcome evil with good." (Romans 12:17, 19, 21)

PRAYER: Dear Father in heaven, please help me to conquer the tyranny of my moods and channel my frustration and anger into a blessing for others and praise for You. Amen.

July 7

TAKING WORK HOME

Somjet Korkeaw, a 43-year-old business executive was burning the midnight oil one weekend. He decided to take his project home rather than wait till Monday to finish it. But as he reached the bottom of his office building – the Taipai 101 – which, at 1,671 feet tall, is the world's tallest building - he realized he'd forgotten an document essential to completing the project. He'd have to go back up to the 99th floor to retrieve it or choose to enjoy his weekend. The problem? The elevators had shut down for the weekend and all the stairwells were locked. All that remained operational was a library service elevator – intended for carrying small loads of books and manuals to offices throughout the towering structure. So Somjet decided to chance it – to use the library elevator to bring him up to the 99th floor. He removed all the books from the little elevator and curled up into its confining little cubicle. Somjet then pressed the "99 Floor" button and listened as the tiny elevator creaked its way up. Unfortunately, Somjet's 150-pound body exceeded the little elevator's lifting capacity by 50 pounds. As the over taxed elevator creaked past the 90th floor it came to slow and final stop – in between two floors. Poor Somjet Korkeaw! In his earnestness to make constructive use of his weekend, he ended up spending the remaining 40 hours of it trapped in a crouched position until maintenance workers could restart the elevator and set him free.

Stories like this remind us that time devoted to rest, recreation and family time is a very wise investment. Being so overzealous for our job so that we cannot rest while things are left undone will bring us to a point of burnout and lead us to do stupid and wasteful things like – spending the weekend in a broken elevator.

In the Psalms King Solomon reminds us: "Unless the Lord builds the house, the workers who build it labor in vain. Unless the Lord protects the city, guarding it with sentries will do no good. It is useless for you to work so hard from early morning till late at night, anxiously working for food to eat, for God gives rest to his loved ones." (Psalm 127:1-4) Victor Hugo once wrote: "Have courage for the great trials of life and patience for the small ones. And when you have laboriously finished your task for the day, go to sleep! God is awake!"

PRAYER: Dear Father in heaven, help me to keep balance in my life – devoting time to my necessary work that is part of my calling. But help me also to give focused time to that which truly defines my core identity: my family, my friends and my faith in You. Amen.

July 8

THE MEASURE OF SUCCESS

Jerry Siegel and Joseph Shuster are a true success story, though you've probably never heard of them. In 1934 they created a cartoon character and spent the next four years trying to find a publisher interested in printing his exploits. After many rejections DC Comics finally purchased their work for $130 ($10 per page for a 13-page cartoon) and hired the two young men as cartoonists and writers. The year was 1938 and Jerry and Joseph's cartoon character was an instant smash hit – and continued to be *for the next 75 years!* Their character has since grossed billions of dollars through comics, radio broadcasts, TV shows, and motion pictures. Who was the character? The ultimate superhero - Superman!

The sad part of this story is that Jerry Siegel and Joseph Shuster received little compensation for their creation. In fact, until Warner Communications voluntarily agreed in 1975 to give these two men annual pensions of $20,000 (increased to $30,000, plus a bonus, in 1981), all these two received for their creation was their initial payment of $130.

Of course, the sadness of this story all depends on how you measure success and failure. *Did Siegel and Shuster make a significant contribution to American culture?* They most certainly did. *Did their work inspire society's faith in the triumph of good over evil?* Most Americans would give an emphatic "yes." *Did their superhero, the epitome of goodness, survive the ravages of the "antihero" era, of cynicism, and of Postmodern negativism?* Obviously, with the stunning success of "Superman Returns," Superman has survived and will evidently be with us for a long time to come. This being the case, then are we not right in concluding that Jerry Siegel and Joseph Shuster were highly successful men? Again, it all depends on how you measure success.

In the Scripture our Lord said, "A man's life does not consist in the abundance of his possessions" (Luke 12:15). Nor is success measured in the abundance of dollars and material things. The measure of success is how our lives have pleased God and how we have benefited our fellow human beings.

PRAYER: Dear Father in heaven, help me to live with eternity's values in mind. Please grant that I may look beyond earthly pursuits and rewards, and strive to do those things that have eternal significance and reap eternal rewards. Amen.

July 9

WHEN WE'RE TIRED OF LIFE'S CHALLENGES

As much as we shrink from challenges, we need them. They're essential to our well-being. That's what one physician says – Dr. Larry Dossey. In fact, Dr. Dossey believes that they very germs that attack and penetrate our bodies contribute to our overall health. How? Because these biological attacks help keep our body on its toes. "Our own body," he writes, "contains the wisdom derived from countless challenges to its integrity. Only through threats to its well-being does the body learn to respond and to be efficient at the business of health."[xlii]

I recall an example of this while touring a submarine docked at Norfolk Naval Base. One of the sailors explained to me that while the vessel is submerged for three months at a time, the air purifiers on board filter out all impurities, airborne viruses and bacteria. "That's great," I said. "You get to breathe in germ-free air." To my surprise the sailor replied, "No, it's not so good. Because the first thing that happens when we return home to our families is that whole crew comes down with a cold." He explained that the human body's defense system, in just three months of *not* being tested and challenged, becomes lax and weaker. It needs to be challenged.

Dr. Dossey goes on to explain that the same is true of us in all the facets of our lives: mental, emotional and spiritual. Tough challenges test us and may be painful, but we thrive on them. If we are to be successful in life we must learn to face our challenges and understand their health-giving powers.

The Scripture concurs. "No discipline seems pleasant at the time, but painful. Later on, however, it produces a harvest of righteousness and peace for those who have been trained by it." (Hebrews 12:11) Whether your personal life, your workplace or your organization confronts you with challenges – realize they are meant to do you good and make you stronger.

PRAYER: Dear Father in heaven, help me to face the challenges of life with faith and a positive attitude. Remind me, O Lord, that you will work all things together for my ultimate good and your glory. Amen.

July 10

WE'VE SEEN TOUGHER TIMES

"It's the worst economy in fifty years! The worst economy in America's history!" Ever hear that before. During election years it seems to be the mantra on the lips of politicians. The trouble is, this unbridled negative torrent can be discouraging, making us believe that we are in the very worst of times. But that is far from the truth.

Few today are old enough to remember "Black Tuesday," October 29, 1929 – the day the stock market crashed, sending stock prices spiraling downward and causing businesses and banks to go bust.

But that dreadful day was just the beginning of sorrows. In the subsequent 50 days, fifty percent of all stock value was lost. But things would get terribly worse. Before the crash General Motors shares were valued at $500 a share. By 1932 they were selling for only $10.

Unemployment before the crash was at a trim 3.2 percent. A year after the crash it had risen to 9 percent. But by 1932 it had risen to a staggering 33 percent. Between the years 1930 and 1932 85,000 businesses closed. In 1930 alone, 1,300 banks closed their doors for good. The following year 2,000 more failed. During this entire period 11,000 banks folded (almost half of the banks in America) – taking billions of dollars of Americans' personal savings with them. A prolonged draught coupled with the fall of agricultural prices led to the foreclosure of thousands of farms. Almost 20% of all Oklahomans fled to California. By 1936 25% of all farms in the "Dust Bowl" had been abandoned and in one year, 1932, 60 percent of all farms in North Dakota were auctioned off. In fact, in a single day in 1932, 25 percent of all land in Mississippi was sold from under its owners.[xliii]

Yes, America has seen worst times than these – and it has survived! Certainly hard times will come again, but we need to view them in light of the entire American journey. If we've survived harder times in the past, we'll make it through whatever lies ahead. But we must have faith in the God who has been there for us and who gives us the eternal promise: "If my people, who are called by my name, shall humble themselves and pray, and seek my face, and turn from their wicked ways; then will I hear from heaven, forgive their sins and heal their land." (2 Chronicles 7:14)

PRAYER: Dear Father in heaven, please forgive our individual and national sins. Please, by your divine Spirit, breathe a revival across our nation and turn the hearts of Americans to you in repentance and faith and to each other in love and unity. Please bless America and heal it of its spiritual and moral sickness. Raise America to true greatness and use it for your torch of freedom and your instrument of peace. Amen.

July 11

THE TOUGHEST AND THE TINIEST

Greenland is a tough place for plants. Eighty-one percent of Greenland's surface is covered with ice. Its interior ice sheet is so thick and heavy, in fact, that it has depressed the land beneath it, creating a basin that lies over 1,000 feet below sea level. Temperatures on Greenland are especially hostile. They routinely plummet to 76 degrees below zero (Fahrenheit) in the winter and barely reach 40 degrees above in the summer. Of course there are no trees on the ice-covered island of Greenland - right? Actually, there are trees on Greenland's southwest coast, and one in particular that thrives in its merciless weather. It is the dwarf willow which grows to just a few inches tall and has the distinction of being the smallest tree in the world. Not only is it tiny, but it cannot compete with other plants in temperate zones where the soil is rich and rainfall abundant. But before you condemn the dwarf willow as a little weakling, remember that it flourishes in the inhospitable climate of Greenland – a climate that kills just about every other kind of tree.

A wimp in one environment, but a champion in another - this is the case for many plants. Though they cannot compete with other flora where sunlight, temperature, and rainfall are favorable to plant life, yet they are tough enough to endure climates that kill most other plants. Many varieties of Cactus and Succulents fall into this category. In places of abundant rainfall and rich soil, cacti often cannot compete with other plants. But in the sunbaked deserts that are lethal to most other plants, cacti are in their element.

The same can be said for people. Circumstances that are intolerable to some are a blessing to others. You may find a certain situation unbearable – yet another person may thrive in the same situation. It doesn't mean you're a weakling and that the other person is a powerhouse. It depends on the way God has gifted you. In different circumstances, you may be in your element, while the other person in those same circumstances might crumble. So stop beating yourself up. Acknowledge your weaknesses and ask God for strength and grace to get you through the tough times. But also acknowledge the strengths God has given you, offer Him thanks, and use those God-given strengths to serve your fellow human beings. The apostle Paul wrote: "I wish that everyone was as I am – yet each man has his own gift from God, one in this manner and another in that." (1 Corinthians 7:7)

PRAYER: Dear Father in heaven, help me not to feel threatened when I see others out-perform me and succeed in situations in which I would have failed. Help me to understand my own strengths and gifts and help me to use them to serve you and others. Amen.

July 12

SETBACKS

Jean Baptiste Reinholdt was a Gypsy. He was raised in Gypsy camp in Belgium and became known by his friends as "Django." But he was also one of the most musically-gifted child prodigies in history. He successfully tried his hand at an assortment of instruments, but finally settled on the six-stringed banjo – a banjo that was tuned and played as a guitar. He was well on his way to a successful career as a musician in Paris when tragedy struck.

Django was only eighteen years old when a fire swept through his wagon leaving him burned on more than 50 percent of his body. Doctors feared his left leg would have to amputated and they knew he would never again play any instrument. Two fingers on his left hand – the hand he used in playing chords - were permanently paralyzed from burns. A tragic fire had robbed him of everything for which he had hoped and dreamed.

But often life's most painful roadblocks can become the gateways to our greatest success. Despite his injuries, Django held tightly to his hopes. And these very injuries that dashed his dreams also forced him to re-learn his instrument and led him to develop an innovative new style: the "Lead Guitarist." Django had great difficulty playing chords, but he could play melodies and went on to become what many believe to be the greatest Jazz guitarist of the 20th Century. His recordings and performances greatly influenced the more famous Jazz musicians like Duke Ellington and Dizzy Gillespie, and Rock stars such as Jeff Beck, Jerry Garcia, Jimmy Hendrix, Carlos Santana, B.B. King, and David Crosby, and even Country stars such as Chet Atkins.

It may seem impossible that any of your setbacks could have any redeeming value. But trust your all-wise, all-loving and all-powerful heavenly Father with your future and your life. If you seek him, he will guide you and open doors of opportunity for you. God is able to turn our hurts into halos, our stumbling blocks into stepping stones, and our curses into blessings (Genesis 50:20; Deuteronomy 23:5).

PRAYER: Almighty Father in heaven, please guide and direct my steps and cause all the pain in my life to become gain. Amen.

July 13

WHEN WE WISH OUR DAYS AWAY

An ancient Arabian legend tells of a band of Bedouin nomads who were retiring for the night. Suddenly in the darkness, an angel of God shone before them. Terrified at his appearance, the angel remained silent and then gave this command to the Bedouins. "Gather as many pebbles as you can in your saddle bags, travel a day's journey, and you will be both happy and sad."

Then as quickly as he appeared, he vanished from their sight.
Puzzled over the angel's command, the Bedouins stared at each other. Then they began to grumble and fume over receiving such a task. "We have too much to carry already. Sure, after a day of carrying pebbles, we'll be both happy and sad – happy the task is over and sad for ever receiving it."

Reluctantly and grudgingly the Bedouins picked up a few handfuls of pebbles each, put them in their saddlebags and journeyed all day. As they wearily unloaded their camels that night, each paused to empty his saddlebag of its worthless contents. But the Bedouins were astonished at what they saw – each of their pebbles had been transformed into a diamond of great value! They were overjoyed at their newfound wealth. But their joy soon turned to regret over the wealth they could have had, if only they had grumbled less and gathered more.

Our days here in Iraq may, at times, seem as worthless as pebbles – fit only to be discarded. But each of them holds some blessing, some joy, some treasure. The Scripture reminds us that "This (today) is the day which the Lord has made, let us rejoice and be glad in it." (Psalm 118:24) Rather than wishing to "fast-forward" through our time in Iraq, take time to smell the roses – they do grow here as well as at home.

PRAYER: Dear God, help me to relish every moment and to cherish every day that you graciously give me as a gift. Amen.

July 14

RUNNING FROM CHALLENGES GETS US NOWHERE

George ran from the fight. He had aspirations for greatness. He had dreams. And he had talent to bring those dreams within his grasp. But in the face of a menacing opponent George ran.

George was a nineteen-year-old "inmate" of Saint Mary's Industrial School for boys - a Catholic reform school. The greatness he sought was as a baseball player. George's talent? He was a pitching sensation. Better than anybody - better than anyone except Bill Morrisette. Bill Morrisette, star-pitcher of rival-school Mount Saint Joseph, was George's "opponent."

Everyone at Saint Mary's was talking about the upcoming showdown between Morrisette and George. They were tired of hearing about Morrisette's no-hitters, of how devastating he was on the mound, of how he had beaten down the best hitters of Holy Cross, Georgetown, and Bucknell. Now the teams of Saint Mary's (a high school) and Mount Saint Joseph's (a college) would clash. But all attention focused on two pitchers - George and Bill Morrisette.

George was scared. The prospect of failure and having to face his teammates was too much to bear. So, ten days before the showdown, George fled. After all, he was just a kid from the slums of Baltimore. He was just a reform school inmate. Everyone was expecting too much from him.

But George didn't get off that easy. A probation officer and night watchman tracked him down and dragged him back. Finally George got a handle on his fear and faced the challenge. Thank God he did. For in that game it was George who pitched a no hitter and struck out 14 players in the process. As for Bill Morrisette, he gave up 6 runs, losing the game 6-0.

Whatever became of these two young men? Bill Morrisette went to the majors. His major league career lasted a total of 13 games. As for George, his major league career lasted a little longer - 22 years! Although, he spent the seven of his pro years as one of the best left-handed pitchers the game has ever known (92 wins against 44 losses), you probably know him better as a gifted outfielder and you certainly know him as one of the most powerful hitters of all time - George Herman "Babe" Ruth. Just think of all he might have missed by running away.

What about us? Are we ever tempted to run from a fight, to flee from a challenge? What greatness will we miss if we run away? God can give us the courage to face our fights and the strength to win them. The Scripture says, "Do not fear, for I am with you; do not look anxiously about you, for I am your God. I will strengthen you, surely I will help you, surely I will uphold you with My righteous right hand." (Isaiah 41:10)

PRAYER: Dear Father in heaven, to You I cling for courage and strength. Empower me by Your Spirit, make me equal to every task, and lead me from victory to victory. Amen.

CHARACTER: ONLY AS GOOD AS THE MATERIAL IT'S MADE OF

Without it we would never have built the pyramids, crossed the oceans or scaled Mount Everest. It has saved countless lives, pulled thousands from the angry seas and stopped the fall of many a mountain climber. What is it? Rope.

Rope had been around for a long time. And throughout its history - from the early Egyptians, through the Industrial Age, down to the present – rope has taken on the same basic pattern: fibers are twisted (clockwise) into yarns, yarns are twisted (counterclockwise) into strands, and strands (clockwise again) into rope. This alternation of the twist is the secret that gives rope its cohesion and strength.

The material for rope has also remained unchanged. Earliest mankind used sinew. But people have always used plant fibers. Today the tough fibers from the bark or leaves of abaca, sisal, jute, or hemp provide the best organic material. The best modern synthetic material is nylon, polypropylene, or Dacron. Far inferior - more easily obtainable - material has also been used for rope. But a rope is only as good as the fibers that go into it.

In a way the quality of fibers that make a rope parallels the quality of the thoughts, words, deeds, and habits that form our character. And character determines our destiny.

The example of an English manufacturer of rope graphically illustrates this idea. The man lived in the early days of the Industrial age. His arduous work and attention to detail earned him the reputation for producing the finest and strongest rope in the world. But the man began to pay more attention to profit than to quality. He sought out cheaper materials for fibers and substituted the inferior for the superior. He amassed a fortune in the process and managed to keep his reputation unstained.

Then one day, as fate would have it, while sailing the Atlantic to America, a tempest-driven wave washed the man overboard. The sailors scrambled to rescue him. They tossed him a rope which he managed to grasp. But as the sailors pulled him through the buffeting waves the rope suddenly snapped. The man drifted hopelessly away from the ship to his destiny.

Upon inspection the seamen observed that the rope was not only new – it was the famous rope made by the very man they had sought to rescue. He had died a victim of his own inferior rope. The inferior quality of his rope, like the quality of his character, had altered his destiny.

Author Frank Outlaw once wrote: "Watch your thoughts; they become words. Watch your words; they become actions. Watch your actions; they become habits. Watch your habits; they become character. Watch your character; it becomes your destiny."

The Scripture says, "Above all else, guard your heart, for it is the well-spring of life." (Proverbs 4:23)

PRAYER: Dear Father in heaven, Please, Dear Lord, even if I must go through the furnace of affliction, make me into the person of value and integrity that you desire me to be. Amen.

July 16

THE DUTY OF ALL LIVING THINGS – TO GROW

The Paradoxical Frog. Yes, there is such a species of frog with that title. It is an olive-green frog that lives in the lakes and lagoons of Trinidad and throughout the Amazon and lays its eggs among water plants. So what's so special about that? These eggs develop into giant 10-inch tadpoles. But the immense size of the tadpoles is somewhat deceiving, and disappointing. Because from this auspicious beginning the giant tadpole grows into a 1 ½-inch adult frog. By the time it reaches maturity, the Paradoxical Frog is only ¼ its original size.

This example of "backward growth" or regression in the Paradoxical Frog has a parallel among human beings. Consider the tragic affliction of many people – people who early in their lives are full of hope, virtue, and ideals, but by the end of their lives they have compromised everything of value for the sake of their comfort and security. They are not only diminished in physical vigor and frame. Their soured and withered soul is but a fraction of its once-youthful size.

In contrast, there are many who understand that the duty of the living is to grow – and never stop until one's dying day. Impossible? Consider General Douglas Macarthur who was commander of all allied forces during the Korean War and pulled off the most brilliant military operation of his 50 year career (the Inchon Invasion) when he was 70 years old. Macarthur went on to make the most profound statement on aging.

"Nobody grows old by merely living a number of years. People grow old only by deserting their ideals. Years may wrinkle the skin, but to give up your ideals, to lose interest, to become timid in the face of challenges - this wrinkles the soul. ...You are as young as your faith, as old as your doubt; as young as your self-confidence, as old as your fear; as young as your hope, as old as your despair."

Consider also the aspirations of the aging, but visionary, Katsushika Hokusai (1760-1849), one of the greatest artists of Japan. His greatest works were produced after the age of 60. He believed it was his duty to grow and never stop. Just a few years before his death he penned these words:

"From around the age of six, I had the habit of sketching from life. I became an artist, and from fifty on began producing works that won some reputation, but nothing I did before the age of seventy was worthy of attention. At seventy-three, I began to grasp the structures of birds and beasts, insects and fish, and of the way plants grow. If I go on trying, I will surely understand them still better by the time I am eighty-six, so that by ninety I will have penetrated to their essential nature. At one hundred, I may well have a positively divine understanding of them, while at one hundred and thirty, forty, or more I will have reached the stage where every dot and every stroke I paint will be alive. May Heaven, that grants long life, give me the chance to prove that this is no lie!"

Never satisfied with his level of expertise and despising stagnation, it is reported that on his deathbed Hokusai exclaimed, "If I had another five years, even, I could have become a real painter." Yes, it is the duty of all living things to grow and to leave this life greater, better, and more filled with faith, hope, and love than when we began. May God grant that our testimony be like that of Paul who, when facing the executioner's sword, could say, "I have fought the good fight, I have finished the course, I have kept the faith; henceforth, there is laid up for me the crown of righteousness, which the Lord, the righteous Judge, will award to me on that day ... and to all who love his appearing." (2 Timothy 4:7-8)

PRAYER: Dear Father in heaven, grant that though my body may diminish in strength and vigor, my spirit may grow stronger day by day. Renew my faith, my hope and my love. Grant that I may not be ashamed when I awake in your presence. Amen.

July 17

THE HAPPIEST PLACE TO BE

Ever hear of the Principality of Sealand? Or of its glorious royal family, Prince Roy, his wife, Princess Joan, and the Heir Apparent, Michael of Sealand (now "co-regent" with his father)? Well, it's all real. Sealand just might constitute the world's smallest island and smallest principality.

Sealand is actually nothing more than an old World War II anti-aircraft battery tower, created by sinking a concrete pontoon in 25 feet of water, seven miles off England's eastern shore, with a small fortress-platform built atop it. In 1967, retired British Army major, Paddy Roy Bates, took his wife and son and inhabited the man-made island. He proclaimed what was formerly known as "Rough's Tower" to be "Sealand" and himself its ruler. In the years to come, Sealand issued its own money, stamps, passports, and other official documents.

But having his own private world has come at a price. Life on the North Sea can be quite miserable and maintenance and upkeep of the tower is a constant battle. By the year 2000, Prince Roy was Sealand's only resident and he has since had to turn the "matters of state" over to his son, Prince Michael. According to Roy Bates, he started this whole enterprise because he was "dissatisfied with the oppressive laws and restrictions" of his homeland, England. But time has proven that his own private world was a far bigger headache and he is quite glad to be back in England.

In a way, this parallels the spiritual journey of many. In our quest for independence, we move away from under the "oppressive and restrictive" protection of our heavenly Father. But our private little kingdom, for which we had such hopes, turns out to be a miserable place, indeed. Over time we find that the center of God's will is the happiest place to be. As the Psalmist said:

"Find rest, O my soul, in God alone; my hope comes from him. He alone is my rock and my salvation; he is my fortress, I will not be shaken." (Psalm 62:5-6)

PRAYER: Dear Father in heaven, help me to come to my senses and return to the God who loves me, believes in me and wants the very best for me. Amen.

DO YOU EVER FEEL WORTHLESS?

That the world's first oil well was dug in 1859 in Titusville, Pennsylvania, by Colonel Edwin Drake is common knowledge. What is less known, is that there were *many previously existing wells* in the area that had struck oil. But these wells had been dug for the purpose of finding drinkable water and when they struck oil, they were abandoned, since the black ooze was considered a terrible nuisance. Amazing, that something we today pay $60-$70 for a barrel was once considered a curse.

But the story continues. Once it was determined that petroleum oil could be extracted from the earth in large quantities, more and more uses for the black crude came to light. The very first commercial product made from petroleum was "rock oil," sold at $1 a bottle as a cure for cholera, corns, toothaches, and neuralgia. But producers saw oil's greatest use as a lubricant in steam engines and machinery. Then a Yale chemist, Benjamin Silliman, Jr., discovered that one of oil's byproducts, kerosene, made an excellent illuminant. Over the next thirty years, producers derived from oil naphtha for cleaning, petroleum jelly for ointments, kerosene for light, and paraffin. In 1870, one company turned 70,000 pounds of paraffin into chewing gum. But during this same period, there was one byproduct of oil that producers considered worthless, even dangerous – gasoline. Then, came internal combustion engine and the automobile in the late Nineteenth Century and gasoline's time finally came. That which was once considered worthless, became the backbone of the industrialized world's economy.[xliv]

You know, sometimes people feel like they're a useless, worthless byproduct of society, as though they have absolutely nothing to contribute to their fellow human beings. But God places no person on this earth whose life does not carry with it a plan and destiny. Like that undervalued byproduct, gasoline, and that misunderstood oil, both of which became invaluable once their time had come, every man and woman will eventually come into their "time," their season of productivity, when they make invaluable contributions to humanity. It behooves us, then, not to give up on life, but to prepare ourselves for some future, yet undisclosed work to which God is calling us.

When he was a struggling attorney in Springfield, Illinois, Abraham Lincoln lived by the credo, "I will prepare myself and perhaps my time will come." And, boy, did it come. So will yours. The Scripture says, "For I know the plans I have for you, says the LORD, plans for good and not for evil, plans to give you a hope and a future." (Jeremiah 29:11)

PRAYER: Dear Father in heaven, my life, my future and my destiny are in your hands. Please grant that your glorious plan for my life may unfold and become reality, and that it will remain unmarred by any stupidity on my part or self-inflicted tragedy. Amen.

July 19

THE ROOT OF THE PROBLEM

Years ago the newspaper, *Tages-Anzeiger*, of Zurich, Switzerland, reported the story of a train conductor who had a rather embarrassing experience. As the train began pulling away from the station, the conductor discovered that the passengers all seemed to have tickets for the wrong destination – a destination in the opposite direction from which the train was traveling. In frustration, he demanded that all the passengers get off the train at the next stop. But the passengers protested. After a heated exchange, the conductor consulted with the engineer to prove his point to the misguided passengers. To his bewilderment, the conductor realized that it was he who was wrong and the passengers who were right. The conductor had simply boarded the wrong train.

There is a wise adage from India which says, "Wanting to reform the world without discovering one's true self and fixing one's own problems is like trying to cover the earth with leather to avoid the pain of walking on stones and thorns. It is much simpler to wear shoes." It is quite possible that much of the hostility we see in our workplaces and in our homes originates from our own hearts. Unresolved conflict, unhealed wounds, and pent up anger keep us at an emotional flashpoint – ready to erupt at any moment. Our wounded hearts distort our view of reality. And too often, they create a frame of mind that sees nothing but evil in the world and demands that it change.

But like the train conductor, the error lies within us. Like the Indian axiom, it is wiser to still the tempest that rages in our own heart before we seek to bring peace to the world. It is better "to wear shoes" than "to try to cover the world with leather." If there is poison in our hearts that makes us spew venom at our spouse, friends and coworkers, ask God to sweeten it. If there are painful emotional wounds, ask God can heal them. But the first major step is to locate the problem – most likely in our own hearts. "Create in me a clean heart, O God," King David prayed. "Renew a right spirit within me." (Psalm 51:10) God will do it, if you ask him.

PRAYER: Dear Father in heaven, it seems I am always at odds with the world, with my spouse, with my friends and with my co-workers. Please remove the bitterness from my soul. Please speak peace to the storm that rages within me. Please create in me a clean and a tender heart, and fill it with your sweet love. Amen.

July 20

WHEN ONE DOOR CLOSES, ANOTHER OPENS

Vasco Nunez de Balboa goes down in history as the discoverer of the Pacific Ocean. He was in fact the first European to see that great ocean – which he named *Mar del Sur* ("South Sea" – it was the Portuguese explorer Ferdinand Magellan who gave its present name), standing in its waters for the first time on September 25, 1513. This was the culmination of a long arduous trek across the Isthmus of Panama with a group of about 90 Spaniards and a large number of Indians – who had told him of a large sea "on the other side."

But Balboa would likely never have seen it, and never have gone down in history, had he succeeded as a planter in Hispaniola (Cuba). His plantation there failed. To escape his creditors, he was smuggled aboard a ship bound for South America where he became governor of a little settlement called Darien, now in the country of Colombia. From there he journeyed west to see the great "other sea" and to his place in the history books.

In a similar way, it was from Nathaniel Hawthorne's failure as a clerk in a customs house – a job from which he was fired – that led to the opportunity to write his renowned novel, *The Scarlet Letter* and embark on a career as one of America's foremost novelists in the Nineteenth Century.

It was James Whistler's failure at the United States Military Academy at West Point, from which he was discharged after failing chemistry that led to his stellar career as a painter.

And it was Mohandas, "Mahatma" (The Great Soul), Gandhi's failure as an attorney that led to his profound role as India's foremost statesman and liberator.

God has a plan for our lives and he often uses our failures to give us direction and open other doors of opportunities to us. The Scripture says, "For I know the plans I have for your, says the Lord, plans for good and not for evil; plans to give you a hope and a future." (Jeremiah 29:11)

PRAYER: Dear Father in heaven, guide and direct my steps; when one door slams in my face, open another door of opportunity for me and show the path I should take. Amen.

July 21

LITTLE DEEDS CAN CREATE A BIG BLESSING

Silk was once worth its weight in gold. Easily transportable, but mysterious to the western world in its origin, silk was the premiere luxury item of the wealthy throughout the Roman Empire.

Once it hatches from its egg, the silk worm feeds on mulberry tree leaves. After its fourth molting it stops feeding and prepares a cocoon. Once it builds a frame of short strands of silk, it then begins to cover the cocoon frame with one single strand of silk that can be up to 900 meters long. The cocoon is then boiled to remove the sticky sericin coating from the strands of silk. The long strands from as many as ten cocoons are twisted together into silk thread, from which silk fabric is woven.

Although Empress Si-Ling, wife of a famous emperor Huang-Ti (2640 BC), is credited with discovering and encouraging the production of silk in China, silk production did not begin in the western world until the 6th Century A.D. Here's how it happened. Two Persian monks, who had long resided in China, learned the whole art of silk worm rearing and brought their knowledge to the Emperor Justinian I. At the Emperor's request (c.550 AD) the monks brought silk worm eggs from China concealed in a bamboo tube. From those few worms were descended all the silk-producing caterpillars in Europe down to modern times.[xlv]

Those monks obviously brought with them a gift that kept on giving. Every human being is capable of leaving such a lasting legacy – an ever-growing chain reaction of good deeds that benefits a widening circle of people. The Scripture says: "Let us not lose heart in doing good, for in due time we shall reap a harvest if we do not grow weary. So while we have opportunity, let us do good to all men." (Galatians 6:9-10)

PRAYER: Dear Father in heaven, in my hand and in my mouth is the power to wound and to heal. Please make me an instrument of your healing and peace. Though my days are short, may the ripple effects of my good deeds go on forever. Amen.

July 22

TIME AND PATIENCE

Never was a project so hopelessly mired in failure, disappointment and doubt. Congress had high hopes for this building that was to measure 170 feet long and 85 feet deep. But when they were handed the estimated cost of $400,000 (in 1790 dollars), the plan was dramatically scaled down. And when construction finally began, a worse building site could not have been chosen - in the middle of farmland and swamps, surrounded by shanties that housed laborers and tents that served as brothels.

As work on this all-important building lagged behind schedule, an inspector found that its main timbers had already begun to rot and needed replacing. Then funding for this "fiasco" ran out and Congress not only didn't know where to find more money. It had serious doubts if the building was worth the effort. But slowly the money came and very slowly construction continued.

When its primary occupant finally took up residence in the building in 1800, he found the roof leaked so badly that the ceiling plaster collapsed and the windows were so drafty that hardly any room was habitable.

Even when it was "new" it was a wreck. Piles of junk and discarded building materials still lay everywhere. The site was a mess. And to add insult to injury, this "Presidential Palace" didn't even come with so much as *an outhouse!* Yes, I'm talking about the Chief Executive's residence in Washington, D.C. – the White House. In fact, while the Capital itself was still a work in progress, officials in New York and Philadelphia so despaired that Washington would ever be completed that they planned federal buildings in those cities, believing they would be the logical sites for the Capital. Yet, despite its rocky and humble beginnings – not to mention being burned to the ground by the British in 1814 - today the White House is one of the best-known and important buildings in the entire world.

Sometimes we forget that many great and wonderful things in our country had such slow and difficult beginnings. Our culture is so conditioned and accustomed to achieving immediate and trouble-free success and instant results that we have forgotten that most things in life require a great deal of time and perseverance. We are in great danger of demanding quick fixes for problems that require long-term solutions. Then, if our endeavors are met with difficulty or detours, we judge the effort a failure and want to scrap the whole project. This tends to be the case with scientific and medical research, health-care and social security reform, the prosecution of war, or even our own personal growth and success. Yes, perhaps the major endeavor for which we lose patience most is with ourselves.

But consider the advice of James Garfield, when he was president of Hiram College and before he became a Civil War hero and President of the United States. The father of one of the students approached President Garfield and asked if his son's course of study could be shortened to allow him to finish as quickly as possible. "Yes, we can do that," Garfield replied. "But it all depends on what you want to make of your son. When God wants to make an oak tree he takes a hundred years. When he wants to make a squash, he requires only two months."

To this we add some advice from another President, Calvin Coolidge: "Nothing in the world can take the place of persistence. Talent will not; nothing is more common than unsuccessful men with talent. Genius will not; unrewarded genius is almost a proverb. Education will not; the world is full of educated derelicts. Persistence and determination alone are omnipotent. The slogan, 'Press On,' has solved and always will solve the problems of the human race."

The Scripture tells us, "You need perseverance, so that once you have done what God requires of you, you may receive what he has promised" (Hebrews 10:36) and "Let us run with endurance the race that is set before us, fixing our eyes on Jesus, the author and perfecter of our faith." (Hebrews 12:3)

It's worth remembering. Outside of some divine intervention, all good things, including our own growth and success, require time and perseverance. There are no shortcuts.

PRAYER: Dear Father in heaven, please strengthen my resolve, stiffen my spine, and help me to persevere toward my own personal growth, development and success. Amen.

July 23

SEE THE POSSIBILITIES IN THINGS AND PEOPLE

On April 6, 1938, Roy Plunkett, an employee of DuPont, was experimenting with cooling gases. Just a few years earlier Willis Carrier had invented a system of air conditioning using ammonia and water as a refrigeration coolant. Now Roy was trying to find a better means of cooling air. On this particular day he left some *tetrafluoroethylene* gas in a container, and upon returning the next day, he noticed it had turned into super-slick waxy substance with impressive properties. Without realizing it, Roy Plunkett had discovered Teflon.

But Plunkett and DuPont were not looking for an excellent no-stick surface for cooking utensils. They were searching for a better coolant and all Plunkett knew was that *tetrafluoroethylene* gas was a failure as a coolant. Consequently this discovery was dismissed.

Marc Gregoire was more open-minded and became the first person to apply Teflon to a useful purpose – he used it on his fishing tackle to prevent tangles and keep it clean. Then his wife suggested Teflon be applied to a cooking surface. "That's a great idea," he thought. And he went on to sell more than a million Teflon-coated frying pans, pots, and griddles every year.

Roy Punkett was only looking for a refrigeration coolant. Consequently, when a very useful discovery –Teflon – fell into his lap, he completely missed its possibilities. But Marc Gregoire valued Teflon on its own merits. He saw Teflon's potential.

What is true of Teflon is also true of people. Supervisors, leaders and parents need to value their subordinates and children on their own merits. Their gifts, talents and potential are not always evident – especially early in life. Their talent and potential for goodness and greatness will be even harder to discern and appreciate if our expectations for them are very narrow. It behooves us, then, to look deeper and to remember that God has called and equipped them for some purpose in this life. They are discoveries waiting to happen. In the Scripture God says, "For I know the plans I have for you; plans for good and not for evil; plans to give you a hope and a future." (Jeremiah 29:11)

PRAYER: Dear Father in heaven, open my eyes to the good and potential in the lives of others. Help me to see and appreciate the gifts, talents and contributions of others. Amen.

July 24

TRUST IN THE GOD WHO GIVES VICTORY

The Scriptures tell us, "Some trust in chariots and some in horses, but we trust in the name of the Lord our God." (Psalm 20:7) Many military commanders would acknowledge the validity of this verse as well, and of the need to trust in God and not just in our equipment and military might. Consider the story of an amateur golfer in Benin, West Africa, Mathieu Boya – the golfer who brought down an entire air force.

Boya was practicing his golf swing in a pasture adjacent to Africa's Benin Air Base. With one swing of the golf club, Boya set off an unbelievable series of events. The shot, described as "a glorious slice," hit a bird, which in turn dropped onto the windshield of a trainer jet whose pilot was taxiing into position for takeoff. The pilot lost control of his plane and plowed into four shiny Mirage jets, totally demolishing the entire air force of Benin within the span of a minute.

Boya was jailed immediately for "hooliganism," and his attorney said he had no chance of winning a trial. The country wanted Boya to pay $40 million to replace the jets. Since Boya made only $275 per year, he figured it would take 145,000 years to pay off his debt to society.

Besides being the ultimate "hard luck kid," Mathieu Boya's calamitous golf stroke demonstrates that the frailty of our machinery and how the smallest and least threatening events can sometimes spell disaster. Naturally, as soldiers we have an obligation to train and plan and maintain our equipment like everything depended on us. But it is also wise to pray like everything depended on God. In the Scripture, David wrote: "It is God who arms me with strength ... he trains my hands for battle so my arms can bend a bow of bronze." (Psalm18:32, 34)

PRAYER: Dear Father in heaven, please bless the men, women and equipment of our Armed Forces and grant them success and safety in their mission to establish your justice, peace and freedom throughout the world. Amen.

July 25

THERE IS A PURPOSE FOR YOUR PAIN

The Industrial Age (c. 1789-1848) was a troublesome time for the millions in Europe and Great Britain. Many rapidly climbed the social ladder and acquired great wealth. But many more sank deeply into poverty. As a child Charles had hopes that he would be among the fortunate, that he would rise above the financial limitations of his father and become a true gentleman. But it was not to be.

When Charles' financially irresponsible father was arrested for indebtedness his world came crashing down. He was only twelve years old at the time his father went to a debtor's prison. To survive Charles had to leave school and find work in a shoe polish factory where he had to slave under the most shocking and humiliating conditions.

Within a year his father was released from jail. Sadly, however, his family did not rescue him from the dreariness of the factory. "We need the money," his mother argued, "let him stay there!" Charles would never forget or forgive this abandonment. He would carry the emotional scars of this period for the rest of his life.

But, as it turned out, these ghosts from the past that haunted him the rest of his life, energized his literary genius and would drive him to become England's most celebrated author of the 19th Century. His name was Charles Dickens. His books – *David Copperfield, A Christmas Carol, Great Expectations, Oliver Twist, A Tale of Two Cities*, to name a few - were so popular that none of them has ever gone out of print. His many novels (more than twenty) are filled with autobiographical elements that gave vent to his pain and resonated in the hearts of millions of readers. His pain became gain as he channeled his hurt and loneliness into writing. His literary works championed the cause of the poor and enslaved in Great Britain and triggered sweeping social reforms.

Many of us carry wounds from our formative years for which we may never find healing in this life. But God is able to turn our scars into stars and our hurts into halos. He can use the very things that haunt us to bless others. As Paul said in the Scripture, "the Father of mercies and the God of all comfort … comforts us in all our affliction, so that we may be able to comfort others with the same help we received from God" (2 Corinthians 1:3-5). So don't lose heart when your hurts go unhealed. God has a purpose for your pain. He can bring about good from the evil in our lives.

PRAYER: Lord, please heal the pain and anguish of my heart. If relief doesn't come as soon as I hoped, please give me comfort and encouragement that I may ultimately pass it on to others. Make me, O Lord, an instrument of Your peace and healing. Amen.

July 26

WHY MUST I SUFFER?

The Battle of Gettysburg raged for three horrific days, from July 1 – 3, 1863, and cost the Northern and Southern Armies nearly 52,000 casualties. Out of this hellish battle came the strange tale of twin brothers, Jack and Jasper Walker, who served with the 13th North Carolina Infantry. On the first day of the battle, the younger brother, Jasper, was bearing the regiment's colors when a rifle bullet struck his left leg and felled the brave soldier. That night surgeons amputated his leg.

Jasper fell into the hands of Federal troops when the retreating Army of Northern Virginia had to leave him behind. During the Southern retreat his brother Jack was also shot through the *left* leg and he, too, had to have his leg amputated. He also captured by Federal soldiers.

Both brothers spent the remainder of the war in separate Northern prisons. After the war both returned home to Charlotte, North Carolina, where they recovered, were fitted with artificial legs made of cork, and went on to marry and live prosperous lives.

Civil War historian Burke Davis relates that on the day his wedding was to take place, the younger twin, Jasper Walker, fell to the ground and broke his prosthetic leg. The accident would have placed a terrible damper on the happy occasion, but his brother Jack came to the rescue. To help his brother, Jack gave his own wooden leg – a perfect fit![xlvi]

Think about it. This man literally gave to his brother "a leg to stand on." Because he had suffered the very same tragic wound, he could give his brother "tailor-made" help, help that fit perfectly, help that caused him to stand.

In a spiritual sense, this is exactly how God causes us to be of help and comfort to others. Paul the Apostle wrote that, "God comforts us in our affliction so that we may be able to comfort others who have similar affliction with the very same comfort we received from God." (2 Corinthians 1:3-4) The adversity and trouble you suffer today will ultimately equip you to help others who suffer the same adversity and trouble. The comfort and encouragement which God gives to you – encouragement that helps you stand in the face of adversity – you will share with others to help them stand as well. There's a purpose in the pain. Through your pain, God is making you an instrument of his peace and healing.

PRAYER: Dear Lord, when the sufferings of Christ are mine in abundance, please grant that Your heavenly comfort to me may be abundant as well. Equip me, O Lord, through my suffering and through Your comfort, to be an instrument of healing and peace in the lives of others. Amen.

July 27

TRADING BLOWS

Rocky Marciano was the World Heavyweight Boxing Champion from 1952 to 1956. He has the distinction of being the only Heavyweight Champion to have retired undefeated both as Champion and as a professional. He left the ring with a flawless record of 49 wins and no losses or draws. And 43 of his 49 wins were by knockouts.

Yet Rocky was hardly an imposing sight. He stood five feet ten and a half inches tall and weighed between 184-190 pounds. The films of his fights reveal that most of his opponents towered over him. He also had the shortest reach of any champion – a mere 67 inches.

But the most troubling thing about Marciano's prospects for survivability in the ring was his style and strategy. In his awkward style, Rocky would routinely absorb five to six punches in order to land one.

Yet Rocky was extremely durable and was a devastating puncher. So it didn't take many of his punches to take out an opponent. True, he would take many punches to land one. But no one can argue with the results – he won every one of his professional bouts.

Sometimes I think God's servants are a lot like Rocky. They take many punches to land one. I'm not talking about physical punches, but emotional blows, insults, abuse, and persecution. The servant of God absorbs all these in an effort to "land the big one." But "the big one" is not a blow, but a blessing. The servant of Christ endures the insults and abuse, in order to someday help that very person who caused him pain.

But who can argue with the results? Throughout its history, the blood of the martyrs has become the seed of the church. And look at our Lord whose chastisement brought us peace and whose unlawful execution brought us eternal salvation (Romans 5:9-10). Jesus believes the best thing to do with sinners is to turn them into saints, not incinerate them. And for us, the best thing to do to enemies is make them friends. That's why we are told to bless when we are cursed and to repay good for evil (Romans 12:17), that we may turn a sinner from the error of his way and thus save a soul from death and cover a multitude of sins (James 5:19).

PRAYER: Lord, make me an instrument of your peace;
Where there is hatred, let me sow love;
  Where there is injury, pardon;
  Where there is doubt, faith;

Where there is despair, hope;
Where there is darkness, light;
Where there is sadness, joy.
Divine Master, grant that I may not so much seek
To be consoled as to console;
To be understood as to understand;
To be loved as to love.
For it is in giving that we receive;
It is in pardoning that we are pardoned;
And it is in dying that we are born to eternal life. Amen.

July 28

MEASURING SUCCESS

What is the *tallest* mountain in the world? Mount Everest? Actually, it is not. True, Mount Everest has the distinction of being the *"highest"* peak on earth. It reaches an altitude of 29,035 feet above sea level. Yet Everest only rises 12,000 feet from its base at 17,000 feet.

The tallest mountain in the world is actually Mount Kea, the highest peak of the Hawaii Islands. It rises only 13,796 feet above sea level. However, from its base at the ocean floor, Mount Kea rises a staggering 33,476 feet!

Perhaps the success of people should be measured the same way. It's not merely how high we rise, but how far we come. Booker T. Washington explained it that way. He was born a slave in Franklin County, Virginia. But from these lowest of circumstances, Dr. Washington rose to become one of the greatest educators, reformers, and activists in America. He once said, "Success is measured not only by how much one achieves, but by how many obstacles one overcomes in the process."

Perhaps someone has done greater things than you. But your achievements should be weighed on their own merits and in light of how far you've come and by the adversity through which you accomplished them. Though your progress seems small, give thanks to God for the distance you've covered, saying, "Thus far has the Lord helped me" (1 Samuel 7:12)

July 29

TRAPPED

At first, it sounded so funny. A man fell waist deep into a vat of chocolate and became hopelessly stuck. But the joke soon turned into a nightmare.

It all started when Donovan Garcia of the Debelis Corporation in Kenosha, Wisconsin, tried to unclog a valve that had been plugged by the extremely thick chocolate. But as he tried to churn the chocolate he slid into the vat and became entrapped for the next two hours. Plant employees and rescue workers tried to free him. But the hot, 110-degree dark chocolate ooze was like quick sand, like glue. Not until Garcia thinned the chocolate out with coco butter could members of the fire department pry him free. He was later taken to the hospital and treated for minor injuries and burns.

Donovan Garcia's experience might seem like a chocolate lover's dream. But it serves as a metaphor for how the things we love can entrap and enslave us. None of us can give free reign to our desires – otherwise they will control and ultimately destroy our lives. All of us must exercise restraint and discipline ourselves, lest our appetites become our master.

In the Scripture, Saint Paul said, "All things are lawful for me, but not all things are profitable. All things are lawful for me, but I will not be mastered by anything," (1 Corinthians 6:12), "but I buffet my body and make it my slave, lest possibly, after I have preached to others, I myself should be a castaway." (1 Corinthians 9:27)

PRAYER: Dear Lord, help me to enjoy life's blessings without becoming enslaved to them. Grant that my thirst for You and for righteousness will be the driving force in my life. Amen.

July 30

WHEN LIFE MAKES NO SENSE

What meaning or sense do you get from an individual piece of a jigsaw puzzle? None at all. A single piece of a jigsaw puzzle, with its asymmetrical shape and irregular dash of colors, makes no sense at all. It only has meaning in relation to all the other pieces of the puzzle. Only when it is fitted together with a thousand other pieces do you see it as part of a beautiful picture. Even so, the individual events of our lives, especially the ugly, painful ones, have no meaning or purpose as isolated events. Only as the years go by and we see those events in relation to the rest of life do they begin to make sense.

How appetizing are the individual ingredients of a cake? Does anyone enjoy trying to swallow 2 cups of flour or a cup of sugar? Can anyone stomach swallowing a teaspoon of salt or slurping down three raw eggs? No, the thought alone is nauseating. But put them all together, add some intolerable heat for 20-30 minutes and all those miserable ingredients make a delicious cake. In the same way, the individual events of our lives may lack savor and beauty when considered alone. But God will put them all together and bring about something very good.

Consider also the "earthwork portrait" of aviatrix, Amelia Earhardt, in Atchison, Kansas. This portrait covers an entire acre and is so large that it can only be appreciated from high above in an airplane (that was Stan Herd's (the artist) intention). But you can walk all over it and be completely unable to make any sense out of the portrait. You have to see it from above. Even so, while we're right in the middle of our circumstances we cannot make any sense of them. But once we view them from above, from heaven's perspective, we can see the beautiful picture that our circumstances create.

Consider Joseph in the Bible. This poor man was hated, disowned and sold as a slave by his own brothers. He was unjustly punished and thrown in jail – for doing the right thing! Then, after showing a kindness to another inmate who was about to be released, Joseph was forgotten, abandoned and left to languish on in prison for years. But on the day, when he rose from a prison cell to sit on the throne of Egypt – second only to Pharaoh – did any of those tragic events make any sense. Then Joseph understood that all his adversity was preparing him to become the savior and ruler of the world. He later confessed to his brother, with whom he was reconciled, "You intended your actions for evil but God intended them for good, … to bring about the salvation of many people." (Genesis 50:20)   The same is true of the painful events of your life. God promises to work all things together for good, for those who love God and are called according to his purpose (Romans 8:28).

PRAYER: Dear Lord, when painful pieces of my life seem to make no sense, have no meaning, and contradict your love – please help me to walk by faith and trust that you will put it all together and from it make something beautiful. Amen.

July 31

YOU'VE DONE HEROICALLY,
BUT DON'T QUIT YET

By the time Edmund Hillary and Tensing Norgay reached the world's highest peak in 1953, more than a dozen previous expeditions to reach the summit had failed, costing the lives of 13 climbers. Frostbite, avalanches, and deep, hidden crevasses had taken a horrible toll.

Then there is the problem of the air. At the top of Everest, 29,028 feet, atmospheric pressure is 33 percent that at sea level – there is 66 percent less oxygen at the world's highest peak! The consequent oxygen deprivation not only makes every step an agonizing effort and robs climbers of their reasoning powers – it can easily kill them.

Hillary himself had failed to reach the summit on at least one previous expedition. Yet, on May 29, 1953, when he became the first man to reach the roof of the world, Hillary spent little time admiring his achievement. In fact, he didn't even take time to have himself photographed by Tensing Norgay. Instead, he immediately took off his oxygen and began photographing nearby, unclimbed mountains – Makalu (27,766 feet) and Kangchenjunga (28,169 feet) and assessing possible routes to their summits. He explains, "Even on top of Everest, I was still looking at other mountains and thinking of how one might climb them."

Sir Edmund Hillary did climb many other mountains, including 10 other peaks in the Himalayas exceeding 22,000 feet and participated in expeditions down the Ganges River and the first mechanized crossing of Antarctica (1958). He also went on to build 30 schools and more than a dozen hospitals and clinics for the Sherpa people of the Himalayas. He never stopped to rest on his laurels, but always looked for another mountain to conquer.[xlvii]

The Scripture reminds us, "Where there is no vision, the people perish." (Proverbs 29:18) It is important that we have direction and keep a goal in view. God can help lift our sights and show us the lofty peaks He wants us yet to climb.

PRAYER: Dear Father in heaven, give me direction and show the path You have chosen for me. Lift my sights to the heights and give me the motivation to reach them Amen.

August

August 1

WHEN OUR RECORD IS TAINTED BY FAILURE

There is something in life that everyone wants but will never have – a perfect record. Sure, everyone wants an unblemished, untarnished, and flawless record. But even the best of us, even the superstars have had their share of glaring failures. Consider some of them:

Babe Ruth was an awesome batter. He knocked out 714 career home runs - a record that stood for thirty-nine years. But he also once held another record – the most career strikeouts – 1330! Ty Cobb was a fierce competitor, batting champ, and once the title holder for most bases stolen in a season and in a career. But did you know that until 1982 he also held the record for being thrown out while attempting to steal in a season (38 times in 1915).

Cy Young was an overpowering pitcher. He still holds the record for most career wins – 511 victories to his credit. However, he also holds the record for the most career loses – 313! And remember, in at least three seasons he racked up twenty or more losses and once had a pathetic seasonal record of 13 wins to 21 losses.

Hank Aaron, one the greatest home run sluggers of all time, hammered a career total of 755 home runs. But O'Henry also holds the record for hitting into the most double plays.

Walter Johnson was one of the greatest pitchers of all time. In fact, until just a few years ago he held the record for most strikeouts in a career – 3508! But he still holds the record for hitting the most batters (204) and is tied for the American League record for most wild pitches in an inning (3) and the most career wild pitches (156).

Jimmy Foxx. Maybe you've never heard of him. Well, until Roger Maris' exploits in 1961, Jimmy came closer than anyone else to breaking Babe Ruth's record of 60 home runs in a season. Jimmy Fox hit 58! He also led the National League in striking out for seven consecutive seasons.

Joltin' Joe DiMaggio, the "Yankee Clipper," once hit into *seven* double plays in a single World Series – a record he still holds.

Reggie Jackson, the Yankees one-time powerhouse hitter, achieved a mark of distinction on May 13, 1983 while playing against the Minnesota Twins. He became the first man in Major League baseball history to strike out 2000 times. But Reggie didn't stop there. He continued to take risks, swing hard at the ball and – miss. By the time he retired his record had climbed to striking out 2,597 times at bat! Jackson once admitted that this was the equivalent to doing nothing but striking out for four consecutive seasons.[xlviii]

So if your record is blemished with failure, be assured that you have plenty of company. The Scripture reminds us that "though a righteous man falls seven times, he rises up again." (Proverbs 24:16).

PRAYER: Dear Father in heaven, when I stumble and fail, help me, Lord to learn from my failures, move on and to grow stronger and wiser. Amen.

August 2

WHEN LIFE GIVES YOU NOTHING BUT LEMONS: MAKE LEMONADE

Jacob Cohen was the son of Vaudevillian comedian, Philip Cohen, aka Phil Roy. He wanted to try his own hand at comedy. So as the age of nineteen, Jacob, now using the stage "Jack Roy," after his father, embarked on a career in entertainment.

But audiences hated him and told him so. And though he continued to persevere and try to improve his performance, the constant rejection cut deeply. For nine years Jack struggled to make the humblest living as an entertainer. He even hired himself out as a singing waiter, but was promptly fired. After years of working for nickels and dimes to eek out a living, only to be rejected by audiences who tromped all over his feelings, Jack quit the business. He vowed to never subject himself to such humiliation again. But nobody seemed to notice he was gone – or care. He would remark later, "When I quit, I was the only one who knew I quit."

For the next twelve years Jacob supported his family by selling aluminum siding. Sure, it wasn't stardom. But it put food on the table. And if people resisted the sale – they were rejecting the siding, not Jacob.

Then, when he was well into his 40s, Jacob thought he'd give comedy another shot. But he knew he'd have to do things differently. He knew he'd have to concoct a certain persona, an image that people could identify with, yet find humorous. Then Jacob realized he had a trunk-full of life experience from which to draw. He took the very memories that had caused him such pain – memories of rejection, humiliation and the heartlessness of others – and used it to his advantage. From his pain Jacob created "the guy" who always gets walked over, always loses out, and who never gets any respect. Borrowing the name of a character from an old "Ozzie and Harriet" show, Jacob transformed himself into Rodney Dangerfield. And people loved him. The guy who never got any respect kept audiences laughing everywhere and reassured them that, in a world where little people get pushed and shoved about, they were not alone.

Rodney Dangerfield went on to headline on such TV shows as Ed Sullivan, the Dean Martin Show, and the Tonight Show (where he appeared 70 times!). He became a comedy staple and showpiece for years in Las Vegas. The man whom audiences once booed off the stage introduced many other comedians to stardom in his own Manhattan nightclub, "Dangerfield's" - talents like Tim Allen, Jerry Seinfeld, Rosanne Bar, Sam Kinison, Rita Rudner, Bob Saget, Jeff Foxworthy, and Jim Carrey.

In a manner befitting the character that made him famous, Rodney Dangerfield once again made the headlines. When Johnny Carson died in January 2005, CNN asked his agent if Rodney would like to make a comment. His agent informed CNN that Rodney Dangerfield had died four months earlier. Even in death, he didn't get "no respect."

Turning our pain into positive gain. Turning lemons into lemonade. Making our hurts into halos. That's what we need to do when people and circumstances wound us deeply. In fact, that's God's purpose for our lives – taking what others intend for evil and designing it for our good (Genesis 50:20). God uses the furnace of affliction to fashion us into his instruments of peace.

In the Scripture, Paul the apostle wrote: "Blessed be the God and Father of our Lord Jesus Christ, the Father of mercies and the God of all comfort, who comforts us in all our affliction that we may be able to comfort others who suffer similar affliction with the same comfort we received from God." (2 Corinthians 1:3-5)

PRAYER: Dear Father in heaven, through the inevitable pain of life, make me an instrument of your peace and healing. Give me the courage and grace to turn my pain into everyone's ultimate gain. Amen.

August 3

WHEN THE WORST THINGS HAPPEN

"Oh no! My wallet's gone!" Not a pleasant discovery, especially in the heart of New York City. But Billy Davis, Jr., of the Fifth Dimension, checked and re-checked his pockets and sure enough, his wallet was gone. The year was 1969 and The Fifth Dimension was performing at the Americana Hotel.

Realizing that the wallet must have fallen from his pocket in a cab, he and the rest of the group contacted the cab company. To his great relief, a man had found the wallet and was trying to get in touch with Billy to return it. But the man wanted no reward, except this: that Billy and the rest of the group - Marilyn McCoo, Florence LaRue, and Lamonte McLamore – attend a new Broadway show that he was producing that year, *Hair*.

They did. And as the group for the first time heard the song, "Age of Aquarius," they remarked to each other, "This is a song that we've got to record. It's just great!"

They took the song to their producer, who agreed to fund their recording of it, provided they combine it with another song from *Hair*, "Let the Sun Shine." They recorded the song-combo that very year and "Age of Aquarius, Let the Sun Shine" became their greatest hit ever. And it all began with a lost wallet.

So often we forget that God is working behind the scenes, often through some of the worst events, to bring about good in our lives. The Scripture reminds us, "God works all things together for good, for those who love God, for those who are called according to his purpose." (Romans 8:28)

PRAYER: Dear Father in heaven, when things go wrong in my life, remind me that You are working behind the scenes, turning my curses into blessings and working my evil circumstances into something good. Help me to do my part by submitting to You and seeking your will for my life. Amen.

WHEN WE FEEL WE CANNOT GO ON

Author and Jesuit priest, Mark Link, tells the story of an infantryman in World War II from West Virginia. He had joined the Army after slaving for years in the coal mines and had, in fact, come from a coal mining family.

Throughout the war, the infantry soldier kept a chunk of coal in his pocket. Whenever things got tough, whenever he reached the end of his rope and felt he just couldn't go on, he'd reach into his pocket, squeeze the coal, and repeat to himself, "If I could take the mines, I can also take this. God got me through the coal mines of West Virginia and he can get me though the battlefields of Europe." That little ritual always gave him the needed courage to go on.

In a way, that is a function of thanksgiving and reflection. When we give God thanks, we remember his acts of faithfulness in the past and find inspiration to trust him for the present crisis. We say in our hearts, "God, if you brought me through all those trials, you'll bring me through this one as well." Consider how David the shepherd boy, when faced with Goliath, explained: "The Lord who delivered me from the paw of the bear and from the paw of the lion will also deliver me from the hand of this Philistine." (1 Samuel 17:37) David reckoned that God's flawless record of faithfulness was proof that he would remain faithful. Take time to remember the challenges and insurmountable problems that you've already successfully overcome. If you got through those challenges, you'll get through this one as well.

PRAYER: Dear Father in heaven, grant that I may not forget your past record of faithfulness in my life. Help me to remember and reflect that, if you got me through those trials of my past, you will get through my present ones as well. Amen.

August 5

WHEN YOU DON'T HAVE WHAT IT TAKES

In the 1994 documentary, *Ben-Hur: The Making of an Epic*, starring actor Charlton Heston recalls his concerns about *the* major scene of the movie – *the chariot race!*

For an entire month Heston worked with secondary project director Yakima Cannut (a famous actor and stuntman in his own right) on his chariot-riding skills. But as comfortable as Heston became with driving the four-horse chariot, he realized he was no match for the other drivers who had been skilled horsemen from their youth. He expressed this concern to Mr. Cannut: "Yak, I appreciate the help you've been giving me, but I've got to confess, I'll never drive as good as the other drivers and there's no way I can win this race." Yakima Cannut assured him, "Chuck, don't worry. You just drive that chariot and I guarantee you'll win the race." Sure enough, Heston won the race.

In a way, this incident is reminiscent of God's assurance to Moses when the frightened prophet raised all kinds of objections to going back to lead Israel out of Egypt: "Who am I that I should go?" "What if the Israelites do not believe me?" "Lord, I cannot speak, I am slow of tongue and slow of speech."

God assured Moses that he would be successful – not because of Moses' qualifications or abilities, but because of God's power and faithfulness. Moses' limitations were very real. But the task to which God called him was far beyond the realm of human ability. God called Moses to do what is impossible for any human being. So Moses' limitations were meaningless. God called Moses only to be faithful and God himself would do the impossible. As Yakima Cannut said to Charlton Heston, "Just drive the chariot and I guarantee that you'll win." So God assured Moses, "Just do as I command, and I will take care of convincing Pharaoh, delivering Israel, and performing the impossible." Moses would only be the instrument, but God would be the agent (Exodus 3-4).

What is God calling and challenging you to do? Don't forget, whatever he calls you to do God will also equip you to do. Success does not so much depend on your ability as on being faithful to what God has called you to do and depending upon his power to do what you cannot. His promise is still valid: "Fear not, for I am with you. Be not dismayed, for I am your God. I will strengthen you; yes, I will help you; yes, I will uphold you with my righteous right hand." (Isaiah 41:10)

PRAYER: Dear Father in heaven, help me to face the challenges and the tasks to which you have called me. Please remind me that I am not alone, but you are with me. Please remind me that you do not call me to do my best, you call me to do the impossible – but that is your department and you will perform the impossible through me. So empower me, O God, and make me greater than myself. Accomplish your purpose through me. Amen.

August 6

OCCUPATIONAL HAZARDS

The popular TV show, "America's Most Wanted," has led to the successful arrest and conviction of hundreds of fugitives from justice. One such arrest was particularly interesting.

While visiting the Nashville County Fair two women spotted David Adams – a man wanted for fraud and arson. They recognized him from that week's episode of "America's Most Wanted." Park rangers wasted no time in nabbing the criminal.

But David Adams insisted that he was not the criminal they were looking for. He showed identification to prove his real name was Christopher Cotton. The park rangers were not surprised – Adams had a reputation for using false IDs and disguises. But as the day wore on, through a grilling interrogation, the police became convinced that they did *not* have David Adams in their hands – they had TV actor Christopher Cotton, who recently played the part of David Adams in a TV reenactment. That's right – the two devoted TV watchers had nabbed the actor that played the criminal's part, not the character himself. When asked by the press if he was bitter over the false arrest, Cotton explained: "No, this sort of thing is just an occupational hazard that comes with the profession."

Sometimes as soldiers we forget that we are not just actors playing a part. We don't have the luxury of saying, "Wait a minute – I'm just an actor." When the duty gets rough, we cannot raise our hand, object, and say, "Hey, guys, this isn't what I signed up for." We are the "real deal" and will be expected to deploy to war and risk our very lives in the defense of our nation.

Sometimes as Christians we also forget that we're not just playing a part. If you want to know what Christ has in store for you, consider his words: "If anyone wants to come after Me, let him deny himself, take up his cross, and follow Me. For whoever wishes to save his life shall lose it; but whoever loses his life for My sake and the gospel's shall find it. For what shall it profit a man if he gains the whole world and loses his own soul? Or what shall a man give in exchange for his soul?" (Mark 8:34-37)   So do not be distressed if adversity comes your way. God can help you in your commitment to your country as a soldier and to God as a disciple and believer.

PRAYER: Dear Father in heaven, help me to grasp the gravity and depth of my commitments to God and country. Help me to keep those commitments. Empower me by your divine Spirit, make me greater than myself, and help me to face and overcome my challenges. Amen.

August 7

WHEN WE REPEAT OUR MISTAKES

Something was terribly wrong. As seaman William Reeves peered into the foggy darkness, he knew something was terribly wrong. Reeves was keeping watch aboard a large steamer as it plowed through the North Atlantic and he was sure disaster lay ahead.

Maybe it was the time of year – April – the time when icebergs drifted south from the Arctic into the paths of many unsuspecting ships. Maybe it was the date - *April 14* – the troubling anniversary of the world's worst maritime disaster, the date in 1912 (twenty-three years earlier) the *Titanic* had crashed into an iceberg and taken more than 1500 of its passengers to their deaths, 12,000 feet down to the icy Atlantic floor. Maybe it was the fact that fourteen years before the *Titanic* disaster, the prophetic book, *Futility*, told the story of another enormous and "unsinkable" ship, eerily named *Titan*, which sank on its maiden voyage after striking an iceberg in the very waters the real "unsinkable" giant had gone down.

Yes, the pieces were coming together and forming a terrifying picture. History was about to repeat itself - he was sure of it. But Reeves was reluctant to shout the alarm for fear of ridicule from his shipmates. Yet he was more frightened of the deadly icebergs he was certain lay ahead. So he did what he had to do – he sounded the alarm. The helmsman ordered engines full astern. The ship churned to a halt – *just a few yards from a massive ice field*, an ice field so extensive and deadly that it took nine days for icebreakers from Newfoundland to clear a path for the mighty steamer.

There was one other frightening detail that alerted William Reeves of the danger that lay ahead, an eerie detail that led him to believe history was about to repeat itself in a terrifying way. You see, the name of his *own* ship was – *Titanian*.[xlix]

William Reeves overcame a common human frailty – the inability to learn from past mistakes and the tendency to repeat past failures and to stumble blindly again and again. Not a human problem, you say? Just consider the Israelites following their Exodus from Egypt. They came to a crisis, with the Red Sea on one side and the charging Egyptians on the other. They cried out and accused God of abandoning them. God delivered them by opening the Red Sea allowing them to escape. Then He drowned the pursuing Egyptians (Exodus 14-15). Then another crisis came – they ran short of water (Exodus 17). Did they recall God's previous acts of faithfulness? No. In fact, every single time they faced a crisis, they forgot their own past pattern of faithlessness and God's own pattern of faithfulness. Instead of reflecting on their disastrous pattern of unbelief and seeking to avoid a future repetition, they stumbled blindly into failure after failure.

We will find ourselves doing the very same thing on both a national and on an individual level – stumbling from failure to failure, seemingly oblivious to the fact that we have gone this way before and made the same mistakes. But like seaman Reeves, we need to reflect on the past, lest we repeat its tragedies. The Scripture reminds us: "All these things happened to them as examples – as object lessons to us – to warn us against doing the same things; they were written down so that we could read about them and learn from them in these last days as the world nears its end." (1 Corinthians 10:11, *The Living Bible*)

PRAYER: Dear Father in heaven, please illumine my heart and help me to gain wisdom from my own successes and failures as well as those of others, so as not to repeat them. Amen.

August 8

ENDURE

One of the most successful and potent U.S. submarines of WWII was the USS Bowfin, which sank some 175,000 tons of enemy shipping (44 ships sunk - unconfirmed) on nine combat patrols. This sub also rescued hundreds of sailors who were lost at sea and downed pilots who crashed or parachuted into the Pacific. In fact, the Bowfin picked up a total of 305 aviators who ditched their damaged planes in the Pacific.

However, conditions aboard the Bowfin were hardly accommodating to the rescued men. The crew of 66 men and officers already lived in hot, confined conditions, where fresh water was always scarce, bunks had to be shared, and the pungent smell of diesel fuel and body odor filled the air. Life was miserable. But it was life. Yet it was not uncommon for the rescued sailors and airmen to be appalled at the living conditions below. In fact, the Bowfin's submariners recall one rescued Australian POW that asked to be returned to the waters of the sea "rather than to stay in this sewer pipe." He completely failed to realize that certain death awaited him outside the submarine and that the combat patrols did not last forever – usually only from 30-40 days. He forgot that they would soon be safely back in port.

This is reminiscent of the Israelites in the Bible who, once delivered from the misery of slavery in Egypt, actually desired to return to their slavery when life became difficult on their journey through the desert. Somehow they forgot the horrific conditions from which God had saved them.

It is also like many Christians who, when facing adversity and temptation, turn back in their hearts to the misery God saved them from. They forget there is nothing to go back to. They also forget that every one of their trials has a limited lifespan and that we all will soon be safely back in port - forever. The Scripture says: "For you have need of endurance, so that when you have done the will of God, you may receive what was promised." (Hebrews 10:36)

PRAYER: Dear Father in heaven, I need endurance and the faith to look beyond my present suffering to see the eternal joys that await me in heaven. Please help me to endure to the end so that I may not be ashamed when I stand before your judgment throne. Amen.

August 9

WHEN OUR TASK IN LIFE SEEMS INSIGNIFICANT

In the Nineteenth Century, Niagara Falls was fast becoming a national sensation and tourist attraction. But transportation from the American to the Canadian sides of the Niagara River and Gorge was very problematic. The river was far too turbulent and the current far too powerful for passage by boat – not to mention the sheer 200-foot cliffs on either side of the gorge made the descent to the river bank impossible. It was obvious that a bridge had to be built.

Horman Walsh became the first man to successfully construct a bridge across the Niagara Gorge. This was a simple, oak plank, iron cable, suspension bridge, completed in 1848. But how did Horman Walsh manage to get those first heavy, iron cables across great expanse of the gorge. Walsh held a contest for the first boy who could fly a kite across gorge, offering $5 as a reward – not a small sum for a boy in 1848. Once the kite had spanned the gorge, a heavier string was tied to the kite string and pulled across. Then a rope was pulled across by the heavy string. Then an iron cable was pulled by the rope. Then multiple, heavier cables were pulled by that first cable. Then, upon those heavy cables, a roadway of oak planks was built.

Eventually, Walsh's bridge was replaced by larger and sturdier bridges, like John Roebling's Niagara Falls Suspension Bridge in 1855, which was replaced by Leffert Buck's steel arch bridge in 1886, which still carries trains across the gorge today. Also constructed for vehicular and pedestrian traffic was the Whirlpool Rapids Bridge, an arch bridge constructed in 1897.

A third and final bridge was the Rainbow Bridge, constructed in 1941 just below the falls. But amazingly, this entire family of steel arch and suspension bridges all began with a boy's kite string flown across a mammoth gorge more than 150 years ago.

And sometimes our simple work for a good cause seems too small, too insignificant for an investment of our time. But we never know, but that the ultimate outcome of our good deed or a kind word may have far-reaching, profound and eternal results. The tender hands of loving parents - cleaning baby bottoms, changing diapers, holding hands of a child taking his first steps, and giving hugs - may be raising a future world leader.

And a soldier - who fulfills his painful duty, fights another battle and bears deprivation another lonely day – may be laying one stone in the foundation for the free world tomorrow. Be faithful in the small things. God is mindful of your labors and He specializes in taking small things and using them to work miracles.

The Scripture says, "The Kingdom of heaven is like a tiny mustard seed planted in a field. It is the smallest of all seeds, but becomes the largest of plants, and grows into a tree where birds can come and find shelter." (Matthew 13:31-32, *Living Bible*)

PRAYER: Dear Father in heaven, help me to be faithful in the little tasks to which you have called me. Help me to see my work, however small, as an essential part of something greater than myself. Amen.

August 10

WHEN TIMES ARE FRIGHTENING

Disturbed by what you read in the newspapers and what you see on TV? Upset about the threat of global warming, war, pestilence and disease? Believe it or not, this world has seen far scarier times than this.

In fact, you might prefer global warming to what many climatologists refer to as "the Little Ice Age" or LIA, which spanned from the thirteenth to the nineteenth centuries. During the height of the LIA, from 1550 through 1850, the northern hemisphere experienced a dramatic plunge in temperatures, creating arctic winters and cool, wet summers. An increase in volcanic activity and a decrease in solar activity are normally cited as the causes of this phenomenon, which led to repeated worldwide crop failures, massive starvation, and the horrific spread of disease. In fact, the most violent volcanic eruption ever recorded occurred during this period – the eruption of Mount Tambora in 1815, which exploded 34 cubic miles of ash and rock twenty-five miles into the atmosphere. The initial eruption killed tens of thousands, but millions more would die as the volcanic dust blocked out the sun's rays, resulting in the virtual loss of the 1816 growing season. The dramatically colder conditions of the LIA resulted in the deaths of tens of millions of persons and also set conditions for the onslaught of the Black Death (1338 – 51) which killed one third of Europe's population – a staggering 75 million people!

The plague of Justinian (beginning in AD 542) killed half the population of Constantinople and unleashed a scourge on Europe that resulted in the deaths of 100 million persons in the centuries to come. The earthquake of Shanxi, China, in 1556, killed 830,000 persons within a matter of minutes. The Mount Asama eruption in Japan in 1783 so polluted the atmosphere that 1.2 million persons died from famine in the following months. The Edo earthquake of 1703 destroyed the city of Edo (modern day Tokyo) and killed 150,000 of its inhabitants. The great Bengal famine of 1770 took the lives of 10 million people in just one year.

Small pox killed 500,000 Native Americans in North America from 1617 through the next two centuries. And in the period of the Spanish colonization of the Americas (1492-1650), conquest and disease took the lives of an estimated 45 million Native Americas – this represented 90 percent of the indigenous population. Influenza, killed 600,000 persons in America alone and 70 million world-wide in the span of just a year, from 1918-1919. And the list goes on and on.[1]

But if there are positive lessons in all this tragedy and death, they include these: First, that the troubles of our times are nothing new under the sun. Mankind has traveled this path before – and survived. That's the second lesson, that although our existence may seem very fragile on this planet, yet mankind's survival is a testimony to human durability and God's faithfulness. God has a future for this world, has insured its survival through the centuries, and has already written its final chapter. In the Scripture we read: "For I know the plans I have for you, says the Lord, They are plans for good and not for evil, to give you a future and a hope." (Jeremiah 29:11)

PRAYER: Dear Lord, though this world is a scary place, remind me of your love and of your promise of a brighter tomorrow. Grant that I may be a partaker of the world to come and that I may faithfully do my part to prepare for it. Amen.

August 11

STUMBLING UPON THE GATES OF HELL

On a hot summer afternoon in 1901, a nineteen-year-old cowboy, Jim White, was riding along a ridge in southeast New Mexico. Suddenly he saw it. It was a menacing sight. Black smoke was spiraling up out of the ground hundreds of feet into the air. "Is it a volcano?" he wondered.

He wound his way toward the funnel-shaped cloud, through cactus, yucca, and rocks. When he reached the source of the smoke, Jim made a frightful discovery - a gaping hole in the earth that resembled the mouth of the netherworld. And if that wasn't enough to spook a cowboy, Jim White realized he wasn't watching smoke billow out of the ground. The "smoke" was *millions of bats* rising from the biggest cave he'd ever seen.

Any other person would have turned and run from this vision straight out of Revelation. But Jim began a quest of exploration that continued for the next thirty years. What Jim White had stumbled upon was Carlsbad Caverns. And because he refused to let his fears snuff out his thirst for knowledge, Jim White opened to the world the largest subterranean chambers, towering dripstone formations, and most fantastic wonderland. Carlsbad Caverns became a National Monument in 1923 and a National Park in 1930, largely due to Jim White's exploration and publicizing of the cave.

At first glance it appeared as a terrifying sight. But Carlsbad Caverns proved to be a national treasure that had waited hundreds of centuries for a brave soul to shed light on its spectacular beauty.

There are times when life ushers us into circumstances we dread. "The thing we feared has come upon us," we tell ourselves. We feel like we're facing the very gates of hell – stuck in the worst place doing the worst job.

But maybe it's not going to be the hell we envision. And, just maybe, we will make the discovery of a lifetime in this hellish place and we will find the curse is actually a blessing in disguise. In these dark, gloomy circumstances God will reveal to us the unsearchable riches of Christ and bless us with every spiritual blessing (Ephesians 1:3; 3:8).

PRAYER: Dear Father in heaven, help me to stop bemoaning my circumstances, resign myself to Your will, and to seek to be a blessing to those around me. Amen.

August 12

WHY BOTHER?

Ray Harryhausen is a towering figure in the science fiction genre of motion pictures. His work as a film director, art director, and especially as a special effects technician is legend. Before the days of computer animation, Ray Harryhausen was unquestionably the very best stop-action animator in motion pictures. *Clash of the Titans, Jason and the Argonauts, The Seventh Voyage of Sinbad, Mysterious Island*, and *The Beast from 20,000 Fathoms* were just a few examples of his work. Harryhausen gave so much attention to every movement and every detail that his monsters and exotic creatures were not only believable. They expressed pathos and evoked sympathy from the audience. Film historians and critics praise him for doing his work *so well* that *his miniature models were better actors than the leading men and leading ladies* of the movies that featured his work.

In an interview Harryhausen expressed the discouragement he sometimes faced in his tedious and painstaking work. While working on the movie, *20 Million Miles to Earth*, he concluded that it was a waste of his time to toil over such details as "breathing" and "blinking the eyes" on his creatures. "Nobody even notices those things," he said to himself. This was a particular temptation when his work was consigned to "B-Motion Pictures" that starred second-rate actors.

But Harryhausen made up his mind to do his very best, regardless of how minor the movie. "That kind of detail is my calling card. It's what distinguishes my work from all others."

His commitment to excellence paid off. All his movies became box office successes – usually on the strength of his animated creatures alone. His miniature monsters stole the show and Ray Harryhausen went on to universal acclaim in the motion picture industry.

The temptation exists for all of us to give less than 100 percent effort, especially when our audience is small or our team is losing. "Why bother?" "No one ever notices." "Nobody cares." But remember this: our character grows by leaps and bounds when we faithfully do our work in the absence of praise and recognition. And Someone *is* always watching, always mindful, and always keeping records of our faithful work. For our Lord reminded us that "Your Father who sees all that we do in secret will one day reward us openly." (Matthew 6:6, 18)

PRAYER: Dear Father in heaven, help me to be faithful in all the work You've called me to do. Remind me in my times of discouragement, that only one life so soon will pass and only what's done for Christ will last. Amen.

August 13

WHEN LIFE SLOWS YOU DOWN

In 1298, 3 years after returning from his 24-year-long adventure to the interior of China (17 years of which was spent in Kublai Khan's court) Marco Polo was captured by the Genoese and imprisoned for a year. Though frustrating for a man who traveled so widely, this imprisonment ultimately gave Medieval Europe *The Description of the World* or *The Travels of Marco Polo.* For it was during his incarceration that he met the writer Rustichello, who insisted that Marco's annuls be recorded. Without this period of imprisonment, the accounts of Kublai Khan, the description of Beijing, and unknown world of the Orient would have been otherwise lost to the Christian world.

Jean Victor Poncelet served as a lieutenant in Napoleon's corps of engineers during France's invasion of Russia in 1812. During the Battle of Krasnoy, he was severely wounded and abandoned as dead. Somehow he lived and managed to recover - even though marched hundreds of miles in the depths of winter to a Russian prison. In these hopeless conditions, which lasted for a year and a half, Poncelet meditated and devised theories on projective geometry. From these theories born in prison, he later published a book, *The Application and Analysis of Geometry*, that is widely recognized as the foundation of modern geometry.

During his two – three-year-long imprisonment, Paul the apostle, received opportunities to share the gospel with governors, kings, the Praetorian Guard, and even the Emperor Nero himself. None of this would have been possible while he was a free man. During his imprisonment he also recorded sacred Scripture for the benefit of millions of Christians to come – his "prison letters" to the Ephesians, Philippians, Colossians, and to Philemon. Paul summed it up by saying: "my circumstances (of imprisonment) have turned out for the greater progress of the gospel." (Philippians 1:12) In fact, Paul refused to call himself a prisoner of Rome. Instead he referred to himself simply as "the Prisoner of Jesus Christ" (Ephesians 3:1; 4:1; 2 Timothy 1:8; Philemon 1, 9).

No one wants to be "confined," "slowed down," or "arrested" by circumstances. We cherish our mobility. But should sickness, family responsibilities, deployment or anything else (even incarceration) bring us to a screeching halt – perhaps it's for a good reason. Maybe God is slowing us down to ultimately make us immensely more productive. The Scripture says, "By repentance and rest you will be saved; in quietness and trust you will find strength." (Isaiah 30:15)

PRAYER: Dear Lord, when circumstances or sickness slow me down, please help me to have the sense to use those times wisely and to receive the blessing you wish to give me. Amen.

August 14

DON'T OVERLOOK THE HIDDEN GEMS

Three starving boys were scavenging for food in their village of Hinnah Malen, Sierra Leone on the African Continent. Their parents had been killed by rebels two years earlier in 1995. Now, they were digging in the dirt for yams to stave off their hunger pains. The oldest boy among them, 14-year-old Morie Jah, found the leafy top of a plant, dug down, and uncovered a large yam. But as he pulled the yam from the ground he found something else lying beneath it – a clear, sparkling rock, about the size of a tennis ball, more beautiful than anything they had ever seen. Sensing he may have discovered a treasure worth many yams, Morie brought the rock to a gem dealer in town. What had he found? A 100-carat diamond valued at $500,000.00! In his quest for a minor meal, Morie Jah stumbled upon a life-changing fortune.

Think about the things we pray about. Life confronts us with challenges and problems that drive us to God for help. He answers, as always, and the crisis is behind us. But little time passes before another need comes out way. Again we plead for God to help us, with a sense of urgency as if He has never helped us before. Again God meets the need and the problem is history. Then another issue arises. And we continue the pattern of seeking divine deliverance from the things we fear and God continues to care for us.

But are we missing something? Something beyond the mere answer to our prayers? Is God trying to reveal a priceless gem of truth, the precious jewel of His unfailing love for us that lies underneath every answer to our prayers? Are we looking for a yam and missing the diamond beneath it? "Behold - look, contemplate, ponder - what manner of love the Father has bestowed upon us," the Scripture commands. In other words "Don't overlook God's love for you." Don't just go from crisis to crisis and miss the love that surrounds you and will never forsake you or fail to care for you.

PRAYER: Dear Father in heaven, please grant that I may not merely take from the hand, but look also into the face of the One from Whom all blessings flow. Amen.

August 15

AT ANY COST

Coffee is a labor-intensive product. Even so, most Americans think it's worth the effort. According to Forbes.com, 80% of Americans drink coffee, with more than half of all Americans consuming it every day. In the U.S. alone, annual retail sales amount to $19.2 billion and $70 billion worldwide.

Yet consider the effort and time that go into a single cup of coffee.

The fruit of the coffee plant are red coffee cherries, each of which contains two coffee seeds or beans. In an entire year, a coffee plant yields enough beans for only about one to one and half pounds of coffee. Since coffee plants remain productive for only 15-20 years of their 60-year lifespan, a very productive coffee tree may only yield about 25-30 pounds of coffee in its life.

There are no labor-saving devices in the harvesting of coffee. All coffee cherries must be picked by hand. This is because a coffee plant will bear unripe, ripe, and over-ripe cherries at any given time. Once workers pick them, the coffee cherry must be dried and crushed. Then the beans must be stripped of their outer fruit and tough "parchment" skin. Skilled workers then hand-select each green coffee bean, eliminating defective beans and grouping the rest into the various grades of coffee.

The select beans are then loaded into 120-pound bags and shipped out to distributors. This all takes place before they are roasted and ground. In the final analysis, it takes 2,000 hand-picked coffee cherries and 4,000 individually selected coffee beans to make a single one-pound bag of ground roasted coffee. That's a lot of coffee beans and a lot of labor to make a cup of the coffee which most Americans say they cannot live without.

As a society we are believers in mass-production. We will only give minimum effort to achieve maximum results – maximum instant results. This is part of the reason Americans have so much trouble investing individual time and effort into relationships – with our spouse, our children, and with God. We may not say it with words, but our actions bespeak that other human beings and God himself are not worth our time and effort. With coffee, however, we make a huge exception. We've got to have it at any cost.

Are we such lovers of pleasure, that we neglect those who give purpose and meaning to our lives for such short-sighted gratification? May God deliver us from the insanity of our ways!

"Be devoted to one another in brotherly love. Honor one another above yourselves. Never be lacking in zeal, but keep your spiritual fervor, serving the Lord." (Romans 12:10-11)

PRAYER: Dear Father in heaven, my actions speak louder than my words. I profess to love you and my family, yet I make no investment of my time and resources in them. Instead I spend myself in selfish and short-term pursuits. Open my eyes to the folly of my ways and help me repent. Help me to live with eternity's values in mind. Amen.

August 16

REMEMBER WHO LOVES YOU

It is common among artists to view their works quite differently from the way the public views them. Often what the public loves and acclaims most, is far from the artist's favorite. This is especially true among songwriters. Often what becomes a number one hit, is far from the songwriter's favorite. On the other hand, what the songwriter loves and cherishes most is frequently unappreciated and ignored by the public.

For instance, consider one of America's greatest songwriters – Irving Berlin. He wrote and composed music for more than 1500 songs. 1000 of these were published, of which 282 reached "top ten" in the nation. 35 of these became "Number One" hits. Among these hits were, "Alexander's Ragtime Band," "There's No Business Like Show Business," "Puttin' On The Ritz," "Blue Skies," "A Pretty Girl Is Like A Melody," "Cheek To Cheek," "Easter Parade," "God Bless America," and "White Christmas" These made Irving Berlin widely recognized as America's greatest song writer. Yet in an interview with the San Diego Union's Don Freeman, Berlin commented, "I wish someone would ask me what I thought about those songs of mine that never became hits – I'd tell them that I loved them all." Like many other artists, Berlin considered some of his more obscure works to be his treasured children – too personal to gain widespread acceptance and recognition.

I think at times of those of God's children who walk this world unloved, unappreciated and largely ignored. I wonder if they are like the artist's favorite songs. I wonder if they bring special delight to their heavenly Father. Truly, many of the greatest men and women of God have been misfits in society – misunderstood and unappreciated. But like the undervalued works of the artist, they are held more nearly to the heart of the God they serve.

If you feel like you're an outcast, if you feel like you're ignored, if you feel like you're invisible – then remember this. Never base your value upon the way others treat you. Never forget that, like the favorite songs of the songwriter, you bring special delight to the heart of your Creator.

"How precious, O God, are Your thoughts concerning me?" wrote David in Psalm 139:17-18. "How vast is the sum of them? If I were to count them they would outnumber the grains of sand." You are in God's thoughts. He loves you and delights in you.

PRAYER: Dear Father in heaven, when I feel the sting of rejection and bigotry, remind me that I am loved by You – and Your love is all that matters. Amen.

August 17

IN PURSUIT OF A DREAM

In 1978 William Smith, of Waukegan, Illinois, won an election for the county auditor in Lake County. However, on the same ballot a referendum passed that eliminated the position of county auditor. The same election that voted him into office, killed the office. Smith described his frustration and disappointment with this analogy: "I feel like I've gone off the diving board and suddenly found that the pool was empty."

Most people would laugh at this, if it didn't strike a note of concern in our hearts – the concern and fear that we may reach our goals too late, that all the good jobs will be taken by the time we finish college, that all prospective spouses will be married off by the time we get financially established, and that all our dreams will go unfulfilled.

Or, perhaps there is an even deeper concern – one that is more difficult to voice or come to grips with: that we will achieve our dreams, but will find them disappointing and unfulfilling. The great Irish playwright, expressed this dilemma in these words: "There are but two tragedies in life. One is not to get your heart's desire. The other is to get it."

Seeing a dream evaporate before our eyes is one fear. Reaching our dream and discovering it is a nightmare is another.

There is a better path. It is this: "Trust in the Lord and do good; … Delight yourself in the Lord and He shall give you the desires of your heart. Commit your way to the Lord, trust also in Him, and He shall bring it to pass. …Rest in the Lord, and wait patiently for Him." (Psalm 37:4-7) No one understands and knows you like the God who breathed into you the breath of life. He knows all about your gifts, your strengths, your talents, as well as your weaknesses, fears, and failures. He also has a blueprint and plan for your life. God alone knows what will make you truly happy. The wisest thing any of us can do is to get to know Him better and seek to do His will.

PRAYER: Dear Father in heaven, please fulfill Your plan for my life. Help me to seek your rule over my own life and incline my heart to do whatever it is You want me to do. Do not merely tell me what to do. Please, also give me the desire and strength to do it. Amen.

WHEN WE'RE SURROUNDED BY DANGER

The aquarium at Orlando's Sea World is like many other famous aquariums. It features exotic creatures of the sea and allows spectators to get a close up view sharks, rays, stinging jellyfish, and eels – with nothing but a four to six-inch-thick shield of Plexiglas between visitors and certain death. But this aquarium allows extreme close-ups. This Sea World features an acrylic tunnel, sixty-feet long and made of 5,000-pound acrylic panels that can each hold back 500 tons of water. The huge acrylic tunnel allows people to walk directly through a huge tank filled with an assortment of hammerhead, mako, and tiger sharks as well as barracuda and venomous fish. In the acrylic tunnel visitors are literally surrounded – above, below, and on both sides - by danger. Yet they are perfectly safe. The transparent barrier is impenetrable. Neither the man-eaters nor the hundreds of tons of crushing water can hurt those in the tunnel.

And many times we sense that we are most definitely surrounded by danger. In the military we're uprooted from home, dragged halfway around the world, and faced with frightening challenges. If we're a freedom-loving person, we hear the relentless threats of terrorism. But even when we are surrounded by danger, if we trust in God, his presence, faithfulness and love serve as an impenetrable barrier through which no evil can pass. God will take care of us. In one of the most beloved of all psalms, David wrote, "Even though I walk through the valley of the shadow of death, I will fear no evil, for you are with me. Your rod and your staff, they comfort me. You make bountiful provision for me, even in the presence of my enemies. You anoint my head with oil. My cup overflows." (Psalm 23:4-5)

PRAYER: When I am frightened, O Lord, remind me that you are a shield all around me (Psalm 3:3) and my refuge and fortress against all of life's dangers (Psalm 46:1). Amen.

WHEN WE SEE NO WAY AROUND OUR PROBLEMS

The city of St. Petersburg, Russia, was founded in 1703 by Peter the Great as an outlet to the Baltic. Czar Peter moved there himself in 1712. It was to become one of the most magnificent and luminous cities in Europe. But during its earliest days, when its streets were being laid out, excavators ran into a persistent problem. The area was covered with boulders left over from ancient glaciers.

One boulder, which lay in the middle of one particular street, was especially large. The government took bids from many contractors to move the boulder away. Since this was long before any heavy earth-moving equipment or high explosives existed, the bids were very high. It would take many teams of horses, a huge labor force, and large wooden hoists and wagons to dislodge and move such a boulder.

Then one peasant came forward who offered to do the job for just a fraction of the cost the others were charging. Though doubtful of the peasant's abilities, the government felt it had nothing to lose. So they awarded the job to him.

The next morning the peasant arrived with a crowd of his fellow peasants, all armed picks and shovels. Beside the large boulder, the peasants began digging an enormous hole. Deeper and deeper they dug the hole and braced it with large timbers. Then they began to dig underneath the boulder, bracing the rock's weight with more timbers. Finally, when the hole was more than thirty feet deep, they excavators removed the timbers that propped up the boulder. Immediately the rock fell deep into the large hole and out of sight. The peasants filled in the hole as best they could and then carted off the excess dirt.

What was the peasant's secret? How did he turn an impossible task into a manageable one? All the other contractors viewed the boulder's massive weight and the force of gravity as obstacles and enemies. The peasant chose to use these to his own advantage. He saw the boulder's enormous weight as a friend to assist him in getting rid of it.

And can't we do the same with the problems of our lives – use them to our own advantage? Don't our greatest problems also provide the means of greatest personal growth? Don't long deployments drive us to appreciate our family relationships more than ever and help us establish right priorities? Don't long separations drive us to write, take family photos, and otherwise document our children's lives much more than if we had never been separated?

The secret of turning our scars into stars, our stumbling blocks into steppingstones and our hurts into halos is maintaining a positive attitude and creative thinking. All around God gives us the means to survive and thrive in adversity. May God open our eyes to the resources and possibilities for good that are all around us! The Scripture reminds us that God turns our curses into blessings (Deuteronomy 23:5) and causes all things to work together for good (Genesis 50:20; Romans 8:28). Life may be against us, but God is for us (Romans 8:31).

PRAYER: Dear Father, my life is filled with so many problems and obstacles. Open my eyes to see that it is also filled with many opportunities and blessings and people to help. Amen.

August 20

WHEN EVIL SEEMS TO REIGN

Tragedy occurred on September 15, 1999 when a gunman entered the Wedgwood Baptist Church in Dallas, Texas, and opened fire on the worshippers. By the time shooting stopped, eight people were dead (including the gunman) and seven were wounded. Far from being a tragic defeat for the church, the deaths of these Christian believers led to tremendous opportunities for the Gospel.

The pastor, Rev. Al Meredith, was invited to Larry King Live and was able to make a beautiful presentation of the Gospel. CNN also broadcast the memorial service live. One of the victim's families lives and works in Saudi Arabia. On this person's behalf, Saudi Arabia, which outlaws even the public mention of Jesus' name, allowed the live memorial service to be broadcast. This constituted the first televised broadcast of the Gospel in that country.

CNN also broadcast the service in Japan, a country that is hardened toward the Gospel, and thirty-five emailed Wedgwood Baptist indicating that they had accepted Jesus Christ. In the wake of the seven deaths, more than 150 students at local schools made public confessions of Christ and hundreds of others heard the Gospel from teachers who found a new freedom to share their faith. Wedgwood Baptist's own webpage received more than 70,000 visits and which displayed a powerful presentation of the Gospel.

From the televised and radio broadcasts, an estimated 200 million persons heard the Gospel and Christian testimonies as a result of this "tragedy" turned inside out by God. Truly, God works all things together for good for those who love him and for the spreading of the Gospel (Romans 8:28). "Be still and know that I am God," the Scripture says, "I will be exalted among the nations; I will be exalted in the earth." (Psalm 46:10)[li]

PRAYER: Our Father, who art in heaven, hallowed be thy name. Thy kingdom come, thy will be done on earth as it is in heaven. Amen.

August 21

REJECT THE REJECTION

John Steinbeck was the most widely-read American author of the 20th Century. His novel *The Grapes of Wrath* earned the Pulitzer Prize (1939) and in 1962 he was awarded the Nobel Prize for Literature in recognition for his life's work.

Yet Steinbeck's portrayal of a darker side of America during the Great Depression also earned him stinging criticism from many in the U.S. who believed his books had Communist overtones. This was particularly true in his hometown of Salinas, California, where the large farm owners felt vilified by Steinbeck. So intense was their hatred toward him that the town of Salinas held a public burning of his books. This demonstrated repudiation cut to the core of the deeply sensitive author.

Yet opinions change. What people discredit as worthless today may be appreciated for its genius tomorrow. Such was the case for John Steinbeck. As it turned out, a generation after the condemnation and burning of his books the people of Salinas erected a museum that honored the name and celebrated the works of John Steinbeck. This museum took twenty years to plan and build at a cost of more than $10 million. It stands today just a short distance from where the city of Salinas had incinerated thousands of his books.

Steinbeck never lived to see his name honored or his works vindicated in his hometown. He died with their criticism still ringing in his ears. But this example is proof that none of us should take to heart the criticism and condemnation of others. We should reject the rejection and continue doing the work to which God has called us. In the Scripture God spoke these words to his trembling servant: "Be strong and courageous. Do not be terrified; do not be discouraged, for the LORD your God will be with you wherever you go." (Joshua 1:9)

PRAYER: Dear Father in heaven, Fortify my spirit and soul so that criticism will not easily discourage me. Help me to look beyond the judges of this life and focus on pleasing you. To you I present my life and work for Your righteous assessment. Amen.

August 22

UNPROFITABLE TRADE-OFFS

"Monk" is the highly successful TV show that follows the trials and triumphs of Adrian Monk, a former San Francisco police detective afflicted with excessive-compulsive disorder (OCD). In an episode from the show's third season, "Mr. Monk Takes His Medicine," Adrian's fears and depression get the best of him. He complains to his psychiatrist, Dr. Kroger, that he can't take the pain anymore. To give him relief Dr. Kroger prescribes medication.

The new medication proves very effective in removing his emotional anguish, but it changes him into another person. He finds relief from his pain, but it's at a price. With his new-found happiness Monk loses his incredible ability to solve crimes. But most disturbing to Mr. Monk is that he loses touch with Trudy, his beloved wife and best friend who died eight years before. His old, depressed self simply had to sniff her pillow and could evoke vivid images of Trudy. But his new upbeat self has lost his sensitivity and creativity. His pursuit of a pain-free existence has come with a serious tradeoff. In the end Mr. Monk decides his old, painful life is better than his undistinguished new life. He realizes that the very things that caused him pain were also a source of great blessing and made him extraordinarily helpful to society.

Monk's example is somewhat reminiscent of the message of Paul the apostle in his Second Letter to the Corinthians. There Paul explains that our afflictions become a fantastic medium through which we can experience God's fellowship and comfort. *"God comforts us in our afflictions,"* writes Paul, *"so that we will be able to comfort others in any affliction with the very same comfort we received from God. For just as the sufferings of Christ are ours in abundance, so also is our comfort abundant through Christ."* (2 Corinthians 1:3-5) Remove the pain from life and we remove the very portal through which we experience God. This is why Paul spoke of knowing Christ *"in the fellowship of His sufferings"* (Philippians 3:10). Paul had learned not to fear or dread the pain of life, for through it he would hear God's voice, enjoy His fellowship, and be blessed with His comfort.

The presence of pain in our lives is neither abnormal, nor evil. On the contrary, our pain can become a great source of blessing. Consider the words of psychiatrist Gerald May, who wrote: *"We have this idea that everyone should be totally independent, that everyone should be totally together spiritually, totally fulfilled. That is a myth. In reality our lack of fulfillment is the most precious gift we have. It is the source of our passion, our creativity, our search for God. All the best of life comes out of our human yearning, our 'not being satisfied.'"*

Don't pursue a pain-free existence. Seek God in the midst of your affliction.

PRAYER: Father of mercies and God of all comfort. Please comfort me in my adversity and affliction. As my trials become more intense and painful, please pour out upon me Your consolation and encouragement. Please grant, O Lord, that I will not come out of my trials empty-handed or empty-hearted. May I come forth from my trials armed with comfort and consolation with which I may benefit others. Amen.

August 23

THE PROBLEM WITH LONG PROJECTS

When it was completed on September 29, 1990, the Washington's National Cathedral constituted the sixth largest gothic cathedral in the world. With towers that rise more than 300 feet and a nave or main corridor that stretches 500 feet, and its position atop Washington D.C.'s highest summit, the National Cathedral is one of the most impressive sights in the Nation's Capital.

But the National Cathedral is a genuine Gothic cathedral, designed and built using medieval methods and technology. The Washington Cathedral possesses all the elements of classic Gothic: flying buttresses, vaulted ceilings, pointed arches, large and elaborate stained glass windows, roofs of lead, and carved-stone gargoyles and grotesques. This awesome cathedral was more than 100 years in the planning and took 83 years to erect (1907-1990).

This may seem like an incredibly long time. But compared to other cathedrals its construction was quite rapid. Consider that the great Cathedral of Notre Dame in Paris took 182 years to build and the Cathedral in Cologne, Germany (which is the world's highest – 515 feet) has taken over 600 years to complete. These cathedrals are simply so ornate and complex that their construction requires vast amounts of time. In fact, the largest cathedral in the world – the Cathedral of Saint John the Divine (in NYC) – is still unfinished, though its construction began 15 years earlier than the Washington Cathedral.

One of the drawbacks of such vast construction periods is that, long before the cathedral is finished, it shows signs of age. When the "brand new" cathedral is complete, much of it is old and requires fixing. Like most cathedrals, the Washington Cathedral is made of limestone. By the time it was finished in 1990, airborne pollutants (including sulfuric acid) had eaten away the outer layers of many of the cathedrals stone carvings. Lichen, a lime consuming fungus, also infests much of the cathedral's carvings, requiring a never-ending restoration process.

Still under construction – yet showing signs of age and needing repair. It sounds like we're describing people, especially people of faith. Believers in Jesus are born again by the Spirit of God. They are new creations in Christ. Yet, they are God's life-long project, requiring a lifetime to complete. And, long before the work is done, much of what was begun needs to be repaired. For the "pollutants" of this life (sins, temptations, and Satan's steady bombardment of flaming missiles) take their toll upon God's work. Thus God must repair and renew the work already accomplished. Ground lost must be regained.

So don't lose heart or be discouraged. It all comes with the territory. It's all part of the long process. And one day, by the grace and power of God, Jesus will finish what he has begun – both construction and repair – and we will be completely transformed. "But our citizenship is in heaven, from where we await a Savior, the Lord Jesus Christ, who shall transform our lowly bodies into the likeness of his glorious body." (Philippians 3:21)

PRAYER: Dear Father in heaven, sometimes it's so hard to have confidence that all the tangles, all the wrinkles, and all the flaws of my body, soul and spirit will one day be corrected. Please finish the good work you began in me and bring it to completion and help me not to lose heart nor be discouraged during the long process. Amen.

August 24

WHAT HIDDEN POTENTIAL LIES WITHIN US?

He was only an average student who distinguished himself at nothing before dropping out of high school. With little ambition to push him forward, this young man became a drifter, working at various jobs from farming to factory work to selling neckties.

His father finally brought him to work on the oil fields of Oklahoma, where he got his first taste of poverty and backbreaking work. But living from-hand-to-mouth with little hope for the future forced him to make a decision – to travel to Hollywood and make a life in pictures.

But he was hardly "movie actor material." He was awkward and insecure around women. Though tall and muscular, he had ears that stuck out like the handles on a sugar bowl and strikingly bad teeth. What hope could such a person have as any kind of actor, much less as a leading man? He went through a string of romances with older women on whom he depended for money, reassurance, and professional guidance. This only reinforced the image of an insecure and ineffectual man.

Yet, as hard as it was to detect any potential for success, there was evidently something within this young man that would eventually make him the undisputed "King of Hollywood," Clark Gable. Gable went on to star in more than 80 motion pictures, earning three Academy Award nominations (winning once for *It happened One Night*). His films include such blockbusters as *Mutiny on the Bounty*, *Call of the Wild*, and *Gone with the Wind*. In 1999 Clark Gable was voted by the American Film Institute to be among the "Ten Greatest Male Stars of All Time."

Human beings are mysterious creatures. Their hidden potential for goodness and greatness never ceases to surprise and inspire us. If you are having doubts about your own worth and potential, put your faith in the God who created you, loves you, and has a plan for your life. In the Scripture, God says "For I know the plans I have for you, says the Lord, plans for good and not for evil; plans to give you a hope and a future." (Jeremiah 29:11) God has a blueprint for your life. As you place your life in God's hands and seek his guidance, He can fulfill his plan for your life.

PRAYER: Dear Father in heaven, as your word declares, help me to trust in you with all my heart and not lean on my own understanding, but to acknowledge you in all my ways so that You will direct my paths. Amen.

August 25

WHEN YOU'RE BROKEN BEYOND REPAIR

In his *Book of Facts*, Isaac Asimov, describes a nickel-titanium alloy known as 55-Nitinol that is nothing short of amazing. It is one of a family of so-called "memory metals." Here's how it gets its name. When it is heated at a high temperature and fashioned into a certain shape, even a very complex shape, and then allowed to cool, the 55-Nitinol will "remember" that shape even when it is crushed beyond recognition. Once it is heated again, it will return to the shape it "remembers." Under extreme heat 55-Nitinol can be shaped into a geometric shape, the number "8," the letter "w," or even into a Crucifix. Once it is allowed to cool, that shape is "fixed in its memory." You can crush that Crucifix to powder. But heat the metal again and it will return to being a Crucifix.[lii]

People are like 55-Nitinol. There are times when we feel that we have been hurt so badly that we will never be the same again? We are so traumatized, violated, and crushed beyond recognition that we convince ourselves our world has no tomorrow. But God has made us more resilient than we realize. Though broken beyond human repair, as we draw near to the flame of his love God will heal us and restore us to our original self – but with a glorious difference. After God heals and restores us, we will be stronger and better than before. We will be enriched with wisdom and grace through the brokenness and the restoration process, so that we are then shaped into an instrument of God's peace and healing to others.

Paul the apostle had this in mind when he wrote these words in the Bible: "What a wonderful God we have – he is the Father of our Lord Jesus Christ, the source of every mercy, and the one who so wonderfully comforts and strengthens us in our hardships and trials. And why does he do this? So that when others are troubled, needing our sympathy and encouragement, we can pass on to them this same help and comfort God has given us." (2 Corinthians 1:3-5)

PRAYER: Dear Father in heaven, in my times of brokenness and pain, please heal me and give me hope for tomorrow. Re-fashion me into a stronger person than I was before and into an instrument of your peace and healing. Amen.

August 26

THINGS ADD UP

It all began when Bill Baker of Redding, California, tried to prepare a meal whose recipe called for 20 ounces of ketchup. But the Heinz 20-ounce bottle he used came up short - by about two ounces. Irritated that such a large company with such a trustworthy reputation had cheated him, Bill complained to California's Division of Measurements. By doing so he triggered a five-year-long investigation that revealed some alarming facts. Because Heinz had routinely shorted its customers - by 0.5% to 2% in each ketchup bottle – Californians had paid Heinz for 78,124 gallons of ketchup that it never received or $650,000-worth of ketchup. After paying a stiff fine ($180,000), Heinz also agreed to overfill its ketchup bottles to compensate for the red stuff it had previously withheld – which added up to 10 million ounces for one year. Little things, good and bad, can certainly add up.[liii]

What are we storing up as our days and hours fly? Wasted moments? Unkind words? Neglected responsibilities? Or, are we accumulating a lifetime wisely-spent opportunities for good? For either good or bad in this life, the Scripture tells us that something else is building in the life to come. We are warned that continued rebellion against God's laws will result in accumulated judgment (Romans 2:5). But we are also encouraged that, by continued obedience to God, and by acts of generous giving and kindness we are storing up treasure in heaven (Matthew 6:20). Something is building up in heaven. Make sure it's something good.

PRAYER: Dear Lord, teach me to number my days that I, at the end of my life, may present to you a heart of wisdom, a life worth living, and a child in whom you delight. Amen.

August 27

WHERE ARE THE PEOPLE?

After Louis Daguerre invented one of the earliest photographic processes in 1837, the French Government declared his invention "Open to the world." Immediately, "Daguerreotypes" began appearing from every continent. Photographs of the great cities of London, Paris, Cairo, and other great metropolises. But when these early photographs of busy city streets were displayed, viewers came away from the galleries

puzzled. There were no people in these photos. Nowhere in these pictures of Paris show any people. It was as if all these cities were ghost towns. Where were all the people?

There were indeed many people when the photos were taken. The reason they did not appear in the pictures is because the people were in motion and it took more than ten minutes for the images to form on the chemically treated plates that were used in the cameras of that day.

Like the Daguerreotype's inability to discern people and animals in motion, so are our feeble senses inadequate to discern the actions of the living God. God is living and active and is light years ahead of our scrutiny as we attempt to "figure out" what He is doing behind the scenes on our behalf. The Scripture says, "His judgments are unsearchable and His ways are unfathomable." (Romans 11:33)

Consider the words of one of England's finest poet, William Cowper.

God moves in a mysterious way His wonders to perform,
He plants His footsteps on the sea and rides upon the storm.
Blind unbelief is sure to err and scan His work in vain,
God is His own interpreter and He will make it plain.
Judge not the Lord by feeble sense, but trust Him for His grace,
Behind a frowning providence faith sees a smiling face.
Fresh courage take you fearful saints, the clouds you so much dread,
Are big with mercy and will break with blessings on your heads.

Can't see God in your circumstances? Don't worry, we are called to walk by faith not by sight. God is there, though you cannot see Him, and He is working out all things for His glory and your good.

PRAYER: Dear Father in heaven, I have worn myself sick trying to figure out what You are doing in my life. Help me to rest in your love, power, and wisdom, as I seek to please You and give You first place in my life. Amen.

August 28

THE SEEDS OF KINDNESS

In the late summer and early fall of 1805, the Corps of Discovery was in serious trouble. Led by Captain Meriwether Lewis and Lieutenant William Clark, the expedition was in pursuit of the headwaters of the mighty Missouri River and the famed "Northwest Passage" – a waterway that supposedly led across the North American continent.

But the men (and one woman – the Indian guide & translator, Sacagawea) of the expedition received the disappointment of their lives as they reached the crest of the Continental Divide. Instead of viewing a descending plain, the navigable Columbia River, and the Pacific Ocean beyond, when they reached the other side of the Divide, they saw nothing but endless towering mountains. Winter was coming and to survive they had to get past them. These were the foreboding Bitterroot Mountains and it took the weary Corps of Discovery eleven days and 165 agonizing miles to get over them.

By the time they stumbled to the base of the Bitterroots, they were dying from hunger, exposure and exhaustion. In this weakened condition, a tribe of Indians found them – the Nez Perce. The chief of this powerful tribe, Twisted Hair, discussed with the elders what to do with the bearded strangers. They decided to kill them and take their treasure of trade goods and weapons, for they had never seen white men before.

But there was among the Nez Perce an old woman by the name Watkuweis, a name which means "returned from being lost." As a young girl she had been kidnapped by an enemy tribe, harshly treated and sold as a slave to another tribe. Finally, she fell into the care of a family of white people who showed her the first kindness she had known since being taken captive. This white family eventually helped her return to her own people. Though many years had since passed, she never forgot their kindness.

Watkuweis was sitting in her tipi when she heard the decision of the elders. And before they could carry out the execution, she cried out to Chief Twisted Hair, "You must not harm these white men. The white people were kind to me when I was a stranger and far away. So you must be kind to them."

The elders listened to her counsel. Instead of killing the men of the expedition, they befriended them, fed them, and helped them build canoes for their trip down the Columbia River.

In the end, when a group of thirty-two men faced certain death and a violent end to one of America's greatest adventures, the seeds of kindness, sown many years before, now bore fruit and saved their lives.

Whether as a nation or as individuals, we must be ever mindful of what seeds we are sowing for generations to come. As you pass through this day, sow the seeds of kindness among those God places in your lives. Someone, perhaps even you or a loved one, will reap the benefits.

In the Scriptures we are admonished to "always abound in the work of the Lord, for nothing you do for the Lord will ever be in vain." (1 Corinthians 15:58)

PRAYER: Dear Father in heaven, today help me to brighten someone's world and lighten someone's load. May poison never spew from my mouth, nor cruelty through my actions, but let me be, at all times, an instrument of your peace and love. Amen.

YOUNG THINGS NEED A CHANCE TO GROW

About twenty years ago the Army entered a phase referred to as "optempo" (optimum tempo). It was precipitated by the fall of the Soviet Union and was characterized by multiple, repeated deployments of soldiers. The chaplains of United States Army Europe conducted a study on the effect multiple deployments were having on marriages. Their conclusion? Bad marriages will get worse, good marriages will survive.

This conclusion not only proved disappointing – since it was hardly "going out on a limb." It also was based on a rather simplistic assumption - that marriages fall into two simple categories: good and bad; that marriages are either dysfunctional or healthy. But that does not reflect reality. The reality is that most marriages are simply at different stages of growth.

What about young marriages? What about marriages in which the couple hasn't had time to bond emotionally, hasn't had time to build some happy memories together, hasn't had the chance to celebrate a single anniversary together - because of multiple deployments? Those marriages seem to break up too frequently. Is that because they're bad marriages or were entered into ill-advisedly?

If you leave a baby on its own in the world and it dies, is that because the baby was a bad or weak person? If you remove a young seedling Douglas Fir from the protection of surrounding adult trees and transplant it to a mountain top and it dies from the blast of the cold and tempest, is it a bad or a weak tree? No, it's because all young living things need the protection of the strong and must be given time to grow.

When Corrie ten Boom, survivor of a Nazi death camp, was five years old, she came into her father's watchmaker shop and asked him: "Father, what is sexual sin?" He just stared at her for a moment and then said, "Corrie, would you please reach over and hand me my toolbox?" Little Corrie tried but couldn't budge it. "I can't lift it Father, it's too heavy." "Yes, Corrie, it's too heavy for any child to lift. And it's the same with sexual sin. It's too heavy for your young mind. But as you grow and become an adult, then you'll be able to handle and understand it." Content with her father's answer, Corrie went on in her little girl's world. Was Corrie bad because she could neither handle the toolbox or the subject of sexual sin? No, she was simply young and not yet grown enough to deal with them.

And what is true for plants and people is also true of marriages. Married couples need to nurture their relationship. They need to spend quality time together. They need to build happy memories together. Of course, at our level, we cannot change the "optempo" of the Army. But we shouldn't add to the misery of broken hearted soldiers by telling them they had a bad marriage or say to them: "Next time, don't marry so soon" or, "It wasn't meant to be." Are we to believe that the Army is totally innocent in this matter? That the fault lies exclusively with the young couples? That if they had a "good marriage" it would have survived?

Marriages are not simply good or bad. They're at different stages of growth and young ones need more nurturing and protection and loving attention if they are to survive. Young married soldiers need the support of their leaders, NCOs, and officers. May God help us to help them!

PRAYER: Dear Father in heaven, all around us are hurting soldiers – soldiers who should be happy about going home, but because their marriages became casualties of this deployment, they have nothing to go back to. Please bind up their broken hearts and fill the void in their lives. Please bless their children, whose worlds have crumbled. Dear Lord, if reconciliation is possible, please heal their marriages. For those whose marriages are battered, but still standing, please strengthen and heal them. And for all of us, rekindle the flame of love in our hearts for our spouses. Turn our hearts to you in faith and to our spouses in love and forgiveness. We ask this according to you great love which has no limit. Amen.

August 30

WHEN WE STRIVE TO DO GREAT THINGS

You've probably never heard of Laurence Gieringer. He built an empire. His construction projects were nothing short of amazing. He built houses, churches, theaters, office buildings, country clubs, cable car systems, roads, bridges, railroads, public utilities, and communities on a scale unmatched by anyone else. He designed the most exquisite church stained glass windows. He designed, built and operated coal mining companies, saw mills, river dams, and airports. He changed the course of rivers. He was an artist, architect, and civil engineer.

Yet Lawrence was no "robber baron." His manifold achievements still remain and continue to inspire and benefit tens of thousands annually. Nor was Laurence Gieringer a millionaire. That's right. For all his accomplishments Lawrence was a gentle and humble man who earned only a modest income.

Remember I said Laurence Gieringer constructed his empire on a scale unmatched anywhere else on earth? Truth is he built things on a very small scale – a scale of only 3/8 of an inch to the foot. Laurence Gieringer is the creator of *Roadside America* in Shartlesville, PA, the *largest* miniature village in the world.

It all began as a boyhood dream inspired as he sat with his brother Paul on the summit of Penn Mountain, looking down on the city of Reading. He dreamt of making his own little city. And what began as a hobby, became his passion. His miniature village also became immensely popular – so popular and so big (half the size of a football field) that he had to build a special building to house and operate his little empire. Laurence died in 1964, but his Roadside America remains a popular attraction that captures in time a panorama of what America used to be.

The true source of Laurence Gieringer's greatness was that he was willing to do little things on a grand scale. He put painstaking care and effort into every detail of every building, vehicle, bridge, and community of his *Roadside America.* The result was a masterpiece and one of the most beloved family attractions in the Northeast.

Our society is filled with people who strive to be the "first" and the "greatest;" to build "the tallest," "the longest," and "the biggest." They jockey for the best and biggest and most prestigious jobs. But rare is the person who takes on the obscure, the tedious, and the small tasks of life and executes them with excellence. Rare is the worker who despises, *not* the little tasks of life, but only doing them in a mediocre way. Dr. Martin Luther King, Jr. once cautioned: "If God calls a man to be a street sweeper, he should sweep streets as Michelangelo painted, or Beethoven composed music, or Shakespeare wrote poetry. He should sweep streets so well that all the hosts of heaven and earth will pause to say, here lived a great street sweeper who did his job well." The Scriptures admonish us: "Whatsoever thy hand findeth to do, do so with all thy might." (Ecclesiastes 9:10)

PRAYER: Dear God, help me to be faithful in the little tasks of life that I may prove worthy of greater things. Show me true greatness is found in doing the little things in a great way. Amen.

IN YOUR MOST DESPERATE HOUR
YOU'RE NOT ALONE

It was the lowest point of Ernest Shackleton's ill-fated Trans-Antarctic Expedition (1914-1916). It was the lowest point of his life. Shackleton had come so far, but he had reached the end of all human strength, only to find another insurmountable hurdle posed against him.

Shackleton had miraculously led the crew of the *Endurance* through hundreds of miles of pack ice – until the ship was entrapped and finally crushed to bits by the encroaching ice. He had led his men on foot across the jagged, frozen wastes of the Weddell Sea. Then he had navigated the three life boats, filled with his starving men, across hundreds of miles of stormy, bone-chilling South Atlantic waters to the bleak, rugged coast of Elephant Island. Then, in desperation to save the lives of his men, Shackleton ventured to sail one of his three lifeboats 800 miles away to South Georgia Island. Under the most horrendous conditions – weathering hurricane force winds and fifty-foot waves, that made it impossible to rest, Ernest Shackleton and four others, reached South Georgia Island after a seventeen-day journey – an unparalleled navigational feat!

But no sooner had the five men reached the shore, than they realized that they were on the wrong side of the island. With what little life and willpower these emaciated men had left in them, they would have to spend it getting across the island's unexplored interior – where jagged mountains and glaciers awaited them. Leaving two of their party behind, who were too exhausted to continue, for the next 36 hours, Ernest Shackleton, Frank Worsley (his navigator), and Tom Crean marched across the island's foreboding interior to the Stromness Whaling Station. Somehow they made it. Years later, Shackleton recorded in his diary, that throughout the long trek he sensed "there were four of us and not three." He kept this awareness of a fourth person with them on that desperate journey a complete secret, until Frank Worsley later remarked to him, "Boss, I know that there were only three of us, but didn't you get the feeling there was a fourth person with us on that journey." The men concluded that there had indeed been a fourth man with them – that God himself had been with them in their darkest hour.

This story is reminiscent of the biblical account of the three Jewish exiles who refused to worship King Nebuchadnezzar's golden idol. As punishment, the King ordered them thrown into a blazing furnace. Then, when he peered into the furnace, the pagan king saw four, not three, men in the furnace of fire – completely unharmed. He remarked, "Did we not throw three men into the furnace, yet I see four men … and the appearance of the fourth is like the Son of God." (Daniel 3:24-25)

Should it surprise us that God is with us at our worst moments? In the Scripture God promised, "Do not fear, for I have redeemed you; I have called you by name; you are Mine! When you pass through the waters, I will be with you; and through the rivers, they will not overflow you. When you walk through the fire, you will not be burned, neither will the flame consume you. For I am the Lord your God, .. your Savior." (Isaiah 43:1-3) If troubles and problems seem to be closing in on you, remember – you are not alone. God himself promises to be with you and to help you if you will call on him.

PRAYER: Dear heavenly Father, in my times of crisis and despair, remind me that you will never fail me or forsake me. Help me to never lose hope nor to abandon my faith in you. Amen.

September

September 1

THE DEADLY ENEMY

It ranks as one of the worst train disasters in history. The death toll was shocking. 521 of its 650 passengers perished. How did it happen? A massive train collision? A terrible explosion? A derailment? *No.* Something far more deadly killed the unsuspecting passengers.

The train was Freight Train No. 8017 of the Balvano Limited. The place was in the inland mountains, near Salerno, Italy. The date was March 3, 1944, among the impoverished days following Italy's fall to the Allies during World War II.

On the March 2, 1944, Train No. 8017, a 47-car freight train pulled by two locomotives, departed Naples with about 100 passengers, and continued to pick up more and more at each of its stops. By 1130 that evening the train had more than 650 passengers. Almost all of these were civilians who had simply hitched a ride to pick up supplies from the farmlands to the north. They never made it.

At about 1 AM the next day Train 8017 chugged uphill into the longest of five mountain tunnels, the *Galleria delle Armi* tunnel. In the middle of the dark tunnel the train grinded to a halt. The engineers sprayed the track with sand. They tried to pull forward, but the train wouldn't budge. Then they tried to back out. Nothing worked. Within a matter of minutes deadly carbon monoxide fumes overcame them and most of their passengers.

When Train 8017 was several hours overdue at its destination, rail officials became alarmed. An immediate search revealed a horrifying sight – the dead bodies of more than 500 people. What made the scene more heart-rending was this. The engineer of the lead locomotive had his gear in "reverse." The engineer of the second locomotive had his gear in "full forward." The train wouldn't move because the two locomotives were pushing and pulling against each other. The two engineers had a fatal disagreement about which direction the train should go. Inspectors concluded that if the two had only pulled together, no lives would have been lost.

Whether it's an organization, a church, or a marriage – the failure of people to pull together is the most deadly enemy. We will not always agree, but we have got to work together as a team in order to survive. The Scripture admonishes us, "Submit to one another out of reverence for Christ." (Ephesians 5:21)

PRAYER: Dear Father in heaven, soften my hardened heart and fill it with your love and forgiveness. Help me to faithfully pray for and support those with whom I disagree. Bless us with unity that we may pull together and survive. Amen.

September 2

THE KEY TO SURVIVAL

Everyone admires a survivor - the kind of person who can stand on his own two feet, weather life's storms, rise up after taking a knockout punch and come back to take out his opponent. Consider what many believe to be a great survivor – the Tyrannosaurus rex, the "king of the tyrant lizards." Popularly known as "T. rex," this giant may have been the largest of all carnivores. It weighed in at 4-8 tons, stood 20 feet tall and 43 feet in length, and may have moved at speeds of 25 miles per hour. Heavily armed with four rows of dagger-like six-inch teeth mounted in massive jaws, T. rex appears to have been the ultimate killing machine.

In stark contrast to the vaunted T. rex, consider also the naked mole rat, perhaps one of the ugliest animals to have ever lived. And, living up to its name, the mole rat does burrow in the ground like a mole and is quite naked. Except for a few scraggly hairs, its pathetic pink prune-like body seems so ill-equipped to survive in a predator's world. Yet what it lacks in looks, the mole makes up for in industry and a cooperative spirit. The mole rat of the African desert builds a massive subterranean mansion, equipped with storerooms, halls, bedrooms, a "wedding chamber" (for mating), and a sealed-off bathroom facility.

But most remarkable about the mole rat is the complex social structure it keeps. As in ants, termites, bees and some wasps, in the mole rat communities, which consist of 20 to 300 animals, there is a queen which reproduces for the entire community and "runs the household." With the exception of a few breeding males, with whom the queen maintains life-long relationships, the rest are female worker-moles who carry out the daily upkeep and supply of the community.

Yes, there is quite a difference between T. rex and the ugly, little mole rat. But the biggest difference is this – one continues to survive and one is long gone. Even the little cockroach has out-distanced every one of those fearsome dinosaurs. In the end, it is not strongest (if we measure strength in muscle and meanness), or the most heavily armed, or the cruelest who survive. The true survivors are those which are industrious and which work together to help each other in a spirit of cooperation. Maybe when Jesus said "the meek shall inherit the earth," he was right. Pulling together as a team and helping each other works. The Scripture also commands us: "Bear one another's burdens and so fulfill the law of Christ." (Galatians 6:2)

PRAYER: Dear Father, help me understand that my key to survival is not "taking care of number one," but "working together with others for the common good." Amen.

September 3

PHANTOM GUILT

A strange affliction torments those who have suffered either the surgical or traumatic amputation of an upper or lower limb – phantom pain! In nearly 82% of cases of arm amputations and 54% of leg amputations, the victim will experience some measure of pain from a limb that no longer exists.

This phenomenon is particularly disturbing in the case of those who sought amputation to escape excruciating pain due to blood clotting or poor circulation. After bowing to the doctor's recommendation for amputation, they still feel the same wracking pain they had before. The source of the pain is gone, but the pain remains.

Doctors do not fully understand the causes of phantom pain, but use an assortment of corrective measures to treat it. These include medications for pain and depression, brain stimulation though surgery, hot and cold therapy, as well as psychological care.

A sort of phantom pain also afflicts many of God's people. There are many sincere believers, who've confessed their sins, put their faith in Christ, and prayed for God's forgiveness. Yet they still are wracked with guilt and a sense of unworthiness. But from what? God's word tells them that He has put away their sins once for all by the sacrifice of His Son (Hebrews 9:26) and that He remembers their sins no more (Hebrews 8:12). Their sins are gone and their slate has been wiped clean. From where, then, does this guilt come? It's a phantom guilt, a residual guilt that can only be erased when the believer learns to put his faith in God's word and not in his feelings.

Believer, if your heart condemns you, remember that God is greater than your heart and He has declared you "not guilty" (1 John 3:20-21). He has made you "the righteousness of God" in His Son (2 Corinthians 5:21). Put your faith in the fact of His word and not your negative feelings.

PRAYER: Dear Father in heaven, thank You for the supreme gift of Your Son, for taking away my sins, and for clothing me in the robe of Your righteousness. Please help me to trust the truth of Your word and not my ever-changing negative feelings. Amen.

September 4

NOT WORTH THE EFFORT?

Assembly-line technology and mass evangelism, both born in the early 20th Century, have the same goal and express similar values: quantity over quality. Success and importance only exist when numbers are multiplied. The ideas of "hand-crafted," "hand-made," and "individual attention" are scorned because they involve investing too much time and energy for so few results. Perhaps the most painful expression of this philosophy is the automated answering service in which a live caller is passed from one digital recording to another until he or she is finally bumped off the line altogether. A human being is not worth even a few minutes of someone's undivided attention. "It's not cost effective," we're told.

But this utilitarian mentality is nothing new. Just look at the outrage vented against Mary, the sister of Martha and Lazarus, when she *wasted* an entire bottle of costly perfume, *on one person* – Jesus (Matthew 26:6-13). "Why this waste?" cried the disciples. "We could have helped many people with this." But Jesus immediately defended Mary and said that wherever the Gospel is preached, what she had done would be spoken of in memory of her. Jesus validated ministry to individuals. In fact, with just one or two exceptions (e.g. when he healed the ten lepers – Luke 17:11-19), Jesus only healed the sick, cleansed the lepers, gave sight to the blind, cast out demons, led tax collectors to repentance, raised the dead, and called apostles *one at a time*.

Yet critics still question the value of wasting time and energy and resources on individuals. The greatest successes in the church only take place when radio and television broadcasts "reach millions" or when "hundreds come forward" at an evangelistic crusade. Building a relationship, establishing trust, and becoming a friend to unbelievers are largely condemned as far too time consuming and inefficient.

Tragically, this scorn for investing so much in so few has not only poisoned church values, but family values. Our own children are not worth the huge investment of our time, patience, and love. We pass that responsibility to minimum-wage laborers while we pursue more worthy endeavors. To my own shame, I am not immune to this flawed thinking.

But Jesus praises and validates the small-scale efforts of individual ministry. He does not measure success and importance by quantity. That's why He said of the poor widow's small gift: "She has given more than all the others" (Mark 12:43). Her gift of two tiny copper coins outweighed all the bags of gold of the rich, because she gave in love and faith and pure devotion. Quantity meant nothing. Quality of motives and character meant everything.

PRAYER: Dear Jesus, forgive me for my worldly values and for neglecting "the lesser" duties to which You have called me. Help me to realize that it's not *what* I do that determines whether my work is sacred or secular, but *why* I do it. Amen.

September 5

WHEN WE PASS THROUGH THE FIRE OF AFFLICTION

The giant Sequoia trees of Sequoia National Park, located in east central California, are the largest living things on earth. For instance, the largest of all Sequoias is the General Sherman tree, which stands 267 feet tall and is a staggering 36 feet wide at its base. It is believed to be about 2,700 years old – it was just a seedling during the days of the ancient Assyrian Empire.

At any given time a single Sequoia will have 11,000 marble-sized cones, each containing about 200 tiny, flake-like seeds – so tiny that 6,000 are required to equal one ounce! Amazing that something so small has the potential of becoming a tree so immense! And, in its vast lifetime, a single Sequoia will probably produce 60 million seeds.

Yet despite its extreme age and super-abundant seeds, a single sequoia will only produce a few offspring that will reach maturity. Why so few?

First there is the problem of its cones. Its cones take two years to mature, but remain on the tree, closed and encased in a wax-like shell, preventing the seeds from escaping. Some tiny forest inhabitants, like the Douglas Squirrel, manage to release some of the seeds by chewing away the outer scales without consuming the seeds. But another major hurdle that prevents the Sequoia seeds from germinating is the dense underbrush, which blocks off both the soil beneath and the sun above, hindering any new growth.

There is one thing that does pave the way for the birth of new Sequoias. *Fire!* That's right. The natural forest fires do *not* ravage the Sequoias. Instead they burn away the harmful dense underbrush, enrich the soil with nutrients, and melt away the waxy covering of the cones, causing their seeds to fall to the fertile ground below. The result? Vast carpets of new Sequoia seedlings.

The way forest fires ensure the survival of the Sequoia groves is akin to the way the trials of life ensure our survival and growth. Human beings do not thrive on prosperity and ease. On the contrary, we need adversity, trials and challenges to spur us on to reach out to God and other people, causing growth in our character and faith. This is why the Scripture tells us: "We boast in our tribulation, knowing that tribulation brings about perseverance" (Romans 5:3) and "Consider it pure joy, my brothers, when you encounter various trials, knowing that the testing of your faith produces endurance" (James 1:2).

Are you going through some difficult times? Allow your adversity to fulfill its intended purpose – to drive you into the arms of God so that your faith and strength may be renewed.

PRAYER: Dear Father in heaven, when I pass through the furnace of affliction, help me to flee to you as my refuge from the storm and as my tower of strength. Please grant that these fiery trials may not harm me, but only consume the dross of my sin and refine the gold of my faith. Amen.

September 6

PRISONERS OF FEAR

Can you think of a worse place to be imprisoned (with the exception of an actual prison) than an airport terminal?

Airport terminals are terrible places: Noisy, dirty, crowded, busy, stressful, inhospitable, and with nothing to eat but fast food. The noise from the jets is bad enough. But the relentless and inescapable repeat-recorded messages about "no smoking in the terminal" and "not leaving bags unattended" will drive a person mad. And there's no privacy, except in a bathroom stall – until the cleaning lady comes. Nor is there any place to lie down and rest. Every eligible bench is riddled with stainless steel armrests that keep anyone but a midget from stretching out one's tired body. And need I say anything about the people? Yes, an airport terminal would be a very bad place to be imprisoned. And if you've seen the motion picture, *The Terminal*, then you'll know what I mean.

But it actually happened. The place was not the John F. Kennedy International Airport, but the Charles de Gaulle Airport in France. The prisoner was not Viktor Navorski from Krakozhia, but Merhan Karimi Nasseri from Iran.

Disowned by his homeland, Nasseri had wandered throughout Europe for years, seeking asylum and legal immigration to the UK, the Netherlands, Germany, France, Belgium, and Yugoslavia. In August 1988, while traveling to the UK from France, Nasseri was mugged and robbed of his identification papers. He somehow talked his way aboard the flight to England, but the UK immigration officers returned him to France, his point of origin. Without passport, visa, or any other identification, Nasseri lacked the authorization to go anywhere. He could not legally step outside the airport terminal.

How did he survive? He washed and shaved in airport restrooms. He ate at the airport fast food stands that would give him handouts. He slept on a red bench in the underground level of the terminal. And he continued this routine for the next *eighteen years!* That's right. Merhan Karimi Nasseri did not leave the airport terminal from August 1988 to August 2006, when he was moved to the Emmaus shelter for the homeless in Paris.

Why did he have to stay so long? Didn't anyone try to help him? Yes, a famous human rights attorney, Christian Bourget, championed his cause. And after years of bureaucratic haggling and stalemate, in 1994 Belgium finally sent documents for Nasseri to sign, offering him asylum in that country. But he refused to sign. Four years later France offered him asylum as well. But he turned them down too.

Why did Nasseri turn down freedom from such an undesirable place? Many have concluded that he had become mentally ill and suffered from paranoia, depression, and anxiety. There was also the simple fact that, even in an airport terminal, Nasseri had a place to sleep, eat, and bathe, *and he had absolutely no responsibilities.* To go out into the world would mean he'd have to work, pay bills, file taxes, set up housekeeping, and be a responsible adult. If that was the cost of freedom, then Nasseri would rather stay in the airport, where he could be free from life's challenges and responsibilities.

The tragedy of Merhan Karimi Nasseri is repeated every day by many people. Every day, all around us, we see people who refuse to risk failure or endanger their personal security to achieve freedom. We see people who flee responsibility and routinely run from challenges. Such people will never reach their God-given potential for goodness and greatness. They will never be the people God created them to be. "Be strong and courageous," the Scripture tells us, "Do not fear or be dismayed, for the LORD your God is with you wherever you go." (Joshua 1:9)

PRAYER: Dear Father in heaven, help me to overcome my fears and my timidity. Empower me to face and overcome my challenges, for You are always with me to bless me and give me success. Amen.

September 7

WILL THIS TASK NEVER END?

The great Notre Dame de Paris Cathedral, with its 112-foot-high vaulted ceiling and its 228-foot-high towers, stands as one of the greatest examples of Gothic architecture. At the direction of Maurice de Sully, Bishop of Paris, construction began in 1163 and was not completed until 1345, 182 years later! This was a significant investment of time as well as of human energy and resources. An important note about the construction of Notre Dame is that, during this period, the average Parisian only lived to be about 45 years old. This means that, if you were one of the craftsmen who started with the project, neither you, nor your son, nor your grandson, nor your great grandson would live to see its completion. You would die before the work, to which you devoted your life, was finished.

Would that indicate failure on your part? Not at all. There are simply many things, many causes, and many endeavors in life that are greater than we are.

When the Scripture refers to the heroes of faith in the Old Testament, people like Noah, Abraham, and Moses, it notes that they all died before witnessing the coming of God's Kingdom and his reign of peace and righteousness on the earth. "All these people," the Scripture says, "died in faith without receiving what was promised." (Hebrews 11:13) Each one of them picked up the torch from his predecessor, held it high in his own lifetime, and passed it to his successor at his death. And each died believing that God would somehow take his small contribution and use it to ultimately build a better world. They did not view themselves, or God, or their cause as a failure.

We also are faced with an endeavor that is greater than ourselves – a task not unlike that of the saints of old – to establish peace, justice and freedom in a war-torn land. We will certainly return to our homeland before the work in Iraq is finished. And perhaps some of us may rest in peace before the ultimate goals of this war are realized, as some already have done. But we can rest assured that we have picked up the torch, and at a great cost in human life have faithfully held it high. Then, when the time comes to pass the unfinished work on to our successors, we will depart in faith, believing that God's justice, peace and freedom will ultimately prevail – and we have been a part of it.

PRAYER: Dear Father in heaven, help me, with the eyes of faith, to see the ultimate victory of your righteous purpose and kingdom, and help me to be faithful in the small part I have to bring it about. Amen.

September 8

WHEN LIFE THREATENS TO CONSUME YOU

Among the favorite foods of the African baboon is the seed of the baobab tree. But this does no harm to the tree. In fact, the baobab tree's progeny depends on it. By being consumed, the outer husk of the baobab seed is eaten away, making it possible for it to absorb water and germinate. The same used to be true for the seeds of the calvaria tree of Mauritius. Its seeds were the favorite food of the now extinct dodo bird. But since the "dodo's demise" no new calvaria trees have sprouted naturally. The same is true for hundreds of plants whose posterity depends upon being consumed – mostly by birds.

These constitute some amazing symbiotic relationships – two separate life forms that mutually benefit each other. But the baboon, the dodo, and all the other fowl only intend to consume and devour. There is only the intent to take and to harm. Yet they help.

This is analogous to the "evil" that befalls those who put their faith in God. Joseph in the book of Genesis, for instance, fell victim to his brother's jealousy and wrath, slavery, the injustice of his master's wife, incarceration, and the forgetfulness of a fellow prisoner. Yet, through it all, God was with Joseph and was using the pain of his life to develop him as a man of faith and character. In the end Joseph told his repentant brothers, "What you intended for evil, to harm me, God intended for good, the salvation of the world" (Genesis 50:20). When we put ourselves, our plans, and our future in God's loving hands he will cause even the evil intentions of others to do us ultimate good.

PRAYER: Dear Father in heaven, this day I put my life and my work in your hands. Please give me strength and wisdom to rise to every challenge and fulfill my mission. Please bring about ultimate good from all the pain and evil that life and others inflict on me. Amen.

September 9

INEVITABLE CONFLICT

The anatomy of a lightning strike is fascinating and illustrative. As a storm cloud develops, negatively charged particles increase and create "stepped leaders" – zigzag paths downward toward positively charged particles on the ground. These stepped leaders stop about 150 feet short of the ground when "positive streamers" rush upward at 60,000 miles per second and – "Contact!" A massive bolt of lightning occurs – passing a current of electricity of up to 200 million volts. The air around the shaft of lightning it is heated to between 45,000 and 60,000 degrees Fahrenheit, causing it to expand so quickly that a large compression wave occurs. Our ears detect this compression wave as thunder. This "clash between positive and negative electrical charges" occurs constantly on the earth. At any given moment between 1,800 and 2,000 thunderstorms are taking place on this planet. And at any given moment an average of 100 flashes of lightning occur in each of these storms. That's a lot of lightning – and a lot of damage. 100 persons die each year from lightning in the United States alone.

But these clashes are inevitable. Wherever negatively charged particles increase and reach down their jagged fingers toward the positively charged particles of the earth, terrifying sparks will fly.

The same is true whenever good is forced to coexist with evil. Whenever evil reaches out its jagged fingers to touch the good, there will be a great clash of currents.

People of faith universally acknowledge the inevitability and the necessity of spiritual conflict. They acknowledge that "our struggle is not against flesh and blood but against … the spiritual forces of wickedness in high places (Ephesians 6:12)." They see no problem with the Apostle Paul charging his young assistant Timothy to "endure hardship like a good soldier of Christ (2 Timothy 2:3)." People of faith freely acknowledge that Good must confront and suppress Evil.

But evil does not only exist in the spiritual realm. It manifests itself in humanity as well. Isn't that why Paul also wrote that God has ordained the human institutions of government, to execute His justice in the world, to deliver the oppressed and punish the guilty, and didn't he also say that God has put a sword in government's hand to accomplish this job (Romans 13:1-7)?

The presence of evil in humanity – rather the coexistence of both moral Good and moral Evil in this physical world - makes conflict inevitable and necessary - necessary because evil must be suppressed. Just as the positively charged streamers must rise up every time to confront the negatively charged stepped leaders, so good must rise up to confront evil. As the great English statesman, Edmund Burke warned, "All that is necessary for evil to triumph is for good men to do nothing." Pacifism at a time when Evil threatens Good is a tragic sin. War, in and of itself, is not an evil, nor is it immoral, for Christ Himself will one day "wage war in righteousness (Revelation 19:11)."

Therefore, let the soldier take heart. Your task is a painful one, a grizzly one, and a thankless one. But it is most certainly a necessary and inevitable one as long as Evil raises its ugly head in our world.

PRAYER: Almighty and merciful Father, we humbly confess our frailty and failures and plead your forgiveness and mercy. Please bless our nation. Make it morally straight and spiritually strong. Guide America on the path of righteousness – for righteousness exalts a nation, but sin is a reproach on any people. Bless also our men and women of the Armed Forces. Please grant them success in their mission, safety in conflict, and a joyous reunion with their families and loved ones. Above all, may Your rule and reign come quickly to our world and may the knowledge of the Lord cover the earth as the waters cover the sea. Amen.

September 10

SICKLY, SENSITIVE, AND SCARED

Sad to say, but most fathers in America would be ashamed to have such a son. He was a sickly kid. He caught every childhood disease there was and frequently had to be quarantined by doctors. He was a sensitive little boy and things that made other people laugh (e.g. the violence of slapstick performers - the Three Stooges) made him cry. And he was the most frightened child you ever saw. Things like getting a haircut, going to a doctor's office, and going to school terrified him. His parents would have to explain things to him to relieve his fears. The average father today would look at this sickly, sensitive, and scared little boy and would shake his head in disgust. "That kid's hopeless. He'll never be able to face life."

But he did grow up and he did face life – and did very well for himself. It all began with a visit to his grandfather. As he was leaving, his grandfather hugged him and said, "You know, Fred, you made this day very special for me – just by being yourself. There's only one person in the world like you, and I like you just the way you are." Fred reflected in years to come, "That went right into my heart and it never budged."

And from the seeds of those kind words planted in his soul came forth a fruitful life that blessed countless millions. I'm talking about Fred Rogers, a.k.a. Mr. Rogers, who created the longest-running and most successful children's program in television history.

Actually, the stunning success of *Mr. Rogers' Neighborhood* is due largely to the very things that plagued Fred as a boy. The loneliness of being quarantined for months forced him to develop his imagination and creativity. His parents' patient explaining of the things he feared became his own model. Many television critics attribute Fred Rogers' success to his style of talking to children about the things they fear and explaining them. Even his sensitivity, which our culture condemns as a weakness, became a source of his success. Disturbed by the pie-throwing and nose-tweaking in other children's programs, Fred Rogers provided something different. He looked kids in the eye and spoke gently to them. And children responded in droves. To this day, years after his death in 2003, Mr. Rogers is adored as a father figure and remains one of the most beloved television personalities ever. It all began with some kind words from his grandfather, Fred McFeely – whose name Fred Rogers used for one of the characters on his show – the "speedy deliveryman," Mr. McFeely.

We never outgrow kind words. They are the bread of life for children and they continue to be health to the soul for adults. Don't underestimate their power. Proverbs 15:4 says, "the tongue that brings healing is a tree of life."

PRAYER: Dear Father in heaven, please make me an instrument of Your peace and healing. Grant that my words will bring comfort to the heart and healing to the soul. Amen.

September 11

GOOD WILL PREVAIL

The year was 1453. Many consider it the darkest year for Christianity. That was the year Christianity's capitol – Constantinople – fell to the Islamic Turks. In a matter of a few months thousands of Christians either died for their faith or were converted to Islam at sword point. To worsen the church's pain, the crown jewel of all churches – Sancta Sophia – was turned into a mosque.

But unforeseen by anyone was the series of events that this tragedy set in motion – events that would ultimately lead to the greatest thrust of the gospel the church had ever seen. For the fall of Constantinople forced explorers and adventurers to find alternate routes from Europe to Asia and restore the flow of its precious silks, jewels, and spices. They sought a way to bypass Turkey to the Spice Island of Indonesia by sea.

Forty years later there appeared a Genoese explorer who was convinced he could reach the East by sailing west. And with a name that meant "One who bears Christ," he believed he had a divine mission – a mission not merely to open trade routes to the East, but to bring the gospel to the heathen. The man was Christopher Columbus. Columbus never did reach the Indies. But he, and all who followed him, driven by the need to find new trade routes to the East, unwittingly brought about the greatest triumph for the gospel of Jesus Christ. For the fall of Constantinople ultimately brought the Christian faith to the new world and planted the seeds that would providentially generate the most powerful champion for the gospel in its 2000-year history – America, which sends more Christian missionaries world-wide than any other nation (127,000 of an estimated 400,000 – Brazil is a distant 2nd place with 34,000 missionaries to its credit).[liv] In the Scriptures God promised, "Be still and know that I am God; I will be exalted among the nations; I will be exalted in the earth." (Psalm 46:10) And never forget Christ's own promise: "I will build My church and the gates of hell will not prevail against it." (Matthew 16:18)

PRAYER: Dear God, help me not to lose heart when evil seems to triumph. Remind me that You shall build your church and the gates of hell will not prevail against it (Matthew 16:18). Amen.

September 12

WHEN THE MISSION SEEMS TO BE GOING BADLY

Renovation. It's the process of taking something with major problems and fixing it. Renovation is a good thing. It brings about significant improvements – whether it's the renovation of a road, a building, a marriage, a person's life, or a country.

There are some problems, however, with the renovation process. First, it's painful. When a counselor digs into a person's past to correct the dysfunction in his or her life – it's painful. When a couple subjects themselves to a therapist's scrutiny and guidance, it's usually painful. Surgery is a form of renovation and because it's so painful the patient must be sedated.

Another problem with renovation is that it's messy. In fact, during the renovation process, the renovated person, marriage, building, road, or nation tends to look worse than it did before. Example: Highway 41A, which runs alongside Fort Campbell, KY, was considered one of the most dangerous roads in America. So great was the public outcry against that road, that the state and local governments of Kentucky and Tennessee finally decided to renovate it. But this involved extensive excavation, the re-routing of traffic into single lanes, and detours. As bad as the complaints had been *before*, during the renovation, people complained even more. "Now the road's worse than ever. It was better before, they should have left it alone."

But renovation also has a finished product that makes *all* the pain and inconvenience worth it. So renovation requires several things in order for it to work: a vision of the finished product, a blueprint of how to get there, and persistence to see the project through.

All of this applies to our own missions in Afghanistan, Iraq, and throughout the world. We cannot judge the success of this mission on the basis of how messy things look now or on how painful these deployments are becoming. Renovation is always painful and messy, especially the renovation of countries. Many will cry and complain as Iraq undergoes its own radical surgery: "Iraq was better off before – we should have left it alone." Unfortunately, we cannot sedate such people to spare them the pain. But we must keep the finished product in view, follow the blueprint established for us, and pursue this mission to its inevitable success. May God help us in that pursuit and let us take courage in his promise: Blessed are the peacemakers, for they shall be called the sons of God." (Matthew 5:9)

PRAYER: Dear God in heaven, please bless the men and women of our Armed Forces as they seek to be peacemakers in war-torn lands. Dear Lord, please give them success in their missions, protect them from all evil and bring them safely back into the arms of the families and loved ones. Amen.

September 13

WHEN OTHERS REJECT YOU

By the end of his life, Giuseppe Verdi (1813-1901) was recognized as Italy's greatest operatic composer of all time. But he didn't begin his career with such success. As a youth, he had obvious musical ability, but in 1832 he was denied entrance into the Milan Conservatory because he lacked the required education and background.

Yet time does strange things. Verdi rejected that rejection, continued to develop his gifts, pursued his career in music elsewhere and finally found success. After Verdi's fame had spread worldwide, this same school that turned him away was renamed the Verdi Conservatory of Music.

God moves in mysterious ways on behalf of those who trust in Him to bring about such twists of fate. The Book of Genesis records how Joseph was rejected by his own brothers and sold as a slave only to ascend to the throne of Egypt and become their ruler (Genesis 37-50). The Scriptures also tell how Jesus Christ was rejected by His countrymen only to become the King of Kings and Lord of Lords (Philippians 2:5-11). Over and over the Scriptures testify that God exalts the humble.

If others have rejected you, reject their rejection. Continue to develop your God-given talents and seek God's blessing on your life. The Scripture says, "Humble yourselves, therefore, under the mighty hand of God, that He may exalt you at the proper time" (1 Peter 5:6).

PRAYER: Dear God, I humble myself in Your sight and submit to Your holy will. Please lift me up and exalt me at the proper time. Amen.

September 14

WHEN YOU FEAR YOUR CHARACTER IS FILLED WITH FLAWS

There is a story about two men, both Italian sculptors of the Renaissance. One was Donatello (1386?-1466), whose real name was Donato Di Niccolo Di Betto Bardi, who is generally considered one of the greatest sculptors of all time and the founder of modern sculpture. The other was Michelangelo (1475-1564), arguably one of the most inspired creators in the history of art.

One day Donatello received delivery of a huge block of marble. After examining it carefully, Donatello rejected the marble because it was too flawed and cracked for him to use. The rejected block of marble lay discarded in a field for the next 40 years, until Michelangelo noticed it. Michelangelo also scrutinized the block of marble. He also noticed the cracks and flaws. But he looked beyond them and saw a powerful masterpiece inside, waiting to be liberated. Because of his superior artistic ability, Michelangelo accepted the "useless" block of marble with all its cracks and flaws. Then, from 1501-1504, he carved it into one of the greatest art treasures of all time - the statue of "David."

Like that piece of marble, many of us have flaws and blemishes in our character, faults that may have resulted in our rejection or disqualification. At those times of rejection we may think there is no tomorrow, no future for us. But God is not finished with us. God knows all about our flaws, but because of His superior artistic ability, He is willing to take us and make us into a masterpiece of a human being - if we will only let Him. The prophet Isaiah declared, "O Lord, You are our Father; we are the clay, and You are the Potter; and all of us are the work of Your hands." (Isaiah 64:8)

PRAYER: Dear Lord, please take the broken pieces of my life and build them into something beautiful for Your glory. Amen.

September 15

WHEN PEOPLE AND THEIR PROBLEMS INTERRUPT US

Ralph Burke was just out having a good time with his high school buddies one winter evening in the mid-1970s. As the group hopped out of their taxi to grab a bite to eat at a restaurant, Ralph spotted her – a ragged-looking girl of about fourteen, standing on the corner, shivering in the cold. Something inside him said, "See if she needs help." So Ralph followed that inner voice and invited her along with his friends to get a meal.

In their conversation, Ralph found out, the teenage girl was from Cleveland, Ohio. She had left home after a falling out with her parents. Now she was cold, hungry, friendless, and broke.

After buying her dinner, Ralph brought her to the bus station, purchased her a one-way ticket home, gave her $20, and left her his address and phone number, with these instructions: "If you ever need anything – please call me." He never heard from her again – that is, not for a long time.

Thirty years later – now married, established and raising a family – Ralph received an unexpected letter. It was from a woman whom he had long forgotten. The woman explained that he had "saved her" at the darkest point in her life thirty years before. She had returned to her parents, finished high school, attended both college and medical school and was now an accomplished surgeon. She was also married and had children. Often she had thought about him and sought to contact him, but had misplaced his address. Then, while one of her daughters was rummaging through her old clothes she found the old piece of paper with Ralph's address and phone number. "What direction would my life had taken if you were not there to help me?" she asked. "Thanks and God bless you for your kindness."

And what course will the lives of others take if we do not show them the kindness and love they need? How many times do we hold the destiny, happiness, success, and life of others in our hands when we're faced with decisions to help or neglect. God help us to be instruments of his love and mercy to our fellow human beings.

PRAYER: Lord, make me an instrument of your peace. Where there is hatred, help me sow love. Where there is injury, pardon; where there is doubt, help me sow faith; where there is despair, hope; where there is darkness, light; where there is sadness, joy. Amen.

September 16

GOD IS WATCHING OVER YOU

CBS News hailed it as a "True miracle." Even skeptics acknowledged it as an amazing coincidence and an incredible stroke of luck. Here's what happened.

In April 2006 Carolyn Holt of St. Charles, Missouri, was driving through town when she suffered a massive heart attack and suffered cardiac arrest. Her car drifted across several lanes of traffic and then crashed into the guard rail.

Among the handful of people who stopped to assist her, two were registered nurses and one was – get this – *a heart-defibrillator salesman, who had a defibrillator in his car.* In case you don't know what that is, a defibrillator is used to "jump start" hearts into a rhythmic beat. The nurses performed CPR on Carolyn and the salesman, Steve Earle, used his defibrillator to restore her heart beat. If that wasn't strange enough, the salesman confessed that he almost never takes his business car (which has the defibrillators in it). For family errands, like the one he was on, he always takes his wife's car. Fortunately for Carolyn Holt, this was a rare exception.

Carolyn was rushed to the hospital, but remembers nothing of the ordeal. She did not regain consciousness until she awoke in the Intensive Care Unit later that day.

This incredible convergence of all the right people at a critical time to save a life reminds us that God is watching over us in those times of our greatest need and helplessness. It also reminds us that God's miracles are manifested just as much through the hands of caring and skilled people as they are without any human intervention. We pray for God to do a miracle in our lives and God may answer with a miraculous healing. But God may also choose people of the medical profession to be his instruments of healing. We pray, but He chooses how He will answer. The Scripture reminds us that people make up the body of Christ – his hands, his eyes, his mouth (1 Corinthians 12:12-20). Through them God often administers the cure.

PRAYER: Dear Father in heaven, thank you for your unfailing love and protection which has preserved me countless times whether I am aware of it or not. Open my eyes and help me to be mindful of Your providential and protective hand. Amen.

September 17

ARE WE HURTING OR HEALING?

She was just a well-meaning, Irish immigrant, who was trying to survive. But everywhere she went she spread sickness and death to innocent people.

Her name was Mary Mallon, a portly 40-year old woman with no particular work skills, except cooking. She had contracted Typhoid fever earlier in life, but apparently suffered only a mild case. Though she survived, she remained a carrier throughout life, and went on to leave a trail of sickness and death from one household, kitchen and hospital after another, earning her the name, "Typhoid Mary." She did try to care for those she unwittingly infected, but apparently worsened their condition in the process.

Mary was eventually tracked down by sanitary engineer, Dr. George Soper. But even when confronted with the evidence, Mary, who routinely prepared and served meals with unwashed hands, refused to believe she had anything to do with the 7 or more Typhoid epidemics that began in every place she had worked. She also refused to give urine or stool samples and drove the doctor away with a clever. Dr. Soper finally returned with the authorities, who arrested and quarantined her in a Bronx cottage.

Three years later authorities released Mary upon her promise to remain a laundress. But she immediately changed her name and returned to cooking jobs. The pattern of sickness and death continued. Dr. Soper finally found her in 1915. This time health authorities quarantined Mary for life. She died 23 years later. An autopsy revealed her gall bladder was still actively shedding the bacterium *Salmonella typhii*. The number of deaths attributed to her has never been determined.

Having the best intentions is not enough. Our world is full of well-meaning, but hurtful people. Insensitivity, social awkwardness, and down-right stupidity have inflicted incalculable emotional wounds in marriages, homes and workplaces. The Scripture commands us to "Speak the truth in love" (Ephesians 4:15) and that "Love inflicts no injury to his neighbor, therefore, love is the fulfillment of the Law" (Romans 13:10). God help us to exercise a healthy measure of emotional intelligence in our interaction with others that we might not hurt, but only help and heal.

PRAYER: Lord, make me an instrument of your peace;
Where there is hatred, let me sow love;
  Where there is injury, pardon;
  Where there is doubt, faith;
  Where there is despair, hope;
  Where there is darkness, light;
  Where there is sadness, joy.
Divine Master, grant that I may not so much seek
  To be consoled as to console;
  To be understood as to understand;
  To be loved as to love.
For it is in giving that we receive;
It is in pardoning that we are pardoned;
And it is in dying that we are born to eternal life. Amen.

September 18

THE TRUE MEASURE OF SUCCESS

The name Charles Goodyear conjures up images in the mind – images of tires, the Goodyear Blimp, and the great tire manufacturer. Yet Charles Goodyear, born in 1800 in New Haven, Connecticut , did not found the industrial giant that bears his name, never envisioned making tires from rubber, and certainly had nothing to do with the Goodyear Blimp.

In fact, Charles Goodyear devoted nearly 30 unproductive years experimenting and promoting the uses of rubber, only to die in abject poverty and $200,000 in debt.

Yet the world is indebted to Goodyear for his contributions. Before he developed the process of vulcanization, rubber could only be used for boots, caps, and wagon covers. You see, rubber had a serious flaw – in hot weather it tended to decompose into a smelly blob and in cold weather it became hopelessly brittle.

Charles Goodyear, however, saw immense potential in rubber. He labored tirelessly and against endless adversity to find a way of making rubber into a durable building material. Goodyear even experimented while serving time in a debtor's prison. Then, in 1839, he unintentionally mixed some boiling rubber and sulfur when the ingredients spilled on the top of his stove. It inspired more experiments until he had perfected the process.

Yet even after this amazing discovery, it took Goodyear five years to acquire the money to exploit his discovery. During that time he was forced to sell his library, even his children's schoolbooks. A neighbor recalled seeing Goodyear's children scrambling in the garden for half-ripened potatoes to eat. Tragedy struck as well, when Goodyear's two-year-old son died unexpectedly. Not until 1844 did Goodyear receive a patent for his vulcanizing process. Yet it never made him rich. Others stole his ideas and attorney's fees drained his profits.

Goodyear did receive some honor for his achievements. In 1855 Emperor Napoleon III of France awarded him the Gold Medal of Honor at the Paris World Exhibition and the Cross of the Legion of Honor. Yet Goodyear was only on hand to receive them because he was serving another term in a Paris debtor's prison.

Five years later, in 1860, Charles Goodyear died. For all his benefits to humanity, Goodyear was benefited little. But he did *not* die an embittered man. Nor did he consider himself a failure. "The success of a career should not be measured exclusively in dollars and cents," he once wrote. He felt that, since so many would reap the benefits from his work, even though he would not share them, he was successful. He explained, "A man should only have regret if he sows and nobody reaps."

In the Scripture our Lord said, "Love your enemies and do good, and lend expecting nothing in return; and your reward shall be great, and you will be sons of the Most High; for He Himself is kind to ungrateful and evil men. Be merciful as your Father is merciful." (Luke 6:35-36) An old gospel song tells the same message:

If I can help somebody as I travel on,
If I can cheer somebody with a word or song,
If I can show some traveler he is headin' wrong,
Then my living shall not be in vain.

PRAYER: Dear Father in heaven, grant that I may not be so foolish as to settle for worldly success – the accumulation of wealth, recognition, and the praise of others. Help me instead to prepare for eternity, that I may become successful in your eyes and hear from You those happy words: "Well done, you good and faithful servant." Amen.

September 19

HANG TOGETHER IN CRISIS

When Germany invaded Denmark on May 9, 1940, the Nazis planned to isolate and remove its Jewish population. Their intent was to do this through the intimidation and force, if necessary, against the Danish government, headed by King Christian X.

The temptation to avoid confrontation and be conciliatory with the Nazis was great. Germany had just demolished the Polish Army and Air Force and ravaged the country the previous fall. Now it was poised to launch a massive invasion against France. This was no time to resist, but rather to find a scapegoat that could bear the wrath of the Nazis - and the 8,000 Jews in Denmark could serve as a very convenient scapegoat.

But King Christian X refused to abandon any of his people. When the Nazis demanded that the Jews in Denmark wear Stars of David to single them out, King Christian, chose to wear one himself, explaining, "*I* am my country's first Jew." He called upon his countrymen to do the same, and they did! Everywhere, everyone, with hardly an exception, the Danes were wearing Stars of David, making it impossible for the Nazis to implement their plan. As a result, almost all of the Jews of Denmark were safely evacuated to Sweden.

In times of crisis, the temptation is for each of us to get a "survivalist" mentality, in which we only seek to preserve our own skin. In that climate, when someone in our midst fails or otherwise falls from grace, we distance ourselves from them in hope that they will draw fire and fury away from us. But this dynamic is deadly to any organization. Solidarity among its members is critical to its survival. In the words of Benjamin Franklin to those reluctant to place their names on the Declaration of Independence, "We must hang together or assuredly we shall all hang separately." The Scripture commands: "Be of the same mind, maintaining a mutual love, being united in spirit, intent on one purpose. Do nothing from selfishness or empty conceit, but with humility of mind let each of you regard one another as more important than himself." (Philippians 2:2-3)

PRAYER: Dear Father in heaven, please bless our organization and bind us together in your love. Deliver us from a self-seeking, self-serving and self-preserving attitude. Help us to hang together lest we self-destruct as a body. Amen.

September 20

WHEN YOU FEEL INADEQUATE FOR THE JOB

"The man's an idiot, incapable of ever being effective or successful as a priest. God only knows how he ever completed seminary, much less received ordination. If he ever becomes a pastor, I pity the poor souls in his parish."

That ominous outlook was the opinion of John's fellow priests and superiors. It had also been the suspicion of most of his professors and instructors throughout school and seminary. John was a terrible student and showed no aptitude for the priesthood. In fact, he failed the entrance exam for seminary on his first try. Once in seminary, he nearly failed Latin – a serious problem when Latin is the language of the Church, the Liturgy, and the Scriptures.

But somehow John Vianney completed seminary and was ordained a priest in 1815. But even then, the pastor of the parish in which he served was afraid to let him preach. Yes, things did not look promising for Father John Vianney in 19th Century France.

Yet the bottom line was this – *God had called John to be a priest and that was the end of it. Whatever God calls us to do, he will also equip us to do.* And John went on to shake France with the gospel. He was made the parish priest of a small village called Ars and by the end of his life he was receiving 20,000 visitors a year who wanted to confess their sins, seek his wisdom, hear his preaching, and have him pray for them. John became recognized world-wide for his miraculous gifts of faith, healing and prophecy.

He founded a large orphanage for destitute girls and "prayed in" the enormous amounts of food, clothing, and funds required to operate it and feed and clothe its orphans. Priests, bishops and statesmen alike recognized his spiritual power and sought his advice. Near the end of his life he was so overrun by penitents, from all over France and beyond, that he was spending 18 hours each day hearing confessions. When he died in 1859, all France mourned their loss.

Saint John Vianney was canonized in 1925 and is now the patron saint of parish priests. Truly, whatever God calls us to do he will equip us to do. God is in the business of taking zeros and making them heroes.

In the Scripture we read, "For consider your calling, my brothers, that there were not many wise according to human standards, not many mighty, not many noble. But God has chosen the foolish things of the world to put to shame the wise, and God has chosen the weak things of the world to put to shame the things which are mighty; and the base things of the world and the despised things God has chosen, and the things which are not, that he may bring to nothing the things that are – that no human being may boast in God's presence. ... as it is written, 'Let him who boasts, boast in the Lord.'" (1 Corinthians 15:26-29, 31)

PRAYER: Dear Father in heaven, though I am weak, strengthen me with your power and make me greater than I am. Use me to do the impossible and I will give the glory for my work unto you. Amen.

September 21

THE MOST POWERFUL TESTIMONY FOR CHRIST

What did Mahatma Gandhi and Karl Marx have in common? Hardly anything, it would appear. Gandhi was a pacifist whose non-violent resistance led to India's freedom from British rule and colonization. Marx's views, on the other hand, inspired Lenin, Stalin and others to kill millions in Russia.

But they did have this in common. At one point in their lives they both became convinced that the Gospel of Jesus Christ held the answer to humanity's problems. As a young man, Marx even wrote a paper praising the virtues of Christ and Christianity. But when he saw hypocrisy and hatred in the lives of professing Christians (including his own father), he concluded Christianity was just one other "opiate" that the rich used to subjugate the poor.

Gandhi started attending church after graduating from a London university and appeared to be truly hungry for God. But he found the haughtiness and bigotry of Christians distasteful and was finally turned away at one church and told to go "worship with people of your own kind." He left this advice for Christians who seek to share their faith with others:

"I would suggest that all Christians, missionaries and all, live more like Christ. If you come to us in the Spirit of Jesus Christ, then we cannot resist you. Do not adulterate Christianity. Give it to us in its rugged simplicity and its high demands, and live out the life. Then we cannot resist you. Put your emphasis on love, for love is a central thing, in Christianity."

PRAYER: Lord, please grant that I will never embarrass You or bring dishonor to Your name. Please help me to help and not to heal and make me an instrument of Your peace. Amen.

September 22

JUST THINK OF WHAT "MIGHT HAVE BEEN"

We often find fault with our country and our government. We need to recall some fiascos that might have become law at the founding of our Constitution were it not for the possible intervention of divine Providence.

For instance, Congressman Elbridge Gerry of Massachusetts felt that one chief executive would be too kinglike and demanded that the United States have not one, but three presidents – one from the north, one from the south and one from the middle states.

Alexander Hamilton motioned that the president's term be *for life!* He believed an ex-president would be a subversive influence.

Congressman Roger Sherman of Connecticut pushed for the president's role to be that of a mere clerk or supervisor to make sure that Congress was doing its job.

Ben Franklin didn't believe that the president should even receive a salary, otherwise the position might merely attract greedy persons.

George Reed of Delaware (afraid that larger states might exert too much power) called for the dissolution of all state boundaries and governments. Other motions called for laws requiring that the number of western states never exceed the number of Atlantic states – greatly inhibiting the future size of America.

And consider Benjamin Franklin's passionate pursuit of what the national bird should be – not the bald eagle, but the turkey!

Just think of how inefficient, impotent, and small our country and government might have been if these motions had passed. But God was present in our nation's founding, giving wisdom to our leaders as they made decisions that would ultimately effect the future of the world. We need to daily pray for our leaders in government that God will guide them and help them to lead our nation on the path of righteousness. In the Scripture the apostle Paul admonished, "I urge, then, first of all, that requests, prayers, intercession and thanksgiving be made for everyone – for kings and all those in authority, that we may live peaceful and quiet lives in all godliness and holiness." (1 Timothy 2:1-2)

PRAYER: Dear Father in heaven, please bless and strengthen our leaders in government – our President, his cabinet, our Congress, our Supreme Court justices, our governors, and our mayors. Fill them with wisdom and courage to choose the right and to reject the wrong and guide them to lead our nation on the path of righteousness – for righteousness exalts a nation but sin is a reproach to any people. Amen.

September 23

GOD: THE GREATEST RECYCLER

In his marvelous, award-winning motion picture, "The Best Years of Our Lives," William Wyler became one of the first directors to address the difficulties returning war veterans experience re-adjusting to civilian and family life.

The film's main character, Fred Derry, descends from Air Force captain to soda fountain attendant upon his return. This amounted to an 80% cut in pay. But the cost was far more painful in human dignity. On his way back from overseas, CPT Derry had actually believed that reunion with his wife and returning home would "fix everything." All his post-traumatic stress, anxiety, and recurring nightmares would go away once he was back in the arms of his wife and again in familiar surroundings – so he thought. But within a few months he was financially broke, unemployed, divorced, and discarded by a nation that wanted to put the war behind it.

In a final scene Fred Derry is trying to escape his hometown. While waiting for a flight he wanders past the airfield into a vast "graveyard" of junked warplanes. Row upon row of gutted B-17 Flying Fortresses and P-47 Thunderbolts – machines that a year before had saved civilization – were now the throwaways of America. Symbolically, those thousands of discarded aircraft represented the millions of unappreciated and undervalued veterans. Like them, Fred Derry's life was now on the junk heap.

But the scene closes with a message of hope. The foreman of a "wrecking crew" tells Derry, "these planes are not junk – we're using them to make prefabricated housing." In the conversation, Derry also manages to get the foreman to hire him.

The message is clear. Those who feel discarded by society, those whose critical skills are no longer needed, those who are broken and considered worthless – have inestimable value as human beings and have a future role to fill and a contribution to make.

Every human being will go through periods of self-doubt and brokenness. We may reach a point when we feel utterly useless and hopeless. We may fear our lives have no tomorrow. But the God who created us put us on this planet for a purpose. He has a blueprint for our lives and, no matter how broken we become, God can transform our lives into something useful and beautiful. To the apostate and broken nation of Israel, God said, "For I know the plans I have for you, says the Lord, plans for good and not for evil, plans to give you a hope and a future." (Jeremiah 29:11)

PRAYER: Dear Father in heaven, redeem my life and my soul. Please take the raw material and the broken pieces of my life and make me the person you created me to be. Please, dear God, bring beauty and wholeness back to my life and fashion me into an instrument of your peace. Amen.

September 24

YOU'VE GOT TO RE-BOND WITH THOSE YOU LOVE

Mithradates IV, known as "Mithradates the Great" (c. 131-63 B.C.), was the outstanding king of Pontus who extended his empire until, in addition to Pontus, he held Cappadocia, Paphlagonia, and the Black Sea coast beyond the Caucasus and consequently became a threat to Rome. Yet his greatest fear was not the Romans, but assassination.

He so greatly feared assassination by poisoning that he self-administered poisons of every kind - systematically increasing the doses until he made himself immune to most known poisons.

Ironically, when he was defeated and cornered by the Romans, he tried to commit suicide by poison, only to find that it had no effect. His efforts to protect himself from being hurt by others became his undoing and cut off his escape from the pain of the sword.[lv]

There is a similar dynamic between Mithradates' fate and the typical human effort to protect oneself from being hurt. People hurt us, reject us, disappoint us, and let us down. So we withdraw from them and insulate ourselves, vowing we will never be vulnerable again. But a painful loneliness results from our efforts to escape pain. Our protection against being hurt becomes our own undoing and causes us an even greater pain.

This occurs in the military like nowhere else. The frequent deployments and family upheavals force most soldiers through an emotional meat grinder. In an effort to escape the pain of separation as an impending deployment looms on the horizon, soldiers typically detach themselves emotionally from their spouses and loved ones. Even worse, after redeployment, they resist re-bonding emotionally with their families lest they make themselves vulnerable against getting hurt all over again. But we cannot cut ourselves off forever from those who love us. If we do a painful loneliness will be our fate. It behooves us all to prepare for reunion now: to correspond, call, communicate and reconcile with our families - rebuilding the bridge between us and our spouses who have pledged to be faithful to us unto death.

PRAYER: Dear God, soften my heart toward those who love me and help me not to shut them out of my life. Restore the emotional bond between me and my spouse and my children. Amen.

September 25

WHEN YOU FEEL INADEQUATE

Ferdinand Waldo Demara, Jr. was a real-life "Great Pretender." Without training, academic degrees, credentials, ordination or a commission, Demara pretended to be (and received payment as) a surgeon, psychologist, college dean, dentist, university professor, Naval officer, and a Trappist monk. Demara's phony life finally caught up with him and landed him an 18-month prison sentence – though he only served six months.

The amazing thing about Demara, was that he actually performed quite well in many of his roles. In fact, while posing as surgeon in the Royal Canadian Navy, this phony "Dr. Joseph Cyr" performed brilliantly during a most critical time – under combat conditions during the Korean War. He removed tonsils, extracted teeth, administered anesthesia, amputated limbs, and - in one life-saving effort - removed a bullet from a wounded soldier that was lodged just one inch from his heart. Demara was successful with every one of his medical procedures and never lost a single patient. He studied medical manuals before such operations and did his very best – saving many lives in the process. In fact, he was so successful that a popular magazine did a feature story on him.

Unfortunately for Demara, the mother of the real Dr. Joseph Cyr read the article and notified the magazine that their "hero" was an imposter. The magazine broke the news to the Canadian Government, but rather than administer military justice, the Navy simply dismissed him - with back pay. He had simply saved too many lives to be punished. In the final analysis, credentials or not, Ferdinand Demara *was* the ship's surgeon.

And how many of us, from soldier to minister to homemaker, may feel a sense of inadequacy or even a sense of illegitimacy – that we are not "the genuine article." Why? Because the role in life we fill does not have the recognition, affirmation and "blessing" of others, because we do not have the education or training or certification others have and we live with the feeling that we are only pretenders. Yet, all the while we are effective in our work – often more effective that the "officially trained and certified" professional. If you can get the education, training, and certification you need, get it. But if you cannot, keep doing the work God has called you to do.

PRAYER: Dear Father in heaven, help me to be faithful in the work you have called me to do – even though I do it without man's recognition, praise or affirmation. Help me to be faithful in secret that you may reward me openly. Amen.

September 26

TAKING CARE OF NUMBER ONE

The Japanese have a special method for growing superb melons. They plant a seed, allow it to sprout and form buds, then remove all the buds, except one. This one bud is allowed to mature into a full fruit. In this way the single fruit receives all the nutrients originally meant for the entire plant. The result? Instead of many normal melons the plant produces one oversized, succulent melon.

In some ways this method of growing fat, rich, juicy melons parallels life for many people. What God intended to be shared and enjoyed by many is consumed by only a few.

What is our purpose in life? Is it to merely survive and to scarf up for ourselves as much as we can? How do we measure success? By the number of possessions and the amount of money we stockpile? The Scripture states that we all constitute "a body with many different members, all having different functions" and that we must serve each other, not just ourselves (Romans 12:4-8). An eye does not see merely for itself, but for the entire body, to guide it. The feet are not two "free wheelers," running about on their own. They exist to provide mobility for the rest of the body. The mouth, the teeth and the tongue do not chew and eat to satisfy and nourish themselves, but they serve to nourish the entire body. And so the Scripture says: "As each one has received a special gift, employ it in serving one another as good stewards of the manifold grace of God." (1 Peter 4:10)

Winston Churchill once noted, "We make a living by what we get; we make a life by what we give." Jim Elliott, Christian missionary who died at the hands of the Waodani Indians in Ecuador, wrote in his journal: "He is no fool who gives what he cannot keep to gain what he cannot lose." Jesus Christ declared, "It is more blessed to give than to receive." (Acts 20:35)

If, in all our plans and pursuits, there is no room for serving God and other people, maybe we should consider how we might experience true success – and happiness. Jesus stated, "There is more happiness in giving than in receiving." (Acts 20:35)

PRAYER: Dear Father in heaven, I want to be a channel of your blessings and not a mere receptacle. I do not want my life to be a mere dead end, leading to nowhere except my own personal gratification. I want my life to count for eternity. So please help me to use my God-given talents and resources to benefit and bless others and to bring honor and glory to your name. Amen.

September 27

THE CONQUESTS OF SELFLESS SERVICE

It was the chance of a lifetime. In 1914 a bright young Navy officer was given a job offer that no sane man could refuse. At a time when the Navy was paying him $3,400 a year, a Midwestern civilian company offered him a five-year contract at *$25,000 a year!* Surely this was a no-brainer.

The young officer measured the pros and cons. He was the Navy's premier expert on diesel engines (a critical innovation – especially for submarines - at a time when all ships burned coal) and the Navy's number one expert on "underway refueling." And it was this expertise that got him this incredible job offer.

Everything seemed in favor of taking the job and kissing the Navy goodbye. He calculated it would take him more than *thirty-five years* in the Navy to earn what this new job offered in *five*. Then there were the hazards of the Navy to consider. The Navy had already cost him his hearing when he was just a midshipman. It also almost cost him one of his hands (luckily he only lost a finger). Then he considered his dismal prospects for promotion in the Navy since a court martial (from running his ship, the USS Decatur, aground) stained his record. Yes, there was no question. Taking the lucrative civilian job was certainly the way to go.

But there were just two other factors to consider. First, how could he best serve his country? The second consideration, for what purpose had God placed him on this planet? Fulfilling that purpose was the true measure of success – not making a lot of money. Therefore, though he would never make large amounts of money and though the prospects for promotion looked bleak, this bright Navy officer, Chester Nimitz, chose to stick it out in the Navy and serve his country in the best way he knew.

It's a good thing he did. For it was Chester Nimitz who took the decimated Pacific Fleet at the beginning of WWII, rebuilt it, conquered the Pacific, defeated the largest and most powerful navy on earth, and saved the fate of America. And what about his dismal prospects for promotion? As it turned out, Chester Nimitz went on to achieve the rank of Fleet Admiral and become the highest-ranking officer in the Navy and its greatest hero of the war. He did all this because at one critical moment in his career, he chose a life of selfless service for his country.

Somewhere in the Bible our Lord said, "Whoever seeks to save his life will lose it, but whoever loses his life for my sake will find it." (Matthew 10:39) May God grant us the guidance to find our purpose in this life and the courage to fulfill it!

PRAYER: Dear Father in heaven, guide my steps and help me to find my calling in life. If it be to bravely serve my country as a soldier, with little financial compensation and recognition, help me to faithfully fulfill Your purpose for my life. Amen.

September 28

ENLARGE YOUR VIEW OF GOD AND HIS PEOPLE

Until the 1920s, the consensus of all astronomers was that the Milky Way, our galaxy, represented the totality of the universe. Yet they had only a vague grasp of its size – so big that, even if you traveled at the speed of light (186,000 miles per second) it would take 100,000 years to travel from one end to the other.

But in 1924, famed astronomer Edwin Hubble - working at the Mount Wilson Observatory, using its 100-inch Hooker Telescope - made one of the most profound discoveries in the history of astronomy. For years astronomers had noticed faint, blurred heavenly bodies in the night sky, which they assumed were stellar dust clouds or uncondensed gases that might be "stars in the making" – but all within our galaxy. Hubble realized that these faint stars were not stars at all, nor clouds of dust, nor "stars in the making." They were *other galaxies* – just like ours and *just as big as ours*, each containing billions of stars. Instantly, the universe became a much bigger place. Not only were there billions of stars in our galaxy. Now we realized there were billions of galaxies in our universe.

Think about it. We have gone from a pre-Copernican/Geo-centric view (that the sun and all the stars and planets circle the earth) to a heliocentric view (that the earth and all the planets circle the sun) and from the view that our galaxy "was everything" to the realization that ours is just one of billions of galaxies.

And as we have had to enlarge our view of the universe, so we (if we are to grow in our faith) must enlarge our view of the church. The church we grew up in and the denomination whose faith we espouse do not define the whole church. My particular conversion experience does not represent the model for all true converts. And the style of worship that I enjoy most is just one of many through which God can move to touch and bless his people.

True, we can go on in our own little world, believing in a tiny universe and in a tiny church. But the bigger our view of the universe, the bigger will be our view of the God behind it. The greater our view of the church, the greater will be our view of Jesus Christ who builds it. The Scripture commands us to "Grow in grace and in the knowledge of Jesus Christ." (2 Peter 3:18). Grow, therefore, in your knowledge of Jesus, the Builder, Savior and Lord of the church – which is the fullness of Christ who fills all in all (Ephesians 1:23).

PRAYER: Dear Lord, please open my eyes to the breadth, height, and depth of your love for humanity. Help me to never compromise the gospel, the love of Christ, and the Christian unity for which Jesus prayed – all in the name doctrinal purity. Amen.

September 29

WE ALL HAVE WHAT IT TAKES TO SUCCEED

Paul didn't stand a chance. That's what most people thought. To most it was obvious that Paul was a poor student, stupid, dyslexic, frequently expelled from school, and already several grades behind the kids with whom he started. Yes, everyone seemed convinced that Paul Orfalea didn't stand a chance.

But his mother believed in him, even though one junior high school administrator told her: "Maybe he can enroll in a trade school and learn to lay carpet." Paul's dad believed in him, too, even though the kids called him "Kinko," because of his curly hair. Finally came graduation day. Paul managed to graduate with a "D" average. He was able to eke his way through the University of Southern California, but showed the same lack of aptitude and promise. The destiny as a common laborer seemed inevitable for Paul "Kinko" Orfalea.

But Paul didn't lay carpet, or work as a truck driver, or slave as a garbage collector. In 1970, Paul started a small copy shop at an old hamburger stand. From that humble beginning, he turned a goofy nickname into an internationally known chain of stores. By the year 2000, Paul Orfalea, at the age of fifty-two, stepped down from his position as CEO of Kinko's. With a personal worth in excess of $225 million, and with 865 stores and 23,000 employees in his portfolio, Paul "Kinko" Orfalea represents the power of encouraging parents and the refusal to accept defeat. Orfalea dismissed his dyslexia, saying, "God gave you an advantage, so work with your strengths." We all have weaknesses. Don't focus on them. Focus on your strengths and use them, with God's help, to fulfill your destiny. Saint Paul declared: "I can do all things through Christ who strengthens me." (Philippians 4:13)

PRAYER: Dear Father in heaven, please empower me by Your Spirit and embolden my heart to overcome my own timidity and perceived limitations, and to face life's challenges. If I do fail, help me to rebound and learn from my failures. Please make me, O God my Creator, the person You want me to be. Amen.

September 30

WHEN WE YEARN FOR STILLNESS AND TRANQUILITY

Everything in space is in motion – both revolving and rotating. But, as astronomer Donald DeYoung explains, this spinning motion is essential to survival of the heavenly bodies. He writes, "Rotation is a universal nature of stars just as it is for all the planets and their moons. … Without these motions, gradual large scale gravity collapse and chaos would occur everywhere in the universe."

All nine planets (or eight if you exclude Pluto) in our solar system rotate. Some, like Mercury – whose *day* is longer than its *year* - rotate slowly. Others, like Jupiter – whose *day* is a mere ten *earth-hours* - rotate very rapidly. But this rotation keeps the planets and stars from collapsing under their own gravity and keeps them from self-destruction.[lvi]

In a way, most people feel like they're in a dizzy sort of motion, in a constant state of agitation, kept spinning by the badgering of adverse circumstances. But as much as we yearn for "stillness" and tranquility, the God-sent motion in our lives is essential to our spiritual health. Without motion and change in our lives, stagnation and staleness of spirit results.

The Scripture agrees with this when it says, "And we boast in our tribulation, knowing that tribulation brings about perseverance and perseverance brings about proven character, and proven character brings about hope and hope does not disappoint, because the love of God has been shed abroad within our hearts by the Holy Spirit who has been given to us." (Romans 5:3-5)

PRAYER: Dear Father in heaven, how I yearn for peace and tranquility in my life. Help me to understand the value of the agitation and adversity that rattles me and sends me spinning. Cause my pain to become my gain. Amen.

October

October 1

A FLY IN THE MOUTH

It is the most popular Hollywood musical ever made – *The Sound of Music*. It has inspired tens of millions of people, generated innumerable visits to the city of Salzburg, Austria (where the story of the Von Trapp Family takes place), and continues to fuel interest in the Von Trapp's thriving lodge near Stowe, Vermont.

But while hundreds of millions have seen the movie, far fewer know that the Von Trapp Family was a highly successful singing group in Europe before fleeing the Nazis in 1938. In fact, they became so popular that Adolph Hitler requested a performance from the group. They refused and promptly fled the country.

But after arriving in the United States success eluded them. Their somber, stoic style of performing classical European folksongs did not appeal to American audiences. They barely survived from one performance to the next. Even after hiring an agent, who tried to get them to lighten up their presentation, audiences did not respond to their music.

Then a very embarrassing event changed everything. During one of their typical somber performances, a fly flew right into Maria Von Trapp's mouth, causing her to cough violently and bring the song to a temporary halt. With teary eyes and a red face, Maria laughed and said, "It's never happened before – a fly flew into my mouth." Everyone - Maria, the Von Trapp Family, and the entire audience - laughed hysterically. The concert continued, but in a far more relaxed and interactive atmosphere. And the audience loved it.

From that moment on, the Von Trapp Family realized their American audiences loved interaction and lightheartedness in their concerts. They would continue it in all their performances. The result – the Von Trapp Family Singers became one of the most popular musical groups in America during the 1940s and early 1950s. Their notoriety led to a best-selling biography of the family, which was made into a popular motion picture (in Germany). Later the book and the movie became the basis for the Toni Award-winning Broadway play and the immensely successful, Oscar-winning (5 Oscars) movie, *The Sound of Music*.

The play has been revived countless times in New York, London, Sydney, Stockholm, and Tokyo. The movie has continued undiminished in its popularity and is second only to Star Wars and Gone with the Wind in the number of tickets sold. And this stunning success all began when a fly flew into Maria's mouth.

Sometimes we fail to see the possibilities that can arise from the painful or embarrassing events of our lives, from the disappointments and failures. But when we place our lives in the hands of the Lord, he will bless them, sanctify all the pain they contain and cause it deepen our relationship with Him and strengthen our faith. The Old Testament records that Joseph, after a life of rejection, obscurity, and disappointment, was able to say: "What you intended for evil, God intended for good." (Genesis 50:20) God does that. He turns our curses into blessings (Deuteronomy 23:5) and works all things together for our good (Romans 8:28).

PRAYER: Dear Father in heaven, here and now I accept your lordship over my life. Guide and direct my steps. Please take all my sorrows, all my pain, and all my disappointments and work them all into something beautiful and good. Amen.

October 2

A LESSON FROM THE INFANTRY

Infantry tactics, techniques and procedures (TTPs) provide a surprising illustration for living. Consider this: when Soldiers prepare individual and team fighting positions along a defense perimeter, Army doctrine dictates that their sectors of fire be angled to their right or to their left, *but not directly to their front*. With a mound of packed dirt providing cover to the front of his position, each Soldier aims at the

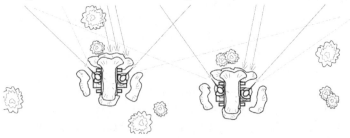

enemy who attacks the fighting position of his fellow Soldiers to his right and left (as seen in the illustration). *He does not cover himself. He covers the Soldiers next to him.* In fact, no Soldier defends his own position. He defends the positions next to his own.

This may seem foolhardy, but it is very effective against opposing forces. For the defending Soldier hits the attacker with flanking fire (i.e. on their side where they are unguarded) and creates interlocking sectors of fire along the defense perimeter. In contrast, if each Soldier aimed directly to his front, the defense perimeter would be easily overcome.

This same dynamic is at work in every team and organization. In a marriage, on a ball team, or in an organization, members ensure their mutual success when they look out for each other, cover each other, and help each other. But if the partners look out only for themselves, the team, organization or marriages crumbles.

The Scripture says, "Bear one another's burdens and so fulfill the law of Christ." (Galatians 6:9)

PRAYER: Dear Father in heaven, deliver me from my selfishness and free me to serve others and to look out for their needs. Let me experience the joy of giving and the freedom of serving others. Amen.

October 3

PERSISTENT PREDATORS

Shark attack. It happened to 22-year-old Luke Tresoglavic while snorkeling off Caves Beach, near New Castle, Australia in February 2004. A small carpet shark, also known as a Wobbegong, latched onto Tresoglavic's leg and thrashed violently. Tresoglavic tried to steady the shark with both hands to keep it from tearing his leg apart. And with this contorted little shark locked onto his leg, Luke had to swim 1000 feet to reach the shore.

But escaping the waters did not end his battle with the shark. The persistent predator continued to clamp tenaciously onto Luke's leg. Other bathers ran to his rescue, but they could not pry the little shark free. So Luke walked to his car and drove to a local surf club – with the 60-centimeter-long (about two feet) shark still attached to his leg. Some of the lifeguards held the thrashing shark steady, while others flushed his gills with fresh water. Finally they were able to pry the persistent predator off of Luke's leg, leaving behind 70 needle-like puncture wounds which were treated at the local hospital. Of course Mark had to drive to the hospital himself, with the dead shark lying beside him.

Strange that a man can escape the shark-infested waters and still be attacked and vexed by a shark. Even so, we can be delivered from lives of sin. We can be saved into a life of fellowship with Christ, moment by moment enjoying the presence of the Holy Spirit. Yet, individual sins from "the old life" may cling tenaciously to us and refuse to let go. Their bite is very real, as is the pain it brings. But their torment is not an indicator that we never left sin behind – any more than that tenacious shark was an indicator that Luke had never left the sea.

The problem for us is this: Christ takes us just as we are. He does not demand we clean up our lives before accepting us into his presence. The moment we cry for help, He draws us from the shark-infested waters. As soon as we call out to Him for salvation and forgiveness, He saves and cleanses us. But sometimes predators from the past continue to hound us and refuse to give up so easily.

But do not be troubled. God knows about your problems and imperfections. He's brought you this far and is not about to "cast you back into the sea where sharks belong." One by one, all such predators will eventually give up – until Christ's final victory at our death and resurrection, when the sins that once plagued us we will never see again – ever.

In the meantime we have this promise in Scripture: "Little children, these things I write that you may not sin. But if anyone sins, we have Someone Who pleads for us with the Father, Jesus Christ the righteous. And He is the atoning sacrifice for our sins; and not only for ours, but also for the whole world." (1 John 2:1-2) God has made every provision to save you, keep you and to bring you safely into His heavenly kingdom.

PRAYER: Dear heavenly Father, please forgive my imperfections and those predators from the past that continue to plague me. Please set me free, deliver me, and help me to win the consummate victory over those shadows from my past. Amen.

HARD DECISIONS

Bill Jeracki, Don Wyman, and Aaron Ralston: What do these three men have in common? All three of them had to make painful, life or death decisions. In the fall of 1993 Bill Jeracki, a 38-year-old anesthetist, was fishing in the Colorado wilderness. As the sun began to set and the temperature began to fall, Bill decided it was time to call it a day. In fact, a snowstorm was in the forecast and Bill knew he had to get going. But as he walked to his truck across the rugged terrain a boulder slipped and pinned his leg to the ground.

What a dilemma he was in! Bill knew if he waited to be rescued he'd die of exposure and hypothermia. So he did the unthinkable. He applied a tourniquet of fishing line above his knee and, with a pocket knife, he cut off his own leg at the knee to free himself. He crawled back to his truck, drove the stick shift to the nearest town, and then was air-evacuated to the Colorado University Hospital. He lost his leg, but he lived.

Earlier that same year in Pennsylvania, Don Wyman had been cutting firewood with his chain saw when a huge oak tree fell in his direction, crushing his left leg. Don tried everything to free himself. But nothing worked and no one came. Finally, Don did what he knew he had to do. He used the pull-chord for a tourniquet and then cut off his leg with a pocketknife, just below the knee. He then climbed uphill to a bulldozer and drove it ¼ mile to his pickup. Since his truck had a manual transmission, Don Wyman had to use a tool to depress the clutch as he shifted gears. He drove to a farmer's house who phoned for paramedics. Don Wyman lost his leg, but he survived.

A few years ago, Aron Ralston had to make the same decision. He had been rock climbing in a red sandstone canyon near Moab, Utah, when a boulder slid and pinned his right arm in a three-foot crevasse. For five days Aron tried to free himself, but to no avail. More than anything this adventurer wanted to save his arm. He had climbed all of Colorado's 14,000-foot peaks as a warm up for his ascent up Mount McKinley in Alaska. But he also wanted to live. And after enduring 30-degree temperatures at night and running out of water, Aron Ralston cut off his own right arm to free himself from the crevasse. He still had to rappel down cliffs and negotiate through rock obstacles to reach park rangers who assisted him. Aron Ralston lost his right arm, but he saved his life.

These horrific stories are a chilling, literal illustration of Jesus words in Matthew 5:29-30: "If your right had offends you, cut it off. For it is better to enter life with one hand than to perish with two hands." In our lives there are things that are precious to us, things that are good in themselves – as good as a left leg or a right arm. Yet those things may be a source of spiritual stumbling for us. Those "good things" may ultimately pin us down and come between us and our family, between us and our military obligation, between us and God. For the survival of our family and for the survival of our faith in Christ, we must cut those things off. It's a hard decision. But the stories above demonstrate that sometimes those hard decisions are inevitable.

PRAYER: Dear God in heaven, please guard me against addictions and destructive behavior. If there is something in my life that is harmful to me or to others, please give me the courage and strength to rid myself of it and live. Amen.

October 5

WHAT'S DRIVING YOU?

Ted Williams played for the Boston Red Sox in a career that spanned 22 years. However, he played for the Sox for only 19 seasons. He missed three consecutive seasons in the prime of his life because he served his country as a Navy flier from the winter of 1942 through 1945. And during almost all of the 1952 and 53 seasons, Ted William's baseball career again took a back seat as he flew combat missions over Korea as a Marine F-9 Panther pilot.

But, regardless of the lost time, his 521 home runs and career batting average of .344 are truly remarkable. Williams' performance at the plate included his record-setting seasonal batting average of .406 in 1942. The fact is, Ted Williams never failed to hit above .300 in a season, *except once* – at the twilight of his career in 1959. Yet in that same year Ted Williams was the highest paid ball player in the majors – though his $125,000 salary is considered peanuts today.

Believing Williams still had another great season in him, the Red Sox offered to renew his contract at the same salary. But Williams declined. He agreed to play one more season, but only on one condition – that they cut his salary by 28% (the highest cut allowed by law) – which amounted to a pay cut of $35,000. His reasoning? "I'm here to make a contribution – not to make a buck."

True to form, in that final season Ted Williams hit well above .300 and slammed in nearly 30 homeruns.

Though cynics will always poke fun at the selfless service, altruism, and bravery of others – our mission, our nation and civilization itself cannot survive without them. True, our popular culture fosters an attitude of *"what's in it for me?"* But all around us are unsung heroes. They sacrifice daily for the good of the mission, wanting only to make their contribution - even though there is little prospect of recognition or reward. They are *driven* not by a lust for glory or material compensation. They are driven by the quality of their character.

The Scripture says that God seeks out individuals after his own heart, who share his values and passion for truth, mercy and righteousness (1 Samuel 13:14).

PRAYER: Dear Father in heaven, by your Spirit turn my heart toward you. Create in me a clean heart that hungers for You and thirsts for righteousness. Amen.

October 6

WHEN YOU CANNOT UNDERSTAND THE "DARK THREADS" OF YOUR LIFE

Corrie ten Boom of Holland was imprisoned in a Nazi concentration camp, along with her father and sister, for hiding Jews in their home. Only she survived; her father and sister both perished. For years following her liberation, Corrie struggled with why God had allowed this tragedy - especially why God had allowed a certain female prison guard to be so cruel to her dying sister.

God gave her an answer while she was touring one of the many European castles. Lying against the wall in the castle was a massive tapestry, mounted and stretched on a wooden frame. But Corrie could only see the underside of the tapestry, not the front side. The underside was un-discernable, a confused spattering of twisted, knotted, and loose dark threads.

Then workers in the castle moved the tapestry to its proper place and Corrie saw its upper side. The tapestry was a glorious picture of mountains, meadows, cathedrals and castles. What a difference seeing the upper side.

Then Corrie realized that the events of this life are like the tangled, confused dark threads of the tapestry - they never seem to make sense. But in heaven we will see the upper side of the tapestry, so to speak. We will see how God, the weaver, has woven the dark threads of this life into something beautiful.

When recounting this story to audiences, Corrie liked to recite the following poem:

My life is but a weaving, between the Lord and me;
I cannot choose the colors. He worketh steadily.
Oft times He weaveth sorrow and I in foolish pride,
forget He sees the upper and I the underside.
Not till the loom is silent and the shuttles cease to fly,
shall God unroll the canvas and explain the reason why,
the dark threads are as needful in the Weaver's skillful hand,
as the threads of gold and silver, in the pattern He has planned. (Anonymous)

The Scripture reminds us, "God works all things together for good, to those who love God, to those who are called according to his purpose." (Romans 8:28) Trust God and do not lose heart when the dark threads penetrate your life. God will bring from them good and beauty.

PRAYER: Dear Father, help me to walk by faith and not by sight, and to trust you as the Weaver of my life. Please take the sorrows, disappointments, and tragedies of my life and weave them into something beautiful. Amen.

October 7

WHEN THE CRITICS PASS JUDGMENT ON YOU

The President would not give the main speech at the special dedication service. The main speech would be delivered by America's foremost orator Dr. Edward Everette and would last two hours. But the President did give a small "side bar" speech that would barely last two minutes and would contain a mere 271 words (202 were just one syllable).

Dr. Everette's speech was met with ovations from the crowds and accolades from the critics. But when the President finished his little speech, a friend turned to him and asked, "Is that all?" The next day one reporter called the little speech, "an insult to the memory of the dead." Another reporter said of it, "We pass over the silly remarks of the President." A third reporter called the President's words "flat and dish-watery."

However, the test of time and subsequent generations of Americans have had the final word. And, guess what? The great two-hour speech by America's foremost public speaker has been entirely forgotten. And the little, dish-watery speech, that was an insult to the memory of the dead? There is hardly an American today who has not heard it, read it, or memorized it. The speaker was President Abraham Lincoln, the dedication service was at the Battlefield of Gettysburg, and the little speech was none other than the Gettysburg Address. In that short little speech, the President ennobled the War Between the States, gave meaning to its tragedy and called the nation to "a new birth of freedom, that government of the people, by the people and for the people shall not perish from the earth."

So if others pass judgment on your work and question your importance, commit what you do and yourself to the Lord and forget about the critics.

PRAYER: Dear Father in heaven, please take my humble work and cause it to touch the hearts of men and turn them to the heights of heaven. Amen.

October 8

"FRIENDLY" FIRE

Not since the War of 1812 had enemy forces occupied American soil. So when a force of Japanese Marines and Soldiers invaded and occupied the Aleutian islands of Attu and Kiska in June 1942, the United States was determined to drive them off.

First came the battle for the island of Attu on May 11, 1943. It was a costly affair: 3,929 U.S. casualties, including 1,481 deaths – many due to the horrifically cold conditions. Only 28 of the Japanese force of 8,500 soldiers survived.

Next came the battle for Kiska Island. This began two months later on August 7, 1943. A force of nearly 35,000 U.S. and Canadian Soldiers landed on Kiska Island. At first they met no resistance. But this was typical of the Japanese defenders – to lure the American invaders into a false sense of security and then suddenly attack. So the wary Allies inched their way forward into the blinding pea soup fog. Suddenly the Americans were hit with volleys of fire, which they returned. The heavy fighting in the blinding, frozen mist lasted for two days until the Allies reached the Japanese fighting positions and found them – empty.

The Japanese had abandoned the island more than a week earlier! But what about the thirty-two soldiers who were killed and the more than fifty wounded? They were all from friendly fire![lvii]

In a similar way, in the workplace and in the church, there are more casualties from friendly fire than from the enemy. Too often it is not the enemy of our souls that breaks the hearts and faith of believers, but the hurtful words and thoughtless deeds of fellow Christians. "Worse than the sin you criticize is the sin of criticism," a wise person once said. This is why Jesus himself warned, "Do not judge or you too will be judged. For the same way you judge others you will be judged and with the measure you use, it will be measured to you. Why do you look at the speck of sawdust in your brother's eye and pay no attention to the plank in your own eye? How can you say to your brother, 'Let me take the speck out of your eye,' when all the time there is a plank in your own eye? You hypocrite, first take the plank out of your own eye, and then you will see clearly to remove the speck from your brother's eye." (Matthew 7:1-5)

PRAYER: Dear Father, grant that I may not criticize my fellow soldier until I have marched a mile in his boots. Amen.

October 9

WHEN WE QUESTION OUR EFFECTIVENESS

A strange tale comes to us from the great Battle of Gettysburg. At a place called Culp's Hill, on July 3, 1863, where some of the fiercest fighting took place, Confederate soldiers had been assailing the Union line from about 4 A.M. until about noon. Unable to drive the federals from the hill, the Confederates began to "hunker down" in front of the Union fighting positions.

Commanders from both sides called upon their snipers to try and pick off any exposed enemies soldiers. One of the best Union snipers was First Sergeant Castor G. Marlin, of Company K, Eleventh Pennsylvania Regiment. Marlin watched as puffs of smoke kept bursting from a hollow underneath barricade of rocks. This trained sniper took aim at center mass of the hollowed recess from where the firing proceeded and fired. No effect. The Confederate sniper kept firing back. Marlin fired a second, third, fourth and fifth time without any effect.

Far more than feeling frustrated, First Sergeant Marlin felt his reputation as the company's best marksman severely tarnished. Worse, the lives of his fellow soldiers were in grave danger from this indestructible enemy. Finally, a sixth shot silenced the Confederate sniper. But why did it take Marlin six shots to take out a single enemy?

After the battle ended, First Sergeant Marlin got his answer. He explored the Rebel fighting positions, especially the hollow underneath the barricade from where the Confederate sniper had fired. To the first sergeant's amazement, he found not one, but five dead Confederate soldiers in that hollow. As historian Gregory A. Coco explains, "As soon as one had fallen another had taken his place, until the shelter would hold no more. The last man had fallen forward dead upon his gun." As it turned out First Sergeant Marlin was far more effective than he thought. Without realizing it, he had overcome an enemy five times larger than he thought.[lviii]

And sometimes we question our own effectiveness in the cause of the Gospel, in our ministry of good works, in our great spiritual conflict with Satan. But Scripture, again and again, encourages us to not to lose heart, for our efforts for Christ are far more effective than we can imagine. "Let us not become weary in doing good, for at the proper time we will reap a harvest if we do not give up." (Galatians 6:9)

PRAYER: Dear Father in heaven, help me to be faithful in my service to you and to humanity. When time goes by and I still see no results from my labor, please help me to continue to do my best and to leave the results with you. Amen.

October 10
WHEN YOU'RE FEELING WEAK

Just about everyone has seen the original film classic, *King Kong*. Although this movie is more than 70 years old (it was released in 1933), modern-day viewers still marvel at its special effects and theatrical power. Yet few people are aware that one of this movie's main characters, Carl Denham – the daring filmmaker who tracks down and captures the giant gorilla, Kong – was patterned after the movie's producer and director, Merian C. Cooper.

Merian Cooper was an incredible man, whose life makes Indiana Jones' look quite dull by comparison. Cooper was a champion boxer and wrestler, adventurer, filmmaker, war hero, soldier of fortune, author, innovator, and storyteller. By the time he made *King Kong*, Cooper had established a reputation for making jungle and wildlife movies on location in far-away and exotic places. His films also exhibit his fascination with aviation. For he had been a World-War I bomber pilot – until he was shot down and presumed dead by the Army. In fact, he spent a year in a German POW camp, recovering from injuries. Undaunted by this experience, Cooper fought and flew again - this time for the people of Poland in their conflict against the Soviet Union (1919-1921). Again he was shot down and endured nine agonizing months in a Soviet Union slave labor camp, until he miraculously escaped and fled to Latvia.

Cooper was a true American patriot and zealot for freedom. His service to his country began even earlier when he enlisted in the Georgia National Guard and served with General Pershing to drive Poncho Villa out of the United States (1916). He also served and flew with General Claire Chennault's American Volunteer Group (the Flying Tigers) before America's involvement in World War II and afterward served his country in other theaters of operations, attaining the rank of Brigadier General.

As a filmmaker, Cooper not only pioneered such innovations as stereophonic sound, Cinerama, stop-action animation, and 2- and 3-strip process color (leading to Technicolor). He is also responsible for many of Hollywood's greatest movies. *King Kong, the Four Feathers, the Last Days of Pompeii, Fort Apache, She Wore a Yellow Ribbon, Rio Grande, the Quiet Man,* and *The Searchers* – just to name a few – are his works. If a task required courage, creativity, and unmitigated drive – Merian C. Cooper rose to the occasion every time.

But for all his towering accomplishments and colorful adventures, Merian C. Cooper showed little promise as a boy and young man. Timid, shy, and physically small, he never grew taller than five foot six inches. When his parents discussed who among their children would achieve success, Merian was never mentioned. Merian was even upstaged by his bothers' mental prowess and described himself as having "a fourth-rate intelligence" and as being wholly undistinguished among all his family members.

How did this shy, small and un-promising boy burst forth into such unparalleled success? In his own words, he compensated for his deficiencies with sheer effort and physical courage. He simply faced his weaknesses and worked harder than his more-gifted counterparts to achieve success. It worked.

Hard work and dedication will always do more than natural ability and intellect. That is the answer whenever we feel inadequate and lacking in natural gifts. Work harder, trust God for strength, and you can overcome any challenge that confronts you.

The Scripture indicates that God can turn the curses of adversity into blessings of achievement and growth (Deuteronomy 23:5; Nehemiah 13:2). Most times it takes a little help from us. It takes our faith, persistence, determination, and hard work.

PRAYER: Dear God, when adversity and challenges confront me, give me the faith and determination to rebound and succeed. Amen.

October 11

THE POWER OF PRAISE

William W. Purkey, the long-time professor of counseling at the University of North Carolina in Greensboro, once told the story of the effect praise and positive affirmation can have in a person's life.

He explained that, in one situation, a mouse had taken up temporary residence in the scoring computer of a company that administers aptitude tests to students. By an incredible stroke of luck, this little critter triggered a key that changed the scores of a mediocre student named Henry Carson – transforming his scores to those of a genius. When the school saw the printout of Henry's phenomenal scores, they were delighted to learn they had such a stellar student in their midst. They expressed regret over any previous misappraisal of his potential for greatness and showered him with praise and bright hopes for his future.

The result of this praise and positive affirmation was dramatic. Henry blossomed as a student and his academic performance soared. And would you believe it, college recruiters invited Henry and his parents out to dinner. New worlds opened up for the exultant youth. His confidence climbed higher and higher and his self-image became more and more robust. To make a long story short, Henry went on to become a leader of his generation – all because of a clumsy mouse who made his home in the computer of a student testing service.[lix]

In the Scripture we are commanded: "Bless those who persecute you; bless others and do not curse them." (Romans 12:14) The Scripture also tells us: "There is one who speaks rashly like the thrusts of a sword, but the tongue of the wise brings healing." (Proverbs 12:18) In your words is the power to wound for life or to bring healing and power to the soul. Be wise and bring healing.

PRAYER: Lord, make me an instrument of your peace;
Where there is hatred, let me sow love;
  Where there is injury, pardon;
  Where there is doubt, faith;
  Where there is despair, hope;
  Where there is darkness, light;
  Where there is sadness, joy.
Divine Master, grant that I may not so much seek
  To be consoled as to console;
  To be understood as to understand;
  To be loved as to love.
For it is in giving that we receive;
It is in pardoning that we are pardoned;
And it is in dying that we are born to eternal life. Amen.

October 12

WHY WE CELEBRATE COLUMBUS DAY

Before 1492, no Englishman ever ate corn, and no Native American ever rode a horse. There were no "amber waves of grain" or wheat fields in the Great Plains of America. Nor could you get your Italian grandmother's recipe for tomato sauce because no Italian had ever seen a tomato. Nor could you find a banana in Guatemala, a peach in Georgia, sugar cane in Cuba, an orange in Florida, or a juicy apple in

Washington. If you ordered fish and chips in England, you only got the fish, because there were no potatoes. And, believe it or not, before 1492, you couldn't even find coffee in Colombia or black-eye peas anywhere in the South.

Christopher Columbus' voyages changed all that. They turned the Atlantic into a thoroughfare and triggered a phenomenal exchange of plants, animals and ideas. When European settlers came to America, they brought with them horses, cattle, sheep, goats, pigs and donkeys. None of these had existed in America before they arrived from Europe. The new settlers also brought new crops with them. They imported small grains like wheat, oats, and barley to the fertile plains. They brought bananas, sugar cane, rice and citrus fruits to the American tropics.

Fruits such as peaches and pears were unknown in the Americas, and the only apples were wild crab apples. Colonists introduced popular flowers like the All-American daisy and vegetables like cucumbers, cauliflower, cabbage and onions.

Native Americans had their own collection of unique crops that the Europeans had never seen before; crops like corn, tobacco, and the tomato. In fact, one crop that came from South America has been called the "perfect food" because of its nutritional value and its role in feeding untold millions in Europe – the potato. Without the New World, Europeans would never have enjoyed sweet potatoes, squash, pineapples, cranberries, or avocadoes. They would have never seen flowers like zinnias, marigolds, dahlias, sunflowers, or poinsettias. And thousands of lives were saved from malaria only after Europeans found they could get quinine from the bark of the cinchona tree. And can you imagine a world without either vanilla or chocolate? They were unknown in Europe before 1492.[ix]

It's right to celebrate Columbus Day and to reflect on its significance. The fact is a great deal of good came from Columbus' voyages of discovery. Though often vilified, Columbus and his successors triggered the exchange of fruits, vegetables, crops, and animals that left neither world poorer, and both worlds richer.

But that is true in all of life. The exchange of ideas and information and of all that is good leaves none of us the poorer, but makes all of us the richer. There is logic to giving and sharing. Do you recall the old adage, "a grief shared is grief a cut in half, but a joy shared is a joy doubled"? Remember also the Scripture that tells us, "There is more joy in giving than in receiving." (Acts 20:35)

PRAYER: Dear God, help me to learn and experience the lesson that giving to others enriches both the giver and the receiver, that there is more joy in giving than in receiving. Amen.

October 13

THE MEASURE OF SUCCESS

Dr. Lydia Emery. You won't find her listed among *Who's Who in America*. She wasn't a famous leader at the cutting edge of medical research and her picture never appeared on the covers of *Time* or *Life* magazines.

No, Lydia Emery, while she was a *bona fide* graduate of medical school and had been practicing medicine since WWII, she and her husband, Cliff Emery (a Marine Warrant Officer) chose to live and work in the out-of-the-way town of Yoncalla, Oregon. What was most amazing about Dr. Lydia is that this 20th Century medical doctor charged 19th Century prices. That's right, until her death at the age of 87, the sick and infirm paid only $1 for an office visit and $2 for a house call. Yes, she even made house calls, and she never raised her fees during her fifty-year practice!

Dr. Lydia made a conscious and deliberate choice. She and her husband struggled financially like everyone else in town, but she reasoned that, if she chose to be a full-fledge wage-earner, she'd lose most of her impoverished clientele and her effectiveness for good would be lost. So Dr. Lydia rendered her services virtually free of charge. She also volunteered in the local school, volunteered as a Brownie and Girl Scout leader, and taught Sunday School in a local church. She never turned her time into money. And for all her giving, she never sought any of the recognition she deserved. In fact, when invited to meet with President Jimmy Carter, she graciously declined to fulfill a promise to help out at a school function. Dr. Lydia Emery chose *not* to "make a living," but she *did* make a life.

News reporter, Charles Kuralt, may have had Dr. Lydia in mind when he wrote these words: "To read the front pages, you might conclude that Americans are mostly out for themselves, venal, grasping, and mean-spirited. The front pages have room only for defense contractors who cheat and politicians with their hands in the till. But you can't travel the back roads very long without discovering a multitude of gentle people doing good for others with no expectation of gain or recognition. The everyday kindness of the back roads more than makes up for the acts of greed in the headlines. Some people out there spend their whole lives selflessly. You could call them heroes."[lxi]

In the Scripture we read that "It is more blessed to give than to receive" (Acts 20:35). Winston Churchill once said, "We make a living by what we get, we make a life by what we give."

PRAYER: Dear Father in heaven, grant that I may not deceive myself by measuring success in the accumulation of wealth and possessions or in the attainment of rank. Help me to see that it is in giving that I receive, that it is in pardoning that I am pardoned, and that it is in dying to self, that I am born to eternal life. Amen.

October 14

DON'T IGNORE THE VOICE THAT SPEAKS

In the depths of the Great Depression, applicants filled a personnel office to apply for a single position as a telegraph operator. Barely heard above the clamor of their conversation was the steady flow of dots and dashes of the International Morse Code. As the applicants heatedly discussed their qualifications for the job, they almost drowned out its faint beeping.

Just then one more applicant entered the office. He didn't even sit down but simply stood and stared, as if deep in thought. Suddenly, the gentleman walked up to an office door marked "Private," knocked and entered. Within minutes an executive came out of that same office and addressed the group of applicants: "We have just found the applicant we want. You may all go at this time."

A storm of protests and complaints erupted. "We've been here for hours. The man you're hiring just walked in the door minutes ago." They demanded an explanation.

The Executive answered: "Listen! Can't you hear the Morse code message we've been transmitting?" So for the first time the group listened in and heard the message, repeated over and over in Morse code: 'If you hear this, come into the office marked 'Private,' the job is yours."

There is a similar message that is piped all around us everywhere. Not the radio waves that fill our world, but the steady message of God's love and goodness expressed everyday by his creation and by the blessings that he pours into our lives. Anyone can tune into God's message. It only requires a listening ear and an attitude of gratitude to hear the message of God's love and blessing. The Scripture tells us: "The heavens are telling the glory of God ... day and night they keep on telling about God. Without a sound or word, silent in the skies, their message reaches out to all the world."

PRAYER: Dear Father, open my eyes and ears to hear the divine message of your love for me that surrounds me every day. Amen.

October 15

FIND A GAP AND FILL IT

This is a geography quiz. Which city is home to the tallest building? New York City? No. Chicago? Nope. It's Taipei, Republic of China, which has the famous "Taipei 101" which stands at 1,671 feet above the ground, making it the world's tallest building.

Another question: Which town has the longest suspension bridge? Is it San Francisco, with its Golden Gate Bridge? Not by a long shot. Is it New York, with its Verrazano Bridge? Nope. The world's longest suspension bridge belongs to the two cities of Kobe and Naruto in Japan. It is the Akashi Kaikyo Bridge which has a center span of 6,529 feet.

And the largest city – based on population? This is somewhat disputed, but most sources identify Tokyo, Japan, with its 32,200,000 inhabitants, as the world's largest city. New York City is a distant second with 17,800,000, followed by Sao Paulo, Brazil (17,700,000), and Seoul, Republic of Korea (17,500,000).

Here are some less renowned "claims to fame" among cities. Which American city is known as "the Sock Capital of the World"? It's Fort Wayne, Alabama. This city boasts 150 sock mills that produce 12 million pairs of socks every year. Every fourth person in the U.S. has Fort Wayne socks on their feet – no kidding!

And what about "the Earmuff Capital of the World"? It's Farmington, Maine, where, in 1873, a fifteen-year-old boy (Chester Greenwood) invented earmuffs.

Here's another "capital." What is the "Casket Capital of the World"? It's Batesville, Indiana, which produces a new casket every 53 seconds.

What about the "Carpet Capital of the World"? That honor belongs to Dalton, Georgia, which boasts more than 150 carpet factories and 100 carpet outlet stores.

Don't forget Alma, Arkansas. Alma's the "Spinach Capital of the World." The Allen Canning Company, which is based in Alma, cans 60 million pounds of spinach each year. That's 65% of all the spinach that American consumes.

This list goes on. There is the Apple Capital of the World – Wenatchee, Washington; the Barbeque Capital of the World – Lexington, North Carolina; the Broccoli Capital of the World – Greenfield, California; the Logging Capital of the World – Forks, Washington, the Garlic Capital of the World – Gilroy, California, etc.

Now, a cynic might poke fun and conclude: "Every rinky-dink town wants to be famous for something." Yet there is a positive lesson here for us. All those medium-sized and small towns across America are doing something that we all need to do in life. We need to find a gap and fill it. Instead of competing with a thousand other cities who all covet the tallest building, the longest bridge, or the world champion baseball team, these towns have found their niche in doing something that no one else does, and they're doing it well.

What about us? Voices come from all directions, telling us we should do what everyone else does and pursue what everyone else pursues if we want to be successful. Those voices tell us we should be like this or that person if we want to be important. We read books on successful people and try to pattern our lives after theirs.

But in reality, it is far wiser to look for what isn't being done. It makes better sense, if you want to be significant, to look for "a gap" – a job that no one else is doing, a need that isn't being met, a vacancy that no one wants to fill – and fill it. Why compete with the glut of individuals who all want to do and be the same thing. In the book of Ezekiel God said, "I looked for a man among them who would build up the wall and stand before me in the gap" (Ezekiel 22:30). Find a gap and fill it.

PRAYER: Dear Father in heaven, open my eyes to the needs of those around me and use me to meet those needs, fix those problems and fill those gaps. Amen.

October 16

SUCCESS AND FAME ARE NOT THE SAME

The Pacific Ocean is the largest body of water on earth stretching nearly 10,000 miles north to south from the Bering Sea to Antarctic's Ross Sea, and more than 12,000 miles east to west from Indonesia to Peru. To sail across this vast expanse of water is heroic, but to fly across it non-stop is nothing short of epic – especially during the pioneer days of aviation.

So, naturally, the man who made the first flight across the Pacific became enshrined in America's history – right? Actually, no. To be honest, most Americans aren't able to recall the names of the first aviators to fly non-stop across the Pacific or probably have never even heard of them. This is puzzling, since Charles Lindbergh, the first aviator to fly solo non-stop across the Atlantic – a considerably shorter distance (3,300 vs. 5,500 miles) – achieved instant celebrity.

Who made this first nonstop flight across the Pacific Ocean? It was Clyde Edward Pangborn, a former WWI pilot and barnstormer, who (along with co-pilot Hugh Herndon) made the historic flight from Misawa, Aomori, Japan to Wenatchee, Washington on October 4, 1931 – just four years after the Lindbergh flight.

Some elements of this flight made it even more heroic than Lindbergh's. For instance, since no aircraft existed with the necessary range to fly across the Pacific Ocean, Pangborn had to overload his plane with fuel. To spare his plane any additional weight and wind-resistance, he rigged his landing gear to drop off after takeoff. However, the landing gear didn't "drop" as planned, so Pangborn had to climb out on the wing struts and detach it by hand – at 14,000 feet above the ocean.

Another obstacle to the aviators was that they were forced to fly without adequate maps and charts. They were stolen the day before by a Japanese nationalist who wanted Japan to be the first to make the non-stop flight. To make matters worse, co-pilot/navigator, Hugh Herndon, fell asleep and caused them to miss their destination – Seattle. By the time they corrected the mistake Seattle was completely shrouded in fog. So he was forced to fly an extra 300 miles across the entire state of Washington to Spokane. However, when he arrived at Spokane, *it was fogged over as well!* With nothing but treacherous mountains beyond, Pangborn was forced to backtrack 170 miles to the small town of Wenatchee where he made a belly landing – 41 hours after leaving Japan.

But there were no tickertape parades awaiting Pangborn. In fact, Pangborn and Hearndon received neither fame nor reward for their accomplishment. Pangborn went from this pinnacle of achievement to abject obscurity, going on to work as an airmail pilot. But he continued to make significant contributions to aviation – as both a test pilot and trailblazer for the emerging airlines. Then, during the early days of WWII he served in the Royal Air Force, ferrying hundreds of American-made aircraft to England to help Great Britain survive during those critical days of the Nazi Blitzkrieg.

By the time of his death in 1958, Pangborn had logged more than 24,000 hours on multi-engine aircraft. Though he spent his life in the realm of obscurity, his contributions to aviation and to victory in Europe equaled those of other famous aviators like Eddie Rickenbacker and Charles Lindbergh. His life goes to prove that success cannot be measured by the amount of recognition our work brings to us. Clearly success and fame are not the same.

Whether recognition comes or doesn't, the scripture assures us that our heavenly Father sees what we do in secret and will reward us openly for our faithfulness (Matthew 6:4, 6, 18).

PRAYER: Dear Father in heaven, if I am called to labor in the land of obscurity, where my life is lived in secret and I receive little applause for my work, help me to be content to be pleasing to You and to faithfully work for that day when I shall hear – "well done, you good and faithful servant." Amen.

October 17

SUCCESS OR FAILURE?

Talk about making significant contributions – this man invented the walkie-talkie. He invented a high-frequency (250 megahertz) spy-radio system that kept the President informed, saved millions of Allied lives, and went completely undetected by the Nazis during WWII. He invented the CB Radio, the radio detonator, the pager, the cordless phone, and the cellular phone. Who was this genius inventor? Al Gross, whose boyhood enthusiasm for radios led him to develop his first hand-held radio in 1938.

He could have *easily* made billions of dollars, if it were not for one important factor that was missing from his life's work – *timing*. Al Gross consistently invented things that were 20-30 years ahead of their time. As a result he was unable to find a market for his inventions – that is, not until his patents ran out and his inventions entered the public domain. For instance, he invented the pager and a paging system in 1949, but it did not become popular until 1974, after his patent on it expired in 1971 and Motorola was able to market it and rake in the billions. Consider that within 20 years more than sixty million people in America owned pagers.

But Al Gross could not cash in on any of its phenomenal success. The same happened with his inventions of the citizens band radio, the cordless phone, and the cellular phone. He had to admit, "I was born 35 years too early."

The happy part of Al Gross' story is that he never became bitter. Even though the fortunes he rightly earned constantly eluded him and that others became rich using his ideas, he never considered himself a failure. Though he did not become rich, the fact remained that Al Gross made staggering contributions to the war effort during WWII. And the constant sight of so many pagers and cell phones was a steady reminder that he had benefited his fellow man – and that was *his* measure of success. "It makes me feel good," he told a reporter who asked him if he was angry that everyone seemed to using his inventions. "It makes me feel like I've had a part in the world."

And isn't that a truer measure of success? That this world is better now than when we found it because of our contributions and life? Even if we have not profited from our own efforts? The Scripture reminds us, "Whoever seeks to preserve his life will lose it; but whoever loses his life for My sake and for the Gospel shall save it" (Luke 17:33-34). As Winston Churchill once said, "We make a living by what we get, but we make a life by what we give.

PRAYER: Dear Father in heaven open my eyes to what is most important in life, especially in the face of eternity. Help me to prepare for Your Judgment Seat that I may hear from Jesus those words, "Well done, good and faithful servant." Amen.

October 18

STANDING ALONE

The 1,500-year-old Dyerville Giant was the world's third-tallest redwood tree. It measured 17 feet in diameter and a staggering 360 feet tall and was the pride of California's Humboldt Redwoods State Park. Sadly, torrential rains felled it in May 1991.

But long before its demise, there were tell-tale signs that all was not well. Not that anything was wrong with the Dyerville Giant itself. It was stronger than ever. The problem was that it stood alone. Many of its adjacent trees had fallen victim to disease, fires and loggers. And standing alone is a bad thing for a giant redwood. That's what brought down the Dyerville Giant.

The park's superintendent, Don Hoyle, explained that redwood

trees depend on each other for support. He said, "It's like a domino effect, with their roots intertwined. Redwoods have relatively shallow roots and they don't have a tap root. Their roots are like a mat and they all help each other to stand up."[lxii]

What a picture of God's design for human beings to lean on and to help each other. The Scripture commands us to "Bear one another's burdens and so fulfill the law of Christ." (Galatians 6:9)

Another author tells the story of a horse-pulling contest he witnessed at a county fair. The winning horse pulled 4,500 lbs. The runner up pulled 4,000 lbs. The owners of the horses were curious as to how much they could pull together as a team. 8,500 lbs.? Wrong!

Together the two horses pulled more than 12,000 lbs. Likewise, we can do so much better and so much more by helping each other and working together as a team.

PRAYER: Dear Lord, in my loneliness and in my weakness help me to reach out to others for help. And help me also to be a blessing. Amen.

October 19

SHARING THE PAIN AND THE PRAISE

The 1960 classic western, "The Magnificent Seven," is possibly the most popular "action-western" of all time and is statistically the second most frequently aired motion picture in US television history. Though it enjoyed immediate success in European theaters, its acceptance came slow in America. But in retrospect film critics unanimously testify to its timeless message and enduring appeal.

Several reasons are cited for the movie's longevity. Most notably is the movie's stirring musical score by Elmer Bernstein. The score he composed is widely considered the best of any western. Another reason for the movie's long-lived appeal is due to its honest treatment of heroes – as did the earlier movie which inspired it – the Japanese classic, The Seven Samurai. In the "The Magnificent Seven" we see the introduction of the anti-hero, the hero that has many flaws and is largely a pathetic figure, but who achieves great things because of a greater measure of good in his soul. But among movie buffs the most appealing attribute of this film is its many clever "one-liners" and "comebacks." Its screenplay is superbly written and does not contain a wasted word.

The man responsible for the screenplay was veteran writer Walter Newman. Walter Newman was such a gifted author that the very greatest of scriptwriters could have learned much from him. But when it came to being a team player and sharing recognition with others, it was Newman who needed to learn – as he demonstrated amply during his association with "The Magnificent Seven."

During the actual filming of the movie, the script had to re-written in several places. Since Newman was unable to travel to the film's on-site location in Mexico, another writer, William Roberts, was brought on board to work as a "script-doctor." Roberts' work was substantial enough for the Screen Writers Guild to grant him recognition as "Co-Author" for the screenplay in the movie credits. Walter Newman was furious at the thought of sharing recognition with anyone else. And when the Guild and the producers did not yield to his "all or nothing" demands, Newman withdrew his name entirely from the film's credits. Consequently, every showing of this splendid motion picture credits William Roberts for the screenplay. Walter Newman is not even mentioned – a victim of his own refusal to be a team player.

Our inability to cooperate with others, to delegate the workload, and to share the recognition can quite often sabotage our own mission and project. It can bring us down personally as well. Lee Iacocca used to caution his young, gifted apprentices, "The reason why many of the most talented people will never succeed in business is that they cannot get along with others." In contrast consider the leadership philosophy of the stellar football coach, Paul "Bear" Bryant: "If anything goes bad, I did it. If anything goes semi-good, then we did it. If anything goes real good, then you did it." The Scripture commands us to "Bear one another's burdens and so fulfill the law of Christ." (Galatians 6:8) What a better way to operate!

PRAYER: Dear Father in heaven, please save me from myself – save me from my own undoing, from my own craving for glory, from my own moodiness, and from my own egocentricity. Please, soften my hardened heart, fill it with your love, and help me work together with others for the good of all. Amen.

October 20

WHEN TEMPTATION COMES

In *Our Daily Bread,* Dave Egner tells about a Cherokee Indian chief sitting with his grandson before an evening campfire. The boy had broken a tribal law and the old chief sought to impress upon him the seriousness of his offense and the need to control the evil impulses within him.

"It's like we have two wolves within us," the old chief explained. "One is good and the other is very evil, and they each fight within us to gain dominance and to demand our obedience."

The curious boy asked, "Which one wins, Grandfather?"

"The one we feed!" replied the wise chief.

The cynic reasons that the only way to deal with temptation is to give into it. But evil desire is fed every time we give into its demands. Temptation is a vicious beggar who, having received from us once, comes back again and again demanding more each time and wreaking havoc in our lives. The way to deal with him is to deny him. The way to deal with evil desire is to starve it. At the same time we must yield to will of the Holy Spirit in our lives, who works in us to will for his good pleasure and to do his good pleasure (Philippians 2:13).

PRAYER: Dear Father in heaven, please empower me and inspire me to say "no" to temptation and to say "yes" to your Spirit. Amen.

October 21

WHEN TRAGEDY TOUCHES US

Of all the children of Simon and Monique, their little son Louis, seemed the brightest and certainly destined for greatness. Even as a toddler, little Louis displayed an aptitude for learning and a gift for music. So it did not surprise his father when, a three-year-old Louis walked into his father's leather harness shop and asked if he could learn the leather trade from his dad. Simon was only too happy to show off his work to his son, and put him in charge of making a few holes in a piece of leather with an awl.

But that day would prove fateful when the awl slipped from little Louis's hands and poked his eye. His horrified father rushed the little boy home, then found a doctor who gave the best care possible for those times. For the year was 1811 in that little French village of Coupvray, not far from Paris.

The injury to Louis' eye did not appear too serious and the relived parents and doctor had hopes for his full recovery. But Louis' eye became infected. The infection then spread to the other eye and within a few days, poor Louis was totally blind. He would remain in total darkness the rest of his life. Life seemed to come to a screeching halt for Louis.

Though he was broken-hearted and angry, blindness did not quench Louis' thirst for knowledge. So at the age ten, his parents enrolled Louis in the Royal Institution for Blind Youth in Paris.

But upon his arrival at school Louis was appalled to find the school's library housed only fourteen books. These books used a system of raised letters so that a blind person could feel them and read the text. But this system consumed enormous amounts of space on the pages, requiring books to be large and cumbersome - and extremely expensive.

Louis was convinced a better system was possible. His memory went back to a time, shortly after the injury to his eyes, when he was handed a pinecone and was impressed by the prickly edges of the pedals and the ease with which they could be detected and counted. From that seed of inspiration, Louis devised a simple alphabet using tiny, prickly bumps made in paper. He arranged these into six-pronged cells for each letter.

This system became increasingly accepted by other schools and libraries, even in other countries, because it allowed for swift, easy formation of words and reading. Louis' system has since gained universal acceptance and today makes it possible for a blind person to read nearly as fast as a sighted person. Louis Braille refused to be one more victim of tragedy. He resolved to turn the curse of his blindness into a blessing that continues to give sight to millions.

The Apostle Paul once wrote, "when we are reviled, we give a blessing in return" (1 Corinthians 4:12). Jesus commanded his disciples to "love your enemies and pray for those who persecute you" (Matthew 5:44). So whether it is with words, thoughts or deeds – take the painful and turn it into something pleasant. Take the bitter and make it something sweet. Someone once said, "If all life gives you is lemons, then make lemonade."

PRAYER: Dear Father in heaven, by your grace and power, help me to turn my curses into blessings, my scars into stars, my hurts into halos and my stumbling blocks into stepping stones. Amen.

October 22

SURVIVING AT THE TOP

The Coast Redwoods of Northern California are the tallest trees in the world. Many measure more than 20-feet across at their base and over 360 feet from top to bottom – nearly as tall as a 40-story building. The tallest known Coast Redwood, the "Hyperion," located in the back country of Redwood National Park, was measured at 379.1 feet tall in 2006. Coast Redwoods are so tall, in fact, that the biggest of these trees have difficulty getting water and nutrients all the way to the uppermost branches. This is why an observer will see many of the tallest Redwoods crowned with dead, gray, barren tops devoid of branches and foliage. They are simply too high to receive nourishment from lower portions of the tree. In order to survive at the top, the uppermost trunk and branches must draw in moisture from the Pacific coastal mists via osmosis. The very tops of these trees must ultimately reach outside themselves for the water and nutrients they need to survive.

"It's lonely at the top," the adage tells us. Indeed, those in leadership may experience feelings of isolation, abandonment, and loneliness capable of killing the soul. Just as there are so many "dead tops" among the tallest Redwoods, so also there are many casualties among leaders. Although at lower levels, one can enjoy moral support from friends and peers, higher up the ladder the leader may find that it is frequently necessary to "stand alone," without that moral support of those we could depend on before.

But how is it possible to survive in such painful isolation? We can survive by reaching outside ourselves to the inexhaustible supply of God's Spirit. God can bring healing to our wounded souls, bind up our broken hearts, and nurture our starving spirits. With the strength that God gives, it is possible to survive and to thrive at the lonely top. The Scripture reminds us, "God is our refuge and strength; a very present help in trouble." (Psalm 46:1)

PRAYER: Dear Father in heaven, restore, heal, and strengthen my wounded soul. Nurture and feed my starving spirit. Empower me, by your Spirit to carry the cross you have called me to bear. Amen.

October 23

WHEN YOU THINK YOU'VE HAD A BAD DAY

Ever have a bad day? Let Joan Murray tell you about hers. And let her also tell you about the time she thought things just couldn't get any worse. Guess what? They did.

Joan was a 47-year-old bank executive and mother of two. A dull, boring life? No. You see, Joan Murray loved skydiving. And although her first 35 jumps were uneventful, number 36 would bring her to the very brink of disaster.

On September 25, 1999 Joan Murray jumped from a height of 14,500 feet. Her main chute failed to deploy. She plunged more than two miles before she managed to get her reserve opened – just 700 feet above the ground. But things continued to go wrong. The reserve failed to properly deploy and Joan spun wildly out of control. She plowed into the ground at 80 miles per hour.

The impact shattered the bones on the right side of her body and knocked the fillings from her teeth. But if things weren't bad enough, poor Joan had the misfortune of landing atop a large nest of fire ants. Before paramedics could rescue her from the angry ants, more than 200 poisonous bites covered her body. The trauma to her body was intense. Joan swelled to more than twice her normal size.

Joan lay in a coma for more than two weeks. She should have died. Her doctors are convinced of that. Why didn't she? What kept her heart beating within a crushed body? Her doctors believe that the very ants that stung her with such fury also shocked her heart enough to prevent cardiac arrest. And she lived and fully recovered. And guess what? She's back to skydiving and enjoys every minute of it.[lxiii]

There's a profound lesson in Joan Murray's ordeal. Don't jump from a perfectly good aircraft? Well, maybe. But the lesson I'm talking about is this one. There are those times in life when we are hit with blow after blow and we're convinced one more burden will crush us, one more painful event will finish us. We look everywhere for mercy, for someone's healing touch. Then it comes – a hard blow to the heart, some hurtful words, another painful event. Yet it does not crush as we thought. Somehow it does the very opposite. The vicious sting of life only serves to strengthen our resolve and anchors our faith more firmly in God.

The old adage becomes reality – if it doesn't kill you it'll make you stronger. And that's exactly what God does with the bee stings and the dog bites of our lives – he uses them to make us stronger, to preserve us. What we expected to kill us ultimately becomes our source of strength. As the Scripture tells us, "The Lord turned the curse into a blessing for you, because the Lord loves you." (Deuteronomy 23:5)

PRAYER: Dear Lord, please turn my curses into blessings, my hurts into halos, and my scars into stars. Amen.

October 24

WHEN WE'RE AFRAID TO BE DIFFERENT

A squash that looks like Elvis Pressley? A zucchini in the image of President Bush? Or, a cucumber in the form of Humphrey Bogart? It's true. They are the creation of toy designer Richard Tweddell III. Tweddell patented a series of plastic molds into which baby zucchini, cucumbers, and squash may be placed. As the vegetables grow they assume the form of the plastic mold, which may be the face of a celebrity, a smiling elf, or the form of a geometric shape. The varieties of faces and shapes are unlimited. In every case the growing vegetable does not develop according to its genetic blueprint. Instead it is squeezed into the ridiculous image the mold provides.

People are comparable to plants in this respect. Their personalities and character can be restricted, stymied, and squeezed into shapes their Creator never designed or intended. God made us with the potential for a distinctive greatness. He wants us to pursue the plan He has for our lives. Too many of us allow the fears, prejudices and dictates of the world to conform us to its own image. Too few of us dare to be different, to go against the current of this world and to march to the beat of a different drum. In the Scripture, the apostle Paul urged: "Be not conformed to this world, but be transformed by the renewing of your mind."(Romans 12:2)

PRAYER: Dear Father in heaven, Your word is a lamp unto my feet and a light unto my path. Grant me the courage and strength to go against the current of this world and follow the guidance Your word provides. Amen.

October 25

WHEN WE TRY AND FAIL

This is a test. I'm going to mention three Pop songs from the 1960's. Try to guess what they have in common. The songs are: "Get Together" by the Youngbloods, "(My Baby Does the) Hanky Panky" by Tommy James and the Shondells, and "Oh Happy Day" by the Edwin Hawkins Singers. What do they have in common? It's this: None of them met with success when first released. Only after two or three years, when released a second time, did they shoot to the tops of the charts.

On its first release in 1967, "Get Together" bombed. It only reached #62 and quickly died. Two years later, the National Conference of Christians and Jews took an interest in the song and used it to advertise the National Brotherhood Week they were sponsoring. Interest in National Brotherhood Week may have been meager, but demands came from everywhere for "Get Together" to be played again and again. The song was re-released in 1969 and sold two million copies.

Tommy James and the Shondells were just a small time group in Michigan way back in 1963 – all of them high school students. When they recorded "Hanky Panky" that same year, hardly anyone outside of Michigan and northern Indiana and Illinois heard it. The group disbanded to the four winds and pursued other things. Two years later, a Pittsburgh, PA disc jockey named "Mad Mike" Metro found a cassette tape of the song in a "Clearance" bin for ten cents. He played it, liked it, and promoted it on his station. It sky-rocketed to the top of the charts, becoming #1 in the nation and catapulting Tommy James to stardom.

Edwin Hawkins had merely assembled an eight-person choir from the larger 46-member Northern California Youth Choir. His purpose was to record and sell copies of an upbeat version of the classic hymn, "Oh Happy Day (when Jesus Washed my Sins Away)" to raise funds for a church. When he sold 600 copies he was thrilled, for he never intended it for any audiences outside the gospel music circuit. But San Francisco DJ Abe "Voco" Kesh, got a copy of the song and promoted it on his station. The result, "Oh Happy Day" went from selling a mere 600 to more than a million copies.[lxiv]

When our efforts do *not* meet with immediate success, it's easy to get discouraged and conclude we've failed. But remember these stories - and thousands of others like them. It's not always on the first try that success comes. If people respond slowly to your ideas – don't conclude that your ideas were no good. Do your best and believe in your work, yourself, and in the God who created you and gifted you. Give yourself and your ideas a chance for success. Their time may simply not have yet come. The great American classic, "God Bless America," by Irving Berlin, was originally rejected in 1918 and sat in a chest for twenty years. Then when released in 1938 it took America by storm and remains one of the most popular patriotic songs ever written.

The Scripture says, "Delight yourself in the Lord and he will give you the desires of your heart; Commit your way to the Lord, trust also in him, and he will bring it to pass." (Psalm37:4-5)

PRAYER: O God of perfect patience, please encourage me and help me not to lose heart when I meet with rejection and failure. Help me to do my best and to believe in you and in the abilities and ideas you've placed within me. Amen.

October 26

BEING FAITHFUL IN LITTLE

As a child George was a grief to his parents and required frequent beatings. As a student he was completely undistinguished. To his prosperous businessman father, he seemed an undisciplined drifter. What hope for success could there be for such a man, without direction or ambition?

Then, after seeing the adulation that returning Spanish American War veterans received, George decided he wanted to become an Army officer. But to his parents, teachers and siblings George was hardly "Officer Material." His grades fell pitifully short of West Point's entrance standards. Undeterred, George then sought entrance into the Virginia Military Institute. But his older brother – himself a student a VMI – proclaimed George unfit for military service and predicted his failure.

That did it. Weary of his own family's dismal expectations, George was determined to prove them wrong and to be successful at VMI. He was. Though he graduated only 15th in a class of 32, he strove to discipline himself and cultivate his leadership and organizational skills. As a result he was promoted to Captain of the Corps of Cadets.

But it was a battle every step of the way, both to get a commission and to get rank. George was consistently overlooked for key command positions. He was consigned to work behind the scenes as a staff officer, while he watched younger officers bask in the limelight and move ahead of him up the career ladder.

Another strike against him was his frankness with superiors and his refusal to "brown nose." For instance, when the fierce and formidable General Pershing openly reprimanded George's own division commander, he went to his defense and highlighted flaws in Pershing's own handling of the war. To all observers this warranted the proverbial "kiss of death" from Pershing. But it had the opposite effect. Pershing valued his candor, took George into his staff, and became a life-long friend.

Again, years later, when he was drawn into the staff of President Franklin Roosevelt, George rebuffed the President's patronizing attitude. Other staff members expected George to "get the boot." But the President did the very opposite. He promoted George to the rank of General and elevated him to Chief of Staff of the Army. Yes, I'm talking about General George C. Marshall, whose organizational genius, cultivated through decades of selfless service and faithfulness in obscure, thankless positions, had made him the most indispensable man of WWII. General Marshall has since been heralded as the greatest soldier America ever produced. Winston Churchill praised him as "the Organizer of Allied victory." He became the first Five-Star General since General Pershing. After the war he was made Secretary of State, Secretary of Defense and was acclaimed world-wide as "the Architect of Peace." His "Marshall Plan" is credited with saving Western Europe from economic collapse and for ultimately winning the Cold War. And, in 1953, George C. Marshall became the first soldier ever to be awarded the Nobel Prize – *for peace!*

Perhaps the limelight and the most-visible assignments have eluded you as well. Perhaps, time after time, you've been forced to labor on in the realm of obscurity. Don't lose heart, nor be shortsighted. By your faithfulness and dedication to inglorious jobs, ultimately assigned to you by a Power greater than the Army, you are becoming a person of value. Remain faithful and God will make you a person of destiny. Consider the words of Jesus, in the Parable of the Talents:

"Well done, good and faithful servant. Because you were faithful with a few things, I will put you in charge of many things. Enter the joy of your master." (Matthew 25:23)

PRAYER: Dear Father in heaven, help me to be faithful in all the tasks You give me. When days, weeks and years go by without recognition or the praise, help me look beyond all earthly rewards to You, who sees in secret and promises to reward all that is done for Your glory. Amen.

October 27

WHO'S IN CHARGE?

Famed boxing manager & trainer Angelo Dundee (born Angelo Mirena in 1923) has the distinction of guiding the careers and serving as the cornerman for the greatest boxing champions of all time. Dundee directed the paths of such formidable giants as Muhammad Ali, Sugar ray Leonard, Jose Napoles, Jimmy Ellis, Carmen Basilio, Luis Rodriguez, and George Forman.

Like all the great trainer-managers of the same period (e.g. Gil Clancy and Emanuel Stewart), Dundee was exceptionally gifted in identifying his fighter's strengths and weaknesses, and then hand-picking opponents to face them – opponents who would most effectively help develop the skills of his own "up and coming fighters."

It may puzzle the casual observer, but Dundee would actually pick opponents who would capitalize on his own fighter's weaknesses. Why did he do this? Out of cruelty? Not at all!

First, Dundee knew that his fighters had to discover their own weaknesses for themselves and this could only be done through the bitter experience of being hit hard by an opponent. Initially all fighters resist the trainer's advice and guidance. Only after being "beat up" a little will fighters become attentive learners.

Second, by constantly facing opponents who take advantage of their weaknesses, Dundee's fighters were driven to correct their deficiencies and to turn their areas of weakness into points of strength. By this masterful management, Dundee took fighters with lots of raw talent and made them into a stable of super champions.

It must be remembered that, in the professional world of boxing, the idea of someone "managing his own training, guidance and growth" is utterly ludicrous. No fighter has the objectivity, skill, or self-knowledge to identify the deficiencies in his own boxing abilities, defense, and fighting style.

There are obvious lessons from the world of boxing for our own spiritual growth and development. As it takes the skill and keen eye of a superb trainer to successfully guide a fighter from the ranks of amateurs to the championship, so also our spiritual growth and development require the divine wisdom of God to guide us from weakness to strength?

The self-help craze of our popular culture has, unfortunately, crept into the church. Today Christians are encouraged more and more to "take charge of their lives" and to "come up with strategies for their own spiritual development," instead of submitting to the discipline of the Lord (Hebrews 12:4-11). Whatever bright ideas we think we have, rest assured that God has better ideas and we'll do well to spend more time seeking Him than reading self-help books.

As the fighter must submit to the manager-trainer, so the believer must submit to God's discipline. I strongly suspect that most human beings are as oblivious to their own weaknesses as any professional fighter is of his. It takes the Lord himself to hand-pick those problems, those trials, and those pressures that will best facilitate our spiritual growth and development. In many cases, God will bring difficult people and difficult times into our lives that will take advantage of our weaknesses. As a result, we will become more keenly aware of those weaknesses and will more fervently trust God for strength. In the process, God will turn those areas of weaknesses into areas of strength.

It all boils down to this: Who is in charge of your life? Are you trying to fill the roles of both manager-trainer and fighter? Or, are you submitting to the guiding hand of the Master Trainer? Is God in charge of your life, or are you? The Scripture says, "Since we respected our earthly fathers who disciplined us shouldn't we submit even more to the discipline of the Father of our spirits, and live forever?" (Hebrews 12:9, New Living Translation)

PRAYER: Dear Father in heaven, I believe You know me far better than I know myself. You know all about my frailty and weaknesses. But I also believe You have a better idea of how to change my weakness into strength and to transform me from what I am into the person You created me to be. Please fulfill Your work in me and help me to submit to Your wise and loving hand. Amen.

October 28

THE STILL, SMALL VOICE

It was the turning point of the Civil War – the war's bloodiest battle that cost both sides 51,000 casualties in three days – 23,000 losses for the North and 28,000 for the South. Civil War historians believe the fate of the nation hung on this battle. The battle? Gettysburg. And the outcome of this battle itself hung largely on the events on a small hill at the very end of the Union line – the Little Round Top, defended by about 300 soldiers of the 20th Maine on July 2, 1863.

The 20th Maine's commander, Colonel Joshua Lawrence Chamberlain had received his orders: "Defend your position or die trying!" If they failed, the Confederate Army could easily flank the entire Union line.

Five times the 15th Alabama, a force twice as large as Chamberlain's, commanded by Colonel William C. Oates, charged up the hill. By the end of the forth charge the 15th Alabama had successfully punched a hole in the 20th Maine's defense. With one third of his men dead and no more men to fill the hole in his line, Colonel Chamberlain himself stood in the gap. On the fifth charge the 20th Maine fought desperately and barely held their ground. Now, out of ammunition and incapable of sustaining another attack, Colonel Chamberlain made a critical decision. He ordered his men to fix bayonets and charge down the hill. This action had a powerful psychological effect upon the 15th Alabama. Thinking they were outnumbered, the Confederate soldiers panicked, broke ranks and ran. Many were captured. And the Battle of Gettysburg was won by the Union and dealt a blow to General Lee from which he could not recover.

But there was a much smaller event that took place that determined the outcome of the battle for the Little Round Top. On that fifth and final charge by the 15th Alabama, a lone Confederate soldier drew his sights on Colonel Chamberlain, got in the prone position, rested his rifle on a rock, took aim and squeezed the trigger. But the strangest thing happened. The soldier felt a terrible sense of guilt and dread. So he lifted his trigger finger, lowered his rifle and cursed himself for his "weakness."

He tried a second time. How easy it would be to end this battle here and now. Shoot the Union commander down and the Little Round Top will be won. Again he aimed and began to squeeze the trigger. But again that same feeling of overwhelming guilt smote his soul –what seemed to be a "still, small voice" forbidding him from killing Colonel Chamberlain.

Believing God was speaking to his heart, the Confederate soldier lowered his rifle and refused to do harm to his enemy.

Reflecting on the battle for the Little Round Top, Colonel Oates went on to comment: "Great events sometimes turn on comparatively small affairs." How true. Hardly could that Confederate soldier have imagined at the time, that simply heeding that still, small voice - his conscience - would ultimately save the Union?[lxv]

It is through our conscience, our spirit, that God speaks to us and keeps us on a prosperous course. The Scripture tells us: "The spirit of man is the candle of the Lord, searching all the inner recesses of his soul." (Proverbs 20:27) To turn a deaf ear to that voice can lead to spiritual deafness. To disobey that voice can have disastrous consequences. To heed and obey that voice can change the course of history for good, even lead to eternal life.

PRAYER: Dear Father in heaven, open the eyes of my understanding and ears of my spirit and help me to hear and obey the still, small voice of your Spirit speaking to my heart. Amen.

October 29

WHEN YOU LOSE HOPE FOR YOURSELF

By 1926 he was an aging, drunken, has-been baseball pitcher – nothing but a pale ghost of his former self. Early in his career a head injury from a hard throw had left him unconscious for two days and with permanent double vision. From the injury he also began to suffer from epileptic seizures. But a few years later his vision inexplicably returned and he went on to become one of the greatest pitchers of all time – Grover Cleveland Alexander. His Major League record of 16 shutouts in a single season stands to this day. He was the only pitcher in Major League history to win the Triple Crown three consecutive years (1915-1917). And he still holds the National League record for most career wins (371) and most career shutouts (90).

But he had been raised in a family of alcoholism and he also yielded to its grip. He used the alcohol to cope with the pressures of the pitching mound and with his epilepsy. But it began to rob him of his pitching performance.

Then came WWI. He served his country as an artillery officer in war-torn France and witnessed such carnage and horrors, that alcohol again became a way of self-medicating. The drink not only soothed his nightmares, but also numbed his shell shock, incurred from relentless blasts of artillery rounds – which also left him almost deaf. Following the war, alcohol tightened its grip more and more, until there seemed to be nothing left of the 40-year-old Grover Cleveland Alexander.

So the Chicago Cubs manager, Joseph McCarthy, did what any sane person would do. He got rid of him. But the brilliant owner of the Saint Louis Cardinals, Branch Ricky, saw something good in Alexander and believed the broken old man still had a future. So he hired him to pitch for the Cardinals. That year Alexander led the Cardinals to the World Series. In the Championship, Alexander had his greatest moments, starting in two games and relieving in one – winning all three games - against the unbeatable New York Yankees. Yes, Grover Cleveland Alexander had his greatest yet to give. He also had someone who believed in him.

Many of us reach a point in life where we're convinced we have no tomorrow and our lives are ruined beyond repair. But there is someone who believes in us, even when we are at our very worst. It is our heavenly Father. The Scripture says, "But God is so rich in mercy, and he loved us so much, that even though we were dead because of our sins, God made us alive with Christ and seated us with him in the heavenly places." (Ephesians 2:4-5)

PRAYER: Dear Father in heaven, when I fail and lose all hope for myself, please take the broken pieces of my life, put them back together, raise me up to newness of life and do good and great things in my life. Amen.

October 30

IF IT TASTES GOOD

The next time you're standing before the bathroom mirror, stick out your tongue and take note of what you see. I admit it's not a pretty sight. I suppose that's why "sticking out your tongue" at a person is an insult. But that pink, muscular, wet, shiny, and bumpy blob in your mouth has a wonderful lesson behind it.

Each of those little bumps on your tongue is a "taste bud." There's about 10,000 of them and each holds a cluster of 30-100 long receptor cells with hair-like sensors on their ends. These sensors protrude through an opening in the taste bud called a "taste pore." At different locations on your tongue "taste-specific" taste buds seem to be grouped together. For instance, along each side of the front of your tongue are tastes buds that detect saltiness. Other taste buds detect sweetness, others sourness, and others – located on the back of your tongue – detect bitterness.

But what is most remarkable about the tongue is that *it can taste "danger,"* i.e. it knows when something is poisonous, "spoiled," or when it will make your body sick. How does the tongue sense danger – *when something tastes bad or bitter.*

On the other hand, the tongue can also sense when a food is wholesome and "good for the body." How does the tongue detect wholesomeness? It does so by picking up a "savory" taste from the food. The tongue knows: if it tastes bad *it is bad* and if it tastes good *it is good*.

Yet, we are so conditioned to believe the very opposite – that if something tastes good, it's probably not healthy, or that if something is bitter in our mouths then it must be good for our stomachs.

And we tend to apply this misconception to the rest of life, especially when it comes to faith. "God's plan for my life will probably make me miserable." "The truth is a bitter pill to swallow." "If I'm happy, I must be doing something wrong." "The right way is always the hard way."

But what does the Bible say? "Oh taste and see that *the LORD is good*," wrote David in Psalm 34:8. "*How happy* is the one who trusts in Him." "Take My yoke upon you and learn from Me," said Jesus, "for My yoke is easy and My burden is light" (Matthew 11:29-30). 1 John 5:3 says, "For this is love for God, to keep His commandments, and His commandments are not burdensome." The truth of God's word is not "a bitter pill." Psalm 119:103 says, "How sweet are Your words to my taste, sweeter than honey to my mouth!"

We have the wrong idea about God and His plan for our lives. "The thief does not come except to steal, and to kill, and to destroy," said Jesus. "I have come that they may have life and have it more abundantly" (John 10:10). The happiest and most fulfilling path for any man or woman is the one which God chooses for them.

PRAYER: Dear Father in heaven, Help me to comprehend the breadth and height and depth of Your love – and to experience it for myself. Spare me from the tragedy of neglecting so great a love as Yours. Amen.

October 31

BE YOURSELF

Trying to be like someone else? That's what the German ocean liner Cap Trafalgar sought to do during the early days of WWI. Naturally, it was not the ship itself, but the German government. In 1914 it sought to disguise the Cap Trafalgar as the British ocean liner, the Carmania, then arm it with deck guns and use it to hunt British ships as a raider. So the ship changed its color scheme to look like the Carmania. It removed one of its three smokestacks to look like the Carmania's profile of only two smoke stacks. Finally, it painted the name Carmania on its bow and the transformation was complete. The German ship Cap Trafalgar was now a dead ringer for the British Carmania.

But the gag failed terribly. For on September 14, 1914 in the Caribbean Sea off the coast of Trinidad, the Cap Trafalgar met another ocean liner-turned raider. This other raider immediately saw through the Trafalgar's disguise and opened fire on her. By some strange twist of fate the other ship was none other than the real Carmania – which, by some strange coincidence, was disguised as the Cap Trafalgar! The real Cap Trafalgar was sunk in a two-hour battle.

Haven't all parents told that to their children? "Don't envy so and so, they probably envy you. Don't try to be like so and so. They're probably trying to be like you." The adult equivalent is, "While you're trying to keep up with the Jones, the Jones are trying to keep up with you." And there is more truth in this than we realize. The truth is, there is something in us all that believes our own identity is not valid or good enough. There is also the truth that while we seek to be like someone else, they seek to be like us. And what is the hard lesson we learn after all our imitating? Be yourself! Be your unique, God-designed self. Even better, Be the person God created you to be. Allow the divine Potter to mold and shape your character that you may become a vessel for his honor and glory. The Scripture says, "But now, O Lord, You are our Father; we are the clay, and You are our Potter; and we are all the work of Your hand." (Isaiah 64:8)

PRAYER: Dear Father in heaven, here and now I place myself in Your loving, skilled, and all-powerful hands. Make me into the person You desire me to be. Fulfill the blueprint You have designed for my life. Please, Divine Master, make me an instrument of Your peace. Amen.

November

November 1

CHRIST'S HOSPITAL

On November 28, 2006, NBC News in Temple, Texas reported that a 70-year-old woman, apparently suffering from near-sightedness, drove her car right through the front window of a local business. The business? It was a Budget Optical of America clinic. The woman was simply showing up for an appointment and had trouble seeing where she was going. The business did not charge the woman with any crime. Police did not even ticket her. All were sympathetic to her problem and gratified she had come to the right place.

As the police and the public did not pass judgment on this woman, so Christians must not pass judgment on one another. People come to the eye clinic out of need, not out of worthiness. It is expected that people with bad vision come to optical clinics. Persons with 20-20 vision do not need corrective lenses. Even so Jesus stated that "It is not the healthy who need a doctor, but the sick. I have not come to call the righteous, but sinners." (Mark 2:17) Consequently, we should not expect the churches to be filled with the healthy, but with the sick, the broken, the bleeding of humanity.

Those who come to Christ, often come as the result of a crisis. Their marriage crashes, their business goes under, or perhaps they find themselves in legal trouble. In the midst of their trouble they turn to their last, but greatest resource – God. So is it any wonder that there are so many troubled people in the church, that the divorce rate among church-goers should be so high? The church is Christ's hospital – a place where sick people come to get well. It never surprises anyone that there is a higher percentage of sick people inside hospitals as opposed to those outside. Why should it shock us that churches have so many of the morally and spiritually sick?

Of course every Christian should strive to be like Christ, to love one's enemies, to bless those who curse, be merciful to those who are hateful. In fact, the standard for which we should strive is perfection: "You must be perfect, as your Father in heaven is perfect." (Matthew 5:48) But the journey to be like Christ takes a lifetime. And all the mending, all the fixing, and all the renovation of our lives can more effectively take place where love and forgiveness prevail and judgment and criticism are absent.

PRAYER: Dear Father in heaven, help me not to judge others – whose guilt is no greater than my own. So often I cry out for justice, yet I remember that I greatly need mercy. Lord, I confess to you my sinfulness, my weakness and my deficiencies. Forgive me, cleanse me, and deliver me from an attitude of self-righteous superiority and a spirit of criticism. Amen.

November 2

WHEN YOUR LIFE IS FILLED WITH PAIN

Abandoned and unloved. That's how Mary felt. Her mother had died just ten days after she was born in 1797. And her father, concerned more with her education than with meeting her emotional needs, drilled his daughter in academic learning rather showing her any affection. As a result, Mary, an exceptionally smart and sensitive child, would go through life yearning to be mothered, loved and cared for. But it was not to be. Not even from her husband, Percy - who despised the notion of marital commitment and fidelity, did Mary find unconditional love. Her deep craving for affection, nurturing, and unconditional love went unfulfilled.

How did Mary deal with the void and pain of her heart? She wrote. In fact, she wrote novels, many of them. True, most of these have been forgotten - novels like *Mathilda, The Life and Adventures of Castruccio, Prince of Lucca*; *The Fortunes of Perkin Warbeck*; and *Falkner*. But there is one particular novel that is known by almost everyone. It tells the story of Mary's own pain – a story of parental rejection and of the disastrous consequences of discarding an unwanted offspring. Of course the "child" in this novel was not a girl named Mary, but *a creature* - made from the body parts of cadavers and brought to life by a young scientist named Victor – *the parent*. Yes, it was the emotional pain of parental abandonment and neglect that fueled the genius of an eighteen-year-old girl – Mary Shelley - to create one of the most widely-read and universally known novels of all time – *Frankenstein*.

And what will we do with the pain that penetrates our hearts? Will we allow it to consume and destroy us? Will we spew the poison of our hearts onto others, hurting as many as we can on a path of self-destruction? *Or*, will we allow God to use the pain of our life to fuel our genius and creativity, so that we may be a blessing to others? Will we allow God to use our pain to be other's gain, and experience God's ultimate healing?

An old adage says, "If life only gives you lemons, then make lemonade." The Scripture says that in all our tribulation, we experience God's comfort, that we may eventually share that same comfort with others who suffer as we have suffered (2 Corinthians 1:3-5).

PRAYER: Dear Father, I do not ask you to remove all pain and trouble from my life. But I do pray that you will turn my stumbling blocks into stepping stones, my hurts into halos, and my scars into stars. Amen.

November 3

WHEN YOU ARE FORCED FROM YOUR COMFORT ZONE

A favorite fish of many hobbyists is the Japanese carp, commonly known as the *koi*. The fascinating thing about the koi is that if you keep it in a small fish bowl, it will only grow to be two or three inches long. Place the koi in a larger tank or small pond and it will reach six to ten inches. Put it in a large pond and it may get as long as a foot and a half. However, when placed in a huge lake where it can really stretch out, it has the potential to reach sizes up to three feet. The size the fish grows is in direct relation to the size of its world.

Doesn't that compare to people? Out growth is determined by the size of our world. Not the world's measurable dimensions, but the mental, emotional, spiritual, and physical opportunities we expose ourselves to.

Realizing that growth comes from moving out of our comfy, cozy, neat little comfort zone can help us accept the upheavals and uprooting that the Army brings upon us. However, look beyond the Department of the Army. God is ultimately in control of your life. It is he who allows people and organizations to pull you from your "little pond" and thrust you into the ocean with all its dangers. But he does this in love and growth will be the result.

"For God knows the way I take," said Job, "and when he has tried me, I shall come forth as pure gold." (Job 23:10)

PRAYER: Dear Father in heaven, when I am pulled out from pleasant circumstances and familiar surroundings and supportive friends, remind me that you are trying to help me stretch and grow. Through all such adversity, strengthen my faith and fortify my character. Amen.

November 4

ODD COUPLES

Odd couple. It's a term we use to describe a relationship between two people as different as night and day, yet who contribute to each other's well-being. All of us can probably think of relationships that fit this category.

The world of nature also has its "odd couples." In fact, nature abounds with them. Biologists and naturalists have a term for these odd-couple relationships: Symbiosis. It means "living together."

For instance, consider an odd couple from Africa: a little bird called "the honey guide" and the ratel, also known as the honey badger. Both have an insatiable taste for - you guessed it – honey. Problem is, neither is capable of getting to the stuff. The little honey guide lacks the strength and claws to break open the honeycombs it can easily locate. The honey badger lacks the sense of smell and, some suspect, the brains to find it. So these two unlikely companions work together. The honey guide finds the honeycomb then finds the honey badger. The honey guide throws a tremendous fuss to get the badger's attention and leads him to the comb. The honey badger's sharp claws easily rip the comb apart releasing its golden ooze to be split between this strange duo.

Sometimes the odd couple includes the volatile mix of predator and prey. For example, the fierce Nile crocodile would normally devour anything within reach of its powerful, dagger-toothed jaws. A stunning exception is the plover, a delicate bird that shares an amazing friendship with this fearsome leviathan. The crocodile provides the plover with food and the plover provides the crocodile with "dental care." As it basks in the sun, jaws opened wide, the crocodile allows the plover to step along its rows of jagged teeth and pick off leeches that infest the croc's gums. The plover provides another benefit to the giant reptile by functioning as an early warning system as it perches itself upon the crocodile's back.

There are many other such friendships between natural enemies. The tropical sea anemone is a thicket of stinging tentacles that will kill and devour any fish that violates its space. A remarkable exception is its toleration of a certain damselfish, as well as its mate and their offspring, that find refuge in the anemone's tentacles. Yet, it will kill and consume any other fish, even other damselfish.

Many animals of different species practice "grooming" and pest-ridding of each other – giving relief to one species and food to the other. For example, cattle egrets feed on vermin embedded in the hide of African buffalo. On the Galapagos Islands, marine iguanas find relief from their misery by the lava crabs that remove pesky ticks. Then there are the amazing cleaner fish that set up virtual "cleaning stations" which rid other fish of parasites. Whole groups of cleaner fish work together servicing "clients" of many species, even dangerous types like barracudas and moray eels – even cleaning inside the mouths of these predator fish!

Another of nature's many odd couples is found in the goby and blind shrimp household. The blind shrimp builds and maintains the hole in which the two strange bedfellows live. In return for lodging the goby provides food, protection and stands vigilant watch over their cozy nest.

These examples only scratch the surface of the world of odd couples that, quite literally, could not survive without each other's contribution and friendship. Think of the many examples of symbiosis between species of animals and plants – plants depending upon animals for pollinating and the successful planting of their seeds - animals depending upon the plants for food and nectar. That they cannot survive without each other's assistance was tragically demonstrated by the man-imposed extinction of the dodo bird of Mauritius. From the time of the dodo's demise (300 years ago), the *calvaria* tree, also peculiar to Mauritius, ceased to reproduce. Scientists now understand that the dodo, which fed on the large calvaria seeds, assisted with the seed's planting and germination. The disappearance of one species doomed the other.

While these odd-couple relationships entertain and amaze the on-looker, they put most of humanity to shame. In nature mutual enemies set aside their differences for their mutual survival. But human beings focus on, even celebrate, their differences and make excuses why they cannot get along. Over differences as simple as color we *homo sapiens* nurture hatred and wage war against each other.

The Scripture reminds us that God made from one blood, every nation under heaven (Acts 17:26). Indeed, we are all made out of the same stuff. Let's set aside our puny differences and, with God's help, work together for our common good.

PRAYER: Heavenly Father, open my eyes to the divine image that You have placed upon every person. Help me to love and appreciate the common goodness and worth that resides in me and in others as your divine workmanship. Amen.

November 5

WHEN YOUR ACCOMPLISHMENTS GO IGNORED AND UNAPPRECIATED

On December 17, 1903 near Kitty Hawk, North Carolina, two Ohio brothers - Wilbur and Orville Wright - reached an age-old dream of humanity. They achieved flight in a heavier-than-air -flying machine.

This was no small feat. Many would-be-aviators around the world were in hot pursuit of developing an airplane that could be flown and controlled by a pilot. Scientists as prominent as Samuel Pierpont Langley – who was being financed by the U.S. Government – had tried and failed to develop such an aircraft.

Naturally, the scientific community rushed to congratulate and herald this pinnacle of technological achievement, right? Wrong. Would you believe that as late as January 1906 the reputable journal, *Scientific American*, expressed disbelief and discredited the reports of the Wright brothers' flight? More than two years after the event! In fact, another year passed before (on December 15, 1906) the *Scientific American* accepted their flight as factual.

But of course, the American military, hungry for innovations and new ideas for weaponry, pursued the Wright brothers to develop their new airplane as a reconnaissance aircraft, as a bomber, and as a fighter – right? Wrong. It's true. The visionary Wright brothers quickly saw the military potential of their invention. But the military leadership did not. Many letters to Howard Taft, then Secretary of the War Department, went unheeded. Not until the end of 1907 – after four years of offers from the Wright brothers – did the military express interest in their plane.

Fortunately, there is one institution in America that is dedicated to the genius and creativity of humanity. Though others failed to recognize and appreciate the Wright brothers' achievement, the Smithsonian Institution did, right? Wrong again. In fact, it wasn't until 1942 – 39 years after the historic flight – that the Smithsonian requested the famed aircraft from the London Museum of Science, whose curator had the good sense to recognize the plane's historical significance.

Like the Wright brothers, our achievements may go unnoticed and unappreciated. But let us follow their example. Despite all the disappointing reactions and all those years of neglect, the persevering Wright brothers continued to develop and refine their stupendous invention. From the humble Flyer I, which traveled only 120 feet for 12 seconds on its maiden flight, the Wrights developed an airplane capable of traveling more than 30 miles at 40 miles per hour. God help us to reject the rejections of others and to pursue our dreams.

The Scripture reminds us: "Do not lose heart in doing good – for at the proper time we shall surely reap a reward if we do not give up." (Galatians 6:9)

PRAYER: Dear Lord, when others ignore and reject my ideas and achievements, help me to reject the rejection and pursue excellence in my life. Amen.

November 6

WHEN YOUR PATH IS FRUSTRATED BY ROADBLOCKS

Life had not been easy for Robert. His life seemed to be an endless string of roadblocks, all of them keeping him from the things in life he longed to do. One of his passions was art and drawing cartoons. But after his father died when Robert was only twelve, he had to abandon his dream of going to art school. So he taught himself how to draw and by the age of fourteen he had sold his first cartoon to *Life* magazine. But his real dream was to play professional baseball. Then, in his professional debut, he shattered the bones in his arm and also his dreams of a career in baseball.

So Robert turned back to his love for art and got a job with the *New York Globe* drawing a daily cartoon for the sports section. Then another roadblock. In 1918, Robert was suffering from a terrible case of "cartoonist block." He was at a total loss for ideas to put onto paper. In desperation, Robert strung together a collage of nine sports oddities from the history of sports and titled it, "Champs and Chumps." He left the office and dismissed the effort as one of his worst.

The following day he was stunned to discover his "Champs and Chumps" of sports oddities was an instant success. Hundreds of requests for more such collections of oddities poured into the Globe and Robert Ripley's "Believe It Or Not" column was born.

For the next half century Robert Ripley traveled to nearly 200 countries combing the earth for strange and fascinating facts about our existence. His efforts left a legacy of columns in hundreds of newspapers, radio and television programs, and dozens of "Ripley's Believe It Or Not" museums. Robert Ripley discovered that life's roadblocks are often God's means of giving us direction and opening unseen doors of opportunity to us. As the Scripture says, "God works all things together for good to those who love him and for those who are called according to his purpose." (Romans 8:28)

PRAYER: Dear Lord, when my path is frustrated by road blocks, help me to be on the lookout for doors of opportunity that you will open and help me to follow your leading. Amen.

November 7

WASTING TIME ON TRAINING?

Robert Pearson was a Veteran airline pilot. But he spent thousands of hours of his personal time on an activity that his fellow pilots considered a waste of time. What was it? He loved to fly gliders.

But what did glider flying have to do with his profession as a high-performance aircraft pilot? Little it would seem. Gliders gain altitude by harnessing the lifting power of thermals, mountain waves, ridge lifts, and wind convergences. Jets gain altitude by the sheer power of their engines. And when gliders do not have thermals or wind convergences to harness - and they are still miles from a safe place to land – the glider pilot must utilize something called "best glide ratio speed" to maximize altitude for distance. Plus gliders use some peculiar methods for braking – slowing down the aircraft. For instance, glider pilots often use a maneuver called a "forward slip" (turning and tilting the aircraft so that it appears to flying sideways) to increase drag, i.e. so that the wings and body of the aircraft create wind resistance. But none of these glider techniques would ever be used in flying a jet. Or would they?

On one fateful day, July 23, 1983, Captain Robert Pearson and First Officer Maurice Quintal became the unfortunate victims of changing technologies and corporate oversights. Through a series of errors, they took off on Air Canada Flight 143, flying from Ottawa, the nation's capital, to Edmonton, Alberta *with only half of their required fuel*. Their aircraft was one of Air Canada's brand new jumbo Boeing 767-200 jets. It was a first of its kind, fully automated aircraft that eliminated the position of flight engineer – the very person who would have calculated fuel requirements. This aircraft also used new metric measurements at a time when all pilots were accustomed to imperial measurements. There were also faulty components and calibrations peculiar with this aircraft, of which Pearson and Quintal were tragically unaware.

But somewhere, 41,000 feet over the province of Manitoba, both engines shut down from fuel starvation. To make a very bad situation much worse, all the jet's dials (e.g. altimeter, air speed indicator, rate of descent indicator) were all digital. Thus, the loss of the engines meant the loss of electrical power and all flight instruments. They had only a battery powered radio and an emergency "ram air turbine" that provided just enough power to run the jet's hydraulic controls.

The pilots frantically scanned the 767's manual for guidance in the event of losing both engines. There was no guidance. The plane was too new and its designers did not anticipate such an emergency.

Suddenly, all those wasted hours of glider training and glider flying became a priceless investment. Captain Pearson quickly determined the best glide ratio speed (220 knots) to be able to reach an old Air Force landing strip in Gibli, Manitoba. But such a speed was far too fast for landing. To do so would blow out all the tires, collapse the undercarriage, and possibly kill all 69 passengers and crew. To make the situation far more critical, the far end of the airstrip was crowded with people and vehicles, assembled for a special sports car event. To slow the hurdling beast, Pearson employed the glider braking techniques he knew so well.

But controls were sluggish. He had to "stand" on the pedals and push-pull with all his might to perform a "forward slip" in the giant 767. But it worked! Captain Robert Pearson safely landed the otherwise doomed aircraft – just a few hundred feet from the unsuspecting crowds! There was not a single fatality. Only a few minor injuries occurred – all from exiting the aircraft.

The many "wasted" hours of glider training and flying proved to be priceless at one critical hour. Even so, our devotion to life's disciplines may make the difference between catastrophe and survival. Soldiers spend countless hours training to survive and be successful in combat. While engaged in this training it rarely seems profitable and never pleasant. But in the terror of battle it suddenly becomes priceless.

So is true of our spiritual disciplines: prayer, study of the Scriptures, meditation, reflection, and witnessing. Our cluttered schedules barely have room for such unprofitable "time wasters." But in the heat of trial and temptation they will give us the edge to survive and be victorious. "Keep watching and praying," Jesus told his disciples, "that you may not enter temptation." (Matthew 26:41) We need to "plug into our Divine Power Source" to recharge our spiritual batteries. It takes time, but it's a priceless investment.

PRAYER: Teach me to pray, O Lord, and to feed upon Your life-giving word. Empower me by Your divine Spirit that I may be equipped to survive the rigors of spiritual warfare. Amen.

November 8

THE TOUGHEST JOBS

When it was constructed in 1937 San Francisco's Golden Gate Bridge was the longest suspension bridge in the world. That distinction has since gone on to other, newer engineering marvels and now belongs to the Akashi-Kaikyo Bridge in Japan. But even 70 years after its completion the Golden Gate remains an impressive sight. Its center span is 4,200 feet (1,280 meters) long and its total length is 8,991 feet (2,740 meters). Its towers reach a staggering 746 feet (227 meters) high and its clearance of 220 feet allows the tallest ships to pass below. But as impressive as the bridge is, equally amazing is the story of its construction and the men who risked their lives to build it – 19 of whom perished in the process. Over the years I have enjoyed many articles and documentaries on the building of this and other bridges and marvel at the ingenuity and vision of the builders who overcame incredible obstacles to erect a monument to man's achievement.

But without denying the builders the credit they are due, I am convinced that theirs are far from the toughest jobs. For the labors of the builders of bridges and towers have advantages over the rest of us. The builders' work has the element of permanence, measurability, and visibility. When they complete this project – it's done. They have a profound sense of "mission accomplishment." And it's permanent. It will not melt away like the great ice sculptures of Finland or wash away like a child's sandcastle on the beach. It's measurable in every way. And the builder of the Golden Gate Bridge will never have to "walk by faith" regarding the effectiveness of his work. He can always stand back and look at San Francisco's most famous and beloved landmark - the mighty Golden Gate Bridge.

What a contrast to the man or woman consigned to the work of maintenance – the person who has the never-ending task of scraping the rust, re-painting the bridge's International Orange, and re-placing its bolts and cables. Those types of jobs go unnoticed, unappreciated, and rarely offer that sense of accomplishment. No one writes books or films documentaries on such unglamorous work. For a person to muster the strength and motivation to scrape the rust and push a paint brush, he must exercise faith and assure himself that his labors count.

Unfortunately, the labors of most people fall into that second category – the work that is fraught with discouragement. Why is the labor of a housewife so difficult? Isn't it due to its never-ending nature? The mess that was cleaned up yesterday must be cleaned up again today. There is no permanence to her work – there is never a "house-cleaning" that lasts for all time. Nor does she ever serve a meal that will nourish a person for a lifetime.

And would you believe that the work of a soldier has the very same occupational hazards – work that goes unappreciated, unnoticed, and is difficult to measure? Just think of the work of the US Armed Forces in South Korea over the last half-century. Did we prevent further aggression and another catastrophic war by North Korea, or not? Most military strategists would give an emphatic yes. But such military success can also be used against the military. A shortsighted logic can conclude, "We've had peace for so long – what do we need the military for?"

Yes, the labors with which most of us are saddled have these occupational hazards. Therefore we must remind ourselves of this: Where would the Golden Gate Bridge be if wasn't for those who continually work on its upkeep? It would have crumbled into the turbulent waters below. And what would become of the homemaker's house if she got weary and went on strike? The home would quickly become a disaster area.

And where would our world be without the men and women in uniform who do the never-ending and unappreciated task of providing vigilance and security for America and for the freedom of the world? There would be a perennial open season for every tyrant to oppress his neighbor and endanger civilization itself.

Therefore, take heart. Your work is indispensable. And it is known and valued by the same God who not only created the world and all that lives within it, but who is eternally working at its upkeep and maintenance. Be faithful in the work God has given you to do – as a soldier, a mechanic, a repairman, a housewife, a caregiver, a preacher. The Scripture encourages us: "Be always devoted to the work of the Lord, for you know that your labor for the Lord is never in vain." (1Corinthians 15:58)

PRAYER: Dear Father in heaven, Help me by faith to dedicate my work to you. Help me to look beyond my earthly supervisor and to do my work for my heavenly master. Help me to look beyond all earthly promotions and rewards, and to labor faithfully in obscurity - that I may one day share in the glory of the world to come. Help me to live and work with eternity's values in mind. Amen.

November 9

SERVICE FOR THE LORD IS NEVER IN VAIN

Within Yellowstone National Park's 3,472 square miles (8,987 square kilometers) are more than 10,000 geysers and hot springs – 62% of the earth's total. The geysers of Yellowstone spew forth an incredible volume of water - 75 million gallons of water – every day! Where does all this water come from? From rain and snow that falls within the park and from beyond. The fallen rain and snows percolate down through the ground into the geothermal network that feeds the super-heated water up into the geysers.

But this trickling down of water takes quite a long time – even centuries. In fact, the water that erupts out of the Old Faithful geyser today is from water that fell to the earth about *500 years ago!*

This amazing "hydrological cycle" has a spiritual parallel. As the water falls to the earth in rain and snow, and seems to be forgotten as it sinks into the ground, only to reappear in a mighty eruption, centuries later, so are the prayers that we pray, the seed of the gospel that we sow, and good deeds that we pour forth. We may go to our graves wondering if we "watered the earth" in vain. We may feel as though we've poured out our lives only to be forgotten. But nothing done for the Lord is ever in vain. Our prayers are registered in heaven and are never forgotten.

The history of the church abounds with stories of mighty moves of God that were fueled by a praying church centuries before. The same is true for the missionary who has poured out his life, sowing the seed of the gospel, without ever witnessing the fruit of his labor. Yet decades later this holy seed suddenly bursts forth in a mighty revival. The Apostle Paul assures us that nothing we do for the sake of the Kingdom of God is ever in vain and that, if we do not lose heart, we shall eventually reap a harvest (1 Corinthians 15:58; Galatians 6:9). Perhaps we may not see it in this life – but we will surely see it in the life to come.

PRAYER: Dear Father in heaven, help me to walk by faith and not by sight. Help me to faithfully invest my time and energy into that great cause that will count for all eternity – the cause of Your kingdom. Amen.

November 10

WHEN YOU SEE NO SOLUTION TO YOUR PROBLEM

Suicide has been defined as a permanent solution to a temporary problem. If you asked the widow of Edwin Armstrong, she would certainly agree.

Edwin Armstrong is internationally recognized as the inventor of many devices related to radio transmission – most notable was his invention to amplify both the transmission and reception of radio signals thousands of times, making long-distance communication possible. But his crowning achievement was his invention of wide-band frequency modulation. What does that mean? He invented FM radio. Until this invention, radio was filled with static and often adversely affected by the weather. Armstrong earned honor from his peers and made a fortune.

But things turned sour for Edwin Armstrong. He became embroiled in court battles with an inferior inventor, Lee de Forest, over patent infringements and with RCA who tried to squelch and then steal his technology when it threatened their own business. Legal fees mounted and brought him to verge of bankruptcy. The constant strain took a toll on his marriage and on his mind. At one bleak moment – after his money was gone and his wife threatened to leave him – this supremely successful inventor who had everything going for him fell into despair. To escape his *unsolvable* problems, Edwin jumped to his death from the 13th floor of his apartment building.

How tragic that a man who experienced such success should take his own life. But his story is even more heart-rending when it turned out that RCA was eventually forced to pay his widow $1 million and other corporations paid her $10 million for their patent infringements. Edwin Armstrong finally was given the recognition and payment his inventions deserved. How sad that he wasn't there to enjoy them.

When we are tempted to despair we need to remind ourselves of the psalmist's words: "Why are you downcast, O my soul? Why are you so disturbed within me? Put your hope in God, for I shall yet praise him – my Savior and my God." (Psalm 42:5, 11; 43:5)

PRAYER: Dear Lord, please help me to pray and to endure the night until the morning dawns and you turn my night into day. Amen.

November 11

PRAY FOR OUR ARMED FORCES

On April 30, 1975 the city of Saigon in South Vietnam fell to the invading forces of the North Vietnamese Army. In the days during the city's demise, hundreds of Americans and tens of thousands of South Vietnamese were evacuated from the city by scores of U.S. Air Force, U.S. Marines, Air America, and South Vietnamese helicopters. Many of these evacuees found refuge aboard the decks of the aircraft carrier, the USS Midway.

At one point more than 100 helicopters and several thousand South Vietnamese civilians (3,071 in a 30-hour period) crowded the Midway's flight deck. In this chaos something took place that left an indelible impression on the memories of the American people: disturbing images of U.S. Sailors pushing American-made UH-1 Huey helicopters overboard into the ocean. These pictures reached the American public without explanation and served to reinforce the views of many that the Vietnam War was a senseless and tragic waste.

In reality those images of discarded helicopters represented something very noble and profound about the U.S. Sailors and Marines aboard the Midway. In their desperation to save as many South Vietnamese evacuees as possible, the Sailors pushed the empty helicopters (which belonged to the South Vietnam Air Force) to make room for other aircraft to land – aircraft that were packed with more people. They valued human beings more than machines and did everything humanly possible to save them.

In that desperate hour there was one particular aircraft – a small, single-engine, airplane (a U.S. O-1 "Bird Dog") that kept circling the Midway. The flight deck crew tried to direct the pilot to ditch his plane beside the carrier, with the intention of rescuing him. But then the pilot dropped a note from the plane onto the deck, wrapped in a leather holster, which read: "Please move aircraft from runway – my wife and five children are on plane and I must land!" In a desperate effort to save the lives of this family, the Sailors pushed empty helicopters out of the way. Many went overboard into the sea. The result: the plane landed safely, and from it emerged a South Vietnamese Air Force major, his wife, and their five small children. A roar of jubilant celebration erupted from the Sailors and Marines.

This story illustrates what the U.S. Armed Forces are all about: making a difference for good in this world. Though often vilified by the very ones they defend, the U.S. Armed Forces remain an instrument of peace, justice, and freedom from oppression throughout the world. Pray for the men and women of our Armed Forces – that God will protect them, inspire them, strengthen them, grant them success in their mission, and bring them back safely into the arms of their families and loved ones. The Scripture says: "By faith they (i.e. the soldiers – David, Jephthah, Samson, Barak, and Gideon) conquered kingdoms, …from weakness were made strong, became mighty in war, put foreign armies to flight." (Hebrews 11:32-34)

PRAYER: Almighty and merciful Father, please bless the men and women of our Armed Forces and the officers who lead them. Please also bless our President, who sends them into battle, and grant him wisdom from above that he may lead our country on the path of righteousness. For righteousness exalts a nation, but sin is a reproach to any people. Bless and protect, O Lord, our Soldiers, Sailors, Airmen and Marines. Please lead them from victory to victory and grant them supreme success as your instrument of justice and peace in Iraq, Afghanistan, and throughout the world. Amen.

November 12

WHEN YOUR EFFORTS END IN FAILURE

Some would call Milton a failure. And if you added up the failures of his life, you'd agree. Milton had failed as a printer's apprentice. Then he failed in his own confectionary business in Philadelphia in 1876. A few years later he tried again to start a candy business in Chicago and again his business failed. A few years later Milton tried once more at the candy business, this time in New Orleans, and again his business went down the tubes. Then, once more, Milton moved out east – to New York City – and tried again to get the candy business to work. But like every other previous effort, this one ended in failure.

But Milton learned from his mistakes. He learned that failure isn't fatal. He learned that obstacles can become stepping stones. He learned that you never become a failure until you stop trying. And all along the journey, from failure to failure, Milton was learning more and more "tricks of the trade," more ways of doing things better, and new ideas and formulas to improve his product.

So with his accumulated knowledge, persistence, and faith in God, Milton tried once more. He started the Lancaster Caramel Company just in time for the Christmas trade. It was a stunning success. But in a short time he sold his business for one million dollars – to finance the true project of his dreams. He built the world's largest milk chocolate manufacturing plant!

Because Milton Hershey refused to quit and toss in the towel, he left a legacy that has blessed the entire earth: a thriving colossal that employs tens of thousands and sweetens life for millions, a medical school that has trained and graduated 2,200 doctors, a K-12th Grade school for homeless children that has a yearly enrollment of over 1,000, and tens of millions of dollars donated every year to charity![lxvi]

Milton Hershey believed the simple truth that God has a plan for each of our lives and that plan is not for our lives to end in painful failure, but to experience success and to be a blessing to others. The Scriptures tell us, "For I know the plans I have for you, says the Lord, plans for good and not for evil; plans to give you a hope and a future." (Jeremiah 11:29) God has a blueprint for each of our lives. Turn your future over to him and seek his guidance that his plan may become your reality.

PRAYER: Dear Father in heaven, you have destined me for a good and glorious purpose – to bring honor to your name and to bless my fellow human beings. Please guide my steps, shape my future and cause your plan to unfold before me, I pray. Amen.

November 13

WHY AM I GETTING NOWHERE?

There is a strange temptation that afflicts people of faith – to be plagued with feelings of guilt because of our lack of spiritual growth. Believers often grieve because they appear to be no closer to God, no more loving to their neighbor, and just as troubled with worry and doubt as when they first believed. The temptations and trials never get easier and they, therefore, conclude that their "net growth" is zero. Yet none of us should rush to judgment.

Consider another group of people what are afflicted with a similar problem – professional boxers. Pro boxers who reach the top of their game are guided by the skilled hands of trainers and managers. These trainer-managers will hand-pick opponents that will push their own fighters to the limits of their abilities. Step by step the trainer selects a cunning boxer, a hard puncher, or a relentless aggressor to face his own fighter. And each successive opponent is a little more difficult than the one before him. The result is that his own fighter improves with each fight. Little by little, the fighter is growing in his defense and fighting style.

But, although he is growing, "the fighting" never gets any easier. He doesn't realize it, but all the while he is getting tougher and better, so are the opponents.

And believers often forget the same thing. God is their Trainer and He is "hand-picking" trials and temptations to confront them and to push them to the limits of their faith and endurance. And each successive trial is a little more difficult than the one before it. The result is that the believer is getting tougher and better, step by step, little by little. He improves with each temptation and trial. Yet, although he is growing, overcoming temptation never appears to get any easier. And the believer can, therefore, conclude that he is not growing, that he is getting nowhere. The believer doesn't realize that, while he is getting stronger, so are his trials.

Therefore, do not lose heart. Commit yourself to God's loving and wise discipline, and leave the results and the measure of your growth in his hands. Don't be self-conscious, be Christ-conscious. "Let us run with endurance," says the Scripture, "the race that is set before us, fixing our eyes on Jesus the author and perfecter of our faith." (Hebrews 12:2)

PRAYER: Dear Father in heaven, here and now I submit to Your all-wise and all-loving will. I leave the complexity of my training and the progress of my growth in Your capable hands. Please make me into the person You created me to be. Amen.

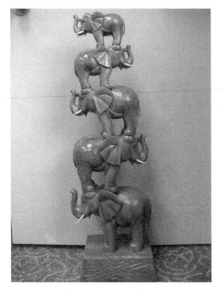

November 14

LESSONS FROM A PYRAMID OF PACHYDERMS

The picture to the left is of a wood carving from the Philippines that I purchased recently. It's a literal "pyramid of pachyderms." It also serves as an illustration of greatness in the Kingdom of God and provides some lessons for military leadership as well.

The first lesson is this: the Greatest (Biggest) is the Servant of All. In the Kingdom, and in the military, the largest and strongest bears the weight and carries the others, serves the others, and puts their needs before his. Doesn't the biggest and strongest soldier on any foot march carry the heaviest equipment? In the Scripture Saint Paul wrote: "We who are strong ought to bear the weaknesses of those without strength and not just please ourselves." (Romans 15:1)

The next lesson is this: the place of power is not for elevating yourself, but for advancing others, developing others, and fostering their growth. In the military the leader seeks to develop his subordinates. That is a huge part of his responsibilities. In the Kingdom, pastors and chaplains must provide for the growth of those in their charge and create opportunities for ministry and for the development of their gifts and talents. We are told in the Bible that God gave to his people apostles, prophets, evangelists, pastors and teachers "for the equipping of the saints for service and for the building up of the body of Christ." (Ephesians 4:11-12).

The third lesson is this: the guy at the top doesn't get there alone. He stands on the shoulders of those beneath him. He rises from the contributions, lessons, and wisdom of many seasoned travelers of life's journey. Alex Haley, the late author of the bestseller, Roots, had a prized picture in his office of a turtle on a fencepost. He'd point at it and say, "Whenever you see a turtle on a fencepost, you know it had some help. Whenever I begin think, 'Isn't it great what I've done,' I look at that turtle and remind myself, 'I got where I am with the help of many others: my family, my friends, and especially God.'"

Whether we are in a position of power or merely aspire to be, remember the words of our Lord: "Whoever wishes to become great among you shall be your servant, and whoever wishes to be first among you shall be the slave of all." (Mark 10:43-44)

PRAYER: Dear Father in heaven, give me a servant's heart, that my pursuits of rank and power may be motivated by the desire to bless and help others and to serve the greater cause of the Army. Amen.

November 15

THE GREATEST DISPLAY OF STRENGTH

The Boston Beaneaters and the Baltimore Orioles dominated baseball in the 1890s. And the fiercest player on either side in that decade was John Joseph McGraw. He was the oldest of 8 children born to Irish immigrant parents. In a diphtheria epidemic, his mother and 4 of his brothers and sisters died. His father took out his grief by beating John mercilessly. So severe was the abuse that young John fled for his life at the age of twelve, vowing never to be bullied again by anyone.

But while the emotional pain of his childhood fired his drive as a ballplayer, it also became a destructive force in his life. His anger got the best of him during a game in 1894, when his team, the Orioles, were battling it out with their nemesis, the Boston Beaneaters. John McGraw got into a fistfight with the opposing third baseman. Both teams joined in, then the stands emptied onto the field and escalated the fight. Then someone started a fire in the stands. The resulting conflagration consumed the entire stadium and 170 buildings in Boston before it was over. This was one fight too many for John McGraw and it illustrated the biblical truth: "Starting a quarrel is like breaching a dam; so squelch a fight before it gets out of control" (Proverbs 17:14).

Yet our popular culture wrongly teaches that angry outbursts and childish temper tantrums are displays of strength, when the very opposite is true. It takes far more strength to subdue our own anger than to conquer an opponent. As the Scripture says, "He who is slow to anger is greater than the mighty, and he who rules his own spirit is greater than the one who captures a city." (Proverbs 16:32)

PRAYER: Dear Father in heaven, everyday I'm tempted to raise my voice and sometimes my fists. Give the strength to lower them. And grant me power, O Lord, to conquer the tyranny of my own passions, anger and moods. Remove the poison and pain from my heart and replace it with your love. Amen.

November 16

YOU CAN DO IT

This is a test. The following men, guess what they all have in common: the famous British playwright, composer, lyricist, actor, singer, novelist, and director Noel Coward, the American inventor Thomas Alva Edison, the Irish playwright Sean O'Casey, the British novelist Charles Dickens, the American Humorist Mark Twain, the American President Abraham Lincoln. They were all grade school drop outs.

In the final analysis, education is not the supreme deciding factor of whether we become successful in life. Some people depend too much on education. They erroneously believe that just "getting a degree" ensures or even constitutes success. Others, who do not have a college education, go through life feeling somewhat "inferior" or "illegitimate" because of their lack of formal training. In the mean time they are driven to achieve the success that many educated people never experience. It boils down to dreaming dreams and paying the price to make them come true.

What excuses do we make for ourselves for not achieving or even trying? Proverbs 13:4 tells us: "The sluggard craves and gets nothing, but the desires of the diligent are fully satisfied."

PRAYER: Dear Father in heaven, as you breathed into the first man the breath of life, breathe into me the drive and motivation to pursue the path you've chosen for me and to fulfill the dreams you've placed in my heart. Amen.

November 17

THE GREATEST VICTORY

The disciple of a renowned Greek philosopher once received a strange assignment from his master: "Pay a *denarius* to everyone who insults you!" Desiring greatly to please his master, the disciple strove to comply. Every time a friend or foe or complete stranger insulted or offended him, he paid the puzzled person a *denarius*. As much as it pained him to be insulted and then pay the person who did it, the disciple discovered that the effect of this gesture was profound: it disarmed his enemies and shamed his friends.

When this rather lengthy trial was over, the master summoned the young man to his quarters and said to him: "You may go to Athens, for you are ready to learn wisdom."

Elated, the disciple set off for Athens. Just before he entered the great city, he saw a certain wise man sitting at the gate insulting all who passed. Naturally, the moment this fellow saw the disciple, he hurled insults at him too.

"Hey!" the man cried, "How did you get to be so ugly and stupid? I have never seen anyone as ridiculous looking as you."

But instead of taking offence, the disciple just burst out laughing.

"Why do you laugh when I insult you?" asked the wise man.

"Because, my lord, for three whole years I have been paying for this kind of thing and now you give it to me for *nothing!*"

"Enter the city," said the wise man, "For you are invincible."

Someone had rightly said, "The greatest victory anyone can win is the victory over his own passions, moods and fears." The Scripture says, "He who is slow to anger is better than the mighty, and he who rules his spirit is better than he who captures a city." (Proverbs 16:32)

PRAYER: Dear God, help me to overcome the tyranny of my own passions, moods and fears. Give me victory over myself. Amen.

November 18

IT'S NOT AS BAD AS YOU FEAR

Can you imagine riding on a space ship that races along at 67,000 miles per hour – more than 1,000 miles per minute? Then suppose this hurdling spaceship begins tumbling end-over-end at a rotating speed of over 1,000 miles per hour– can you imagine what that would be like? Then suppose this hurdling, tumbling spaceship gets caught in a vortex that whirls around at 45,000 miles per hour and this vortex gets caught in a bigger whirlpool speeding at an incredible 500,000 miles per hour! What a crazy, wild ride that would be! Such a ride would be lethal to our constitution – to say the least! The maniacal motion would drive us mad! The G-forces would crush and disintegrate us, right?

Actually, such a ride would not be so bad. How do I know? Because every day of our lives, we *are* on that ride. That's right. We are on a spaceship called Earth that flies through space around the sun at 67,000 miles per hour and "tumbles" at 1,040 miles per hour. And the solar system, of which we are a part, moves through our galaxy at 45,000 miles per hour. And while we are moving along at such breakneck speeds within the outer wing of our great spiral galaxy, this outer wing itself moves at an incredible 500,000 miles per hour! But as scary as it sounds – you'd hardly even notice it.

"There have been a great many terrible things in my life," Mark Twain once wrote, "only a few of which have *actually* happened." True. It's not the actual living that is so terrible. It's our fears and dreadful anticipation of what the journey holds that we find unbearable. Our fears of tomorrow cause an anthill to cast the shadow of a mountain. We anticipate tomorrow to be immensely worse than God will ever allow it to be. And if the journey God has mapped for us is "fast-paced" and "tumultuous," don't worry. God will *so shield* and *strengthen* us that we'll hardly notice the speed.

"Fear thou, not," says God, "for I am with thee. Be not dismayed, for I am thy God. I will strengthen thee; yea, I will help thee; yea, I will uphold thee with the right hand of my righteousness." (Isaiah 41:10)

PRAYER: Dear Father in heaven, keep me as the apple of your eye and protect me safely in the hollow of your almighty and all-loving hand. Amen.

November 19

WHAT ON EARTH ARE WE HERE FOR?

Raoul Wallenberg had everything going for him. He came from a wealthy and distinguished family. His father was an officer in the Swedish Navy, his grandfather an ambassador for Sweden, and his brothers and cousins were powerful bankers and industrialists. And now he obtained the position of first secretary of the Swedish diplomatic mission in Budapest, Hungary.

But Wallenberg found himself in perilous times. The period was March 1944 and the infamous SS General, Adolf Eichmann had just arrived in Budapest to eliminate the entire Jewish population. But these were other people's problems, right? Wallenberg was coming from a neutral country and he could have easily coasted through the war. But he didn't.

With the help of the U.S. War Refugee Board (WRB) and the backing of Swedish government, Raoul Wallenberg turned his plush position into life-saving mission. Instead of being the traditional diplomat, "Wallenberg was a con artist who bribed, bullied, and blackmailed Hungarian and German officials to save Jews." He felt compelled to do so – Adolf Eichmann had already sent 400,000 Jews to the death camps and there was no time to wait.

Wallenberg designed and massed-produced phony Swedish passports that had no real authority, but, coupled with his imposing presence and authoritative tone, fooled Nazi officials and saved the lives of thousands. At times Wallenberg would even leap atop train cars loaded with Jews, pass arms-full of passports to those inside, then hop back to the ground and demand the train stop and that those Jews "under the protection of the Swedish government" be released. It worked again and again. Eventually, Wallenberg sectioned off a city-block of buildings, draped them with Swedish flags and declared it a "Swedish district" in which up to 15,000 Jews at a time found refuge.

Naturally, Eichmann ordered Wallenberg's death. But no matter how many times the German soldiers fired on him, Wallenberg always escaped. But it wasn't the Nazis who got Wallenberg. It was the Soviets. They imprisoned him in 1945 and he presumably died in captivity in 1947 – a tragic end to one who, instead of playing it safe, risked everything to save the lives of others. But in Budapest at the end of the war there were 120,000 Jews who had survived. Most of them owed their lives to Raoul Wallenberg. Perhaps he took to heart the biblical passage that warns us: "If you remain silent at this time, be assured that deliverance for the Jews will arise from some other place; but you shall perish. And who knows whether you have come to the kingdom for such a time as this." (Esther 4:14)

PRAYER: Dear Father in heaven, please help me make the most of my days and my opportunities. Grant that I may not fail in my hour of crisis. Amen.

November 20

WHEN YOU'VE TRIED AND FAILED

Nothing is a failure if we learn from it, glean a lesson from it, and use that lesson to persevere to success. That's what author Paul G. Stoltz writes in his book, *Adversity Quotient*. He tells the story of Thomas Edison's long, arduous effort to create a durable, portable and efficient battery as an independent power source. To achieve this invention, Edison took *more than 20 years and 50,000 experiments!*

One of his many critics blasted this methodology, stating, "Mr. Edison, you have failed 50,000 times. What results can you ever hope to get from such an inefficient method?" Edison replied, "Results? Why I've gotten plenty of results. I now know 50,000 things that won't work!"

And isn't it wiser for us to learn from our mistakes than to grieve over them. God is in the business of forgiving and redeeming our lives. We cannot erase our failures, but the blood of his Son can blot out our sins (1 John 1:7). And God's power, love and wisdom can even use our most tragic failures for good in our lives. The Divine Artist can interweave the darkest, ugliest threads of our lives into the most beautiful tapestry. "And we know," says the Scripture, "that God causes all things to work together for good to those who love God, to those who are called according to His purpose." (Romans 8:28)

PRAYER: O dear Father in heaven, please gather up the broken pieces of my life and build them into something beautiful for your glory and for the good of mankind. Amen.

November 21

GIVE YOURSELF A CHANCE

Several years ago I finally discarded a useless tool. For the longest time it was allowed to "hang out" in the tool box without doing any useful service. It was a "Torx Screwdriver" - similar to a Phillips head, though its head consisted of a six-pointed star. I had never seen any other like it. More important, I had never had any use for it, nor had I ever seen a screw that it would fit. Then, one day, when I was in the mood for cleaning, I finally scrapped that worthless thing. It had taken up room in the tool box too long. I was certain it would never serve any purpose.

Within the space of a week one of my car head lamps burned out. So, on the way home from work I stopped at Walmart, picked up a new headlamp, and prepared to change out the old one. With toolbox and lamp in hand, I knelt down to inspect the number and types of screws I'd have to remove to do the job. As I peered in at those screws I had an immediate sad, sick feeling. All around the housing for the lamp were a dozen Torx screws, which demanded nothing else but a Torx Screwdriver to remove them. "If only I had my old screwdriver back," I whined. "If only I hadn't thrown it away."

I've thought about that incident many times since and how it parallels people. Many people feel like that "useless" screwdriver that will never find any meaningful purpose in this world. Then, convinced they will never find their niche in life and that they only serve to take up space, they give up on life and throw themselves away. I recall the heart-breaking story of John Toole, an Army veteran, who couldn't find a publisher to buy the novel he had worked on for so long. Already prone to self-doubt and depression, the nine consecutive rejections from publishers convinced him he'd never find success or serve any useful purpose. He took his own life. How sad - sad both because suicide is a terrible tragedy and sad because he was wrong about himself, life, and his novel. It was a good one. In fact, eleven years after his death, his mother succeeded in getting it published and it became a Bestseller. In fact, in 1981, it won the Pulitzer Prize for fiction.

I also recall another despondent man named Sammy. Sammy had finally realized his dream of becoming a riverboat pilot in the mid Nineteenth Century. But when the Civil War shut down all commercial traffic on the Mississippi, Sammy's job faded away. He traveled west with his brother and tried his hand at numerous jobs – as a secretary, as a prospector, as a newspaper reporter and journalist. He failed or was fired from them all. Then, in the mid-1860s - without a job, a penny or a friend – Sammy lost the last thing he had left – hope that he'd ever find happiness or success in life. Sammy put a revolver to his head and came within a breath of pulling the trigger. The only thing that held him back was the suspicion that he might be wrong about life, that he might *not* be thinking clearly. Good move for Sammy. For within a matter of months Samuel Clemens would begin a stunningly successful career as a journalist, a humorist, a lecturer, and especially as an author. Most important, Samuel Clemens, aka Mark Twain, would soon meet the woman who would become his soul mate – Olivia Langdon.

I can think of many others who reached such low points in life, convinced that they would never find happiness, never know love, and never serve any useful purpose. Like that Torx Screwdriver they, and sometimes all of society, reach the verdict that they are useless and should be discarded. Don't give in to doubt. Hang on to hope. Give yourself, and God, a chance. God has put no one on this planet who cannot serve some good and great purpose and who cannot be a blessing to others. Give the Divine Author a chance to bring you to that fruitful chapter in your life when he answers all your conflicts and perplexing problems.

PRAYER: Dear Father in heaven, I believe and confess here and now that You have created me for a purpose. Throughout my sojourn in obscurity and fruitlessness, help me have faith in You and never lose hope. Amen.

November 22

WALKING BY FAITH

Nearly everyone has gone through this ritual. It's late at night and you're about to turn off the lights in the living room before going to bed. You walk across the room, find the switch and reach out to turn it off.

But before you plunge the house into darkness, you map out your path back across the living room floor. You note that you must move to the right of the footstool and be careful of the toys the kids left on the carpet. Then, with the flip of a switch, all is dark. But *what you saw in the light* you now use to guide you through the darkness. And it works. You make it across the dark room without tripping or stubbing your toe.

This is an analogy of what it means to walk by faith, to walk in the light of what God has revealed to you and to use that inner light to get you through the darkness. Walking by faith has also been likened to taking an evening stroll through the forest during a thunderstorm. You grope in the dark, trying to feel your way along the path. Then suddenly there is a brilliant flash of light and in an instant you can see the path. For just a moment you see how the path turns to the left, then to the right, then straight over a foot bridge. And at once it's dark again. But you can walk through the darkness by *what the light revealed to you.* You go as far as you can with the light you have received until the next flash of lightening gives you more guidance.

But this is not only an illustration of our "faith walk," but also of *our responsibility to the light*. *First*, we need to heed the light and all that it reveals. The Psalms remind us that God's word is a lamp to our feet and a light to our path (Psalm 119:11). The Scripture reveals the direction our lives should take and gives guidance on the choices we should make. It "turns the light on" in our darkened souls and reveals the truth.

But it's not enough *to see* the path, the turns, and the bridges. *We must walk* that path, negotiate those turns and cross those bridges. In the same way, it's not enough to study the light of the Scripture, we must live our lives by its light. We must be doers of the word and not just hearers (James 1:22).

And when all is dark we must hold on to the light. As someone has said, "Don't doubt in the darkness what God has shown you in the light." In other words, when bitter circumstances tell you that God has abandoned you, keep believing in his promise, *"I will never leave you nor forsake you"* (Hebrews 13:5). When fears torment you, believe his word that says, *"I sought the Lord and he heard me and delivered me from all my fears"* (Psalm 34:4).

When it seems that you will be overwhelmed by the pressures and burdens of life, believe God's promise that says, *"Fear not, for I have redeemed you; I have called you by name, you are mine. And when you pass through the waters, I will be with you, and through the rivers, they will not overflow you. When you walk through the fire you will not be scorched, nor will the flame burn you. For I am the Lord your God, the Holy One of Israel, your Savior"* (Isaiah 43:1-3). Give heed to the light, walk by the light, and keep believing in the light.

PRAYER: Dear Father in heaven, open my eyes to behold wonderful things in your word and help me to walk by the light it sheds on my path. Amen.

November 23

WHO WANTS WHAT THEY DESERVE?

"God has not dealt with us according to our sins, nor rewarded us according to our iniquities" (Psalm 103:10)

Preachers and churchmen often decry this generation for always seeking to avoid the consequences of its bad choices. They criticize it for casting off restraint and then being unwilling to owe up to the recompense of its actions.

Is that so out of character with the human race? Is that so different from any of us fellow sinners who once cried to God for mercy? Were we seeking justice from God when we knew we had broken his commandments and were found guilty in the court of heaven?

No, in one glorious moment we realized God doesn't deal with us as our deeds deserve or reward us according to our sins. He delivers us from the consequences of our sins – particularly the eternal consequences – and we gladly accepted His free gift of forgiveness.

We've somehow forgotten the grace that was freely poured out upon us and become overly focused on the fact that others do not measure up to the standard.

Historian and author Shelby Foote once told the story of a soldier, a private, in the Confederate Army who was brought before General Robert E. Lee for some infraction of the rules. The young man trembled before the formidable Commander. And who wouldn't? Lee was the highest ranking officer in the Confederate Army and lived by the highest standards. In his four years at West Point Robert E. Lee had the distinction of being the first cadet to have never received a single demerit. His flawless record earned him the title "The Marble Model." And on the battlefield Lee was ruthless. No wonder the poor private trembled.

Seeing the private's fear, General Lee told the young man, *"Don't be afraid, son. You'll get justice here."*

"I know, sir," replied the private. *"And that's what I'm afraid of."*

Like that soldier, *none of us* wants justice. We need God's mercy and with great joy we hear the words of Christ, "God does not deal with you according to your sins, nor reward you according to your iniquities."

PRAYER: Dear Father in heaven, I will never outgrow my need for Your love and forgiveness. As long as I breathe I will always need Your power to live righteously and Your forgiveness when I fail. Help me to forgive as I have been forgiven. Amen.

WISDOM FROM A USED CAR SALESMAN

"There's no such thing as a perfect car." That's what a used car salesman once told me as I began to point out deficiencies in a car I had just purchased from him. He was right. That car was flawed – but so also has every other car I have subsequently owned. And his words have come back to me again and again – concerning all of life.

Life is not perfect and we have to take life on life's terms, not ours. There's no such thing as a perfect or pain-free life. "No pain" is not an option. The options are "more pain" or "less pain." No one has a pain-free existence. We can make choices in life that will help us avoid unnecessary pain – i.e. stay free of substance abuse, keep physically and spiritually fit, nurture marriage and family relationships, obey the law, etc. But we cannot escape all pain.

There's no such thing as the perfect spouse. Why? Because people have flaws, unmet needs, fears, and their own share of selfishness. It's inevitable that couples clash from time to time. But husbands and wives grow and mature by learning to accept each other as they are – flaws and all.

There's certainly no such thing as the perfect job. Sure, we all envision that occupational position in which all our gifts and talents will be utilized and appreciated, where we will never be called upon to do anything for which we're inadequate or poorly trained, where we'll get along with all our co-workers. No human being has ever had such a job. Besides, such a comfort zone would stymie our personal and professional development. We grow and develop by being challenged and "stretched."

Nor is there any such thing as the perfect political candidate. Ever think to yourself, "I'm so disgusted with *all* the candidates, so I'm not going to vote at all?" Again, "no pain" is not an option. So choose the course that brings less pain. You'll never find a candidate who perfectly represents all your ideals and values. So choose the one who comes closest to the way you think and believe. Remember, *not* to decide, *is* to decide. And also, *not* to vote *is* to vote – for the candidate that you despise the most.

There's no such thing as a perfect car. Yes, nothing in this life is perfect. Life is to be accepted and enjoyed as God gives it. It's one of life's hardest lessons. Perhaps the hardest lesson of all is accepting that which seems most flawed and least perfect – our own selves.

God accepts and loves us as we are, yet loves us too much to leave us that way. Therefore, he sends us the imperfect, the painful, the hard to accept – that we might grow and develop by it.

What, then, is our task? To take life as it comes. Do what we can to improve it. Seek God to do that which is beyond our power. But accept that which remains imperfect – including ourselves - for our own growth and development. The apostle Paul admonished: "*In everything give thanks, for this is the will of God in Christ Jesus concerning you.*" (1 Thessalonians 5:18)

PRAYER: Dear Father in heaven, I am so accustomed to rejecting what is flawed. In my immaturity I demand perfection from people, from life, and from myself. But only you are perfect. Help me to accept life as it comes and to be thankful in all circumstances. Please grant me the serenity to accept the things I cannot change, the courage to change the things I can, and the wisdom to know the difference. Amen.

November 25

FOCUS ON LIFE'S BLESSINGS

Not long ago, fifteen-year-old Jennifer Mee of Florida made the headlines for having been plagued with a bad case of hiccups. Hiccupping at a rate of fifty times per minute, she endured them for a period of nearly six weeks. Life became an ordeal as the hiccups disrupted her sleep and made it impossible for her to attend school. Then, after thirty-seven straight days of hiccupping, Jennifer inexplicably awoke one morning – hiccup-free.

Hiccups result from uncontrollable spasms of the diaphragm. Their causes and cures are not fully known. But at one time or another, they afflict everyone – some, like Jennifer, more than others.

But Jennifer's is hardly the worst case on record. That record belongs to Charles Osborne of Anthon, Iowa. After slaughtering a hog in 1922 he began to hiccup and continued to do so for the next 68 years – an estimated total of 430 million hiccups! Yet Charles Osborne somehow managed to live a long, productive, and happy life – dying at the age of ninety-eight.

What's the point? That even when life has "hiccups," "wrinkles," and "waves" - from small ripples to big billows - it's not the end of the world. Nobody's life is perfect. No one has the perfect spouse, the perfect child, or the perfect job. The key to survival and happiness is to focus on life's blessings, not on the hiccups. Sure, the hiccups may never leave you. They may seem to cry out for your attention. But learn to ignore them and give your attention to the good in your life. Develop an attitude of gratitude and you will do well. The Scripture says, "Bless the Lord, O my soul, and forget none of his benefits." (Psalm 103:2)

PRAYER: Dear Father in heaven, help me to overlook life's blemishes and adversity. Help me to be mindful of your blessings and mercies that are new every morning. Amen.

November 26

TITLES AND POSITION
DO NOT EQUATE TO SIGNIFICANCE

His motion picture career spanned more than six decades. During this time he produced and directed over fifty feature films and established himself as the undisputed king of suspense. Who was he? Alfred Hitchcock, who generated such classics of the horror-suspense genre as *Suspicion, Shadow of a Doubt, Rear Window, Dial M for Murder, Vertigo, North by Northwest, The Birds*, and *Psycho*.

But there is another person behind these landmark films whose name never appeared in the film credits. Alfred Hitchcock depended so much on this person's opinion, that he would never seek the screen rights to a book, approve a screenplay, or accept the final cut of a film scene unless he had her approval. This person was none other than Alma Hitchcock, Alfred's wife.

In a documentary on the making of the thriller *Psycho*, Pat Hitchcock, daughter of the famous film-maker, noted that her father would ask Alma to read novels and peruse screen plays for him. If she did not think they were any good, Hitchcock would abandon them. The screenplay writer for *Psycho*, Joseph Stefano, commented that he knew his work had "passed the test" because Hitchcock told him that "Alma liked it."

Alfred Hitchcock depended on his wife's input for nearly every phase of the motion picture, including the casting and editing of the film. The documentary notes that, at the time of her death, Charles Chaplin of the *Los Angeles Times* said, "The Hitchcock touch had four hands and two of them were Alma's."

During this entire period, Alma Hitchcock made significant contributions to the success of the film industry as well as to her own husband's work. And she did it all without any official title, position, or formal recognition. This is amazing, because our culture tries to tell us that we can have neither identity nor significance without them. To say, "I am the director" means something. To say, "I help the director" means nothing. But this is not so in God's Kingdom. Jesus said that our heavenly Father sees the good that we faithfully do behind the scenes, in secret, and without any credit, titles, or position. He is mindful of our loving, but secret labors and He will most certainly reward us openly at the end of the age (Matthew 6:2-6, 16-18).

PRAYER: Dear Father in heaven, sometimes it is difficult being the "water boy" for the "real players" on the field, supporting others who labor in the limelight and frequently receive praise. But I would rather be a doorkeeper in Your house than to dwell in the tents of the wicked. Please, dear Lord, as I continue to labor in this land of obscurity, teach me humility and purify my motives. Help me to look beyond my earthly masters to You, O God. For You will surely make all earthly suffering worth it all. Amen.

November 27

WHEN WE TOLERATE SIN IN OUR LIVES

Dr. Paul Lee Tan tells the story from ancient China about King Huiwang of the state of Qin who wanted to attack the state of Shu, but was prevented by the unassailable mountains of that region to the southwest.

Then the king came upon an idea. He learned that his opponent, the king of Shu, was a very greedy man and he intended to use this vice against him. King Huiwang quickly commissioned skilled stonemasons to carve four beautifully ornamented stone oxen. Then he had his men spread the rumor in the enemy kingdom that these four oxen produced "golden manure." He even overlaid the oxen's hindquarters and tails with gold to add credibility to the rumor.

When the rumor reached the ears of the king of Shu, he immediately sought to purchase the oxen from King Huiwang. "Buy them? I'll give them too you. I only ask that you prepare a road from your kingdom to mine to allow the safe transport of the oxen."

In his eagerness to take possession of the "magic oxen," the king of Shu mobilized his kingdom into a workforce that leveled rocky hills, cut and tunneled through mountains, and traversed deep ravines with bridges – paving an easy route between the two kingdoms. And once the road was complete King Huiwang fulfilled his evil intent, invading the kingdom of Shu in a surprise attack and slaughtering its subjects.

Like King Huiwang, the enemy of our souls plots our destruction. But preventing his attack are the unassailable mountains of God's grace and provision that protect us in the hour of temptation. But what opens the door for Satan into our lives? Our weaknesses and our vices, if not overcome, will provide an open road for Satan into our lives. The Scripture tells us in Ephesians 4:27: "Do not give the devil a way to defeat you."

PRAYER: Dear Father in heaven, help me to be alert and vigilant against the enemy of my soul and all of his schemes to use my weaknesses against me. Fill me with your Spirit and empower me to overcome my weaknesses and temptation. Amen.

November 28

THE LEAST LIKELY TO SUCCEED

William Henry, born in 1937 in a rough Philadelphia neighborhood, was the son of an African American Navy mess steward and the oldest of four children. Although he was good at sports and well-liked by other students, this young man was too much of a class clown and was performing poorly in his classes. After failing the tenth grade and dropping out of school, he (like his dad) also joined the Navy.

While working as a Navy medic during the Korean War, William realized he needed to get an education if he wanted to get anywhere in life. But what could a high school dropout, the son of a Navy cook, ever amount to? He didn't even have high school under his belt, where was he to start?

William started by taking correspondence courses to get his high school equivalency. Then he applied and was accepted to Temple University on an athletic scholarship. He had to work hard, not only at his studies and sports. William had to work hard to earn money – quite often as a bartender - to pay for his education. It was during his bartending that his talent for comedy began to surface. His clientele repeatedly suggested that he become a standup comedian.

Finally, the day came. William graduated from Temple University, then again from the University of Massachusetts – with his *Doctorate in Education!* He became the first in his family to earn such an advanced degree and has since made significant contributions in the field of education, particularly in children's education.

But you probably don't know him for his academic achievements. Most people know William Henry Cosby, a.k.a. Bill Cosby as the famed standup comedian and television actor from such shows as "I Spy," "The Bill Cosby Show, "Fat Albert and the Cosby Kids," "The Electric Company," and many others.

Like Bill Cosby, many of us come to those places in our lives when we've failed and find ourselves in a rut. *"Where do we go from here? How can we get ahead? Who are we to think we could ever amount to anything? It's such a long way to go, where do we begin?"*

Bill Cosby had those same questions. And like him, we need to set goals for ourselves and start at the beginning. No one gets into a taxi and says, "Take me anywhere." We need to establish an objective or goal to shoot for.

And then we need to start at the beginning. The longest journey begins with a single step and beginning is half the battle. Once we begin and build momentum, our daunting task will seem so much more manageable.

If our educational goals seem *so far off* – even years in the future - *then remember this.* Those years will pass regardless of how we spend them – nothing can keep time from passing. *"Ten years from now,"* will pass no matter what. If we fill those years with hard work and stay focused on our goals, we will come out of those years with high achievement and proud accomplishments. But if we simply "coast along" and drift through life, we will come through those years empty-handed, empty-headed, and profoundly disappointed with ourselves.

Consider the message of Longfellow's poem, "Saint Augustine's Ladder."

We have not wings, we cannot soar;
But we have feet to scale and climb

By small degrees, by more and more,
The cloudy summits of our times.

The mighty pyramids of stone
That wedge-like cleave the desert airs,
When nearer seen, and better known,
Are but gigantic flights of stairs.

The distant mountains, that uprear
Their solid bastions to the skies,
Are crossed by pathways, that appear
As we to higher levels rise.

The heights by great men gained and kept
Were not attained by sudden flight,
But they, while their companions slept,
Were toiling upward in the night.

Someone said, "Our days are identical suitcases – all the same size – but some people can pack more into them than others." Make the most of your days, your talents, your life. Ephesians 5:15-16 tells us: "Be very careful, then, how you live, making the most of every opportunity..."

PRAYER: Dear Lord, though my strength is small and my talents seem few, help me to make the most of what You've given me. Amen.

November 29

DECEPTION

After wintering in Cambridge, Massachusetts, in the winter of 1775-76, George Washington succeeded in driving off a large British force of 10,000 soldiers from Boston in March 1776. Early one morning soldiers of the British garrison in Boston awoke to find the hills of Dorchester Heights bristling with enemy cannon. In a major engineering feat, Washington had moved the newly captured cannon from the Saratoga battlefield to the hill tops overlooking Boston. Clearly at a profound disadvantage, Lord Howe, commander of the British forces, chose to evacuate the city rather than risk destruction.

The amazing thing about this American victory was that there was really no threat at all to the British forces. For, unknown to the British, General Washington didn't have the gunpowder to fire his cannon. In fact, when he took command of the Army in 1775 there was such a shortage of gunpowder within the ranks that the average soldier only had enough to fire about 5 shots apiece. Washington had pulled off a major deception.

Deception was also present during the Peninsula Campaign in the early stages of the Civil War. This was particularly so during the Battle of Yorktown, where Major General John Magruder, who commanded a Confederate force of 12,000, held off General McClelland's force of 120,000 for a month (April 5 – May 4, 1862). He did this by emplacing phony cannon made of logs and by ostentatiously marching small forces past the same spot over and over to give the appearance of a much larger force. It worked. McClelland wasted precious time emplacing massive artillery and building huge siege works and fortifications to deal with the Confederate force he believed was larger than his own.

Deception was largely the reason why General Arthur Percival, commander of the Allied forces in Singapore, surrendered his Army of 120,000 to the Japanese commander, General Tomoyuki Yamashita in February 1942. Percival believed himself hopelessly outnumbered and outgunned when General Yamashita, pounding his fist on the negotiation table, demanded his immediate surrender - "to give up this meaningless and desperate resistance." In reality, Yamashita's Army was dangerously low on supplies and, with only 30,000 soldiers, was but a fraction of the size of Percival's force.

And how often do we capitulate to the enemy of our souls because we believe "the temptation is just too much" and "we're not strong enough" and "we don't have what it takes"? Too often we surrender to temptation without "firing a shot" and without putting up the smallest fight. Too often we forget that "greater is He who is in us, than he who is in the world" (1 John 4:4).

PRAYER: Dear Father in heaven, open my eyes to see the strength and the victory that are mine through Jesus Christ. Help me to remember that no temptation has come upon me except what is common to everyone and that you will never allow me to be tempted beyond what I can bear. Help me, through Christ, to gain the inevitable triumph. Amen.

November 30

WHEN SOLDIERS ARE WEARY OF TRAINING

Automaker Henry Ford asked electrical engineer genius Charlie Steinmetz to build the generators for his factory. One day the generators ground to a halt, and Ford's repairmen couldn't find the problem. In desperation, Ford called Steinmetz, who tinkered with the machines for about an hour and then threw the switch. Sure enough, the generators whirred to life. A few days later Ford was shocked to receive a bill from Steinmetz for $10,000.00. Flabbergasted, the tightfisted carmaker demanded to know why the bill was so high. He insisted that Steinmetz itemize the bill so he could see exactly what he was paying for.

Steinmetz sent his reply: $10.00 for tinkering with the generators. $9,990.00 for knowing where to tinker. Ford paid the bill. Knowing what to do in the time of desperation and crisis is what made the cost worth it.[lxvii]

In the same way, knowing how to survive in the desperate times of combat will make all the endless hours of training worth it. The tough training gives soldiers the critical edge they need in the ultimate game in which only the winners survive.

But what about our spiritual training? General George C. Marshall once wrote:

"The soldier's heart, the soldier's spirit, and the soldier's soul are everything. Unless the soldier's soul sustains him, he cannot be relied on and will fail himself, his commander, and his country in the end. It is not enough to fight. It is the spirit that wins the victory. ... With it all things are possible, without it everything else – planning, preparation, and production – count for nothing."

"It's morale - and I mean spiritual morale – which ultimately wins the victory; and that type of morale can only come out of the righteous nature of a soldier who has the spirit of religious fervor in his soul. I count heavily on that type of man and that type of Army."

Are we trained to survive in combat? Do we also have the spiritual edge that can help us in crisis and the desperate times of combat? God help us to strengthen and under-gird our spirits through prayer, worship and the reading of Scripture that we may have the spirit and heart to survive the troublesome times to come. The Scripture tells us: "Put on the full armor of God, that you may be able to stand firm against the schemes of the devil. For our struggle is not against flesh and blood, but against … the spiritual forces of wickedness" (Ephesians 6:11-12).

PRAYER: Dear Father in heaven, help me to strengthen and fortify my faith and spirit that I may be able to survive the trials of life and rigors of combat. Amen.

December

December 1

WHEN YOU FEEL OVERWHELMED

Have you ever felt like you're in over your head? Ever feel like a task is so large that you cannot even begin? If so remember these simple thoughts:

1. The longest journey begins with a single step. The greatest accomplishments all begin with a dream and the courage to try to make it reality. Most people never begin because they fear failure. But it is better to try and do something imperfectly than to do nothing flawlessly. As Joshua stood at the threshold of the Promised Land, realizing the great and hazardous task that lay before him, God told him:

"Just as I have been with Moses, I will also be with you; I will never leave you or forsake you. Only be strong and courageous" (Joshua 1:5-6).

2. Beginning is halfway there. Just getting started is half the battle. Once you get started you will gain momentum. Robert Shuller states that "the one battle most people lose is the battle over the fear of failure ...Try, start, begin...and you'll be assured you won the first round!" Many others, with less talent and ability than you, have come this way before and have made it. So can you. Get started!

3. Inch by inch, anything's a cinch! God had told Joshua he did not have to conquer the Promised Land all in one year, but "little by little" (Exodus 23:29-30). So God also commands us to take just one day at a time, to only bear today's burdens and to place tomorrow's concerns in His almighty hands (Matthew 6:34; Psalm 55:22).

4. God promises to give you only what you can bear! In 1 Corinthians 10:13 God tells us that He only allows trials to enter our lives that everybody else must face and that He will never push us beyond our limitations. Put your trust in God; He will not let you down.

5. There is an end to every task, every trial, every test, and every ordeal - this will all soon be history! Robert Shuller states that, "Every problem has a limited life-span" and that "Tough times don't last, but tough people do!" More important, though our trials are not forever, God's power *is.* Isaiah 40:28-29 tells us that the Everlasting God never grows weary, but gives strength to the weary and weak. Saint Paul tells us that "our light affliction is but for a moment" (2 Corinthians 4:17). Hang in there and this task or trial will soon be behind you.

6. As you accomplish what you once thought "impossible," you will move from weakness to strength and be transformed. Phillips Brooks once said,

"Do not pray for easier lives, pray to be stronger men. Do not ask for tasks equal to your powers, but for powers equal to your task. Then not only shall the doing of your work be a miracle, but you shall be a miracle. Every day you shall wonder at yourself at the richness of life which has come in you by the grace of God."

PRAYER: Dear God, may I not shrink back in fear, but march on in Your strength, and experience Your transforming power. Amen.

December 2

WHEN WE CALL OURSELVES A CHRISTIAN

Imposter. We all know what the word means. The very mention of the word probably brings someone to mind – someone who pretends to be someone better, more interesting, more significant than he or she actually is.

Does anyone remember Rosie Ruiz. In 1980 she was once heralded as the world-record-breaking women's Boston Marathon champion – for a day or so. Then it was discovered that Rosie had hopped aboard public transportation early in the race and hopped off near the finish line. She crossed the finish line ahead of every other woman in record time. An investigation disclosed she had taken a similar shortcut in a previous New York Marathon. Besides being a cheat, Rosie pretended to be a marathon champion, relishing in all the glory she never earned.

Our world abounds with such pretenders. More than twenty years since his death, Elvis Presley still has many men impersonating him. They steal some of "the King's" glow to enjoy the limelight they are not willing to work for and to conceal the barrenness of their own lives.

There have also been many outlaw impersonators. Historically, Jesse James seems to have been a favorite with imposters. One James-pretender, who hadn't done his homework very well, rolled into a Kentucky town to ply his trade – a town in which the James Gang had robbed a bank many years before. A U.S. Marshall confronted the imposter, pulled a yellowed document from his pocket and declared: "I have here a warrant for your arrest, charging you with the robbery of the

Bank of Columbia and the murder of the cashier." When the imposter turned pale, the Marshall added: "However, on the chance that you may not be the real Jesse James, I'm giving you ten minutes to get out of town." The man was gone in five.

But of all imposters, the worst may have been the "Great Pretender" himself – Ferdinand Waldo Demara. Without training, academic degrees, credentials, ordination or a commission, Demara pretended to be (and received payment as) a surgeon, psychologist, college dean, dentist, university professor, Naval officer, and a Trappist monk. Demara's phony life finally caught up with him and landed him an 18-month prison sentence, one of the few things in life he actually earned.

Maybe we should add some of our own names to the list of phonies. How many of us relish in the name "soldier" yet do not share the Army's values of selfless service, courage and integrity? How many wear a starched uniform and spit-shined boots, yet scheme to avoid the sacrifices, training, and hardship our duty requires? Far too many, I fear. Far too many do everything to serve and protect themselves in a profession that may require them to lay down their lives.

Then there are the religious imposters among us, who name the name of Christ, yet never live as He lived. The Scripture tells us, "Let everyone who names the name of the Lord abstain from wickedness." (2 Timothy 2:19)

PRAYER: Dear Lord, help me to be honest with myself and with others. Grant that the faith I profess with my mouth will express itself in the way I live. Amen.

December 3

PRACTICING WHAT WE PREACH

Dr. Marshall Seper was called "the old country psychologist." For eleven years his radio program drew a "high listening audience" in mid-America.

He not only popularized psychology but also practiced it successfully. A huge portion of the American public turned to one man for answers to their personal problems – Dr. Seper. And Dr. Seper always seemed to have the answer. Even for the "hard cases," those who had lost the will to live, Dr. Seper proved very effective. "On the air" he talked numerous suicide callers out of taking their own lives.

Then one Monday morning he got into his red convertible, drove ten minutes from his home, took out a gun, and killed himself. A fan of his radio program asked the ultimate question: "Why couldn't he follow his own advice?"[lxviii]

A strange dilemma often befalls those in leadership or instructor positions. They possess a wealth of knowledge and expertise from which they never benefit, because it's all intended for "the other guy." They can devote all their energy to giving the best advice or delivering instruction in the most effective way. But they forget to apply it to their own lives. They dichotomize life into the professional and the personal. But it doesn't work. We must practice and live what we preach.

Paul the Apostle wrote, "I discipline my body with blows and bring it under complete control, lest while preaching to others I myself may become disqualified." (1 Corinthians 9:27)

PRAYER: Dear Father in heaven, I don't want to be disqualified from life's race or fail the very principles for which I profess to stand. Please help me to practice what I preach and to first apply my learning to me, before I preach it to others. Amen.

December 4

THE GOSPEL ACCORDING TO ABBOTT AND COSTELLO

There is hidden wisdom in an unlikely place - the 1951 movie, *Abbott and Costello Meet the Invisible Man*. In this comedy, Bud Abbott and Lou Costello play two bumbling detectives who try to help a professional boxer, Tommy Nelson (Arthur Franz), wrongly accused of killing his manager. The real murderer is a corrupt boxing official and crime boss, Boots Morgan (Sheldon Leonard).

In their investigation detectives Abbott and Costello discover a vial of serum in a laboratory that has the power to turn a person invisible. Tommy Nelson gets the idea of injecting himself to avoid the police as well as to trap crime boss Morgan. To infiltrate the boxing world, Costello poses as "the new up and coming contender" – with a whole lot of help from Nelson.

The fight scenes are funny but hardly believable. Lou Costello's pudgy profile is the antithesis of a fighter's physique. Yet, with his invisible companion by his side, the short and plump Costello hammers one opponent after another with "such incredible speed" that his blows look like "phantom punches." And that is exactly what they are. Nelson is the real power behind the little man. The little guy's punches rarely connect, but it doesn't matter. The invisible power-puncher is at his side, doing the real damage to Costello's opponents. The invisible heavy-hitter, Tommy Nelson, creates the illusion that Costello is a dangerous fighter, with fists of fury and blinding speed. But it's all illusion. Without his invisible partner he wouldn't stand a chance.

We live with the same illusion. Unbroken success in our many tasks leads us to believe that we can handle things just fine by ourselves. But our self-sufficiency makes us very weak in faith and wholly unprepared to face the emotional, moral, and spiritual conflict pitted against our souls. We are, all of us, very much like Lou Costello trying to survive in the ring and we badly need the unseen presence and power of Jesus. But don't worry. The Bible promises, "the battle is not yours, but God's," (2 Chronicles 20:15) and "the Lord himself will fight for you." (Exodus 14:14). The Lord is in the arena with us. He will empower us, make us equal to the task, and grant us success in our work. And when credit and praise is lavished upon us for being so good at our job, we will pass the praise on to God to Whom it truly belongs.

PRAYER: Dear Father in heaven, please help me with the challenges I face. Fill me and empower me by Your Holy Spirit. Lift me above all human limitations and make me more than equal to the task with which You've honored me. Amen.

December 5

WHEN WE FEEL UNAPPRECIATED

Throughout his life, Gregor Johann Mendel (1822-84) went un-noticed and un-appreciated. He was a brilliant student, but too poor to afford college. So he entered the Augustinian Monastery for an education.

When he wanted to teach at the University of Vienna, he was rejected. Three times he failed the entrance exam – not because of incompetence, but due to originality of thought. In fact, his examiner completely misunderstood him and concluded that Gregor Mendel lacked scientific "insight and the required clarity of knowledge." So Gregor was consigned to teaching science in high school. But he continued with his own experiments and observations of plants.

Then, after completing his seven-year-long pioneering experiments on heredity, he sent his results to a Swiss botanist, but received an icy rejection of his work. When he finally published his findings in *Experiments with Plant Hybrids* in 1866, no one noticed or seemed to care. The truth was that Mendel's work was so far ahead of its time that *it took thirty-four years, sixteen years after his death*, for the scientific community to "catch up" and recognize the significance of his work. Today, Gregor Mendel's theories on heredity are foundational and he is universally recognized as the "Father of Modern Genetics."

Gregor Mendel went through life un-noticed and un-appreciated, and went to his death totally unaware of the significance his life's work would have on the future. In the same way most of us live our lives in obscurity and may have no idea of the profound legacy we'll leave behind. Therefore, we should never judge our lives a failure based on the apparent success or failure of our efforts in this life. In fact, the Scripture tells us not to pass judgment on our own lives or on anyone else's prematurely. For not until the day of eternity will God bring to light the quality of our life's work and the hidden impact it has had on others (1 Corinthians 4:5).

PRAYER: Dear Father in heaven, help me to do my best to do my duty and to leave failure, success and recognition in your hands. Amen.

December 6

UNSUNG HEROES ARE STILL HEROES

You've heard of Paul Revere and his famous "Midnight Ride" on the 18th of April, 1775. And why not? Paul Revere's 20-mile trip to alert the countryside of the approaching British invasion just before the Battles of Lexington and Concord contributed to the outcome of the conflict – a catastrophic rout of the British.

But the real reason you're familiar with Paul Revere is that his journey, cut abruptly short by the British who captured him, was immortalized by the great American poet, Henry Wadsworth Longfellow.

But have you ever heard of Israel Bissell? Every American should have. For his mad-dash mission to alert America of the British threat in Massachusetts covered nearly 20 times the distance as that of Paul Revere's. Israel Bissell was a 23-year-old dispatch rider for the Massachusetts Provincial Congress. On April 19, 1775, Colonel Francis Smith marched his brigade of British regulars into Middlesex County to confiscate stockpiled weapons of the Massachusetts Militia.

That very day Israel Bissell bolted off with orders to alert the rest of the colonies that one of their own was under attack. In record time Bissell traveled more than 350 miles in five days (wearing out several horses in the process), going as far as New York City and Philadelphia, alerting towns and hamlets along the way and delivering a written plea for help and a call to arms. Revere alerted Middlesex County. Bissell alerted the nation and brought news that unified the northern colonies and impelled them to "get off the fence" and make the fateful decision – to fight for independence.

Yet for all his heroics, Israel Bissell was largely forgotten. Not until 1926 – the year of America's Sesquicentennial celebration - did one historian, Abram Wakeman, take note of Bissell's profound contribution. Little has been written about this unsung hero since. But the fact that Israel Bissell received little recognition and praise does not diminish his achievements and contributions. Sung or unsung, Israel Bissell was a hero.

All of us can identify with Israel Bissell. There are times when our labor goes unnoticed and unrewarded. To make things worse, we might even be subjected to having to listen to praise directed to others whose sacrifices and achievements are small in comparison.

But success is not measured by the amount of praise or recognition we receive. Success is measured in having completed our mission and done our best to contribute to the cause of freedom and the good of our country and other people. It behooves us all to settle the matter in our hearts – to seek true success, to look beyond our earthly masters to our heavenly One, and to strive to please Him. In the Scripture our Lord said, "Watch out! Don't do your good deeds publicly, to be admired by others, for you will lose your reward from your Father in heaven." (Matthew 6:1)

PRAYER: Dear Father, help me this day to do my best to complete your mission for my life. No matter is my task seems small, unimportant and unnoticed, help me to do my best – that I may be true to You, to others who depend on me, and to myself. Amen.

December 7

NO END IN SIGHT?

On December 7, 1941, 350 Japanese warplanes in two massive waves virtually destroyed the air and naval forces of the United States at Pearl Harbor. In less than two hours they sank or heavily damaged all eight of the Pacific Fleet's battleships, 3 of its cruisers, and five of its other ships. On that day Japan's carrier-based aircraft also destroyed or damaged 343 U.S. airplanes, most of them parked in tight groups in the center of the airfields to protect them from sabotage.

Most grievous among the losses was the sinking of Admiral Kimble's flagship, the USS Arizona, which accounted for nearly half of all those who died – 1,177 of 2,390 deaths. To this day the un-recovered remains of nearly 900 sailors are still aboard the sunken ship, making it a virtual graveyard in the clear waters of Pearl Harbor. To commemorate the courage of these brave men and to memorialize their deaths, the USS Arizona Memorial was constructed in 1987, just above the sunken ship, spanning its beam.

Positioned just a few hundred yards from the sunken Arizona is another famous battleship, the USS Missouri – known as "Mighty MO." Its close proximity to the Arizona is no mistake. For it was aboard the decks of the Missouri in Tokyo Bay that General Douglas Macarthur and Admiral Chester Nimitz accepted Japan's unconditional surrender on September 2, 1945, which officially ended the greatest and most costly war in human history. Hence, these two sites respectively represent the beginning and the end of America's involvement in WWII, the darkest day in US military history and the brightest, America's catastrophic defeat and its consummate victory.

Perhaps to this meaning we can add another for the believer– that no matter how dark the hour, no matter how deep the valley, and no matter how fierce the conflict, God will bring our trials to an end and a shining morning to our nights. Truly, for God's faithful people, every problem has a limited lifespan and every trial a certain death. If we will only remain faithful we will gain the inevitable triumph, so help us God!

The Scripture reminds us, "Therefore, let us not grow weary in doing good, for in due time we will reap a harvest if we do not give up." (Galatians 6:9)

A visitor to Pearl Harbor observes the two profound "bookends" of the Second World War – the USS Battleship Arizona Memorial (right) and the USS Battleship Missouri (left)

PRAYER: Dear Father in heaven, please sustain me in every trial and help me to endure every battle to the inevitable triumph. Amen.

December 8

WHEN LIFE IS AGAINST YOU

He didn't stand a chance. He was born to a poor family in rural Japan, at a time when no one but the industrial aristocracy had any opportunity for success. Then came the Second World War, which devastated the economy. To make things worse, Soichiro did not have an education, nor did he desire one. He was certainly ambitious and dreamed of making motorcycles, but the powerful ruling families of the motor industry stood in his way and threatened to squash like a bug any competition.

Nevertheless, against all the opposition and without formal education, Soichiro pursued his dream of making motorcycles. And he did. He began by using small military generator motors to power bicycles. By 1952 he produced the Cub, an easy-to-operate motorcycle that proved very successful in Japan. But the system was still against him. Because he was not "blue blood," he was not allowed to employ any of the leading engineers as Mitsubishi, Nissan and Toyota could. The system also made it difficult for him to obtain permits or get loans.

But Soichiro's biggest "downer" was failure. Endless trial and error, roadblocks, wasted time and effort, dead end projects all sapped him of strength, motivation, and hope. Yet, Soichiro reconciled himself to failure and came to acknowledge it as a necessary part of the pursuit of excellence and success. The Result, by 1989, Soichiro Honda's Honda Motor Corporation had the best-selling car in America – the Honda Accord. Today, Honda sells more than a million cars and more than eleven million products annually in the U.S. alone.

Does he grieve over his many failures? No, in fact, he has incorporated them into his philosophy of success. This is what he said:

"Although I made one mistake after another, I never made the same mistake (twice) and I always tried my hardest and succeeded in improving my efforts."

"To me, success can be achieved only through repeated failure and introspection. In fact, success represents 1 percent of your work and results from the 99 percent that is called failure."

It's painful to fail. If you have failed at some project, try to understand that God will incorporate failure into his plan to bring good things into your life and he will use failure to teach you your greatest lessons. So if your record is blemished with failure, be assured that you have plenty of company. The Scripture reminds us that "though a righteous man falls seven times, he rises up again." (Proverbs 24:16).

PRAYER: Dear Father in heaven, when I stumble and fail, help me, Lord to learn from my failures, move on and to grow stronger and wiser. Amen.

December 9

YOU'RE NOT A FAILURE IF YOU FAIL

In a recent article in *Leadership* magazine, J. Wallace Hamilton cautioned: "The increase of suicides, alcoholics, and even some forms of nervous breakdowns is evidence that many people are training for success when they should be training for failure. Failure is far more common than success; poverty is more prevalent than wealth, and disappointment more normal than arrival." The good news is this, though failure occurs far more frequently than success, failure is not the final chapter and failure is actually part of success – failure, trial and error, is the often the path for reaching success.

Consider the following. Charles Dickens, famed author of *A Christmas Carol*, *Oliver Twist*, *Great Expectations*, and *David Copperfield*, was the highest paid writer of his time. Yet he did not receive a single cent for the first nine stories he published. Lawrence Tibbet became a Metropolitan opera star. Yet the first time he was the inside of the Metropolitan Opera House was in the standing-room-only section, because he couldn't afford a seat. John D. Rockefeller attained legendary proportions because of the fortune he amassed. Yet he started life hoeing potatoes at four cents an hour.

Frederick Austerlitz (not exactly a household name), was born in Omaha, Nebraska. He went to Hollywood with stars in his eyes. He landed a film test in 1933. The director's assessment: "Can't act, can't sing, balding; can dance a little" and advised him to go back to the corn fields of Nebraska. Yet Frederick Austerlitz recovered from this rejection and went on to star in such movies as "Top Hat," "Swing Time," "The Gay Divorcee," "Holiday Inn," "Easter Parade," "On the Beach," "Finian's Rainbow," and many others. This man who "couldn't sing" went on to sing and croon his way into hearts everywhere. And though he could only "dance a little" in 1933, Frederick Austerlitz, a.k.a. Fred Astaire, went on to be recognized world-wide as a consummate dancer.[lxix]

Though failure and disappointment come your way, don't let it stop you. With God's guidance and help and your own persistence success is inevitable. The Scripture says, "For I know the plans I have for you, says the Lord; plans for good and not for evil, plans to give you a hope and a future." (Jeremiah 29:11)

PRAYER: Dear Father in heaven, fortify my spirit so I may stand firm when those days of failure and disappointment come. Guide me in the path I should travel and help me to persistently pursue my life's goals until they become reality. Amen.

December 10

YOU HAVE WHAT IT TAKES TO BE SUCCESSFUL

Israel Isadore Baline was born to Jewish parents, on May 11, 1888 in Temun, Siberia, Russia. His family immigrated to the United States in hopes of a better life, but "Izzy" grew up in abject poverty in New York City's Lower Eastside. After his father died Izzy went to work full-time. But when he failed to earn as much as his brothers and sisters he left home at the age of 13 because he didn't want to be a burden to his family. Now homeless, Izzy slept in stairwells and on park benches. He tried a series of odd jobs; selling newspapers, working the docks, etc., but just couldn't make anything work.

Finally Izzy got a job as a singing waiter and dreamed of making a career in music, especially as a song-writer. But there were a few problems. First, Izzy was uneducated. He had only reached the third grade. Second, although Izzy taught himself to play the piano, he could only play it in one key - F sharp. Third, Izzy couldn't read music - throughout his life he would have to rely on a "musical secretary" to compose music as he thought out the melody in his head.

Years later, while serving in the Army during the First World War, Izzy composed a patriotic song and sang it for his musical secretary, Harry Ruby. Ruby listened to the song, frowned and said, "Geez, not another patriotic song!" A discouraged Izzy, now called Irving, threw the song into his trunk of rejects.

There the rejected song stayed for 20 years until on the eve of the Second World War, when he gave it to singer Kate Smith to use. The song was an instant success and became so popular nation-wide that most Americans wanted to make it the National Anthem. The reject-song was "God Bless America."

The song-writer was Irving Berlin. And despite his limitations in music, education, and opportunities he went on to write more than 1,500 songs and publish nearly 1,000 of them. One half of these became hits, 100 went to the top ten, and 35 reached "number one" in the nation.

Hits like "Alexander's Ragtime Band," "There's No Business Like Show Business," "Puttin' On The Ritz," "Blue Skies," "A Pretty Girl Is Like A Melody," "Cheek To Cheek" and "White Christmas" made Irving Berlin, the poor Russian-Jewish immigrant, with little education and no training in music, widely recognized as America's greatest song writer.

What limitations do we think we have? What excuses are we making for ourselves for not succeeding, for not even trying? God is our Creator. He is able to take the raw material of our lives and fashion us into something great. Let us ask Him for His help.

The Scripture says, "O Lord, You are our Father. We are the clay and You are the Potter; we are all the work of Your hands." (Isaiah 64:8).

PRAYER: Dear Father in heaven, please take me, with all my weaknesses and problems, and make me into the person You want me to be. Make me into the person You created me to be. And give me the courage and strength to face and overcome all my limitations. Amen.

December 11

IS LIFE OUT OF CONTROL?

Pierre Wilson directed movies of the most spectacular events ever witnessed. From the 1940s through the early1960s he filmed these spectacles in the cutting edge technology of the day - 65 and 70-millimeter Cinemascope and Vista-Vision – directing the most powerful movies ever made. Why have you probably never heard of him? His work was classified Top Secret. Pierre Wilson was one of the unsung heroes who documented many of the United States' atmospheric atomic bomb tests conducted in the Nevada Test Site, near Bikini Atoll, in the Marshall Islands, Johnston Island, Christmas Island and in outer space.

Peirre's work has led to some frightfully unpredictable experiences. One such example of the unexpected comes from the test, Operation Castle Bravo, one of the early hydrogen bomb tests in 1954. In Castle Bravo scientists anticipated a bomb "yield" of about 6 megatons (i.e. the explosive force of six million tons of TNT).

Instead the bomb took everyone by surprise, and had a runaway yield two and a half times greater than what was expected. Within a mere six minutes the explosion sent a mushroom cloud 130,000 feet into the atmosphere, vaporized an Island, and scoured a crater more than a mile and a half wide. Its unanticipated power led to the tragic contamination of soldiers and civilians, among them the crew of a Japanese fishing boat.

This is why Pierre Wilson hesitates to refer to himself as a director, for he knows by experience how helpless human beings are in the face of atomic bombs. In an interview from the documentary, "The Atomic Filmmakers: Behind the Scenes," he made an insightful comment: "No one directs an atomic bomb going off. Once somebody presses the button - it's out of control!"

An atomic bomb out of control – what a frightening thought! Yet just as frightening is the thought of life getting out of control, of being at the mercy of merciless circumstances.

We do everything to get a handle on life. We plan, we build, and strive to insulate ourselves against the flood of disappointments and tragedies that befall other people. And we live with the illusion that we will be exceptions to the rule. Nothing will touch us, *we* are in control. But sorrow and tragedy show no partiality. None of us is immune to their sting, nor beyond their long reach.

But this is not the whole story. For the person who puts their faith in Jesus Christ and entrusts their life and future in his almighty and all loving hands, the story is brighter. Sure, the Christian believer has his share of pain and sorrow – just look at what his Master endured. But nothing of the pain and tribulation that the believer endures will separate him from God's love. And God's love, not fate, becomes the prevailing force in his life. God's love transforms his pain into gain, his hurts into halos, his curses into blessings, and his scars into stars. God's love may not separate the believer from tribulation, peril, and death. But none of those things can separate him from God's love. God's love may not separate him from tragedy, sorrow, and pain. But God's love will protect him from their evil effects. (Romans 8:31-39) Therefore, entrust your life and very self to God's unfailing love.

PRAYER: Dear Father in heaven, as Jesus my Lord prayed and as countless saints of God before me have prayed, I now pray: 'Father, not my will but Yours be done.' I entrust myself, my life and my future to Your almighty and all-loving hands. I entrust myself to Your unfailing love. Guide and direct my steps and have Your way in my life. Amen.

December 12

THE SECRET OF TRUE SUCCESS

In 1975 the Sony Corporation introduced the first affordable home video player system, using its Betamax format. The next year JVC (Victor Corporation of Japan) introduced its own VHS (Video Home System) format. Both systems used reel-to-reel video-audio tape in plastic cassettes. But Sony's Betamax cassettes were less bulky than JVC's and they produced a superior quality picture. Why then, thirty years later, do we still have VHS cassettes everywhere, yet Betamax cassettes are nowhere to be found?

The reason is simple. JVC shared its technology with many companies – licensing them to manufacture its VHS system – Zenith, RCA, Matsushita, to name a few. Sony, on the other hand, tried to keep a monopoly on its technology and refused to allow any other company to make Betamax video players. The result – not only did many more VHS video players hit the market. A far greater selection of movie titles and TV shows in the VHS format appeared in stores. Sony's business scheme backfired. By 1988 the Sony Corporation admitted defeat and itself began producing VHS video players.

Sharing breeds success. This truth extends to the totality of life. Sharing knowledge does not make us ignorant. It enriches those who receive. A candle does not diminish its flame if it lights others. It serves its purpose by spreading the light. Even when we give of our material wealth, we are not the poorer. The Scripture tells us over and over that God loves a cheerful giver (2 Corinthians 9:7), that if we give to the poor we are lending to the Lord and He will repay us (Proverbs 19:17), that if we give we shall receive many times more (Luke 6:38), and that when we give to those in need it is the same as giving to Christ (Matthew 25:40).

On the other hand, Christ warns that those who greedily cling to life and its possessions, will lose everything in the end – worst of all our own soul (Matthew 16:25-27). A wise person once wrote: "He is no fool who gives what he cannot keep to gain what he cannot lose." Be generous with you time, your resources, and yourself in the cause of good and of the gospel. By doing so, you will preserve them for eternity.

PRAYER: Dear Lord, show me that it is in giving that we receive, that it is in pardoning that we are pardoned, and that it is in dying to self that we are born to eternal life. Amen.

December 13

WHEN YOU FEEL ALONE

Thor Heyerdahl won fame in 1947 by navigating a small raft, called *Kon Tiki*, across 4,300 miles of the Pacific Ocean, voyaging from Peru, South America to Polynesia. He reached land just as his raft was sinking – the raft of balsa wood and bamboo had become too waterlogged.

Oddly enough, Thor once had a deathly fear of water. He overcame it in the most unlikely way. Would you believe that, after he had mustered the courage to get out on a canoe in the turbulent waters of a Canadian river, his worst fear came upon him – his canoe *capsized?* To make matters worse, the rapids swept him toward a huge waterfall. He recalled thinking, "Now I will know which of my parents is right, my father who believed in God or my mother who did not." Lost in the overpowering torrent, the Lord's Prayer suddenly flashed through his mind. So he prayed in his mind to God for strength and fought with his body to swim to the river's bank. Then something strange happened. A burst of energy surged through him. He detected an unseen force empowering him from within to swim like never before and an unseen hand pulling him to the shore. As he rose from the river and stood on the solid ground, Thor lifted his eyes heavenward and thought, "My father is right – there is a God who is ever present and with us in trouble." His fear of water, and every other specter, was gone.[lxx]

That day Thor experienced the reality of the biblical promise: "God is our refuge and strength, a very present help in trouble" (Psalm 46:1).

PRAYER: Almighty and merciful God, make your abiding presence real to me. Grant that I may never ignore you and help me to turn to you in trouble. Amen.

December 14

WHEN YOU'RE ALL ALONE IN YOUR SUFFERING

"He was with the wild animals and the angels attended him." (Mark 1:13) Why in the world would John Mark insert such extraneous information? So what if, during his 40 days for being tempted by Satan in the wilderness, he was among wild beasts and the angels were attending him? Why mention such things?

Actually, Mark had a very good reason. For at the very time of this writing Christians were being marched into the Roman Coliseum and were facing the wild beasts – being fed to lions and sewn up in animal skins and thrown to wild dogs. Mark knew the Christian believers would be comforted by the fact that Christ had already been in their shoes and knew by experience what they feared and were suffering. Christ was with the wild beasts too.

An example of the comfort that Christ's suffering brings is displayed in a Time magazine article that reported on a priest who was imprisoned in Romania for years. He was locked up in an underground cell in total darkness. A stench pervaded it 24 hours a day because it was next to an open drain into which five floors of toilets flushed. His bed consisted of two boards on a damp floor. Rats ran across him at night. How could anyone endure these conditions for such a long period of time? The priest said that his greatest source of strength was meditating on the crucifixion of Jesus. At times during these meditations, he was filled with such a deep sense of God's presence that joy overflowed in him.[lxxi]

Whatever it is that you're going through – there is someone in the universe who knows by experience exactly how you feel. The Scripture says, "For we do not have a high priest who cannot sympathize with our suffering, but one who has been tempted in every way as we are, yet without sin." (Hebrews 4:15)

PRAYER: Dear Lord Jesus, please remind me that I am not alone in my suffering, but you are with me. As my path seems all uphill and shadows fall across my way, help me to see your footprints every step of the way. Amen.

December 15

POOR NIGHT VISION

I run a lot at night. I do this because I like the solitude, not because I see well in the dark. In fact, my night vision is very poor and I frequently mistake the shapes and contours of tree trunks for people. I mistake a lone leaf on the sidewalk for a grasshopper, a curved stick for a snake, and a small rock for a toad. Why do I distort reality so much at night? I sense it's because my eyes are only picking up fragmentary information – just bits and pieces of reality – and my mind is trying to make sense of them. It's like trying to visualize the picture of a jigsaw puzzle with only a few of the pieces on hand. At night my mind tries to find meaning from the few pieces of an incomplete picture.

The other day I overheard my NCOIC, SSG Desmond West, say to our chapel secretary, Mrs. Nobuko Motegi, *"Nobu, the next time you go shopping, please pick me up a car(pet) ...for ...my office."* I was immediately incensed. "Why does SSG West need a carpet? Is he so much better than the rest of us who settle for having the bare essentials to do the job?" But as I headed for his office to question him, I picked up more of the conversation. Then I saw Nobu-san and SSG West looking at the printer in his office and it dawned on me. He didn't ask for a **car**pet for his office. He asked for an ink *cartridge* for *the printer* in his office. I only picked up bits and pieces of the message – and my mind was trying to make sense of the fragments of what my ears heard.

So what's the point? That I should have an eye exam, or a hearing exam, or a mental exam? Maybe. But it struck me that, what my mind tries to do with the fragments of information that my eyes and ears pick up, we all tend to do with the painful events of our lives. In the Scripture the Apostle Paul admitted that in this life "we only see as through a dim window and only have a partial understanding." (1 Corinthians 13:12) In other words, we are not getting the whole picture. When tragedy or disappointment darkens our path, our limited view can only detect a few pieces of what is really happening. As a result our troubled minds try to give meaning to the few fragments of discernable reality. It's like when I run in the dark – we are distorting the meaning. We draw the wrong conclusions. Tragedy comes and we conclude that God has failed us, abandoned us, and has been cruel to us and our loved ones. We're trying to see and understand in the dark.

In such times we must cling to the only sure light that we have – the testimony of Holy Scripture. When life is cruel, the Scripture assures us that God is for us, not against us. The Bible promises that nothing can separate us from God's love, which turns our curses into blessings and causes all things to work together for our ultimate good and for His glory (Romans 8:28-39).

PRAYER: Dear Father in heaven, in this life, when I only know in part and see in part, help me to cling to the light of Your word and to find insight and strength from its promises. Amen.

December 16

IRRECONCILABLE DIFFERENCES

In his book, *The Whole Ten Yards*, Frank Gifford relates an amazing story from the early days of "Monday Night Football." The evening before a game in Los Angeles, Gifford had met former Beatles superstar-lyricist and lead vocalist John Lennon at a social event. On a whim the former football star invited Lennon to the next day's game. Surprisingly, Lennon accepted, but cautioned Gifford that he knew nothing about football.

The next evening, Frank Gifford became alarmed when he realized he already had a guest for the game – the former actor and Governor of California, Ronald Reagan. Besides the embarrassment of "doubling up" on two prominent guests, Gifford worried about a possible confrontation. Reagan and Lennon were two generals on opposite sides of a cultural war – both fixed at extreme ends of the ideological, cultural, and political spectrum. Their differences were irreconcilable.

But the evening went off without a hitch. And just before half-time Gifford witnessed a sight he will never forget. He turned to see the two adversaries standing behind him, away from the mikes, monitors, and attention of the audience. He writes, "and there's Reagan, explaining what's going on down on the field. And John looked absolutely enthralled. ...(the two of them) acting like father and son!"

Stories like this remind us that our differences do not make us irreconcilable. We read how the torrential hatred of WWI was brought to a screeching halt by the spirit of the Christmas Season in 1915. We hear of the unbridled prejudice among the 1947 Brooklyn Dodgers against the first African American Major League player being conquered by team spirit and the common goal of winning. Amid the flurry of angry words it's easy to lose hope that people can ever be brought together. But these examples show us that there is much more that unites us than divides us. We are bound by our common needs for love, appreciation, respect, significance, and intimacy. Those are the things that define us as human beings – not color, ethnicity, or political views. But we are most defined by our common need and hunger for God. Though many feel religion is a divisive element, it is more accurate to say that mankind is incurably religious and that God represents the greatest force in reconciling enemies.

Consider two of the most natural enemies that ever lived. One was a political and religious zealot, Simon the ardent Zionist. The other was a collaborator with the enemy, who sold out all national loyalty for monetary gain, Matthew the tax collector. Under any other circumstances Simon would have slit the throat of Matthew. But the power and love of Christ proved a far greater force than anything else in the lives of these men. Jesus Christ called both men to be his apostles. Despite the chasm between them, Christ brought them together. Their Heavenly Father healed all the hurt of their hearts and satisfied all the hunger of their souls. In the arms of their Heavenly Father, they became brothers.

If our common humanity can bring us together - demonstrated in sports, teamwork, and holiday seasons - then surely the God who made us and knows us intimately can reconcile us to each other. The Scripture reasons with us, "If someone says, 'I love God,' and hates his brother, he is a liar; for one who does not love his brother whom he has seen cannot love God whom he has not seen," (1 John 4:20) and "I say to you, love your enemies, and pray for those who persecute you, in order that you may be sons of your Father who is in heaven." (Matthew 5:44-45)

PRAYER: Dear Father in heaven, please heal the hurts of my heart and satisfy the longing of my soul. Open my eyes to the kinship I have with my fellow human beings. Reconcile me to the rest of humanity, by the power of your love. Amen.

December 17

TROUBLED THIS HOLIDAY SEASON?

Ever have a gloomy holiday season? Be encouraged, you're not alone. A famous American General passed through his darkest valley during one Christmas season.

In 1776 Thomas Paine had written, "These are the times that try men's souls." Never truer words, especially for General George Washington - especially as the holiday season approached.

Things could not have been worse for the Commander and Chief of the fledgling Colonies in December of 1776. General Washington had not won a single victory in the War for Independence. He had been driven from the field at the Battle of Long Island and had narrowly escaped total destruction at New York. From battlefield casualties, expired enlistments, disease and desertion, Washington had lost *ninety percent* of his forces. Popular support for the American cause stood only at *thirty-three percent* – the same proportion of the country that favored British rule.

On top of the gloomy strategic picture was Washington's personal suffering from the criticism and schemes of subordinates. Three of his generals - Horatio Gates, Charles Lee, and Thomas Conway, all British-born, had served in foreign commands and two had attained the rank of general officers. These men all openly criticized Washington and believed themselves far better qualified for his job.

And now Washington was in retreat, west of the Delaware River, with the vestiges of his ill-clad, ill-equipped and ill-fed, demoralized Army. In a letter to his brother, Washington confessed, *"I think the game is pretty near up."* But no letter revealed the depths of his despair as did this note to his cousin, Lund Washington.

"If I were to wish the bitterest curse to an enemy on this side of the grave, I should put him in my stead with my feelings - and yet I do not know what plan of conduct to pursue. I see the impossibility of serving with reputation, or doing any essential service to the cause by continuing in command, and yet I am told that if I quit the command, inevitable ruin will follow... . In confidence, I tell you that I never was in such an unhappy, divided state since I was born"

But Washington knew that the country needed more than popular support for the war to be won. America needed leadership – leadership to exercise courage and commitment to the cause in the face of such a crisis.

In a bold move, Washington pulled off a surprise attack on the Hessian Regiment at Trenton *on Christmas Day* and won a stunning victory – capturing over 900 Hessian soldiers, and suffering only two American casualties. Less than two weeks later (on January 2-3, 1777) Washington won two more victories against British forces under General Cornwalis at Trenton and Princeton. These decisive American victories so boosted the morale of the country that within weeks 8,000 new recruits enlisted and reenergized the Army to fight on. Six more years of bloody fighting would follow. But Washington had learned the lesson – that everyone passes through deep, dark valleys of despair, but we will once again reach the heights of joy. He also learned that courage and perseverance in the face of conflict and danger will gain the inevitable triumph.

If this holiday season presents you with some challenging tasks, then be encouraged from the example of a brother in arms from the past. Consider also the encouragement from the Scripture: "Don't be afraid, for I am with you. Don't be discouraged, for I am your God. I will strengthen you and help you. I will hold you up with my victorious right hand." (Isaiah 41:10, *New Living Translation*)

PRAYER: Dear Father in heaven, when people and circumstances are against me, please give me the courage and strength to do what is right and fulfill the work You've called me to do. Amen.

December 18

WHEN HATRED POISONS OUR HEARTS

James Montgomery was a shiftless vagrant. He had failed in school and had dropped out of his apprenticeship as a baker's assistant. He was orphaned at the age of twelve when his Christian missionary parents, whom he hardly knew, died in the West Indies. And, now, with no ambition, no job, no money, and no family in 18th Century England, it was clear that James had no future.

James had another strike against him – he was Irish. And the incessant persecution he faced from the English brewed in his heart the only driving force in his life – bigotry.

James Montgomery did have one love - writing. So when he teamed up with a fellow Irishman-editor of the pro-Irish newspaper, the *Sheffield Register*, James appeared to have found his element. Eventually James took over as editor and used his paper (now the *Sheffield Iris*) as a weapon for Irish independence. Twice his scathing, anti-English editorials landed him in prison. But this only strengthened his resolve to fight.

Yet for all the anger that filled his heart, James Montgomery sensed a deep emptiness in his life. He turned to the faith of his parents, began reading Scripture, and eventually found peace of soul in place of the tempest that raged within him. The first sign of this came with one significant editorial printed on Christmas Eve, 1816. This editorial was actually a poem entitled, "Nativity."

Angels from the realms of glory, Wing your flight o'er all the earth;
Ye who sang creation's story, Now proclaim Messiah's birth.
Come and worship, come and worship, Worship Christ, the newborn King.

Shepherds, in the field abiding, Watching o'er your flocks by night,
God with us is now residing; Yonder shines the infant light.
Come and worship, come and worship, Worship Christ, the newborn King.

Though an Infant now we view Him, He shall fill His Father's throne,
Gather all the nations to Him; Every knee shall then bow down:
Come and worship, come and worship, Worship Christ, the newborn King.

All creation, join in praising, God, the Father, Spirit, Son,
Evermore your voices raising, To th'eternal Three in One.
Come and worship, come and worship, Worship Christ, the newborn King.

Montgomery's "Nativity," took all his readers by surprise. One person in particular took notice – Henry Smart. Smart was a devout Christian and composer of hymns. He had forsaken a promising career as a British lawyer and politician to devote himself to revising the worship of the Church of England. Henry Smart took Montgomery's

"Nativity," composed a stirring melody for it, published it, and made it one of the most beloved hymns of the church.

But this was a strange collaboration. Henry Smart was no Irishman. He was an upper class Englishman, at the center of everything that James Montgomery had fought against. Under any other circumstances these two men would have been worst enemies. But the message of the humble Christ, born in a stable, who died on the cross to reconcile all people to God and to each other, took the sword from James' heart. The holy Child of Christmas brought these two enemies together to produce one of the most beloved of all Christmas carols.

Jesus Christ can do that. The same Lord who commanded us to love our enemies and to pray for those who persecute us, who prayed for his own murderers from the cross, can heal our angry hearts and remove the hatred.

PRAYER: Dear Father in heaven, please heal my angry heart. Reconcile me to God and my fellow human beings. Make me an instrument of your peace. Amen.

December 19

DEADLINES

In the Army we call them "suspense dates." When you get a written task from higher headquarters, the first thing you look for is the infamous "S:" at the upper right-hand corner of the document, followed by a date. That date tells you when the mission must be executed.

Lewis Redner received such a "suspense date" or deadline – 24 December 1868! The task – compose a melody for a poem that the famous 19th clergyman, Phillips Brooks, had written during his trip to the Holy Land three years earlier. The "song" was to be sung at the midnight Christmas Eve service, just a few days hence.

Mr. Redner was the church organist and Phillips Brooks was his pastor. Phillips Brooks was a towering figure, both physically and intellectually, and was one of the most influential preachers of the 19th Century. He had officiated over President Lincoln's funeral and that same year had made a trip to the Holy Land. From that trip experiences Rev. Brooks had composed a five-stanza poem about the birth of Jesus Christ. And now he wanted his poem put to music and so he gave the task to his organist, Lewis Redner.

But Redner kept drawing blanks. Try as he did, he could not come up with a decent melody that would do justice to Rev. Brooks' poem. As the time approached, Mr. Redner became more desperate. This song was to be sung at the church's most important service for the entire year. To fail would be catastrophic. Finally, the last day had come – December 23, 1868 – and he still was unable to compose a melody. Feeling as though he had failed miserably, Lewis Redner finally put the whole matter in the hands of God, praying that God would somehow "work things out." God did. That night, after Redner had prayed himself to sleep, he was awakened from his sound sleep with a haunting tune ringing in his mind, a tune no human being had heard before.

Quickly, he composed the music on paper. The next morning he taught that song to the church's children's choir and it was sung that very evening. When all his own efforts had failed, God came through for Lewis Redner. To his dying day Mr. Redner believed that melody of *"O Little Town of Bethlehem,"* was a gift straight from heaven.

What inhibits us from asking God for help when we are faced with tasks and challenges? God can help us. And, like any parent, God yearns to hear from his children. Why not ask the Lord today for strength, wisdom and guidance to help you with the tasks you have? As he did for Lewis Redner, he will come through for you also. The Scripture tells us, "If anyone lacks wisdom let him ask of God who gives to all men liberally." (James 1:5)

PRAYER: Dear Father in heaven, Please help me today with the tasks and challenges I will face. Raise me above my own inadequacy and limitations and make me more than equal to the task. Amen.

December 20

LOSER!

His name was William Sidney Porter. By his 48th birthday in 1910, he would be dead from cirrhosis of the liver – the culmination of years of alcohol abuse, hard living, and tragic choices.

Some would say his wrong choices included his failure to keep a steady job. Though trained as a pharmacist, William would go through an array of different jobs – bookkeeper, newspaper editor, draftsman, ranch hand, journalist, shepherd, and clerk. But he couldn't get any of them to work.

Some would say his bad decisions also included his choice of a bride. When he eloped in 1887, against the advice of both his in-laws and his own family, he married a woman who was just as infected with tuberculosis as he was. Some would also say his bad decisions included some outright dishonesty. After being fired from his job as a bank teller in the First National Bank of Austin, Texas in 1895, he fled the country pending charges of embezzlement. When he returned to the U.S. in 1897, the authorities were waiting for him. He received a five-year prison sentence.

But William Porter didn't bring all his troubles on himself. He couldn't help it that his mother died from tuberculosis when he was only three – getting his life off to a terrible start. Nor could he stop his wife's death, leaving him a single parent at the beginning of his prison sentence.

To his credit, inmate William Porter tried to do his best to provide for his eight-year-old daughter, Margaret. But what can a jailbird do from prison? *He could write!* And that's just what William Porter did. He began to write short stories – the genre for which he became famous. He wrote and had published no less than a dozen short stories while still behind bars. Of course, he had to conceal his identity. Who would read something from a convict? So he adopted the "pen name," *O. Henry*.

O. Henry was released after serving three years of his five-year sentence. Having discovered his literary gift and first love, O. Henry went on to become the 20th Century's foremost master of the short story – famous for their surprise endings. You're probably familiar with one of them, which is especially popular during the holiday season: *The Gift of the Magi*. It is the love story of a struggling newlywed couple. In it the husband sells his watch in order to buy a comb and brush set for his wife, who has also sold her hair to buy her husband a gold chain for his watch. In the end the young couple realizes their greatest gift is their love for each other.

And it is for this heart-warming story, and hundreds of others like it, that we remember O. Henry. We do not remember him or define his life by his failures, his prison sentence, his indebtedness, his alcoholism, or his times of moral weakness. We remember him and define his life by his contributions and by the joy his stories brought to millions.

In the same way we remember Babe Ruth for his 714 career home runs, not for his 1330 career strike outs. Nor do we remember Thomas Edison for his myriads of failed experiments. We remember him for his 1093 patented inventions – still a record today! Consider what Soichiro Honda, founder of the Honda Motor Company, used to say: *"Success is 99% failure."*

If your record is blemished by failure, take heart. So is everyone else's. "If at first you don't succeed," the old adage says, "you're doing about average." It's better to try to do something and fail, than it is to try to do nothing and succeed. As Babe Ruth once said, "Don't let the fear of striking out hold you back from hitting homeruns." The Scripture reminds us that, "though a righteous man falls seven times, he rises up again." (Proverbs 24:16). Even good people fail – over and over.

PRAYER: Dear Father in heaven, when I stumble and fall, help me, Lord, to learn from my failures, move on and grow stronger and wiser. Amen.

December 21

REGRET

An ancient Italian legend tells the story of a woman named Befana, who was visited one night by the Magi. They asked her directions to the newborn King of Israel. Befana could not show them the way, but did offer them lodging for the night. The next morning the Magi girded themselves for the day's journey and pleaded with Befana to accompany them – for they sought the King of Kings to bring him gifts. Something within the woman yearned to go with them and find the Christ child. But instead she made excuses: "I cannot go. I have too much work here to do."

The Wise Men bid her farewell and left. However, soon Befana regretted her decision. She had given up a once-in-a-lifetime opportunity for the routine details of life. Quickly Befana gathered armfuls of gifts and ran out the door to join the Three Kings in their search for the Christ child. But her quest was unfruitful. Though heartsick, she continued on, day and night. And as her pursuit of the Magi went unfulfilled, she found poor and destitute children along the way. To them she began to give the very gifts intended for the Christ child. According to the legend, she continues to this day, though now an old woman, to give her gifts to poor children, on her way to find the Christ child.

This legend oozes with a theme that resonates in every human heart – the sense of regret. We regret missed opportunities. We regret unkind words and hurtful deeds to others. We regret deeds we can never undo. Regret is painful.

But there can be something redemptive in regret. Consider the story told by Ben Burton of his childhood cruelty to a little boy, Andy Drake. Little Andy Drake's father was in prison. His mother took in laundry, and men, to make ends meet. Andy always seemed to be dirty and dressed in raggedy, over- or under-sized clothes. His rusty, one-of-a-kind bike, had sections of garden hose wired to the wheels in place of tires. Ben Burton and his buddies befriended Andy – but always kept him at a distance. And just to let Andy understand the difference between him and them, they cooked up a little jingle:

Andy Drake don't eat no cake, and his sister don't eat no pie,
If it wasn't for the welfare dole, all the drakes would surely die.

But nothing seemed to dampen Andy's spirits. He remained a cheerful boy and an intensely devoted friend. Then the day came when Ben Burton and his upper middleclass friends decided Andy was not worthy of them. On the happiest day of Andy's life, during a campout with "the gang," Ben and his friends heartlessly mistreated Andy, kicked him out of the group and sent him home crying. His family moved away soon after and Ben Burton would never see Andy again.

But the memory of those events would linger on to torture Ben for years to come. Try as he might, Ben was unable track down Andy. He could not undo "the martyrdom" of that little boy. Ben went on to become a business executive, author, columnist, and high school coach. And in the face of every disadvantaged child and outcast person, Ben saw Andy Drake and vowed to never again betray him. In an open letter to the boy he could never find, Ben confessed that his sins of so long ago had driven him to accept and serve all the Andy Drakes of this life. In a true sense Ben's regret had driven him to turn his own evil into good.[lxxii]

As in the legend of Befana and the Magi, regret for past sins and failures can put us on the path to redemption. And Befana would be pleased to know that her quest of the Christ child *was fulfilled.* For in her giving to the poor she ultimately gave to Christ: "What you have done to the least of these my brothers," said Christ, "you have done unto me." (Matthew 25:40)

PRAYER: Dear Father in heaven, I cannot undo the evil of my past. Please forgive my many sins and grant that my regrets will put me on the path of redemption for my own soul and blessing to others. Amen.

December 22

SUCCESS OR FAILURE?

In 1943 author Philip Van Doren Stern wrote a short story with a Christmas theme that he entitled. *The Greatest Gift*. Try as he did to sell the story, no publisher was interested in buying it. So what Van Doren couldn't *sell* he decided to *give away*. At his own expense the disappointed author printed 200 copies of *The Greatest Gift*, placed them inside Christmas cards, and mailed them to his friends and family. His efforts to publish a story seemed to be a failure.

But not quite. One of Stern's Christmas cards fell into the hands of an RKO Pictures executive who convinced the company to purchase the story for $10,000. But, although RKO executives saw potential in *The Greatest Gift*, none of them knew what to do with it. They commissioned three different scriptwriters to work independently on possible screenplays for a film based on *The Greatest Gift*. All three screenplays were less than satisfying, so a movie-version of *The Greatest Gift* was never made. The story sat on the shelf for the next three years. Again, it seemed like a failure.

But not quite. RKO finally brought *The Greatest Gift* to the attention of veteran director, Frank Capra who immediately saw the story's potential. He bought it for the same price that RKO had paid - $10,000 – who threw in the three screenplays for free. Though he kept elements of both the original story and the three RKO screenplays, Capra created a new script of his own and gave the story a new name – *It's a Wonderful Life*. Convinced he had a fabulous hit on his hands, Capra openly confessed, "This is the film I have waited all my life to make!" Frank Capra finished the film just in time for the 1946 Christmas season. But to his profound disappointment, this "greatest film" opened to mixed reviews from the critics, a disappointing show at the box office (the film barely broke even), and not a single Academy Award.

Within three months from its opening day, *It's a Wonderful Life* was out of sight and mind and its actors and director went on to other projects. Though the movie was re-released in theaters several times in the next decade, for the next 28 years *It's a Wonderful Life* remained largely "on the shelf" – unviewed and forgotten. Again, the story seemed like a failure.

But not quite. By a strange twist of fate *It's a Wonderful Life* was given a rebirth. In 1974 a clerical error prevented the film's copyright from being renewed and the film entered the public domain. *It's a Wonderful Life* could now be purchased and viewed by any TV station. Almost immediately, every TV station across America began showing the film multiple times in a single holiday season and its popularity rapidly grew. The movie's message of hope and the significance of every person's life was powerful. And from the 1970's to the present, watching *It's a Wonderful Life* became an indispensable Christmas tradition for millions of Americans. Though it never won an Oscar nor made a fortune for its creator, movie historians and critics consistently rank *It's a Wonderful Life* among the ten best movies of all time.

Like its main character, George Bailey, this movie could have easily judged itself a failure. Time and again, success seemed to elude this project. Yet today *It's a Wonderful Life* is widely recognized as the most beloved movie ever made. Like George Bailey and the movie, we also may feel as though our life has been a failure. But don't judge yourself prematurely. God will bring all things to light and will reveal the true significance and success of our lives. Our part is to be faithful in our daily tasks and to leave success with God.

PRAYER: Dear Father in heaven, help me to work faithfully in the work to which You have called me. Help me to walk by faith, not by sight, and to leave the results of my work in your hands. Amen.

December 23

WHEN PEACE SEEMS GONE FROM THE EARTH

Things couldn't be darker in those cold December days of 1914. Five months had passed since Europe had rushed head-first into war and already the frightful toll of casualties had reached 800,000 dead and wounded. Millions more would join the ranks of the maimed and dead.

And now the huge war machines of Germany and France were slugging it out, toe-to-toe, just 50 miles from Paris. Already, the Germans, French, and British alike were heart-sick from war. And the approaching holidays only promised to trigger more unbridled bloodshed and killing.

But something strange happened on that Christmas Eve in 1914. Much to the outrage of their high command, British soldiers raised "Merry Christmas" signs above their trenches, wishing "good will" to the enemy. The Germans responded with an outburst of Christmas carols. The French and British echoed back with carols of their own. The feelings of brotherly love and good will seemed to get out of hand. Against the protests and direct orders of their officers, both German and British soldiers left their trenches, greeted each other with Christmas songs and exchanged gifts. At some spots along the Western Front, soldiers from opposing sides played games of soccer together. That day on the bloody plain called "No Man's Land" in war-torn France, the Prince of Peace reigned supreme. Even the next day, this spontaneous truce could not be overturned. Neither side seemed willing to fire the first shot.

Only when fresh troops arrived and the high command threatened to punish such kindness toward the enemy as treason did the war resume.[lxxiii]

How profound that even mankind's professional killers were softened by the celebration of Christ's birth. Yet the Bible promises that, one day Christ, the Prince of Peace, will return to earth to establish His Kingdom. On that glorious day peace will cover the planet. The prophets foretell that the lion will lay down with the lamb, swords will be beaten into plowshares and spears into pruning hooks, and no longer will men learn war.

But the peace of Christ can always begin in our own hearts, families and work places. Scripture tells us that the Prince of Peace knocks at the door of each heart seeking to still the storms that rage within us and melt away the hatred that consumes us. Pray for world peace. But seek peace within your own soul by allowing the Prince of Peace to come in and sit upon the throne of your heart. Let his reign of peace begin in your life today.

PRAYER: Dear Lord, please forgive my failures, be enthroned in my life and bring peace to my war-torn heart. Amen.

WHEN YOU FEEL LIKE A MISFIT

Bob May, depressed and broken-hearted, stared out his drafty apartment window into the chilling December night. His 4-year-old girl Barbara sat on his lap quietly sobbing. Bob's wife, Evelyn, was dying of cancer. Little Barbara couldn't understand why her mommy could never come home, why she could never play with her mommy, why her mommy could never tuck her in bed or even give her a hug. Barbara looked up into her dad's eyes and said, "Why isn't mommy just like everybody else's mommy?"

Bob's jaw tightened and his eyes welled with tears. Her haunting question brought waves of grief, but also of anger. It had been the story of Bob's life. Life always had to be different for Bob. Small and frail as a child, Bob was often bullied by other boys. He also proved too small to compete in sports. He was often called names he'd rather not remember. From childhood, Bob was different and never seemed to fit in.

Bob did complete college, married his loving wife and was grateful to get his job as a copywriter at Montgomery Ward during the Great Depression. Then he was blessed with his little girl. But it was all short-lived. Evelyn's bout with cancer stripped them of all their savings and now Bob and his daughter were forced to live in a two-room flat in the Chicago slums.

Evelyn died just days before Christmas in 1938. Bob struggled to give hope to his child, for whom he couldn't even afford to buy a Christmas gift. But if he couldn't buy a gift, he was determined a make one – a storybook! Bob had created an animal character in his own mind and told the animal's story to his girl to give her comfort and hope. Again and again Bob told the story, embellishing it more with each telling. Who was the character? What was the story all about? The story Bob May created was his own autobiography in fable form. The character he created was a misfit outcast like he was. The name of the character? A little reindeer named Rudolph, with a big shiny nose.

Bob finished the book just in time to present to his little girl on Christmas day. But the story doesn't end there. The general manager of Montgomery Ward caught wind of the little storybook and offered Bob May a nominal fee to purchase the rights to print the book. Ward's went on to print the storybook, *Rudolph the Red-Nosed Reindeer* and distribute it to children visiting Santa Claus in their stores. By 1946 Ward's had printed and distributed more than six million copies of *Rudolph*.

That same year, a major publisher wanted to purchase the rights from Ward's to print an updated version of the book. In an unprecedented gesture of kindness, the CEO of Ward's returned all rights back to Bob May. The book became a best seller. Many toy and marketing deals followed and Bob May, now remarried with a growing family, became wealthy from the story he created to comfort his grieving daughter.[lxxiv]

But the story doesn't end there either. Bob's brother-in-law, Johnny Marks, made a song adaptation to Rudolph. Though the song was turned down by such popular vocalists as Bing Crosby and Dinah Shore, it was recorded by the singing cowboy, Gene Autry. "Rudolph the Red-Nosed Reindeer" was released in 1949 and became a phenomenal success, selling more records than any other Christmas song, with the exception of "White Christmas." The gift of love that Bob May created for his daughter so long ago kept on returning back to bless him again and again. And Bob May learned the lesson, just like his dear friend Rudolph, that being different isn't so bad. In fact, being different can be a blessing.

PRAYER: Dear Father, thank you for making me different from everyone else. Please help me to accept myself and appreciate my differences and to use them to benefit others. Amen.

December 25

CHRISTMAS: A TIME OF HOPE

Noel Regney was deeply discouraged. He had reason to be. His dreams of writing classical music had gone unfulfilled and now, in his fifties, it looked like they never would be. Besides all this, his recurring nightmares, born out of the horrors he witnessed in World War II, became intensified by the subsequent wars in Korea, Vietnam, and the ever-present tension between America and the Soviet Union.

Noel was born and raised in France. His sensitive heart loved and nurtured one thing – music. But his dreams of one day composing classical music were dashed to pieces when the Nazis conscripted him into their army. Horrified by the cruelty and atrocities of the German war machine, Noel deserted, fled back to France and became a fighter for the resistance. But Noel's sensitive nature, unfit for the pain and heartbreak of war, suffered the deepest emotional scars from his experience.

Then life seemed to lead Noel on a brighter path when he immigrated to the United States and married a beautiful and talented pianist/songwriter, Gloria Shayne. Gloria enjoyed a measure of success as a writer of Rock and Roll songs. But for Noel, there was neither success nor peace of mind. And now, in the 1960s - with the Rock and Roll as the undisputed king and classical music a mere relic - all hope of success was fading. Far worse than the discord in his own heart, was the fading hope for world peace in the shadow of the Soviet and nuclear threats.

In this time of despair, Noel's mind went back to the Bible stories he had heard and read as a child. He recalled the story of a star that appeared in the East announcing of the birth of the long-awaited Prince of Peace and the Savior of the world - the holy child of Bethlehem. Noel realized that with the birth of every child comes a message from God that He is not yet finished with us. How much truer with the birth of Christ, our Redeemer!

From his re-discovered faith Noel found inspiration to write the following words, that his wife Gloria put to music.

Said the night wind to the little lamb,
do you see what I see
Way up in the sky, little lamb,
do you see what I see
A star, a star, dancing in the night
With a tail as big as a kite
With a tail as big as a kite

Said the little lamb to the shepherd boy,
do you hear what I hear
Ringing through the sky, shepherd boy,
do you hear what I hear
A song, a song, high above the trees
With a voice as big as the sea
With a voice as big as the sea

Said the shepherd boy to the mighty king,
do you know what I know
In your palace warm, mighty king,
do you know what I know
A Child, a Child shivers in the cold
Let us bring Him silver and gold
Let us bring Him silver and gold

Said the king to the people everywhere,
listen to what I say
Pray for peace, people everywhere!
listen to what I say
The Child, the Child, sleeping in the night
He will bring us goodness and light
He will bring us goodness and light.

Within a matter of days after the husband-wife collaboration that produced *"Do You Hear What I Hear?"* Noel and Gloria's song was recorded by the Harry Simeone Chorale and became a phenomenal success. Author Ace Collins explains, "The couple could not have dared imagine the effect (this song) would have on the nation. At the height of the Cold War, millions, like Noel, were yearning for peace and hope. This Carol's combination of words and music powerfully voiced those prayers. Newspaper stories of the time wrote of drivers hearing it for the first time on the radio and pulling their cars off the road to listen. ... It was sung by church choirs, became an integral part of television specials, and inspired numerous magazine features and even sermons."

In our times of discouragement and profound fear, remember the message bound up in the babe of Bethlehem. God is not yet finished with us. He will bring us goodness and light.[lxxv]

PRAYER: Dear Father in heaven, turn our hearts and minds to the Child of Bethlehem, the Prince of Peace, this holiday season. May his kingdom and peace fill the world and bring healing to the nations. Amen.

December 26

WHEN YOUR CONTRIBUTION IS NOT APPRECIATED

The internal combustion engine in your car represents the epitome of consumption and ingratitude. It has an insatiable lust for gasoline and consumes all you feed it. But don't expect your engine to give thanks for all your supply of gasoline. Of course, it's just a machine – but it's a hungry machine. And no matter how much you try to feed it, you will never flood it or overwhelm it with fuel. On the contrary, if you floor your gas pedal, your engine will surge with power, use everything you give it, and then demand more and more.

Sometimes people in "support roles" may feel a little like the guy at the gas pedal. They support people, units, and organizations that take freely, consume, and then demand more and more. Supplying them what they need doesn't satisfy them for long. In fact, your support to others only empowers them to do more and then to ask for more at an increasingly accelerated rate. And, should you dare to falter in fulfilling their demands, don't expect any gratitude for past support. You will only hear outcries and complaints over your lack of support. The role of supporting others can certainly be a thankless job.

The unsurpassed Italian conductor Arturo Toscanini was once asked which is the most difficult instrument to play. He replied, "Second fiddle." He ought to know, he played second fiddle in obscure South American orchestras for years.

Maybe you're stuck in a support role, playing "second fiddle" to others and receiving little credit but lots of grief. Be faithful in your work. God is mindful of and measures your success on the basis of your faithfulness. The Scripture says, "God is not unjust so as to forget your work and the love which you have shown toward his name and by serving others ..." (Hebrews 6:10)

PRAYER: Dear Father in heaven, help me to be faithful in the obscure and thankless task to which you've called me. Help me to look beyond all earthly reward and recognition to seek after an eternal reward with you. Amen.

December 27

ONE SOWS, ANOTHER REAPS

It was Veterans Day when Demos Shakarian, founder of the Full Gospel Businessmen's Fellowship, was traveling by air from New York to Los Angeles. His journey was divided into several connecting flights, from New York to Chicago, from Chicago to Denver, and from Denver to Los Angeles. The trip was stressful because he was racing to a speaking engagement in LA and was forced to change planes at every airport. Shakarian had to literally run from one gate to another in a mad dash to catch his flights.

At the JFK Airport Shakarian was confronted by an elderly Veteran seeking donations and giving traditional poppies. But Shakarian was in a big hurry. He apologized to the old Vet as he dashed passed him, "I'm sorry, I'm late for my plane." At Chicago's O'Hare Airport, he again had to run past a Veteran who was asking for donations. "I'm very sorry, sir. I can't stop. I've got to run." In the Denver airport the same scene repeated itself, with Demos Shakarian feeling increasingly remorseful each time he rejected the Veteran's request.

So by the time he landed at the LA International Airport, Demos Shakarian was determined to find a Veteran and give a generous donation. And so he did. The first Veteran he saw received his gift. In fact, the Veteran didn't even have to ask. Shakarian's heart, softened by all the previous Veterans, was eager to give.

That night, as he spoke to a group of businessmen, Shakarian told the story and then asked the question: "Which Veteran sold me the poppy? You might be tempted to credit the last Veteran for the sale, but I assure you that his effort was the smallest. In truth, all four Veterans sold me the poppy. For although I turned the first three Veterans down, they all tugged at my heart and finally convinced me to give a donation."

Shakarian's point was this: "One sows and another reaps" (John 4:37), but they are all part of the same work. Jesus explained to his disciples, "I sent you to reap what you have not worked for. Others have done the hard work, and you have reaped the benefits of their labor" (John 4:38) – just as the other three Veterans had done all the hard work and the fourth reaped the benefits of their labors.

Sometimes we get discouraged because we seldom, if ever, seem to lead anyone to put their faith in Christ. We faithfully share the gospel with others but, as Demos Shakarian turned away the Veterans, our efforts seem unfruitful. But don't lose heart. God is using you to do the hard work – the hard work of sowing the seed of the Gospel and preparing the heart of the sinner to finally open his heart to God and put his faith in Jesus.

PRAYER: Dear Father in heaven, please help me not to lose heart, but to be faithful in sharing my faith – through my actions as well as my words. Amen.

December 28

WHEN WE FEAR THE UNKNOWN

The unknown. What is it? It is an un-scalable mountain, an unbearable burden, an impregnable barrier. The unknown is something we approach with great anxiety and apprehension. We inch toward it, like a man shuffling forward in the dark, fearful of stubbing his toe, of falling headlong into a ditch, of stepping off a cliff.

Actually, experience teaches us differently. The unknown – the thing we cringe before – rarely meets our fearful expectations. Consider the experience of the unknown in one man's life – fighter ace and test pilot, Captain Chuck Yeager.

Chuck Yeager had been recruited in 1947 to test the experimental rocket plane, the Bell X-1, and hopefully to push it beyond the sound barrier (Mach 1 or 760 miles per hour at sea level). Although designed to fly twice the speed of sound, the Bell engineers and pilots who had flown the X-1 demanded extreme caution in Yeager's X-1 tests - and with reason. Many other pilots who approached the speed of sound in conventional aircraft usually paid a severe price. They all experienced extreme buffeting and turbulence and were forced to slow their aircraft down. Scientists feared that, as a plane flew faster, the air to its front would be compressed so much so that the aircraft's controls would freeze and its wings would rip off. Early in 1947 Geoffrey DeHaviland died when his jet, the Swallow, disintegrated as he approached supersonic flight. This tragedy solidified the idea of a real "sound barrier," an impregnable wall in the sky.

So in his X-1 test flights Chuck Yeager was only allowed to inch forward – increasing his speed by a mere two hundredths of a Mach from one flight to the next. Over a period of months his flight speed creeped forward from Mach 0.82 to Mach 0.84 to Mach 0.86 – closer and closer to the unknown, toward the sound barrier.

Then came the day – October 14, 1947. Yeager reached Mach 0.92. Then he pushed the X-1 faster, to Mach 0.96, and noticed something. After some initial buffeting, at around Mach 0.94, the faster he pushed his plane the smoother his aircraft rode.

Suddenly his Speedometer went off the scale and fluctuated wildly. What was going on? *He had reached supersonic flight! Chuck Yeager had broken the sound barrier!*

Yeager felt a mix of relief and let-down. He explains, "After all the anxiety, breaking the sound barrier turned out to be a perfectly paved speedway. …And that was it. I sat up there feeling kind of numb, but elated. After all the anticipation to achieve this moment, it really was a let-down. It took an instrument meter to tell me what I'd done. There should've been a bump in the road, something to let you know you had just punched a nice clean hole through that sonic barrier. The unknown was a mere poke through Jello."[lxxvi]

And so it is with most of our fearful "unknowns" – they rarely meet our expectations. They are not the burdens or the barriers we fear.

The Scripture gives more than one hundred commands *not* to be afraid. For instance, "Fear thou not, for I am with thee; be not dismayed, for I am thy God. I will strengthen thee; yea, I will help thee; yea, I will uphold thee with the right hand of my righteousness." (Isaiah 41:10) Someone said: "Fear knocked at the door. Faith answered. No one was there." Answer your fear of the unknown with faith.

PRAYER: Dear Father in heaven, help me to face the unknowns of my life with courage and with faith in You. Remind me that there is nothing in this world that You and I cannot handle. Amen.

December 29

WHAT SHOULD OUR PRIORITIES BE?

On August 24, AD 79, more than 1900 years ago, the 4200-foot volcano called Mount Vesuvius, erupted following weeks of tremors and smaller eruptions. The nearby cities of Pompeii and Herculaneum were engulfed by pyroclastic flows of super-heated ash. The complacent inhabitants, who had ignored the volcano's warnings, all perished.

Decayed bodies of the people trapped by the disaster have left cavities in the hardened ash. By pouring liquid plaster into them, archaeologists made casts of the victims.

Many of these human casts are deeply moving to look at. Some reveal parents sheltering children and couples in a final embrace before death. But one of these cavities in Pompeii is quite puzzling. The cast is of a man holding a sword. His foot rests on a pile of gold and silver. Scattered about him are five bodies, probably would-be looters. In his final moments before death he was clinging to and fighting keep this world's possessions.

Someone once asked the question, "If you were on the Titanic - after it struck an iceberg and was sinking - would you trouble yourself by straightening the deck chairs? Before hopping into one of the life boats, would you run back to make sure your cabin door was secure?" Obviously you would not. Saving your life and the lives of those you love is all that matters in such a desperate situation.

Yet when we devote our fragile existence to the pursuit of wealth and materialistic success - at the expense of our family relationships and to the neglect of our souls – we are just as foolish as the man straightening deck chairs on the Titanic. In the Scripture Jesus said, "Do not lay up for yourselves treasure on earth, where moth and rust corrupt and where thieves break through and steal. But lay up for yourselves treasure in heaven, where no moth or rust destroys and where thieves do not break in and steal. For where your treasure is, there will your heart be also." (Matthew 6:19-21)

PRAYER: Dear Father in heaven, open my eyes to the things in life that matter most and help me to pursue them. Remind me that this life is heaven's dressing room and its purpose is to prepare for the life to come. Amen.

December 30

THE POISON WE CONSUME

They call him *Monsieur Mangetout* – "Mr. Eat-it-all." His real name is Michael Lotito and he is also known as "the man with the iron gut." Why? Because he is renowned for consuming huge amounts of 'indigestibles." Since he began his bizarre diet in 1959, Lotito has eaten eleven bicycles, seven shopping carts, a cash register, a washing machine, a television, nearly 1,000 feet of chain, and a metal coffin. But Lotito assures us, "The coffin was empty – no one was inside." Probably the most impressive of his meals was his consumption of a *Cessna 150 airplane* – 2,500 pounds of steel, rubber, aluminum, and Plexiglas.

How does he do it? He cuts the metal and Plexiglas into tiny pieces about the size of a thumbnail. The rubber tires he eats are cut into thin strips and consumed in "a stew." And he lubricates his gastrointestinal track with castor oil for the broken glass he swallows. All in all, up to present Michael Lotito has devoured over ten tons of metal and other junkyard debris. Lotito's ability to eat and digest things that are poisonous to most people continues to baffle doctors.

But consider the steady diet of media violence, hatred, cynicism, moral ambiguity, and concentrated sex that most Americans consume. By comparison Lotito's menu doesn't seem so bad. He poisons the body. Most of us poison the soul.

In the Scripture God says to His children: *"Why do you spend your money on what is not food and your labor on what does not satisfy? ...Give ear and come to Me; hear Me that your soul may live."* (Isaiah 55:2-3) Why do we feed on "foods" that sicken our souls, turn us into spiritual wimps, and fuel our bigotry and racial hatred?

Are you hurting and hungry? Listen to the words of Jesus: *"I am the Bread of life. He who comes to Me shall never hunger. He who believes in Me shall never thirst."* (John 6:35)

PRAYER: Dear Lord, please heal my sin-sick soul. Cleanse me, forgive me, transform me, and fill my poor heart with Your love, by the power of Your Holy Spirit. Amen.

December 31

WHY WE SHRINK FROM CHALLENGES

In his *Memoirs*, General Ullyses S. Grant explains the fear he felt as a young man about to begin his first year at West Point. "I really had no objection to going to West Point, except that I had a very exalted idea of the requirements necessary to get through. I did not believe I possessed them, and could not bear the idea of failing." He goes on to explain, "I would have been glad (while *en route* to West Point) to have had a steamboat or railroad collision, or any other accident happen, by which I might have received a temporary injury sufficient to make me ineligible, for a time, to enter the academy. Nothing of the kind occurred, and I had to face the music."[lxxvii]

Isn't it amazing that the very man who would someday command the most powerful army on earth and fight in history's bloodiest battles would shrink from the first challenge that confronted him! Yet his words are insightful as to the basic reasons we all shrink from challenges in life: 1. We have an exalted view of the challenge; 2. We have an inferior view of ourselves; 3. We have an unrealistic view of the options; 4. We have no view of God, only of our fears.

The nation of Israel was also faced with such a challenge. In the book of Numbers (chapters 13-14) we read of how Israel came to the threshold of the Promised Land. Now, after 400 years of slavery, all their hopes and dreams were about to be realized. Tragically they backed away from the challenge of taking the good land which the Lord had promised them. Why?

First, they had a distorted view of the challenge. In Deuteronomy 1.29 we read of how they wanted to send spies into the Promised Land to check it out before entering.

As a result of their inspection they received a panoramic view of every problem they would face for the next 20 years. They became overwhelmed. They saw too much all at once.

The Lord had already promised them that He would fight their battles for them and that they did not have to take the land all at once, but "little by little" (Exodus. 23.27-30). Even our Lord Jesus told us to handle only today's challenges and leave tomorrow's alone (Matthew 6.34).

Second, Israel had an inferior view of itself. Numbers 13.33 tells us that the Israelites saw themselves as "grasshoppers" next to the "giants" who lived in the Promised Land. How sad! They momentarily forgot how special they were as the people of God. They also forgot a fundamental lesson we all must learn. The challenge that awaits us has been conquered by many people before us - none of them any better than we are!

Third, Israel had an unrealistic view of its options. They forgot they had nowhere else to go. Just think of what U.S. Grant would have missed if he shrank back from going to West Point! His only other option was to live a life of regret. Israel spent the next 38 years grieving over its act of cowardice. Let's face the music and avoid their example!

Fourth, Israel had no view of God, only of its fears. U.S. Grant feared failure. So did Israel. Yet the road to every success is paved with many a failure. Consider the following: Babe Ruth hit 714 home runs; a record that stood for 38 years! But who remembers that he also once held the record for strike outs - 1,330?

Thomas Edison, America's greatest inventor, created the first practical light bulb. Yet this single invention was preceded by 2,500 failures! In the words of Robert F. Kennedy: "Only those who dare to fail greatly can ever achieve greatly."

We must take risks. Fortunately we do not have to take them alone - the Lord Jesus tells us that He will never leave us or forsake us (Hebrews 13.5) and that we can do all things through His power (Philippians 4.13).

PRAYER: Loving Heavenly Father, Your faithfulness to me in the past gives me confidence for the present. Help me not to doubt You, but to take the risks I must and rest in Your unfailing love. Amen.

END NOTES

[i] Information from *Isaac Asimov's Book of Facts, 2201 Fascinating Facts*
[ii] Information from *2201 Fascinating Facts* and *Uncle John's Bathroom Reader Plunges into the Universe*
[iii] Information from *Uncle John's Extraordinary Book of Facts*
[iv] Information from *The Greatest Stories Never Told*, Rick Beyer
[v] Information from Kevin Conrad, *Wisdom for Faithful Living Today*
[vi] Stories from *The World of Ripley's Believe It or Not*
[vii] Quote from Harold Kushner, *Becoming Aware*
[viii] Quotes from Donald T. Phillips, *Lincoln Stories for Leaders*
[ix] Quoted in *Christus Approximus*, Jerry McCulley
[x] Information from Robert Harris, "Fallacies, Assumptions, and Creative Thinking," *C120 Critical Reasoning and Creative Thinking*
[xi] From Steve Jobs' 2005 commencement address at Stanford University
[xii] Information from Paul Lee Tan, *15,000 Illustrations*; "Dwight David Eisenhower, The Centennial," *U.S. Army Center for Military History;* Stephen Oates, *With Malice Toward None*
[xiii] Information from *Uncle John's Biggest Ever Bathroom Reader*
[xiv] Information from *Isaac Asimov's Book of Facts* and "The Magnificent Migrating Monarch," *Creation ex Nihilo* 20(1):29-30
[xv] Information from *The Handbook of Texas*
[xvi] Information from *Bits and Pieces*
[xvii] Information from Paul Harvey, Jr., *Destiny*
[xviii] Information and quotes from *Isaac Asimov's Book of Facts* and from *Uncle John's Bathroom Reader Plunges into the Universe*
[xix] Information and quotes from Robert Schuller, *Daily Power Thoughts*, and *Isaac Asimov's Book of Facts*
[xx] Information and quotes from "Girl with Rare Disease Doesn't Know Pain," *CNN.com*, 11-1-04
[xxi] Information from *Stories Behind Everyday Things*
[xxii] Information from *The World's Worst Historical Disasters*
[xxiii] Information from "Heaven's Gate," in *Amazing Stories of Survival*
[xxiv] Information from William J. Bausch, *60 More Seasonal Homilies*
[xxv] Information from Paul G. Stoltz, *Adversity Quotient*
[xxvi] Information from *2201 Fascinating Facts*; "Halley's Comet," by Calvin Hamilton; "What we have learned about Halley's Comet," *Astronomical Society of the Pacific*, Fall, 1986
[xxvii] Information from *Above and Beyond*
[xxviii] Information from Goldman, M. Hirsh, *The Blunder Book*
[xxix] Quote from Harold Kushner, *Becoming Aware*
[xxx] Information from *The Experts Speak*, pp. 193, 307
[xxxi] Information from *Above and Beyond*
[xxxii] Information from *Uncle John's Extraordinary Book of Facts*
[xxxiii] Information from M. Hirsch Goldberg's *The Blunder Book*
[xxxiv] Information from *Isaac Asimov's Book of Facts*
[xxxv] Information from John Maxwell, *Failing Forward*, and Frances Heerey, *Biographies: God at their Sides*

[xxxvi] Information from *Isaac Asimov's Book of Facts* and *Sower's Seeds: Sixth Planting*
[xxxvii] Information from *Isaac Asimov's Book of Facts*
[xxxviii] Information from *Stories Behind Everyday Things*
[xxxix] Information from *Uncle John's Biggest Ever Bathroom Reader*, *A Treasury of Bible Illustrations; Breaking Through to the Next Level*
[xl] Information from *Isaac Asimov's Book of Facts* and Raymond McHenry, *Something to Think About*
[xli] Information from William J. Bausch, *A World of Stories*
[xlii] Quote from *How Your Church Family Works*, Peter L. Steinke
[xliii] Information from *Uncle John's Bathroom Reader Plunges into History Again*
[xliv] Information from *Isaac Asimov's Book of Facts* and "The Story of Oil in Pennsylvania," *The Paleontological Research Institution*
[xlv] Information from *Isaac Asimov's Book of Facts*
[xlvi] Information from *The Civil War: Strange and Fascinating Facts*
[xlvii] Information from *The Greatest Adventures of All Time*
[xlviii] Information from *The Blunder Book*, M. Hirsh Goldberg
[xlix] Information from *Strange Stories, Amazing Facts*
[l] Information from Chris McNab, *The World's Worst Historical Disasters*
[li] Information from J. John and Mark Stibbe, *A Box of Delights*
[lii] Information from *Isaac Asimov's Book of Facts*
[liii] Information from *Uncle John's Ahh-Inspiring Bathroom Reader*
[liv] Information from Derrick Johnson, *The Wonder of America* and "In a 200-year tradition, most Christian Missionaries are American," *Reuters*, February 20, 2012.
[lv] Information from *Isaac Asimov's Book of Facts*
[lvi] Information from *365 Fascinating Facts from the World of Discovery*
[lvii] Information from *The Greatest Military Stories Never Told*
[lviii] Information from Gregory A. Coco, *War Stories*
[lix] Information from Mark Link, *Jesus: A Contemporary Walk with Jesus*
[lx] Information from *Uncle John's Bathroom Reader Plunges into History*
[lxi] Information and quotes from Donald R. Nelson, *The Business Journal*, and Charles Kuralt, *On the Road with Charles Kuralt*
[lxii] Information and quotes from Mark Link, *Mission: Praying Scripture in a Contemporary Way* and *Our Daily Bread*
[lxiii] Information from *People*, August 5, 2002
[lxiv] Information from *Uncle John's Biggest Even Bathroom Reader*
[lxv] Information from *Uncle John's Bathroom Reader Plunges in History Again*
[lxvi] Information from *Bits and Pieces* and the Milton Hershey website
[lxvii] Information from Roy B. Zuck
[lxviii] Information from Mark Link, *Mission: Praying Scripture in a Contemporary Way*
[lxix] Information from Mark Link, *Action: Praying the Scripture in a Contemporary Way*
[lxx] Information from Mark Link, *Challenge: Praying the Scripture in a Contemporary Way*
[lxxi] Information from Mark Link, *Mission: Praying Scripture in a Contemporary Way*
[lxxii] Information from *A Second Helping of Chicken Soup for the Soul*
[lxxiii] Information from Dr. Paul Lee Tan
[lxxiv] Information from Ace Collins, *Stories behind the Best-Loved Songs of Christmas*
[lxxv] Information from Ace Collins, *Stories behind the Best-Loved Songs of Christmas*
[lxxvi] From *Yeager: An Autobiography*

[lxxvii] Ulysses S. Grant, *Memoirs*, pp.11-13

BIBLIOGRAPHY

Unless cited in the text or in the endnotes, most of the information used in this book is from the following sources.

"Admiral Nimitz: Thunder of the Pacific," in the documentary, *The History Channel Presents Pearl Harbor: The Definitive Documentary of the Day That Will Forever Live in Infamy*, 1996.

Bouzereau, Laurent, "All About 'The Birds,'" documentary on the making of "The Birds," Universal Studios, 2000.

Anderson, Nancy Scott and Dwight, *The Generals: Ulysses S. Grant and Robert E. Lee*, Wings Books, Avernel, NJ, 1987.

Aron, Paul, *Unsolved Mysteries of American History: An Eye-Opening Journey through 500 Years of Discoveries, Disappearances, and Baffling Events*, John Wiley & Sons, Inc., New York, 1997.

Asimov, Isaac, *Isaac Asimov's Book of Facts*, Bell Publishing Company, New York, 1981.

Benn, Colleen, "Creating Special Effects (for "A Beautiful Mind")," Universal Pictures, 2002.

Beyer, Rick, *The Greatest Stories Never Told: 100 Tales from History to Astonish, Bewilder, & Stupefy*, Harper Collins, New York, 2003.

Beyer, Rick, *The Greatest War Stories Never Told: 100 Tales from Military History to Astonish, Bewilder, & Stupefy*, Harper Collins, New York, 2005.

Bausch, William J., *60 More Seasonal Homilies*, Twenty-Third Publications, Mystic, CT, 2002.

Bausch, William J., *A World of Stories for Preachers and Teachers and All Who Love Stories that Move and Challenge*, Twenty-Third Publications, Mystic, CT, 1998.

Bausch, William J., More Telling Stories, Compelling Stories, Twenty-Third Publications, Mystic, CT, 1993.

Bausch, William J., *Once Upon a Gospel: Inspiring Homilies and Inspiring Reflections*, Twenty-Third Publications, Mystic, CT, 2008.

Bausch, William J., *Still Preaching After All These Years: 40 More Seasonal Homilies*, Twenty-Third Publications, Mystic, CT, 2005.

Bausch, William J., *The Word In and Out of Season: Homilies for Preachers, Reflections for Seekers*, Twenty-Third Publications, Mystic, CT, 2000.

Bausch, William J., *The Yellow Brick Road: A Storyteller's Approach to the Spiritual Journey*, Twenty-Third Publications, Mystic, CT, 1999.

Bausch, William J., *Timely Homilies: The Wit and Wisdom of an Ordinary Pastor*, Twenty-Third Publications, Mystic, CT, 1990.

Cavanaugh, Brian, *The Sower's Seeds: One Hundred and Twenty Inspiring Stories for Preaching, Teaching and Public Speaking*, Paulist Press, Mahwah, NJ, 2004.

Cerf, Christopher; Navasky, Victor, *The Experts Speak: The Definative Compendium of Authoritative Misinformation* , Villard, New York, 1984.

Chambers Book of Facts, New Edition, Chambers Harrap Publishers, Edinburgh, 2005.

Cheatham, Craig, *The World's Worst Cars: From Pioneering Failures to Multimillion Dollar Disasters*, Barnes and Noble Books, 2007.

Collins, Ace, *Stories Behind The Best-Loved Songs Of Christmas*, Running Press Book Publishers, 2004.

Colson, Charles; Morse, Anne, *How Now Shall We Live Devotional*, Tyndale House Publishers, Wheaton, IL, 2004.

Delaney, John J., *Dictionary of Saints*, Doubleday & Company, Inc., Garden City, NY, 1980.

DeYoung, Donald, *Fascinating Facts from the World of Discovery*, New Leaf Press, Green Forest, AR, 2000.

Dougherty, Martin, The World's Worst Weapons: *From Pioneering Failures to Multimillion Dollar Disasters*, Barnes and Noble Books, 2007.

Dupuy, Trevor N.; Johnson, Curt; Bongard, David L., *The Harper Encyclopedia of Military History*, Castle Books, Edison, NJ, 1992.

Edelman, Joe; Samson, David, *Useless Knowledge: Answers to Questions You'd Never Think to Ask*, St. Martin's Griffin, 2002.

Freeman, Allyn; Golden, Bob, *Why Didn't I Think of That: Bizarre Origins of Ingenious Inventions We Couldn't Live Without*, John Wiley & Sons, Inc., New York, 1997.

Gilbert, Rob, *Even More of the Best of Bits and Pieces*, The Economic Press, Inc., Fairfield, NJ, 2000.

Gilbert, Rob, *More of the Best of Bits and Pieces*, The Economic Press, Inc., Fairfield, NJ, 1997.

Gillis, Michael, "The Quiet Man: The Joy of Ireland," a documentary on the making of "The Quiet Man," Artisan Home Entertainment, 2002.

Goldman, M. Hirsh, *The Blunder Book: Colossal Errors, Minor Mistakes, and Surprising Slipups That Have Changed the Course of History*, Quill/William Morrow, New York, 1984.

"Gothic Cathedrals: Notre Dame to the National Cathedral," *The History Channel*, 1994.

Graham, Billy, *Just As I Am: The Autobiography of Billy Graham*, Harper Collins Publishers, New York, 1997.

Grant, Ulysses S., *Personal Memoirs of U. S. Grant,* (Da Capo Press, New York, 1982.

Gregory, Leland H., III, *Great Government Goofs*, Bantam Doubleday Dell Publishing Group, Inc., New York, 1997.

Harris, Robert, "Fallacies, Assumptions, and Creative Thinking," *C120 Critical Reasoning and Creative Thinking, Fort Leavenworth, KS*

Harvey, Paul, Jr., *Paul Harvey's The Rest of The Story*, Bantam Books, New York, 1977.

Harvey, Paul, Jr., *More of Paul Harvey's The Rest of The Story*, Bantam Books, New York, 1980.

Harvey, Paul, Jr., *Paul Harvey's For What It's Worth*, Bantam Books, New York, 1991.

"The Heroic Chaplain," *Soldier*, November, 1995.

Hutchins, Brian, *Webster's New World Book of Facts*, Webster's New World, 1999.

John, J.; Stibbe, Mark, *A Barrel of Fun*, Monarch Books, Oxford, UK, 2001.

John, J.; Stibbe, Mark, *A Box of Delights*, Monarch Books, Oxford, UK, 2003.

John, J.; Stibbe, Mark, *A Bucket of Surprises*, Monarch Books, Oxford, UK, 2003.

Kerr, Paul, "Guns for Hire: The Making of the Magnificent Seven,"Metro-Goldwyn-Mayer, 2005.

Lenehan, Arthur F., *The Best of Bits and Pieces*, The Economic Press, Inc., Fairfield, NJ, 1994.

Link, Mark, *Action: Praying Scripture in a Contemporary Way – Year C*, Thomas More Association, 1997.

Link, Mark, *Challenge: A Daily Meditation Program Based on the Spiritual Exercises of Saint Ignatius*, Thomas More Association, 1993.

Link, Mark, *Jesus: A Contemporary Walk with Jesus*. Thomas More Association, 1997.

Link, Mark, *Vision: Praying Scripture in a Contemporary Way – Year B*, Thomas More Association, 1998.

Louis, David, *2201 Fascinating Facts: 2 Vols. in One*, Gramercy, New York, 1988.

Lloyd, John; Mitchinson, John, *The Book of General Ignorance*, Harmony Books, New York, 2006.

Mackay, Harvey, *We Got Fired! And It's the Best Thing That Ever Happened to Us* Ballantine Books, New York, 2004.

Maxwell, John C., *Failing Forward: Turning Mistakes into Stepping Stones for Success*, Thomas Nelson Publishers, Nashville, TN, 2000.

"Modern Marvels: Mount Rushmore," *The History Channel*, 1994.

"Modern Marvels: More Engineering Disasters," *The History Channel*, 1999.

"Niagara: A History of the Falls," *The History Channel*, 1998.

Oates, Stephen B., *With Malice Toward None: The Life of Abraham Lincoln,* Harper & Row, Publishers, Inc., New York, 1977.

Osbeck, Kenneth W., *101 Hymn Stories,* Kregel Publications, Grand Rapids, MI, 1982.

Osbeck, Kenneth W., *101 More Hymn Stories,* Kregel Publications, Grand Rapids, MI, 1982.

Osbeck, Kenneth W., *Amazing Grace,* Kregel Publications, Grand Rapids, MI, 1990.

Peale, Norman Vincent, *Words That Inspired Him,* Inspirational Press, New York, NY, 1994.

Pearlman, Myer, *Knowing The Doctrines of The Bible,* Gospel Publishing House, Springfield, MO, 1937.

Phillips, Donald T., *Lincoln Stories for Leaders,* Book World Services, Sarasota, FL, 1997.

Powell, Colin, *My American Journey,* Ballentine Books, New York, 1995.

Rosas, John Paul, "Remembering '20 Million Miles to Earth,'" Columbia Pictures, Rosas Productions, 2007.

"Scourge of the Black Death," *The History Channel,* 1997.

Sherwood, Dane; Wood, Sandy; Kovalchik, Kara, *The Pocket Idiot's Guide to Not So Useless Facts,* Alpha Books, 2006.

Smith, Douglas B., *Ever Wonder Why?,* Fawcett, 1991.

Tan, Paul Lee, *Encyclopedia of 15,000 Illustrations,* Bible Communications, Inc., Dallas, TX, 1998.

The Best of Uncle John's Bathroom Reader, Portable Press, Ashland, OR, 1995.

"The Brooklyn Bridge," *The History Channel,* 1995.

"The Incredibles," A Pixar Film by Disney, 2005.

"The Plague," *The History Channel*, 2005.

"The Von Trapp Family: Harmony and Discord," *Biography* on the *A&E Network*, 1998.

"To the Moon," Nova, 1999.

'Transcontinental Railroad," *The History Channel*, 1995.

Uncle John's Absolutely Absorbing Bathroom Reader, Portable Press, Ashland, OR, 1999.

Uncle John's Ahh-Inspiring Bathroom Reader, Portable Press, Ashland, OR, 2002.

Uncle John's Bathroom Reader Plunges into Great Lives, Portable Press, Ashland, OR, 2003.

Uncle John's Bathroom Reader Plunges into History, Portable Press, Ashland, OR, 2001.

Uncle John's Bathroom Reader Plunges into History Again, Portable Press, Ashland, OR, 2004.

Uncle John's Bathroom Reader Plunges into The Universe, Portable Press, Ashland, OR, 2002.

Uncle John's Bathroom Reader Plunges into National Parks, Portable Press, Ashland, OR, 2007.

Uncle John's Bathroom Reader Tales to Inspire, Portable Press, Ashland, OR, 2006.

Uncle John's Bathroom Reader Wonderful World of Odd, Portable Press, Ashland, OR, 2007.

Uncle John's Biggest Ever Bathroom Reader, Portable Press, Ashland, OR, 1996.

Uncle John's Curiously Compelling Bathroom Reader, Portable Press, Ashland, OR, 2006.

Uncle John's Extraordinary Book of Facts, Portable Press, Ashland, OR, 2006.

Uncle John's Fast-Acting, Long, Lasting Bathroom Reader, Portable Press, Ashland, OR, 2005.

Uncle John's Legendary Lost Book of Facts, Portable Press, Ashland, OR, 1999.

Uncle John's Monumental Bathroom Reader, Advanced Marketing Services, Ashland, OR, 2007.

Uncle John's Slightly Irregular Bathroom Reader, Bathroom Readers' Press, Ashland, OR, 2004.

"USS Bowfin: Avenger of Pearl Harbor," *The History Channel,* 2005.

"War of the Worlds," A Steven Spielberg Film by Dreamworks and Paramount Pictures, 2005.

Wikipedia: The Free Encyclopedia (Numerous articles)

Winchester, Jim, *The World's Worst Aircraft: From Pioneering Failures to Multimillion Dollar Disasters* (Barnes and Noble Books, 2007)

Thankfulness	May 17	Trust in God	March 30
	June 21		May 3
	July 5		July 1
	November 24		July 24
	November 25		August 5
Temptation	October 20		September 20
Time	May 2		October 27
	August 26		November 9
Tolerance	April 6		December 1
	July 1		December 4
Tolerance	November 1	Tragedy	February 27
	May 1		April 22
	May 25		December 31
	July 30	Truth	November 29
	August 3	Unappreciated	March 23
	August 20		August 16
	August 25		December 5
	October 6		December 26
	October 21	Unity	September 1
	December 15	Unsung Heroes	October 16
	December 24		November 5
Training/Discipline	November 7		November 8
	November 30	Unsung Heroes	November 26
Tribulation	May 3		December 5
	July 30		December 6
	September 30	Values	January 17
	October 23		August 15
	November 3	Veterans	September 23
	December 11	Witnessing	August 20
	December 18		September 21
Triumph of Good	September 11	World Peace	December 23
Trust in God	January 5		December 24
	January 11	Worry	March 30
	January 18		April 15

Made in the USA
Middletown, DE
07 October 2018